The Chomsky Effect

The Chomsky Effect

A Radical Works Beyond the Ivory Tower

Robert F. Barsky

The MIT Press
Cambridge, Massachusetts
London, England

MIT Press books may be purchased at special quantity discounts for business or sales promotional use. For information, please e-mail special_sales@mitpress .mit.edu or write to Special Sales Department, The MIT Press, 55 Hayward Street, Cambridge, MA 02142.

This book was set in Sabon by SNP Best-set Typesetter Ltd., Hong Kong, and was printed and bound in the United States.

Library of Congress Cataloging-in-Publication Data

Barsky, Robert F.
the Chomsky effect : a radical works beyond the ivory tower / Robert F. Barsky.
    p.   cm.
Includes bibliographical references and index.
ISBN 978-0-262-02624-6 (hardcover : alk. paper)
1. Liberalism. 2. Anarchism. 3. Chomsky, Noam—Influence. 4. Chomsky, Noam—Criticism and interpretation. 5. Political science—Philosophy. I. Title.
JC574.B374   2007
320.51′2—dc22

                                                              2007000654

10 9 8 7 6 5 4 3 2 1

This book is dedicated to my parents, Pat and Syd, for their basic decency, to my boys, Ben and Tristan, for their wisdom and their humor, and to Marsha, for ever.

People are dangerous. If they're able to involve themselves in issues that matter, they may change the distribution of power, to the detriment of those who are rich and privileged.
—Noam Chomsky

I'm not as remote from the popular culture as I sometimes pretend.
—Noam Chomsky

Dear Bob,
Your friend reminds me of a time about 30 years ago, when my kids were little, and one of them came into where I was working and looked at the books on the table, all with titles about torture, genocide, . . . and mumbled something like: now I see why you look so sad sometimes.
—Noam Chomsky, personal correspondence to author, October 3, 2001

Contents

Preface

Noam Chomsky is one of the most recognized names of our time, and in 2005 he was voted the most important public intellectual in the world today, the result of his winning 4,827 of 20,000 votes cast in a poll conducted jointly by a British monthly called *Prospect* and the Washington-based journal *Foreign Policy*.[1] This result is hardly surprising; his contributions to linguistics and his theories regarding the workings of the human mind have rocked the intellectual world for more than fifty years, beginning with the critical reception of his early work on syntactic structures and his appeal to what he called the Cartesian approach to language. His crusade against the Vietnam War and his on-going critique of American foreign policy, his analyses of the Middle East and Central America, his long-standing local and international activism, and his assessment (sometimes with Edward Herman) of how media functions in contemporary society have made him a darling of political dissenters around the world who take from Chomsky both useful analysis and, moreover, a whole approach that is valuable in the struggle against oppression. He is at once a beacon to the downtrodden, and, as much of the world witnessed on September 20, 2006, from a televised speech delivered at the United Nations General Assembly, he is also an inspiration to the likes of President Hugo Chavez of Venezuela, who recommended to representatives of the governments of the world that they read Chomsky's recent book *Hegemony or Survival*.[2] Chomsky's vicious and persistent attacks against "Stalinist" politicians, "commissar" academics, greedy members of the managerial classes, poser liberals, "scientific" Marxists, self-aggrandizing social scientists, authoritarian pedagogues, lackey media types, and fanatical sports fans has also created a vicious set of adversaries who commit remarkable amounts of effort to discredit, admonish, critique, or ignore Chomsky's approach. In the face of it all, Chomsky stands forth, now eighty years old and yet as energetic, fearless, and courageous as ever, perhaps even more so as the years bring him new kinds of experience, optimism and disgust; he is indeed, as U2's Bono has called him, the "rebel without a pause." As a consequence, most everyone has strong feelings (positive and negative) about Noam Chomsky, and the effect that he has upon people extending across national, social, and institutional lines is a fascinating phenomenon, and is a remarkable testament to what an intellectual can accomplish when engaged beyond the ivory tower.

One realm in which he has found himself alienated from the majority, particularly in his own country, is spectator sports, and this single example is illustrative of the complexity of his effect. Noam Chomsky is the Niles from the popular sitcom *Frasier* in regard to contact sports, gloriously and also willfully disconnected. This has had a remarkably negative effect upon many people from all walks of life, a testament to the importance of sports not only in this society, but more generally, and it may be an example where the application of a general principle finds itself counterproductive in the overall objectives. For him, the basic social role of sports is diversion aimed at "Joe Six Pack," rather than, say, relaxation, aimed at forming and sustaining families, communities, and friends. In the film *Manufacturing Consent,* for example, he suggests that there is a range of ways in which popular culture seeks to divert people, to "get them away from things that matter," to "reduce their capacity to think." From this standpoint, sports is for him "an example of the indoctrination system," "something to pay attention to that's of no importance," which keeps people from worrying about things that matter to their lives that they might have some chance to do something about. A scene recorded in the film is as follows:

You know, I remember in high school, already I was pretty old. I suddenly asked myself at one point, why do I care if my high school team wins the football game? [laughter] I mean, I don't know anybody on the team, you know? [audience roars] I mean, they have nothing to do with me, I mean, why I am cheering for my team? It doesn't mean any—it doesn't make sense. But the point is, it does make sense: it's a way of building up irrational attitudes of submission to authority, and group cohesion behind leadership elements—in fact, it's training in irrational jingoism. That's also a feature of competitive sports. I think if you look closely at these things, I think, typically, they do have functions, and that's why energy is devoted to supporting them and creating a basis for them and advertisers are willing to pay for them and so on.[3]

I think that in terms of the negative "effect" that Chomsky can induce, sports has been at or near the top of the list for the naysayer, just below his views on Israel and his unpatriotic and ungrateful attitude toward his country. But careful examination of what he says, even in this short quote, reveals a basic attitude one can discern and probably admire outside of the example that he provides: he hates arbitrary authority and submission thereto, he has scorn for irrational beliefs and jingoistic replies to complex issues, and he looks for ways in which corporate America abusively incurs into our lives in search of new ways to make profit. He doesn't look to the ways in which such diversions help bridge generation gaps between parents and kids, how attention to strange rituals like NCAA tournaments teaches us about communities and individuals far from home, the virtues of kids who might not otherwise be interested in reading suddenly gobbling up sports pages written by quite creative and often humorous journalists. What he sees instead is submission and rituals that recall the horrors of what nationalism or patriotism have led to this century. That's one side. Another side is the unadulterated humor of the quote, as indicated by the audience reaction, which is laughter and uproar (followed, perhaps, by much more divisive discussions after the talk among people who took the comments personally). This humor both drives the point home and also allows him to make the move from the example to the deeper message:

But the point is, this sense of irrational loyalty to some sort of meaningless community is training for subordination to power, and for chauvinism. And of course, you're looking at gladiators, you're looking at guys who can do things you couldn't possibly do—like, you couldn't pole-vault seventeen feet, or do all these crazy things these people do. But it's a model that you're supposed to try to emulate. And they're gladiators fighting for your cause, so you've got to cheer them on, and you've got to be happy when the opposing quarterback gets carted off the field a total wreck and so on. All of this stuff builds up extremely anti-social aspects of human psychology. I mean, they're there; there's no doubt that they're there. But they're emphasized, and exaggerated, and brought out by spectator sports: irrational competition, irrational loyalty to power systems, passive acquiescence to quite awful values, really. In fact, it's hard to imagine anything that contributes more fundamentally to authoritarian attitudes than this does, in addition to the fact that it just engages a lot of intelligence and keeps people away from other things.[4]

Still another aspect is his noting from the example of professional sports the real creativity, intelligence, and concentration that people devote to their assessment of sports, which leads them to call into radio stations and grill with carefully articulated approaches the erroneous assessments made by coaches and "authorities," a point he reiterates:

In fact, I have the habit when I'm driving of turning on these radio call-in programs, and it's striking when you listen to the ones about sports. They have these groups of sports reporters, or some kind of experts on a panel, and people call in and have discussions with them. First of all, the audience obviously is devoting an enormous amount of time to it all. But the more striking fact is, the callers have a tremendous amount of expertise, they have detailed knowledge of all kinds of things, they carry on these extremely complex discussions. And strikingly, they're not at all in awe of the experts—which is a little unusual. See, in most parts of the society, you're encouraged to defer to experts: we all do it more than we should. But in this area, people don't seem to do it—they're quite happy to have an argument with the coach of the Boston Celtics, and tell him what he should have done, and enter into big debates with him and so on. So the fact is that in this domain, people somehow feel quite confident, and they know a lot— there's obviously a great deal of intelligence going into it.[5]

If only, he thinks, people would do the same with their politicians, if only they'd stand up to their "commander in chief" when he lies to them, or if they'd call their "leaders" when the strategy they are using is leading to obvious failure. Some people admire Chomsky for his consistency, finding in this assessment the basic values that guide all of his work, while others find in him a haughty disregard for rituals held most dear to the population. And never the twain shall meet.

I am concerned with such issues that display the range of reactions to Chomsky's arguments because, taken together, they contribute to what I have come to think of as the "Noam Chomsky Approach." This approach, and the effect that it has, is important not only for those interested in understanding Noam Chomsky as a person, but also for those who hope to change the current situation of systemic inequality in the direction of the "good society" he describes. Positive change is not going to come about thanks only to Noam Chomsky or others whose work has led to ethical and responsible action beyond the ivory tower; indeed any such suggestion would be worrisome since it implies either a quest for a personality to revere, or a high level of adherence to some preconceived dogma. If society is to change, then attitudes toward it must change, hopefully in response to rational and informed decision making effected for the good of the individual and the associations into which she or he freely enters. Chomsky plays a role here not solely on account of his specific analysis of particular events but, moreover, the attitude that he brings to his work, the approach that he applies to issues he considers important, and to the catalyzing effect that he has upon others who are witness to his behavior and knowledgeable about his approach. From this standpoint Noam Chomsky may seem to some people to be a guru or an ideologue, but the fact is that he scorns such an image in favor of the idea that he tries to help infuse energy or support to work that is or could be done to improve society. If he could just serve this purpose, the catalyst who encourages peoples' curiosity and willingness to be the "dangerous" people they can be by fostering interest in matters that should concern them, his self-assigned role would undoubtedly be easier to fulfill. But any dissident or dissenter comes up against power, and interests, and, accordingly, considerable resources dedicated to the maintenance of status quo power relations, so it is incumbent upon him to offer up credible sources, "indisputable" facts, and convincing rhetoric to guide people along the path to understanding not only the world but even their own self-interest. We ought to be concerned about how the government is spending our money, that is, the rationale for spending a huge percentage of the federal budget on military and Pentagon expenses rather than upon the kind of social projects and programs that promote a higher standard of living for the majority of the population. This is self-interest, and informed involvement in political discussions by that measure is the exercise of our individual interest, in the same way as figuring out how our monthly income is being spent is in our interest. But given that such self-interest conflicts with a power elite interest, because government officials like corporate managers would generally prefer to act with impunity (the cloaks of secrecy that surround our own government's actions on a range of fronts is testament to this), it's likely that attempts to become engaged in our own affairs will be met with resistance or scorn. As regards Chomsky, this produces a large contingent of retractors, particularly among those who possess significant resources or power, and therefore who have a lot to lose. Many of them are eager to jump on any miscue that could be used to undermine their power, creating, shall we say, a "self-interest effect." For this reason, there is likely to be a range of reactions against Noam Chomsky, depending upon where one sits on the power spectrum, which are in fact in evidence in reviews of his books (or books about him) or in the commentaries that one hears about his importance, the accuracy of his work, his ongoing legacy, or the value of his contributions to the range of fields his work impacts. These conflicting assessments are evident on a range of fronts but come together around particular debates, which is why I will discuss in some detail certain key moments that come up when people talk about Chomsky's work, which variously include his views on why the United States was in North (and South) Vietnam, the false pretensions of much of the research in the "social sciences," Robert Faurisson's denying the Holocaust, why East Timor was downplayed in the Western press in favor of Cambodia, the U.S.-supported militarization of Israel, and so forth.

In short, this book attempts to answer some of the questions most frequently asked about Chomsky's work by assessing how he approaches the various subject areas to which he contributes, notably language studies, media, education, law, and politics, and by noting the references he makes, implicitly and explicitly, to the precursors from whom he draws. The reception of this approach is discussed as well under the rubric of the "Noam Chomsky Effect," which speaks of his positive and negative popularity, and the impact he has on both accounts. I begin, therefore, with a discussion of Chomsky's popular appeal, the use made of his persona in popular culture such as rock music, film, and theater, and the links that exist between him and other popular academics/social thinkers. In the second chapter, I discuss the resistance to Noam Chomsky from various standpoints, including contemporary Zionists, mainstream political thinkers, and certain communities of scholars (especially in linguistics), and I also undertake an in-depth assessment of the Faurisson Affair and the Pol Pot Affair. Chapter 3 is a systematic survey of the individuals and movements that have influenced Chomsky's work: from the "Cartesian" thinkers (Descartes, von Humboldt, Montesquieu, Rousseau, Voltaire) to the Scottish Enlightenment (notably Hume and Smith); from American classical liberals (Dewey, Jefferson, Madison,

Thoreau) to anti-Bolshevik Marxists (Gramsci, Korsch, Luxemburg, Mattick, Pannekoek); from anarchists (Bakunin, Goldman, Kropotkin, Rocker) to anarcho-syndicalists (notably the Spanish example from the 1930s); from Zellig Harris to Bertrand Russell. I focus somewhat unevenly upon certain precursors who have been more subject to neglect in our culture, (Zellig Harris, Rudolph Rocker, and Wilhelm von Humboldt) because in my opinion Chomsky's personal and intellectual traits are best understood and contextualized with reference to these figures.

The second half of the book assesses Chomsky's approach to specific domains and milieus that are crucial and often misconstrued in discussions about the value of his work. Chapter 4 is a discussion of the legal side and legal implications of his political work, and therein I undertake a sustained assessment of his approach to ethics, classical liberalism, international law, human rights, and the function of law in the "good society." Chapter 5 is an overview of his views of education, including its role in contemporary society and the role it should or could play in the good society. This chapter also contains a survey of the education theories from which Chomsky draws inspiration, or about which he has commented, including those of Michael Bakunin, John Dewey, Emma Goldman, Wilhelm von Humboldt, Bertrand Russell, as well as contemporary efforts on the internet (ZNet, etc.). Chapter 6 assesses Chomsky's approach to the study of language and discourse and focuses upon the basic questions he asks in his own linguistic work, followed by an assessment of how his work on language has been appropriated outside of the linguistic domain, media studies, and various approaches to language research. Chapter 7 discusses creative discourse, with the specific example of literature and its associated questioning and refusal of knowledge claims. This rebelliousness on the part of the fiction writer, who often seems the type who might show up drunk at a party and tell everyone there that they really don't know what they're talking about, leads naturally into a meditation on the role of humor, in the broad sense and in Chomsky's work and in the many talks he gives. And in the end, I offer a survey of approaches to the "public intellectual," historically and contemporaneously, with an eye to assessing how Chomsky came to mean so much to so many and, therefore, what he may mean to the generations to come.

One of the reviewers of the manuscript for this book suggested that I reflect upon the voice, or more accurately the voices, that narrate the different chapters in this book. I admit to being conflicted as regards this issue, in part because it's doubtlessly clear to those who have read my work that I am extremely sympathetic to "Chomsky's approach," and the ten years I have devoted to this book is as tangible a sign of this as I could possibly produce. On the other hand, when I finished the final revisions it struck me that this book, which was originally entitled "People are Dangerous," is on the one hand a book about Noam Chomsky, but on the other hand is not, or not solely: *The Chomsky Effect* is a reflection, sometimes critical, of what Noam Chomsky has taught me and others, that is, it is a very tangible example of the "Chomsky Effect" in a whole series of registers and realms. So what I think has emerged as the compendium of ideas that Chomsky has inspired or promoted is a reflection upon how people relate to each other when placed into relationships of all kinds—loving, fearing, hating, admiring, loathing, desiring—via Noam Chomsky. For this reason the reviewer was absolutely correct and very helpful in drawing attention to the fact that there isn't a single "voice" in this text but rather a collection of assertions, analyses, attacks, defenses, explanations, and, moreover, an array of thoughts that are situated between two lives, Noam Chomsky's and my own, which meet and diverge in ways that I hope are inspiring, not necessarily in themselves, but in other venues and spaces between the voices, that is, in worlds not yet imagined. In short, this is a dialogue, a "dialogic" text, to invoke the oft-mentioned work of Mikhail Bakhtin, which tries through a range of speech genres to provide more than just the background for a system of ideas by showing the tangible imprints that these ideas have upon an array of people in all sorts of fields and worlds.

This work follows in the line of studies undertaken, primarily, by Carlos Otero, and works within a similar framework as the one he articulates in his introductions and excellent footnotes for books like *Critical Assessments: Noam Chomsky, Radical Priorities*, and *Language and Politics*. It also follows from the inspiring corpuses of work on anarchists by Paul Avrich and George Woodcock, the wonderful writings and publishing work of those associated with AK Press and Black Rose Press, and the range of excellent works about Chomsky's approach to society by his friend David Barsamian, by Mark Achbar and Peter Wintonick through the film and the book called *Manufacturing Consent*, Fred d'Agostino's *Chomsky's System of Ideas*, Milan Rai's *Chomsky's Politics*, Raphael Salkie, *The Chomsky Update: Language and Politics*, and, of course, the truly astonishing work that Michael Albert and his collective have undertaken on Znet and in *Z Magazine*. I owe debts of gratitude to a range of persons who have generously commented on various versions of this text or on ideas presented herein, indeed way more than I can possibly even recall at this point. I would like to say, however, that Sam Abramovitch, Saleem Ali, Stephen Anderson, Marc Angenot, Marion Appel, Jill Brussel, Karl Brussel, Murray Eden, Alain Goldschlager, John Goldsmith, Elizabeth Harvey, David Heap, Denise Helly, Henry Hiz, Henry Hoenigswald, Michael Holquist, Russell Jacoby, Martin Jay, George Jochnowitz, Konrad Koerner, Julia Kristeva, Seymour Melman, Bruce Nevin, Juvenal Ndijirigya, Christopher Norris, Mark Pavlick, Michel Pierssens, Larry Portis, Marcus Raskin, Nicolas Ruwet, Tiphaine Samoyault, Elise Snyder, George Szanto, Darko Suvin, Jeff Tennant, Clive Thomson, Lisa Travis, and Michel Van Schendel offered invaluable assistance for this project, sometimes unwittingly, and Alham Usman brought me to the final corrections by patiently listening to and commenting upon the entire text one last time. I have also learned a tremendous amount from organizations such as the Chomsky Reading Group at Vertigo Books in Washington, D.C., The Palo Alto Peace and Justice Center in California, David Barsamian's public radio show in Boulder, Colorado, and Znet. I have also thoroughly enjoyed reading the words of the many unsung Internet heroes who read Chomsky's work and react to it in their blogs, reading lists, and posted messages. Support for this research has taken many forms, and I owe special debts of gratitude to a range of people affiliated with particular institutions in which this work was written, notably Columbia University, the Massachusetts Institute of Technology, University of Pennsylvania, University of Western Ontario, Vanderbilt University, and Yale University. I owe special gratitude to current and past members of the MIT Press, notably Carolyn Anderson, Amy Brand, Gita Manaktala, Sandra Minkkinen, Marney Smyth, Ben Williams, and especially Tom Stone, and, for funding, the Canadian Social Sciences and Humanities Research Council. Jeffrey Weston's comics depicting Chomsky and Predicate have been a constant source of entertainment and wisdom, and I'm grateful for his contributions to this book. None of this would have made any sense without my remarkable boys, Tristan and Benjamin, who show the wonderful and exciting sides to being "dangerous" with their creativity and their force. And to Marsha, whose magic exceeds reason, whose dance defies gravity, and in whose presence I have found ecstatic, passionate, sublime calm.

I

Dissent

1

The Chomsky Effect Within and Beyond the Ivory Tower

Noam Chomsky's commitment to work beyond the ivory tower, which has made him the occasional target of popular media (in terms of his having been idolized, vilified, ignored, misrepresented, or censored), is based upon a truly radical conception of society, and his work places him in the excellent company of intellectual figures who have pursued radical political work. Some of these figures are professors or academics who chose to work beyond the confines of academia, even as they made lasting and original contributions to their respective fields, and those with whom Chomsky has the strongest affinities, include Zellig Harris (linguistics, University of Pennsylvania), Seymour Melman (engineering, Columbia), Anton Pannekoek (astronomy, University of Amsterdam), Bertrand Russell (philosophy, Cambridge University), Edward Said (English literature, Columbia) and Howard Zinn (history, Boston University). Chomsky is not terribly excited about putting himself into the company of academics, however, and when he does mention antecedents to his work he explicitly and implicitly recalls ideas proposed by anarchists and anarcho-syndicalists like Michael Bakunin and—especially—Rudolph Rocker, anti-Bolshevik Marxists like Karl Korsch or Rosa Luxembourg, classical liberal thinkers like Wilhelm von Humboldt and Adam Smith, and those who offer up conceptions of the "good society" or critiques of existing phenomena found, in varying ways, in the efforts of his close collaborators Michael Albert, David Barsamian, Edward S. Herman, and Carlos Otero. His views on Israel and Palestine hearken back to idealist conceptions about the socialist state that was to be erected in Palestine by proponents of the Kibbutz Artzi, and by various organizations that favored increased cooperation

Figure 1.2
"I'm Drawn To Noam" by Patricia Storms.[1]

I need to keep my quick sketch skills limber, so with this in mind, I've created a new category, I'm Drawn To You. Every now and then I'll do quick caricatures of personalities in the media who fascinate, intrigue, inspire and even disgust me.

I've always been drawn to faces. As a kid I would stare at people's faces for long periods of time, trying to memorize every line and curve, as well as the spirit in their eyes and their smile (that is, if they were the smiling type). When I was first in college studying Library Techniques, I used to stare at all the faces of the women in the class (it was 95% women who took the course), and would often secretly draw them because their faces were fascinating, but also because I was usually bored out of my fucking mind. It eventually got back to me that some people in the class thought that I might be a lesbian since I stared at the women so much. Seems like a strange connection to make to me, but whatever.

So if you recognize the face, you will see that my first choice is none other than Noam Chomsky. I hope I have done him justice. I think he is one of the most important voices of reason in the world right now, even though I find his droning voice so damned annoying. His written work is, for me, a tough slog, but I'll keep trying. If you've never encountered him before, I highly recommend the videos *Manufacturing Consent, The Corporation*, and the newest one, *Noam Chomsky: Rebel Without a Pause*.

Mr. Noam Chomsky, I'm Drawn To You. But tell your wife not to worry.

between oppressed Arabs, Jews, and Palestinians in the Middle East and beyond, such as Avukah, Hashomer Hatzair, and the League for Arab-Jewish Cooperation.[2] These ideas have great currency for Chomsky because of his early influences, notably some intense discussions to which he was privy on account of his visits, beginning in his teenage years, with a remarkable uncle who ran a newsstand and a kind of spontaneous literary political salon on 72nd Street in New York City. This model of intense, open-ended discussion remains for him critical and is in fact one of the legacies of his own approach when he meets with individuals, whether in his Massachusetts Institute of Technology (MIT) office, or in the course of rallies, talks, or discussions beyond the ivory tower. Commenting upon his approach to linguistics research, Chomsky has remarked that "very few people do scientific work by sitting alone in their office all their lives. You talk to graduate students, you hear what they have to say, you bounce ideas off your colleagues. That's the way you get ideas, that's the way you figure out what you think. That's the way, and in political life or social life, it's exactly the same thing."[3]

Chomsky was born in 1928 in Philadelphia into a remarkable family. His father, William, was described in a 1977 *New York Times* obituary as "one of the world's foremost Hebrew grammarians," and his mother, Elsie, who taught alongside his father at the religious school of the Mikveh Israel congregation, is still remembered for her brilliance and her uncompromising and serious approach to Zionism, the Hebrew language, and, of course, Jewish cultural affairs. The array of formative influences on Noam was expanded through his readings of anarchist and anti-Bolshevik writers and, beginning in 1945, through direct contact with people at the University of Pennsylvania, most notably his teacher and early mentor Zellig Harris. Harris's influence upon Chomsky's general approach to questions of language and politics is substantial, and indeed a huge array of people I've met over the last few years (in the course of researching this book and a forthcoming study of Zellig Harris) claim equal debts to this towering figure. What all of this suggests is that to understand Noam Chomsky demands that one invest in careful research into his formative influences and into the ways in which he has updated historical approaches (inspired notably by Enlightenment thinking and anarchist work) to accord with the complexities and challenges of contemporary society.

The study of historical works alongside Chomsky's own thinking helps contextualize Chomsky's approach to the "good society," and the extreme distance we have to travel if we hope to see a manifestation of these ideals in our lifetime. But not only does Chomsky consider that these goals could be achieved, he also insists in his historical writings (and there are many) that we look back to past moments when concrete advances were made in this very direction—notably in Catalonia until the victory of Franco's fascists, a consequence not only of Franco's own efforts but of the many direct and indirect contributions made by the Nazis, the British, the Soviets, and the Americans, who all chipped in to destroy populist movements and free associations set up in variance with the more brutal model of contemporary capitalism. In other words, Chomsky is popular among people for a variety of reasons, but I suspect few people comprehend that his objective, like that of the Catalonians earlier this century, is nothing less than a radical overturning of society as we know it today. He is, therefore, quite different from most of the so-called public intellectuals to whom I will refer in the conclusion of this book, and indeed some of his earliest writings outside of the field of linguistics were critical of the "New Mandarins" who are regularly summoned by elites to legitimize or explain (justifiably) unpopular legislation to those deemed too ignorant or stupid to understand that whatever is best for elites is and should be the law of the land: "Contrary to widespread belief and self-serving doctrine produced by the intelligentsia themselves, the fact is that, by and large, intellectuals have tended to be submissive and obedient to one or another state—generally their own, though naturally episodes of apologetics for foreign states tend to receive more attention, conformity to domestic power being tacitly assumed as the norm."[4]

Many people who are unfamiliar with anarchist movements express surprise when they learn that Chomsky's views are *this* radical, are "anarchist," because most people have come to equate anarchy with violence and chaos, or with some brand of unattainable, and therefore undesirable, idealism. Chomsky persistently emphasizes the anticapitalist, procooperative and spontaneous roots of anarchism and the many ties it has, especially in the United States, to the history of the working class. The spontaneity of anarchist uprisings is important because it suggests a natural accord between anarchy, actual human needs (when they are freely expressed), and the natural propensities of human beings for creativity and cooperation. Perhaps this is the reason for the historically valid perception that if allowed to spread, true anarchy has deeply rooted popular support. And Chomsky hastens to point out that this occurs despite the consistently negative press that anarchism has received over time, press that has made a rather convenient link in people's mind to that which is violent, uncontrollable, and menacing.

There are historical reasons for the link frequently made between anarchy and violence, including the justifiable lack of an institutional basis for anarchism and a collective amnesia about the fact that many anarchist ideas grow out of actual examples from history, such as solid friendships or good marriages, or in the loose and free association of groups in ancient Greece (described by Rudolph Rocker in his masterpiece *Nationalism and Culture*) and, more recently, the workings of certain segments of Spanish society in the 1930s. Instead, the legacy that remains grows out of memories of its so-called terrorist phases, including one that lasted from March 1892 until June 1894, during which time nine people were killed and numerous others wounded in eleven separate detonations in France, all linked in some way to anarchists. As Mina Graur suggests in a recent biography of Rudolph Rocker, "that was the time when the stereotype of the vile anarchist, a dagger in his hand and a fuming bomb in his pocket, was planted in the public's mind. The press and the police did their best to reinforce this image and frighten the public with the specter of the 'great international anarchist conspiracy'."[5] Examples like this could be multiplied with references to similar events in different periods throughout the world. The point is that the image is far from the anarchy proposed by the likes of Chomsky, who in turn has been influenced by a range of anarchists such as Rudolph Rocker, whose views on this point and many others are probably closer to Chomsky's than anyone else's.

If Chomsky's anarchy has been cause for confusion, his Jewish heritage and views on Israel have been for many a source of veritable bewilderment. Once again, though, Chomsky's views on Israel and Palestine hearken back to a corpus of idealist historical works, notably conceptions about the nonreligious, inclusive socialist state that was to be erected in Palestine by proponents of the Kibbutz Artzi (a federation of kibbutzim founded upon progressive socialist ideas by the Hashomer Hatzair youth movement)[6] and by various individuals and organizations that favored increased cooperation between the oppressed (Arabs, Jews, Palestinians) in the Middle East and beyond. Many of those involved with this effort would be unfamiliar to most readers, but—if only to remind ourselves of others who have had these ideas and have not been accused of being anti-Semitic on their account—it is worth invoking the clearly deified Albert Einstein. It is seldom mentioned that Einstein supported a region in Palestine that would be home to a broad array of oppressed peoples, not just Jews; indeed, he gave a talk, published along with four others given between 1921 and 1933 as *Mein Weltbild*,[7] which already set out a major theme of an approach to Jews and to Zionism that would might place his ability to stay in Germany into question. In a prescient statement, particularly as we continue to witness Israeli military incursions into Arab territories, Einstein warned:

We need to pay great attention to our relations with the Arabs. By cultivating these carefully we shall be able in future to prevent things from becoming so dangerously strained that people can take advantage of them to provoke acts of hostility. This goal is perfectly within our reach, because our work of construction has been, and must continue to be, carried out in such a manner as to serve the real interests of the Arab population also. In this way we shall be able to avoid getting ourselves quite so often into the position, disagreeable for Jews and Arabs alike, of having to call in the mandatory power as arbitrator. We shall thereby be following not merely the dictates of Providence but also our traditions, which alone give the Jewish community meaning and stability. For our community is not, and must never become, a political one; this is the only permanent source from whence it can draw new strength and the only ground on which its existence can be justified.[8]

Just as Chomsky's anarchism resonates with a particular set of ideas and principles drawn from historical sources, which I will document in chapter 3, Chomsky's approach to Zionism also has an earlier foundation. In this respect as well Chomsky is quite similar to Rocker, who befriended a series of radical Jewish groups, notably in Paris and London, which were quite distant from what today would be considered "Zionist" organizations and which, even then, stood quite apart from other organizations or Jewish radicals:

Unlike the Bund, which supported Otto Bauer's formula of an extraterritorial autonomy as a solution to the Jewish national problem, or the Zionists, who favored political self-determination in the form of a Jewish state, the radical Jews in Paris treated Jewish national self-determination as an essentially non-national issue. Instead, they regarded the problem as part of a more general social question, which would, accordingly, be resolved by means of an all-engulfing social revolution. Rocker was fascinated by these anarchists who embodied in their very existence the Bakuninist type of revolutionary, dedicating themselves, body and soul, to the idea of the revolutionary.[9]

In fact, Chomsky has much in common with a range of early radical Zionists about whom most people, including contemporary Zionists, know very little, largely because their ideals have been replaced by organizations and individuals who actively link Zionism to organized religion or Israeli state politics. And as the son of one of this century's great Hebrew scholars, and himself a highly trained reader of Hebrew texts, Chomsky is also very much the Jewish intellectual, who speaks of his admiration for the general questioning approach of Jews to their world and to the types of close readings proposed by, for example, scholars of the Talmud. He recalls:

I was raised in a Jewish tradition and I learned Hebrew very young. My parents were both professors of Hebrew. They observed religious customs without being themselves very religious. It is necessary to realize in fact that Judaism is a religion founded upon the carrying out of certain rights, but it does not require an act of faith. You can be an observant Jew while at the same time be an atheist. My wife was raised in the same milieu as me. Neither of us are either believers nor observers. I continue to read the Hebrew press and Hebrew literature, and I am profoundly implicated in questions that were of concern to me during my childhood.[10]

This will sound strange to some readers who have come to associate Chomsky, notably on account of the Faurisson Affair, discussed in the next chapter, with a complex anti-Zionism or even anti-Judaism, charges which we can evaluate further alongside documented information.

Chomsky is unlike other popular academics, particularly figures from the sciences such as Jacques Cousteau, Stephen J. Gould, Stephen Hawkins, Carl Sagan, or David Suzuki, because his views are simply more contentious. There are linguists who feel that they haven't received from him their due, Zionists who consider his views on Israel painfully similar to those upheld by anti-Zionists, and a range of people who have been swayed by arguments suggesting that his approach to East Timor, academic freedom, Pol Pot, the United States, Israel or, moreover, Faurisson, are unacceptable. One point I would insist upon, however, is that as much as Chomsky tries to convince people that his views on some specific point or another are accurate, he does not prescribe a formula for appropriate behavior or accurate thinking beyond, say, paying attention and not succumbing to authority. What is interesting about his belief in a recognizable and (eventually) knowable human nature is the concomitant effort everywhere apparent in his work beyond academia to postulate a set of cognitive tools, intrinsic to all humans, that can be employed to unleash our potential. The link between his postulating these ingrained abilities and his political work is his confidence that a world free of oppression, authoritarian structures, and "leaders," whatever form it might take, would be a vast improvement over the present situation. In this sense Chomsky has the effect of a facilitator, a catalyst, an inspiration, rather than the leader of some form of anarchist vanguard; so I would suggest that support for Chomsky's approach should not be equated with blind allegiance to specific comments he makes or to the battles he has chosen to wage, but to the values he upholds. To the degree that we consider our own values in accord with his, we are likely to feel more or less sympathetic to him.

What I myself find inspiring about Chomsky is the positive effect he has upon so many people who are dissatisfied with the world as they themselves experience it. We are encouraged in schools, religious institutions, the workplace, and in the society at large to respect the views of those empowered to dictate how we should react to events (teachers, journalists, "experts"), so when someone of Chomsky's intellectual and academic stature comes and says that what seems to us unfair, unjust, or prejudiced in the workplace, the household, the neighborhood, or the world is indeed aberrant by standards of decency or justice—that is, when he confirms in plain and simple English that bombing innocent civilians and then starving them over a prolonged period in Iraq is perverse, that invading Granada, bombing Tripoli, or supporting murderous Contras is obscene, and that not assisting those in need for obviously corporate-inspired reasons while preaching freedom and equality is hypocritical, we become empowered. For obvious reasons we've come to expect that the great and well respected are going to either shy away from basic issues or else use obscure terms and convoluted reasoning to legitimize perverse trends, like ever-growing corporate profits, insane military budgets, the "streamlining" of industry, or the "paying down" (with money from the poor even as we reduce taxes for the rich) of our "national debt." To hear Chomsky talk about these matters generates genuine amazement and even gratitude from those taught or, through various means forced, to accept what seems to them intrinsically wrong. As an anarchist, he has taught us to be wary of movements or "solutions" proposed from above, movements that, in the end, have turned out to be ineffectual or (as in the cases of brutal, unregulated environment-destroying capitalism, state Marxism, or Maoism) downright murderous.[11] This approach is one of the reasons Chomsky is admired and one of the ways that he serves to popularize ideas beyond the scholarly community.

An examination of Chomsky's career could also be a source of inspiration for those with some degree of power both inside and beyond institutions, such as the university (intellectuals, writers, teachers), because he offers a concrete example of how one can employ a privileged position (in his case Professor at the famed Massachusetts Institute of Technology) to advance the cause of the downtrodden against forces of oppression. Despite his having been arrested, threatened, included on Nixon's "most wanted list" and marginalized by some groups or institutions, he has been compensated both by the sense that his own decisions have been formulated on the basis of consistent adherence to what I would consider decent values (rather than careerism, the profit motive, or the will to power) and by triumphs in the public domain, evidence for which can be found at any of his well-attended public lectures. Wherever he goes (and he travels extensively; indeed since retirement his schedule of talks seems only to have accelerated), Chomsky fills auditoriums with admiring devotees, he is swarmed by curious onlookers, and he is swamped by demands that he grant interviews, accept honorary degrees, and speak to local activist groups. An article called "Chomsky Swims Against Mainstream"[12] makes reference to the "millions of Americans [who] have been drawn to the books and speeches of Chomsky the political analyst. His vast knowledge, clarity and strong commitment to humane values make Chomsky an appreciated speaker—and an energizing catalyst for social activism. At frequent appearances across the country, overflow audiences of thousands are routine." He is for these people a beacon, an inspiration, a catalyst for action in a world where marginal groups find themselves ignored and despised. Of course not everyone who shows up for these talks leave in agreement. The *Los Angeles Times* reported in "The Unbridled Linguist" by Kathleen Hendrix[13] that in the course of one such talk "one man yelled out he'd bet $100 that one of Chomsky's claims about National Security Council policy would turn out to be 'a lie' ("I'll take that bet," actor Ed Asner called out). One woman angrily called out 'Why do you live here?' and another man was overheard saying after the talk that 'wanting to ask Noam Chomsky a question is like wanting to walk into a buzz saw'."

I had the pleasure of meeting some of these audiences in the course of the book tour for *Noam Chomsky: A Life of Dissent* and was constantly amazed by the array of people who came out for talks, from welfare mothers to famous philosophers, from local activists to former classmates of his, and of course students. An excon claimed to have shared a cell with Chomsky, although unlike Norman Mailer, whose similar experiences are recorded in his *Armies of the Night*, this man had been incarcerated for something quite unrelated to Chomsky's dissension against the status quo. These people came out not only to hear about him, but to talk about *their own* Chomsky, their experience of him and his work, because whatever their views, they all felt passionately about his approach to the world. As a linguist friend, David Heap, has pointed out in conversation, no matter where one stands on the issues Chomsky discusses, it is impossible to be indifferent about him. So many people I met on that tour, and ever since, recall with great fondness the positive repercussions that Chomsky had left behind long after the microphone was turned off and the hall dimmed; for this reason, Chomsky seems to leave a trail of energy behind him by the very force of his talks and the manner that he employs. He is known as a lecturer who is still willing to discuss long after the event ends, who is always ready to take one more question, to learn about one more activist group, to have one more beer with those willing to stay on at the pub into the evening hours. For those audiences and organizations he is as an intellectual hero, a valiant and able combatant who is willing to donate his energies, his time, his life, to the battle against oppression in all forms. This is a longstanding effort on his part, as was clear already from a December 30, 1969, *New York Times* article by Robert Reinhold titled "Moral Question is Raised At Conference in Boston," which describes a by-now very familiar scene: "Dr. Shilling's remarks [regarding whether universities should accept money from the U.S. Defense Department] were greeted with less enthusiasm than Professor Chomsky's by many of the young people in the audience, who wore buttons with red fists of protest and passed out leaflets."

Not only is the Chomsky Effect longstanding, it is also remarkably diverse—including, somewhat incomprehensibly, an architect designing a house, as we discover in a 2002 *New York Times* article: "Mr. Eisenman and Mr. Falk shared an interest in Noam Chomsky's theories of language and mused about what Mr. Eisenman called a Chomskyesque house. 'I don't know what it meant,' Mr. Falk said in a recent interview, 'but it sounded good.' "[14] When it comes to sounding good, however, the real stage is music, as we shall see.

Rockin' Chomsky

In the last 10 years there have been some frenzied attempts to censor certain kinds of music and certain artists. Do you think that within the realm of entertainment that there are things which are threatening to the system of domination and the veil of disinformation?
Noam Chomsky: There is, well, I should say that I don't know much about this part of the world. But there can be no question that part of the revival of independence and dissidence and breaking of constraints, much of which was extremely healthy, which took place in the 1960s, was very closely tied to the developments in the music world, and that frightened people. Elites want to put things back in control and order.[15]
—Tom Morelo (guitarist, Rage Against the Machine)

His venomous message is spread on tapes and CDs, and the campus lecture circuit; he is promoted at rock concerts by superstar bands such as Pearl Jam, Rage Against the Machine, and U-2 (whose lead singer Bono called Chomsky a "rebel without a pause").
—David Horowitz[16]

Chomsky's following has expanded seemingly exponentially over the years and now extends in surprising ways into the domain of popular culture, notably punk and rock music.[17] A May 24, 1996, article by Mike O'Neill in *The Tampa Tribune* cites U2's Bono saying that Chomsky is the "Elvis of academia," the evidence for which includes a single called "Noam Chomsky" by the Horsies, an homage to him by Midnight Oil, and the fact that *Rock and Roll Confidential* refers to him as "a quote machine with all the rockers." K. L. Billingsley (author of *Hollywood Party: How Communism Seduced the American Film Industry in the 1930s and 1940s*) has documented the array of bands that use Chomsky's lyrics and persona as muse to their own music or political aspirations in his article provocatively titled "Noam Chomsky, Punk Hero."[18] For example, when Pearl Jam was preparing a tour of the United States in 1996, much ado was made of their attack against Ticketmaster's monopoly over the concert trade: "Eddie Vedder knows what it feels like not to have enough money to be able to buy a T-shirt at his favorite band's show and he wants to turn this thing around," said Pearl Jam's manager, Kelly Curtis, and they wanted to do so by charging $20 for the best tickets to their shows. Then, "as part of its small economic rebellion against the way rock and roll does business, in fact, Pearl Jam set up a 75-watt 'pirate' radio station on every stop on its tour. The station broadcast selections from their albums. But there was something else besides the crashing chords, and this is what was interesting about Pearl Jam's venture into radio. In between cuts, a male monotone voice oozing vulgar Marxism droned on about manipulation of the media, the evils of corporations, and the sins of America generally. The recorded voice belonged to Massachusetts Institute of Technology professor Noam Chomsky, the linguistic theorist and hard-core leftist whose career has bizarrely branched into the music business."

The reference in Billingsley's work to "vulgar Marxism" indicates that all the popularity in the world won't necessarily yield accurate readings. Nevertheless, he does correctly note that Pearl Jam is not an isolated example of this phenomenon: REM wanted Chomsky to tour with them to open their act with a talk (he turned them down), the punk band Bad Religion added a Chomsky talk to the B side of one of its records, Rage Against the Machine included a photo of a Chomsky book inside the

CD cover of "Evil Empire," and a former producer for the Rolling Stones and Bonnie Raitt (at the time when Billingsley was writing his article) were working on an album by well-known (but unnamed in this article) rockers "pounding out rhythms to back Chomsky's lyrics." And so, asks Billingsley, "What gives? Noam Chomsky has always had his admirers, but to become a hero of the Slackers crowd and a figure in the rock and roll mass cult in his sixties? This is, to say the least, a curious development. But then the emergence of Noam Chomsky as a guru to the hardcore Left has been somewhat curious." His explanation for this "guru" status (which Chomsky, as we've seen, specifically refuses) relates to a very tangible sense that Chomsky has indeed been tenacious, out there when everyone else had already gone home:

For some of his former leftist comrades, Chomsky was simply an eccentric, a sort of Doctor Dementia of the far left afflicted by a radical logorrhea which seemed embarrassingly passé. But there was also at the same time, the growth of a legend which made of Chomsky a cult hero. . . . Indeed, to his small cult of followers, Chomsky was heroic because he alone had kept up the attack when the rest of the left had lapsed into embarrassed silence. For them, he was the only figure radical America could offer who bore comparison to the European intellectual—that engagé figure whose opinions were backed by intellectual achievements whose significance could not be denied even by the most ardent opponents of his politics.

One of the reasons for Chomsky's popularity in the music world is, according to Billingsley, the fact that some rockers, who learned of his work in "ghettoes" at universities, are now musicians. He cites Charles Young, who writes about music for *Playboy* and *Musician* (and who wrote the cover story for *Rolling Stone* on the Sex Pistols), who notes that Chomsky's "influence is growing all over the place," and that "the seed was planted by the Sex Pistols, and Noam Chomsky is the blossom on the plant now." Young's own interest in anarchy grew through listening to punk music, and he found Chomsky on a shelf devoted to anarchists' writings. Says Billingsley: "For Young, discovering Chomsky 'was truly a life-changing experience.' Galvanized by the conversion experience, he became positively evangelical, with his own musical milieu proving the ideal mission field: 'Rock and roll is a fruitful area to spread it because rock musicians are natural anarchists in terms of their personality, even if they don't know it. It makes complete sense to me that

Chomsky has been picked up in these circles rather than among Hollywood moviemakers.'" Trying to get a sense of the popularity of Chomsky's thought, Young is cited as saying "It's not just fuck-youism. Punk has always been an attitude and not a philosophy. He [Chomsky] had a philosophy that went with the attitude. The emotional appeal of punk fades as you grow older and intellectual appeal comes along to fill it up. The American ruling class feels no obligation toward anything like a social contract anymore. With communism defeated, they can lay off everybody they want and turn the United States into the Third World. It's happening everywhere now. Chomsky is addressing that. He offers an explanation and offers facts. People are very grateful for that. They want to find out who he is." This quote is a great example of the Chomsky Effect, and Young himself has used his own influence to spread the word, says Billingsley: "When he interviews musicians, he gives them copies of Chomsky's books. Young 'turned on' the band Live, which sold six million albums last year, to Chomsky. He also gave Chomsky books to Rancid, an 'avowed leftist band.' And he convinced Jan Wenner to let him interview Chomsky for *Rolling Stone*, stained-glass window to the rock culture. What emerged was not so much an interview as a duet."

Chomsky's influence in the musical world extends further, into the "punkzine" punk magazine *MAXIMUMROCKNROLL*, which ran one of his lectures with the caption: "This is reality," and which has Chomsky as part of its "Project Braintrust (along with Tim Yohannan, Grendl M, Dave S, and FAIR, the New York-based leftwing media group"). Says Billingsley, "Around the time of the [first] Gulf War, *MAXIMUM-ROCKNROLL* released a record called "New World Order." On one side is "music of resistance" by the group Bad Religion. The song "Heaven is Failing," by Mr. Brett (Brett Gurewitz), has these lyrics: "As I walk beneath the valley / I shall fear no evil / For thanks to King George and his rainbow cabinet / Today murder is legal." On the flip side Chomsky takes a solo: "The U.S. Air Force is pounding large parts of Iraq and Kuwait into dust, killing no one knows how many people" and "American troops walking into what could be a meat grinder."

Interestingly, according to Billingsley, "This seven-inch vinyl release may have been the inspiration that made Chomskyites of Pearl Jam. The group's leader, Eddie Vedder, 'is a big Bad Religion fan,' according to

Andy Kaulkin of Epitaph records, a label owned by former Bad Religion member and Chomsky devotee Brett Gurewitz. The label negotiated with AK Press of San Francisco, which Kaulkin describes as 'kind of anarchist,' for the rights to release Noam Chomsky CDs such as 'Class War: The Attack on Working People'; 'Prospects for Democracy'; and 'The Clinton Vision'—all based on lectures recorded at the Massachusetts Institute of Technology. 'It makes sense for us to produce it,' says Kaulkin. 'Epitaph is the foremost label. The kids respect Epitaph and will buy anything that is on Epitaph. The kids will want to know more about Chomsky. It's got our logo on it.' Other bands on the Epitaph label, it is worth noting, include Offspring, Voodoo, Glow Skulls, Wayne Kramer, NOFX, Down By Law, Joykiller, Total Chaos, Red Aunts, Rancid, Gas Huffer, Ten Foot Pole, Claw Hammer, and RKL (Rich Kids on LSD). Lest this seem an arcane list, a Los Angeles record retailer confirms that he sells 'boatloads' of Epitaph material, new and used. Kaulkin says that his Chomsky project will help AK Press, but that it is also a commercial project that will make money."

Further, Don Was (who has a portrait of Chomsky above the drum kit at his studio, which he calls "the Chomsky Ranch") worked "on an album that combines Chomsky readings with original music by REM, Pearl Jam, and other groups. X has already laid down one track. Proceeds of the album will go to FAIR. And what does Professor Chomsky himself think of rock and punk bands pushing his stuff? Chomsky says he had never heard of *MAXIMUMROCKNROLL* or Bad Religion but complied with their request for material. " 'Seemed fine to me,' he said, 'but I know very little about this scene.' His devotee Charles Young, however, says that Chomsky is 'completely in favor' of these musical adaptations and notes that calls from bands are pouring into the professor's MIT office at a surprising rate. 'It has been explained to Noam what a potential tool rock can be for organizing', says Young, and Chomsky is presumably intrigued by the idea of building a cadre among a new lumpen youth audience since he has failed to build a cadre audience anywhere else. Young is optimistic about prospects for getting the word out. He notes that Tom Morello of the band Rage Against the Machine studied at Harvard: 'They are smart guys. They have been reading Chomsky for years. Between Pearl Jam and REM, Rage Against the Machine, it is spreading out there. It might be wishful projection but I believe that music will be going into a political period again' ":

> But if Noam Chomsky will not likely be touring with Pearl Jam any time soon, for now, however, the Chomsky-rock dialectic remains. Perhaps it is just retribution that after a lifetime of leftist fundamentalism, Chomsky's most eager acolytes turn out to be the subliterates of *MAXIMUMROCKNROLL*, where Bad Religion, bad politics, and bad music converge. It is also strangely appropriate that he has finally found favor with a kind of ruling class. Every member of Pearl Jam, after all, is a multimillionaire with a fan base that, as one producer put it, "will buy anything they put out" and which hangs on their every word. The various producers and even many of the punk bands are also wealthy and powerful, enjoying the rewards of the American society, although they too posture as members of a downtrodden proletariat.

Interesting as always is the degree to which the Left is expected to abide by some rigid set of principles (Maoist? anticonsumerist? ascetic? abstinent?), while the rest of society can happily gorge itself with wanton disregard for any restraint. It would seem that at least part of the idea of this music is to inform those who feel that there's something amiss on society's playing field, and that perhaps we ought to level it out rather than erecting one luxurious version for the rich and another paltry one for the poor.

Despite what feels like a decline in popular culture activism, as anticonsumption grunge gives way to Bentley-backdropped hip-hop videos featuring, say, G-Unit, or the sickening consumerist celebration of wealth and excess by Paris Hilton or those featured on television shows about billionaire's lifestyles, there remains a strong antiestablishment sentiment across the musical horizon. This is very much a bottom-up phenomenon, whereby bands come to be inspired by certain political ideas, and then promote them to eager fans, in a process not unlike the creative move from the bottom up, as we see in an interview titled "Monopolies, NPR, & PBS," between Robert McChesney and David Barsamian:

> It's actually ironic, given all the claims made about the market. It's a very poor mechanism for creativity. Look at popular music. These record companies are desperate to make money. So they want to give people what they want, the five companies that sell 90 percent of the music now, all but one part of these huge giants we just named. The problem they have is that the commercial impulse isn't always very good for creativity. All the great breakthroughs in rock and roll and popular music in the last 40 years have been outside of their web. It happens in the nooks and crevices. Once these corporate guys get hold of it, they try to recreate it. Real creativity can't be sparked on Wall Street.[19]

More surprising than this kind of resistance to corporatization among the bands and the fans is where this sentiment comes to play out, such as in the Texas band the Dixie Chicks, or in the Indigo Girls, which in both cases contain band members speaking out not only to a status quo in their immediate environments, but to their own personal past and family members. In a November 1999 interview with Sandy Carter, Amy Ray recounts:

Sandy Carter: Can you talk some about experiences and influences that gave birth to your views and social vision?

Amy Ray: From an early age, I had a sense of community involvement. But my family background was very conservative. My father was a product of the 1950s, very conservative, very smart, and hard to argue with, but also very charitable and giving. By college, I was gay and had broken away from a lot of that background, become an environmentalist, and was into social welfare and down on the military. But some of my biggest changes came when I met Winona LaDuke in 1990. Through her I was able to bring environmental and indigenous activism together and that opened doors to other connections. Reading Noam Chomsky helped me see the interconnections between a broad range of issues and how the whole paradigm of society needs to change. Later, meeting the Zapatistas in Mexico and seeing change happen at the grassroots level, bottom-up, that was certainly an inspiration.[20]

As a resident of Nashville, I am constantly amazed at the heartfelt appeals by country, folk, and blues stars, presumably with many Republican supporters in the room, for a reconsideration of or downright rejection of current administration policies. We expect such introductions from Joan Baez or Emmylou Harris, and we get them, but there's a much stronger moral and sometimes religious-inspired discourse in musical performances than one might expect in the so-called red states. And the 2004 election certainly galvanized a large array of voices, from the stage to the public and back again. Moby, Eddie Vedder, Bono and others maintain their resistance, but they're joined by committed rockers and aficionados; the www.interpunk.com site, for example, remarks the flowering of spoken word resistance through discussion of Jello culminating, once again, with AK Press's involvement with the production of accompanying text:

The surprise Green Party presidential nomination and the growing rebellion against corporations has aroused interest in JELLO's spoken word side as never before. This election year special combines fresh reflections on the WTO convention in Seattle; democracy; e-issues; the Green Party & other election issues;

post Columbine High School backlash on kids who think; and our ever more interesting times taken from recent live performances in Boulder, Seattle and Denver. JELLO BIAFRA's Become The Media is the sixth installment in his spoken word albums. JELLO BIAFRA is the former leader of DEAD KENNEDYS and collaborator in the ongoing LARD project. JELLO's last spoken word release If Evolution is Outlawed, Only Outlaws Will Evolve was released in November 1998 to rave reviews. Recently, Alternative Tentacles Records released THE NO WTO COMBO Live From The Battle In Seattle LP/CD which featured JELLO BIAFRA, Kim Thayil and Krist Novoselic protesting & rocking against the World Trade Organization last December. This release will be available to the book world via AK Press.[21]

Reviews on the interpunk site offer some humorous anecdotal reactions to Jello; an April 10, 2003, review by Stian Nygard, for example, states: "great spoken word by a great man. hours of listening. easy listening that is. jello speaks very clearly. not like noam chomsky, he mumbles too much. im not saying noam chomsky is worse than jello, just that he speaks more dull and you have to pay more attention to him. maybe the problem is that im from norway. anyway, this is interesting stuff."[22] Or the August 7, 2001, call to reflect and consume the right stuff, from Rob in Illinois, who on December 29, 2001, states "Support Alternative Tentacles and keep buying Jello's stuff! I'd recommend to get this to learn how the other members DK were trying to ruin the name and Jello. Good cd otherwise, if your interested in political scandals and whatnot check this out," and Kent in Las Vegas on August 7, 2001: "Classic Jello Biafra. I think all the punks who are all anti-authority and all anti-government should listen to some stuff by Biafra, and read some things by Noam Chomsky. Instead of just being ignorant towards what they hate. Buy BUy BUY! yea!" The point of course is that this music inspires understanding or at least curiosity among a marginalized population who would benefit from alternative insights, as Andrew from New Jersey suggested on February 5, 2002, "this cd is about basically one that exposes the politicians for what they are gives hope the underground and just is good."[23]

Perusal of alternative reading lists on such sites as amazon.com further reinforce this link between music and dissident views. One guide, by James O'Blivion,[24] a self-described political junkie (subversive), begins with an introduction to the problem:

Tired of sweating and slaving for minimum wage (or slightly above) whilst the billionaires acquire more billions? Tired of violent crime that makes your neighborhood a dangerous place to live? Tired of giving 1/5 of your income to your government while corporate executives (who can AFFORD to give 1/5 of their income) receive tax break after tax break? If so, be aware that your enemy has a name . . . and it is Capitalism. See . . . this is how it works: Corporations own EVERYTHING. They own the media, they own the government, they own the war machines, they own the country . . . don't let them own YOU.

His antidote is "anti capitalist reading," such as Noam Chomsky's works in both book form and in the CD form mentioned previously. He also invokes Daniel Guerin's *Anarchism: From Theory to Practice*, and, "above all," Robert McChesney's *Corporate Media and the Threat to Democracy* and a Benjamin Bagdikian book titled *The Media Monopoly* (the cover of which appears on a Rage Against the Machine album, "The Battle of Los Angeles"), along with other works by Noam Chomsky, Che Guevara, Marx and Engels, Jean-Paul Sartre, Malcolm X, and Franz Fanon.

Appropriately, in response to the site's own questions, "So what now?" and "Where do you go from here?" there's a section on "anti-capitalist music":

Well, allow me to recommend a few items for your listening enjoyment. First, you'll want to get ahold of a few Dead Kennedys albums . . . I'd say that "Bedtime for Democracy" is a good place to start. After listening, you may also want to check out their lead singer Jello Biafra's spoken word. "I Blow Minds for a Living" and "Become the Media" are my highest recommendations. Up next, curl up and settle into Anti-Flag's brilliant anti-corporate opus, "A New Kind of Army." Pay extra close attention to the lyrics of "The Consumer's Song" . . . they're calling out to you. Next, grab some Rage Against the Machine, preferably their 1991 album, "Rage Against the Machine." That should give enough fuel to the fire of your discontent. And quite possibly the most important album on this list: "A New Morning, Changing Weather" by The (international) Noise Conspiracy. This is where it's really at. When you hear "Capitalism Stole My Virginity," you'll know what I'm talking about.[25]

The "Effect" is clearly set out here, for, according to O'Blivion, "after checking out a few of the items mentioned, I'm sure you'll be well on your way to fighting the system which holds you down. From there on in, you should have no problem finding similar works which expound upon the ideas of socialism and anarchism. Thanks for reading . . . and good luck. Solidarity."

The most trenchant effect of this music-politics link, though, is that when dissent occurs in a popular musical venue, Chomsky is invariably invoked, generally as an example of what can be said, or of a reasonable place to turn to when in search of information. At a 2003 concert in Denver, Colorado, Eddie Vedder of Pearl Jam angrily impaled a mask of George Bush on his microphone stand and then slammed it to the stage. The results, in addition to a "few dozen" people walking out, were long sequences of discussions on various sites about the event. An individual self-titled "European" wrote, on November 5, 2004, the following blog:

the thing is, you people who go on about oh, what's wrong we are just trying to save the world from bin laden, and sadam was such a fuck and deserved to die and get kicked out etc. . . . try and get a proper perspective on it all . . . someone talked about ed vedder having no tact. well does george W? does the US government? what about all these countries it goes into in the name of freedom and democracy? don't you think there is more to it than your government claims? the UShas been trying to get a better grip and hold on the middle east for over fifty yes 50 years. do some proper research before you get involved in this subject man. get a grip of your own perspective before you start trumpeting on about the good will of the US government. the USis currently run by a radical rightwing extremist group that has managed to go around conquering and manipulating whatever country it can in the name of peace. don't believe everything they tell you. wake up and try and see the truth. of course they're gonna go on about what an awful guy he was . . . and sure as shit he was, but's it's their perfect excuse to go and milk the land, to gain another base in the middle east . . . to spread themselves across the planet . . . and who's gonna benefit? you can't be serious to claim the iraqis are gonna benefit? I mean sure maybe a bunch of them will no longer get pulled out of society and thrown into jail to have their balls electrocuted, but lots of shit is gonna happen that is just as bad . . . the country will end up owing billions of dollars to the US and will have to pay it back for the next century, there will still be shit loads of poor people barely able to eat, while a bunch of white, private school educated, elitists get fatter or higher on coke which ever one gets them through the night. the rest of the world is trying to help in a neutral way without benefits and the US just says step aside, or get yourselves an army big enough to stop us . . . that's exactly what they said, except maybe in more eloquent terms yet disguised with more gloss and varnish . . . wake the fuck up . . . and eddie vedder is one of the few in the states who can see through all this . . . if you had any sense you'd do yourself the favour of doing some proper research outside of switching on your TV and listening to the news, the US news channels are the most biased media signals outside of north korea . . . i mean some proper research . . . try noam chomsky . . . he is possibly the most free thinking american the US currently has . . . good luck on your voyage out of the dark forest . . . i hope you make it.[26]

One of the suppositions that guides all of this, from blogs to radical reading lists to the desire to purchase books by Noam Chomsky in record stores, is the sense that the right is going so far as to raise serious questions, even among those who might have been or remained uninterested in the workings of government. Many people suggest, with the newly composed Supreme Court, the growing presence of hardened religious fanatics in positions of power, the unquestioned and ever-growing rise of the Pentagon budget in the face of massive tax cuts to the rich and concomitant reductions in social aid across the spectrum, that a new backlash is brewing. One such galvanizing point was the 2004 reelection campaign of George Bush, and whole sites are devoted to bringing politics to the punk and rock scene. For instance, www.punkvoter.com features discussions about U.S. politics, considerable Bush-whacking, and articles by members of bands such as The Frisk, The Criminals, Blatz, The Gr'Ups, Tsunami Bomb, Midtown, The Dwarves, The AKAs, Jawbreaker, Jets To Brazil, Lunachicks, Sick Of It All, Operation Ivy, Common Rider, Authority Zero, Trans Am, Kool Arrow Records, Goldfinger, Jello Biafra, Good Riddance, Anti-Flag, Pennywise, Bad Religion, The Lawrence Arms, Razorcake Fanzine. Jesse Luscious, of The Frisk, The Criminals, and Blatz. The Gr'Ups, for example, writes about just coming "home from a Punkvoter.com meeting with a ton of folks including Fat Mike, Jello Biafra, and San Francisco Supervisor Matt Gonzalez. We figured out the next steps for PV—and it's going to be a blast!"[27] Among the prioritics named at the meeting?

Another PV priority is the continuing assault on Roe vs. Wade and related choice issues. Obviously the Supreme Court and other judicial appointments will be key to the survival of legal, accessible abortions and other basic sexual health and sexual education programs. A third is a combination of fighting media consolidation and encouraging media literacy. Less corporations owning more and more media outlets combined with rampant ethic problems within those media outlets (Fox News anyone?) leaves us vulnerable to the rabid demagogues salivating on right wing talk shows and websites. Fight them by checking out books like "The Culture of Fear: Why Americans Are Afraid of the Wrong Things" (by Barry Glassner) and "Manufacturing Consent" (by Noam Chomsky)![28]

Jesse Michaels, of Operation Ivy and Common Rider, has another approach to being just "informed" by the likes of Chomsky and Zinn, worth quoting at length:

Before I say anything else, I want to say again, all these radical things are great and very important. But in a time when things are going from just scary to really terrifying, at a time when we are actually looking down the barrel of worldwide feudalism, it may be a good point to take stock and look at what really works, what could really change things and what is really practical. People on the left, particularly young people, need to be RICH. They need to have the means to start networks such as FOX. People on the left need to understand the language of the rich. It is of much greater importance to understand economics, technology and how the people in power actually create policy than it is to understand Che Guevara's philosophy of agrarian uprising. Howard Zinn is fantastic and does the world a great service but the left has a thousand Howard Zinns and not enough Rupert Murdochs. Noam Chomsky is a fine researcher and disseminator of information but the left desperately needs some Diebolds, some Cheneys, some Bushs etc. I don't mean the left needs some reactionary pricks that want to drag the world back into the dark ages, I mean the left needs some people with strong convictions who actually have the means to put their ideas into practical action and who are willing to fight dirty. My vision for the future isn't a million kids with liberal arts degrees and "Anti-Capitalist readers" tucked in their hemp shoulder bags, my vision for the future is a million kids with technology and business degrees from M.I.T. living the good life and using their power and influence to ACTUALLY MAKE CHANGES IN GOVERNMENT AND PARTICULARLY IN THE MEDIA. Why is this anathema to progressives? Fear of money on the left is the ultimate ally of the robber barons. Kids calling bands or writers "Sell outs" when they become successful benefits an elite who don't want the riff raff living next door to them. Worst of all, this naively anti-money attitude limits the one pointing their finger to a mental ghetto of limited means, limited power and even limited personal happiness. MONEY won/stole the last two elections. MONEY created Fox News. MONEY created the Iraq war. MONEY created the oil lobbies, the MIC, etc. A good example on the positive side is somebody like Fat Mike of fat records. Fat Mike is not a real political guy but he took his power ($) and put it to real, tangible use with Rock Against Bush. This tour went on for months and planted seeds in the minds of an enormous mall-culture generation that wouldn't go anywhere near a protest march. This is not condescension on my part, its simply the truth. What if somebody more sophisticated than Mike did the same thing with even more means?[29]

As one might imagine, the array of political views aired on such sites is vast, although I would venture to say that if there is a theme among those who mention someone to whom they turn for help and information, it's that people should be reading Noam Chomsky, and the overall view of how his work has affected them, or should affect others, is to motivate them to seek out alternative sources of information, and to use their minds to productively and with curiosity try to understand the world. In an interview by Jackie Renn for Real Change News, recorded as "A

Tradition of Troublemaking Punk Grandad Joe Keithley on post-grunge music and People Power,"[30] Renn recalls that "before MTV's Rock the Vote, there was punk music's Rock against Reagan. Now the base ingredient of punk music, rebellion, is putting new blood into election 2004." Reminding readers that "punk rock is not only a musical style but a culture, an anti-establishment movement born from the economic downfall of Great Britain in the 1970s and the policies, foreign and domestic, of the U.S. in the 1980s." Keithley recalls his own political activities in the interview, including running for the Green Party, but now mostly takes action by playing acoustic guitar on the picket line: "I have lots of friends in the union movement up there. We played a couple of really big anti-war rallies. It was great; Noam Chomsky came and spoke. We've done other things like anti-globalization. Whatever comes along. I don't put one brand of politics on what we do or what I do personally. I kind of go with the people. People Power." The motivation for inviting Chomsky, therefore, was to motivate this people party, because, in his words, "People can overthrow governments if they put their minds to it."

Presumably, the appeal of being anti–status quo for a punk band is intrinsic in the very exercise in which they engage when they play music; however, when one moves more mainstream, one immediately recalls the fervor with which the Dixie Chicks were attacked for their vocal outpourings against Bush. In a May 26, 2003, article by Matt Schild titled "Fight the Power,"[31] NOFX's Mike Burkett commented: "Now everyone is scared of being 'Dixie Chicked,'" Burkett says. "You say one thing bad about your government and you might lose a large portion of your fans. Good. Who wants a bunch of idiots for fans, anyway? Besides all that, I feel that it is the artists responsibility to speak out. Noam Chomsky recorded an entire speech on the same subject. If artists don't speak out, who will?"

And finally, it seems incumbent upon us to consider the role that music has played for Chomsky. The Znet site has a considerable library of folk, antiwar, populist, and activist music, but Chomsky himself has little engagement with such things. In an interview with David Barsamian, in the 2001 collection of interviews published as *Propaganda and the Public Mind: Conversations with Noam Chomsky*, Chomsky says: "Part of the genius of the system of domination and control is to separate people from one another so that [collective action] doesn't happen. We can't 'consult our neighbors', as one of my favorite Wobbly singers once put it back in the 1930s. As long as we can't consult our neighbors, we'll believe that there are good times. It's important to make sure that people don't consult their neighbors." And who was that Singer? "T-Bone Slim." Barsamian, clearly surprised by the musical reference, asks, incredulously, "You were listening to T-Bone Slim?" Chomsky's reply is more of what one might expect, notably "I read about these things. I'm not attuned to the auditory world"(!) (146–147). Not prepared to let a sleeping dog (bone) lie, Barsamian recalls the discussion at a later date: "In our last interview, you actually surprised me by mentioning a song by T-Bone Slim. Apparently you had read about it in some book. Are there any other musical references in your writing?"

NC: It just shows you really haven't read what I've written carefully (laughs). I actually quoted that in print—but I'll leave it to you to find out where. I read it in a collection of T-Bone Slim's songs which was put out by one of the anarchist publishers a couple of years ago. I kind of liked that one.

DB: Going back to the thirties and forties and that whole period of Woody Guthrie and the Weavers, were you ever connected to any of that music?

NC: Not much, I used to listen to Leadbelly years ago. I heard it but I was not much part of it.

DB: Some music groups today take inspiration from you, like Rage Against the Machine, U2, Chumbawamba, and Bad Religion, with whom you've actually recorded. Are they in touch with you?

NC: Just for interviews now and then. I had an interview with a musician from Rage Against the Machine a couple of weeks ago. I hear about it now and then, but I honestly don't know anything about it. (203–204)

Here, as throughout Chomsky's work and words, is that dry and sometimes ironical sometimes sarcastic wit, also mentioned by Barsamian ("His rich and wry sense of humor often goes unnoticed in the fusillade of facts," ibid. ix). This is a complicated characteristic, which combines self-deprecation, a strong sense of self-worth and limitations, along with a healthy dose of sarcasm:

Tom Morello (guitarist, Rage Against the Machine): Are you a fan of any particular kind of music, and can we play a request for you?

Noam Chomsky: If I told you what my tastes were, it would shock you.

TM: Oh no, you go right ahead. Shock me.

NC: Almost nothing. I am very much restricted to things in my childhood or before. Far before.

TM: Our CD catalog is pretty large, try me.

NC: I wouldn't even know what to say. Beethoven's Late Quartets.

TM: Anything in R&B or pop music. Anything that rings a bell?

NC: I am so ignorant, it isn't even worth asking me. I sort of knew something when my kids were around, but that's a lot of years ago.

This humorous way of speaking ("it would shock you," "far before," "It isn't even worth asking me"), in evidence throughout Chomsky's talks and writings, is indeed a powerful part of what makes the Chomsky Effect, and I'll return to it in some detail in the concluding chapter. Notice as well the direct collaboration that Chomsky has undertaken, for Chumbawamba's album "For Free Humanity, For Anarchy," Bad Religion's "New World Order: War #1" (released by the U.S. magazine *Maximumrocknroll* to protest the first Gulf War), and a track by Chomsky entitled "Capitalism Speech" appears on The Marcia Blaine School For Girls—School Disco Volume 2 (released by Metal-On-Metal). On the Bad Religion site (http://www.badreligion.com/titles/) we learn from a June 8, 2004, note that Epitaph Records "The Empire Strikes First" contains "14 songs that are fresh, focused, and absolutely alive in the way that great rock 'n' roll energizes everything it touches. It's been a long road from their early-80s beginnings, but these days, the primary concerns of Graffin and Gurewitz are not the band's intricate (and subtle) years-long evolution; they're first and foremost topical songwriters focused on domestic chaos and its global manifestation. Bad Religion is, after all, the outfit that, during the first Gulf War in 1991, shared a Maximum Rock 'n' Roll split seven-inch with radical MIT professor Noam Chomsky, who, like them, is locked into the tense present and dedicated to exposing the forces who lie and disguise to deepen and enforce human misery." In an interesting art/politics link, the blurb then goes on to suggest that "It's tempting to say—though impossible to prove—that the *The Empire Strikes First* is a such a terrific album because vocalist Graffin and guitarist Gurewitz, the band's most important creative forces, are responding to the death, desolation, and destruction of war, and to the concurrent attacks on the Bill of Rights; it seems more than just a happy accident that the band has just delivered one of its most charged and inspired records in years." One could only hope that this would be one of the Effects of engagement!

Dissidentiwood

With Mark Achbar and Peter Wintonick's 1992 *Manufacturing Consent: Noam Chomsky and the Media*, and, more recently, with Will Pascoe's 2003 *Rebel Without a Pause*, Noam Chomsky has come to the big screen. Both films, particularly the former, have been popular with audiences around the world, although, as we'll see later, their international appeal may be relatively stronger than their domestic pull, particularly in the case of the broadly diffused *Manufacturing Consent*, even though as Billingsley notes: *Manufacturing Consent* "was shown widely on college campuses and broadcast recently on PBS, which offered a tape of the show and a copy of *The Chomsky Reader* as bonus gifts for donors." The film itself contains a series of scenes reflecting the range of the Chomsky Effect; on the positive side we see thousands of people in audiences anxiously awaiting his words, and we hear the power of his analyses as he moves with grace through a plethora of different topics for different interviewers. But in a June 10, 1993, *Seattle Times* article, John Hartl recalls that the down side is represented as well: "During the course of the movie's 167 minutes, Chomsky is shown expressing his ideas with everyone from William F. Buckley (who threatens to smash his face in) to Boston University President John Silber (who calls him 'a systematic liar')." But as was the case with Michael Moore's *Fahrenheit 9/11*, a chord was struck, and audiences responded with enthusiasm. In an interview with Pat Dowell, on National Public Radio, a sense of the film's effect, and indeed the effect that being filmed had upon Chomsky himself, is made clear:

Dowell: Only the mall shoppers aren't watching. They're playing miniature golf, seemingly oblivious to Chomsky's looming image discussing thought control, the Gulf War, or spectator sports as training for irrational jingoism. Audiences who've seen the finished film in theaters have been more responsive. Chomsky says he's gotten lots of mail, much of it angry about his analysis of sports. More gratifying to him is the fact that the movie has proved useful to activists raising public awareness of East Timor. And that makes Chomsky glad

he agreed to let Wintonick and Achbar follow him with a camera, literally for years.

Chomsky: In fact, for a while, I couldn't get off an airplane in some foreign country without seeing those two smiling faces there, and my heart sinking. It felt [like?] the first scene of "Dolce Vita" a bit.

Dowell: Noam Chomsky goes to the movies? Fellini movies?

Chomsky: Yeah, I'm not as remote from the popular culture as I sometimes pretend.

There is a line here, however, with which Chomsky feels uncomfortable, and it relates in some way to the genre of film, as we will see. First, of course, is the intrusive nature of the biographical genre, or indeed any production that showcases the work of an activist who is trying to encourage people to do things together or on their own, and not to worship authority of any sort. As to the former, Chomsky notes: "My wife, particularly, laid down an iron law that they were to get nowhere near the house, the children, personal life—anything like that—and I agreed with that. I mean, this is not about a person. It's about ideas and principles. If they want to use a person as a vehicle, okay, but, you know, my personal life and my children and where I live and so on have nothing to do with it." As to the second issue, on the nature of the genre as "entertainment," Chomsky begins by stating that he has not seen the film *Manufacturing Consent*, and never will, "partly for uninteresting personal reasons, namely, I just don't like to hear myself and mostly think about the way I should have done it better, and so on. There are, however, some more general reasons. Much as the producers may try to overcome this, and I'm sure they did, there's something inevitable in the nature of the medium that personalizes the issues and gives the impression that some individual—in this case, it happens to be me—is the, you know, the leader of a mass movement or trying to become one, or something of that kind."

In an era of sound bites and reality TV, people (including public intellectuals) are often willing to do or say the most obscene kinds of things to simply have their coveted five minutes of fame; from Chomsky's perspective, this is not only wrong, it is a lost opportunity to make connections and build community. Chomsky is in this sense an exception, for a precise set of reasons: "There's very little in the way of political

organization or other forms of association in which people can participate meaningfully in the public arena. People feel themselves as victims.
They're isolated victims of propaganda, and if somehow, somebody
comes along and says, you know, the kind of thing that they sort of have
a gut feeling about or believed anyway, there's a sign of recognition and
excitement and the feeling that maybe I'm not alone."[32]

So the effect of *Manufacturing Consent* was powerful, and to the
degree that it has generated this "recognition and excitement" it would
seem to be a useful tool for organizing and diffusing ideas. But as time
passed, Chomsky became more and more reticent about its effect in ways
that are both complex and revealing. In discussions with several individuals, including Mark Achbar, which took place in Woods Hole, Massachusetts between 1993 and 1996, Chomsky is asked about the film, why
he refuses to see it, and what role it played—or could play—in advancing the kinds of ideas he hopes to promote. Here, some of his concerns
are predictable in light of what I have described so far; if his hope is to
catalyze people to think through things for themselves, and to hook up
for creative interaction with individuals to explore issues and ideas, then
he wouldn't want blind allegiance to what he himself is saying: "I get a
ton of letters about it—like I get a letter from some steelworker in
Canada saying, 'I took my friends three times, we all saw it and it's great,'
and so on and so forth. Well, that's all fine. But the standard letter, the
standard letter, is something like this: it says, 'I'm really glad they made
this film; I thought I was the only person in the world who had these
thoughts, I'm delighted to know that somebody else actually has them
and is saying them.' Then comes the punch-line: 'How can I join your
movement?' That's why I'm ambivalent" (319).[33]

There are several points here. First, he is but the speaker for a much
broader effort undertaken by, say, the group who has invited him, and
therefore his very presence there is a sign of the hard work that has been
done to organize the event, and it's this hard work that ought to be recognized: "somebody else organized the talk, and the real work is being
done by the people who organized the talk, and then followed it up and
are out there working in their communities. If they can bring in some
speaker to help get people together, terrific, but that person is in no sense
'the leader'" (319).[34]

But at this point it seems reasonable to ask about where these ideas come from, that is, doesn't Chomsky present *his* ideas, and therefore someone might come out to hear *him* speak? In many writings, he points out that much of what he has to say in the political realm, and even in the linguistic work, emanates from early oft-forgotten sources (as we will see in chapter 3), which is part of the answer; but here he addresses another point, about hero worship and deferring to higher authority:

Woman: But the critique of the media in the film is taken from speeches that *you* gave.

Chomsky: Yeah, but that's because other people are doing important things and I'm not doing important things—that's what it literally comes down to. I mean, years ago I used to be involved in organizing too—I'd go to meetings, get involved in resistance, go to jail, all of that stuff—and I was just no good at it at all; some of these people here can tell you. So sort of a division of labor developed: I decided to do what I'm doing now, and other people kept doing the other things. Friends of mine who were basically the same as me—went to the same colleges and graduate schools, won the same prizes, teach at M.I.T. and so on—just went a different way. They spend their time organizing, which is much more important work—so they're not in a film. That's what the difference is. I mean, I do something basically less important—it *is*, in fact. It's adding something, and I can do it, so I do it—I don't have any false modesty about it. And it's helpful. But it's helpful to people who are doing the real work. And every popular movement I know of in history has been like that. In fact, it's extremely important for people with power not to let anybody understand this, to make them think there are big leaders around who somehow get things going, and then what everybody else has to do is follow them. That's one of the ways of demeaning people, and degrading them and making them passive. I don't know how to overcome this exactly, but it's really something people ought to work on.

Woman: As an activist for East Timor, though, I have to say that the film put our work on a completely different level. Even if you have some trouble with it personally, it has gotten people doing a lot of real work out there.

Chomsky: I think that's true; I know that's true.

Another woman: Now I've got to admit it—I felt odd having you sign a book for my friend earlier today.

Chomsky: Yeah, it's crazy—it's just completely wrong. In a place like San Francisco, it gets embarrassing: I can't walk across the Berkeley campus—literally—without twenty people coming up and asking me to sign something. That doesn't make any sense.

Woman: It does feel unnatural.

Chomsky: It is, it's completely missing the point. It's simply not factually accurate, for one thing—because like I say, the real work is being done by people who are not known, that's always been true in every popular movement in history. The people who are known are riding the crest of some wave. Now, you can ride the crest of the wave and try to use it to get power, which is the standard thing, or you can ride the crest of the wave because you're helping people that way, which is another thing. But the point is, it's the wave that matters—and that's what people ought to understand. I don't know how you get that across in a film (cited in *Understanding Power*, 321–322).[35]

Some of the same issues pertain to the second full-length feature Chomsky film, *Rebel Without a Pause*. This documentary offers the movie-going audience another approach to the Chomsky Effect, and some of the reviews are quite revealing relative to issues discussed to this point. John Danziger, in *Docurama*,[36] opens with:

You've got to be pretty seriously committed (to say nothing of having basically no interest in music) to think of Noam Chomsky as a rock star, but that's sort of the premise of this documentary, a worshipful portrait of the influential linguist and professor in the months before the Iraq war. The documenting of Chomsky minutiae and comings and goings has apparently become something of a cottage industry—a sticker on the cover of the case of this DVD, for instance, crows that this is the most important Chomsky documentary since *Manufacturing Consent*, which may make you wonder just how many horses are in that race. Still, along with all the noise about Chomsky's celebrity is a good amount of Chomsky himself, articulating a point of view that gets abysmally short shrift in the mainstream media; even if you disagree with him vehemently, you'd have to admit that he's well read, well informed and hugely influential.

A number of reviewers have pointed out that *Rebel Without a Pause* did not have the impact of *Manufacturing Consent*, but was rather more like what one finds when surfing through the many sites devoted to videos and tapes of him speaking. Christopher Long writes, in *DVD Town*, for example:[37] "You probably already know if you're going to be interested in the movie. If you love Chomsky, you'll want to see it. If you can't stand him, you'll avoid it like the plague. *Rebel Without a Pause* doesn't match up to Mark Achbar's *Manufacturing Consent: Noam Chomsky and the Media*, the definitive Chomsky documentary, but it's still a worthy effort and of value even just as historical record. It's not exactly exciting viewing but Chomsky himself admits that he's not really a dynamic speaker; he just has a message many people want to hear."

On a much smaller scale, there is as well *Power and Terror: Noam Chomsky in Our Times*, which could be classified among what is probably dozens of works put together by film students or Chomsky aficionados. Mickey Z[38] adds his sense of the cinema effect with a discussion of *Power and Terror*, this "short, sparse film," which he saw at Film Forum in the West Village. The review doesn't talk much about the film, but rather focuses upon the new wave of interest in Chomsky that has developed among musicians, previously discussed. For him, the film itself "succinctly lays out the post 9/11 geo-political realities of the day," offering "information we all need to hear; information that goes far beyond fashionable poses or indecipherable theories. As usual, our favorite dissident linguist has done the tedious work of compiling the statistics, the quotes, and the headlines. From there, as always, it's up to us." This is a common theme. But what he also emphasizes is that Chomsky speaks in a "language that would have most rock stars regurgitating their p?t? [*sic*] into their kidney-shaped pool," so "Besides urging you to see this movie and spreading the word long and far, I'd also like to encourage music fans to demand more from your chosen idols. If Bono and others want to wear the hat of political rebel, let's get more for our entertainment dollar." It's an interesting argument, in light of all that we've seen in this chapter, but rather than celebrating the diffusion of Chomsky's ideas through the endlessly popular medium of music, Mickey Z bemoans the appropriation of Chomsky's works in an unthinking way: "As was inevitable, rock stars awash in capital were using the only internal reference point they know: their massive ego. The highest form of praise they can muster is to elevate another human being to the same level of blind adoration they wallow in (I can see it now: Noam stage-diving at his next lecture). The only possible result of such self-centered drivel is the personalization of Chomsky as a youth 'hero' with very few of his ideas coming along for the ride. With most anti-corporate tyranny tenets being checked at the door by the pop music elite, members of the well-bred gentry class can now welcome a 'dissident linguist' with open arms, conveniently leaving the rest of us behind." This, says Mickey Z, "is class war for the polite crowd." So what does he expect? "Instead of just whining about the disappearing rain forest, why not educate the masses about the role corporate America, the U.S. government, and the meat-based diet plays in the domestic affairs of Brazil? Why just write a song for starving Somalis when you have the influence to mobilize hundreds of thousands of people to examine the social conditions that allow for poverty in a world of plenty? If not, we can simply stop buying their music, going to their concerts, and wearing their overpriced, sweatshop-produced t-shirts."[39] This is an interesting approach, reminiscent of Jean-Paul Sartre's demand that authors be engaged in the issues of the times in his (immediate) post–WWII book *Qu'est-ce que la littérature* (*What is Literature*), and in his writings in and about his journal *Humanité*, as we will see in the last chapter. The degree to which we can expect this kind of engagement from artists is a complicated issue, hearkening back to discussions of the avant-garde and modernism, and one might wonder if, as we saw earlier, this would really make for better music. Probably not. But it's clear that the musicians themselves, and the audiences present for the performances, are turned on and tuned in to a distinctly anti–status quo discourse; where it leads them, when the amplifiers and headphones are turned off, is another matter, which we will pick up in chapter five.

Professional Popularity

Given the broad popular appeal for Chomsky and his work, and the range of people who want to hear what he wants to say, there are of course many anecdotes about his life. Some of the stories about him are true, though perhaps distorted by the passage of time or the views of the person telling the story, and some of them are simply far-fetched, but they are part of a collection of positive and negative impressions recorded through anecdote. In one frequently cited example, it is said that during a demonstration he was being hustled off by billy club-wielding cops when suddenly someone shouted out "Don't hit him in the head!". Another recalls an observation when he arrived in Japan to accept his prestigious Kyoto Prize and someone noted he was wearing the same tie he had worn on his previous visit, years earlier, to a U.S. campus. His response? "Why would I need two?" This response was echoed in a comment he made to me, while folding his suit and placing it in my car after receiving an honorary doctorate from the University of Western Ontario, when he said that he had to take good care of it, since he only owns one. There exist as well numerous anecdotes recounting to his ability to work constantly, including stories of late-night telephone calls to students or researchers to check specific facts or make comments, a report about the Chomskys' tearing out the kitchen in their house to make room for more books, an account of his car breaking down and him walking into a dealership and asking for another "blue one," and a story that when a doctor suggested he lose some weight, Chomsky responded with the welcome idea that he could save the time normally accorded to eating lunch.

These episodes are perhaps rooted in some event or another, and for the most part they are positive depictions, images of a man whose effect is deemed desirable. But given the radical nature of his views, and the fervor with which he defends or promotes them within his field and beyond the university environment, we find at least as many people who describe him as abhorrent, malicious, subversive, and dangerous, as we will see in the next chapter. For people on all sides, however, there is agreement that Noam Chomsky's oratorical skills are legendary, and virtually without equal (especially among his opponents!), and that he has a stubbornly tenacious argumentative side. As one colleague at MIT said, "he does tend to stomp on arguments. . . . He's not a grand old man, in terms of sitting back and letting 100 flowers bloom or letting the young people carry the torch."[40] This may be so, but it does not speak to the way that Chomsky, to follow the metaphor, has prepared the soil so that people are encouraged to bloom; these are the efforts that represent his force, his legacy, his Effect, and on this point, even those who have been critical on some levels of Chomsky's work tend to agree. John Goldsmith (professor of linguistics at the University of Chicago and author, with Geoffrey Huck, of *Ideology and Linguistic Theory; Noam Chomsky and the Deep Structure Debates, 1996*), in personal correspondence, writes: "This is the most defensible position, from where I sit, with regard to Chomsky's beneficial effects. His effects as a teacher (both direct—his effects on the students who have spent time around him in Cambridge— and indirect, through his writings) have been great. As I've said repeatedly, in this respect I owe him a great deal. But the contrast between his espoused anarchism and his practical stance in cognitive science is one that's difficult for me to feel comfortable with."[41] For Goldsmith, like others, there is also another side to this Effect, the negatives of which I will explore in the next chapter, from a range of perspectives and according to a range of variables.

The Chomsky Effect is not only multifaceted, it is also variable across disciplines, genres, and classes of people. Two examples, one professional and one political, suggest the depth and range of reactions to Chomsky's approach and Effect. Within the professional linguistics community, there are hoards of scholars, from all around the world, who have been and remain devoted to studying the implications of Chomsky's insights and advancing the current research. There are also groups, notably the generative semanticists, who feel that Chomsky has betrayed them, lied about their work, or obfuscated the story of the rift that was formed between them in the 1960s and 1970s. These quarrels can make for some interesting and even valuable reading, when the focus is on something other than professional jealousies, the demarcation of territories, the will to power, inner or inter-disciplinary rivalries, gossip, innuendo or falsification (alas, as in any other professional domain, such activities are disturbingly easy to find). In noting these effects, I'm not going to adjudicate on one side or another, especially in the details of personal rifts that have opened up in linguistics, noted by Goldsmith, Harris, and elsewhere; nevertheless, no examination of the Chomsky Effect would be complete without some mention of the effect that he has had upon the field of language studies, which will come up in different sections of this book. His ideas revolutionized the field which, when he entered it in the 1950s, was dominated by discussions about matters (distributionalism, behaviorism, structuralism) now considered retrograde or, at the very least, of marginal interest. It was the power of this work, undertaken from the time he was a graduate student, that provided the credibility and credentials for him to speak out as an intellectual on affairs of public concern, matters to which I will return in depth in chapter seven.

The presence of such a powerful personality at the great scientific research institution, MIT, coupled with the visibility of other towering intellectual figures like Roman Jakobson at Harvard and Zellig Harris at the University of Pennsylvania, has contributed to making linguistics recognizable to a public who otherwise would have little concern for such research. Chomsky and Harris, and their quite well-known parting of ways, or the early relation between Jakobson and Chomsky (Jakobson got Chomsky his first job at MIT) has created a veritable mystique in the field and has perhaps been a force for promoting interest beyond the academic realm. This is not to suggest that high-profile linguists or linguistics-inspired researchers are household names, but many people have probably heard of Henry Hoenigswald, John Goldsmith, Joan Gopnik, Henry Hiz, Konrad Koerner, Leigh Lisker, Fred Lukoff, Robin Lakoff, or Stephen Pinker. Ray Jackendoff, a former student of Chomsky's, now at Brandeis University, says that "Chomsky set the field on quite a different course, and most people wouldn't have gone into the field had it not been for him. I can think of one other person who has dominated in one field, and that's Freud."[42] The downside of this situation is that contemporary linguists now wonder what will happen to the field now that Chomsky is emeritus (he's 80 years old). Linguistic programs are already under attack in North America, and the loss of such a figure as an active participant therein, given that he has lent both credibility and a kind of sexiness to the field, is of great concern to some. Others claim that people like Chomsky or Harris have been detrimental to those areas deemed by them as being of lesser importance, while still others foresee the rapid decline of the whole field (or its being folded into other traditional areas like anthropology, or newer areas like cognitive sciences).

David Heap offers another scenario, which would see the convergence between the generative paradigm and its various rival or competitor frameworks: "I tend towards this vision not only because I am an irrepressible optimist (gotta be!), but also because I have seen evidence (in this country at least) of former sectarian enemies who now at least talk (and sometimes even listen) to each other. The convergence scenario is also a viable one outside of North America, notably in the UK and some places on the European continent, where generative linguistics is seen as an interesting and important contribution but not the final word. France is (of course) another story" (personal correspondence, August 20, 1998). No matter what side one stands on, however, it is clear that Chomsky's Effect in this domain is of tremendous importance worldwide. What will be his legacy? This is harder to determine. John Goldsmith responded at length to my inquiry in this regard:

For a number of years now linguists have been playing the "What do you think will happen to the field when Chomsky retires?" game. It's followed closely by the "How will history remember Chomsky? game." My guess, on the latter question, is that he will be remembered in fifty years much like Ernst Mach was by mid-century. Do you know Ernst Mach? He was one of the most important, and certainly prestigious and influential, scientists in the second half of the 19th century. "Mach speed" is named after him, as are Mach bands, which one learns about in intro to psych courses. The founders of logical positivism, the Vienna Circle, originally called their group the Machkreise, the Mach Circle, debating issues that arose out of his scientific philosophy. He believed in sensory impressions, and he believed that all there was in addition to these sensory impressions were elegant methods for reducing the complexity of our descriptions of these impressions (you can see that this influenced Russell considerably, for example). There is much more that could be said about his ultimately influential ideas about the simplicity of certain kinds of descriptions—there's a continuous thread leading to Chomsky's simplicity metric of the 1950s and 1960s. But Mach's greatest influence, perhaps, was on the young Einstein and others of his generation, because Mach argued that Newton's notion of "absolute" space and time were errors; space and time do not exist, but are notions we use to organize our sense impressions. This philosophy freed up people like Einstein, and allowed them to rethink the character of space and time in radical new ways. But at the same time Mach's view was less than liberating—he could never accept the idea of atoms, for example; they seemed to be so small that we'd never really encounter them in sensory data, so they couldn't be real. Mach, and true followers of his work, simply didn't accept the mounting evidence for atoms (of which the most impressive was Einstein's analysis of Brownian motion in 1905). In sum, Mach's greatest contribution was methodological and not substantive (though historians of science know about his contributions in a range of areas, including psychophysics); he is not remembered the way the greats of his generation are, such as Maxwell, Boltzmann, and Gibbs. But his overall philosophy had galvanizing effects on quite a few important figures, for both the good and the bad (as we see in hindsight).[43]

The second example regarding Chomsky's long-term Effect comes from outside of the linguistic domain, where the Effect is more complicated and the legacy more tied to the current moment. Here, discussions regarding Chomsky's work vary significantly not only across time, but also from place to place, and group to group. Within the Zionist community, for example, there are individuals who feel that Chomsky stands up for a version of socialist Zionism (related to groups like Avukah, Hashomer Hatzair, Kibbutz Artzi), which for them was (and remains) an inspiration in their struggle to establish a society erected on non- or anticapitalist principles. Variations exist, of course: there are Jews (and Gentiles) who consider that Chomsky's decision to speak on behalf of the Arabs or the Palestinians in Israel is a sign of his consistency as regards human rights abuse, which makes him a rare example of someone who insists upon the consistent application of classical liberal principles of justice, as we'll see further on; there are those who use his approach to justify their attacks against Israel, unrelated to any desire to uphold international law; there are those who insist that all nationalism is prejudice, but find in Chomsky's work suggestions that he insists upon the prejudice of Israeli nationalism while playing down other examples in the world; and there are those who consider that one constant in Chomsky's approach is his pervasive desire to speak on behalf of the underdog. This leads to another truism: One can learn a lot about groups by watching their reaction to Chomsky, often more about them than about Chomsky's ideas, which are nuanced in ways that refuse easy categorization and misconstrued in such debates.

Other variables include personal animosity that arises out of Chomsky's disregard for benefits that for some people are lifelong objectives, like material wealth or professional success. Chomsky is notoriously dismissive of those who denounce his work for careerist purposes, and indeed would be distraught if he suddenly found favor with the intellectual or political elite. He is of course deeply ensconced in the elite in some ways, being a graduate of the prestigious University of Pennsylvania, a former fellow at Harvard, a well-paid full professor and holder of a named chair at MIT, and the recipient of countless professional awards. But in other ways he feels deeply at odds with elites for reasons that can also be traced to his political views, and he is scorned by some for this reason. As an anarchist, he believes in the elimination of arbitrary authority, because this would create the conditions whereby the creative potential of all persons can be manifest, in its own way and on its own terms. He constantly fights against the wholesale condemnation of the world's rabble and the concomitant promotion of particular vanguards. His teaching and lecturing styles reflect these views as well, something that is evident from his paying attention to and taking seriously the views of all persons. Given this stance, the idea of a "popularizer" does not refer to the messenger who comes down from the mount to explain to the ignorant masses the meanings of his (or others') great teachings; instead, he speaks to others on the basis of his direct experience with the matters at hand and he seeks out the opinions of those with whom he is engaged.

For this reason, an astonishing number of people with whom he has corresponded expressed to me their amazement when the well-known Noam Chomsky came into their world by responding to their questions or comments with detailed and serious letters. I myself first communicated with him while still a student in comparative literature, and was astounded by his willingness to engage my diverse concerns (refugees, language theory, anarchist movements) with devotion and care that far exceeded polite recognition. He is not singular in this respect; indeed a measure of the decency of those in the teaching profession is their generosity, and my own experience is that those with the most integrity and concern tend to be the most generous with their time and respectful of others. But given the range of issues that concern him, one can only imagine the number of letters that occupy the twenty hours per week Chomsky devotes to writing correspondence. Nathan Glazer refers to this quality as "wearying": "It's his indefatigability. He always writes the last letter. You just have to give up; he's more energetic than any of us."[44]

There is another point that deserves some elaboration because it leads us to the central concerns that underwrite Chomsky's approach. Chomsky is fundamentally worried about the rising fascism and Stalinism in Western society, something that in his sense can be demonstrated by certain legal decisions on many levels (as we will see in chapter 4), American foreign policy in, for example, Latin America, French foreign policy in Rwanda or Algeria, or through careful analysis of corporate culture. In other words, it would be erroneous to think that the end of World War II led Western society away from the impulses that led to Nazism and fascism. On the contrary, we must be on guard in our daily lives against all forms of behavior in any way similar to what has been conveniently appropriated to certain countries or certain eras. We have enough evidence to suggest that the active French collaboration on a plethora of fronts, the Swiss collaboration through banking practices, the American collaboration through their refusal to act on early knowledge of the Nazi death camps, the Vatican collaboration if only through their silence, the Soviet collaboration with Hitler through the Hitler-Stalin pact, even the Canadian collaboration that came as a result of Mackenzie King's refusal to grant asylum to Jews, was well known and systematically carried out during World War II.

So another effect that Chomsky has upon those willing to entertain his speculations is that the society in which we live is not the liberal Mecca we would like to think it is. This of course flies in the face of the "feel good" attitude promulgated by contemporary politicians, and by many versions of popular culture (especially cinema). This is not necessarily a positive realization for all citizens, who'd like to feel that they have some say in the government, and that it does, or at least aspires to, act in the interests of those who have empowered it. It may seem to some that we are safer and more secure when blinded, and gagged, by the sand in which our heads are buried.

But not for Chomsky.

Resisting and Reviling the Chomsky Effect

Friends, there is treason among us . . . at least if you believe the right wing. Noam Chomsky is the inspiration of all the evil that is arising on American campuses, the inspiration of the misguided, the comforter of the wicked, the ally of the cruel. He gives aid and comfort to the enemy, which everyone knows is the definition of treason. Who is making these charges? David Horowitz. So there you have it. The intellectual leader of worldwide forces against America, the man who provides the academic framework for terrorism, the man who provides the foundation for hatred for America, is not Osama Bin Laden. It is not Saddam Hussein. It is Noam Chomsky.[1]

To gain a true measure of the Chomsky Effect requires that we engage with the Web sites, articles, blogs, and popular discourse deriding Noam Chomsky, lest we display willful disregard for the considerable number of real enemies he has, or fall into the kind of blind worshipping that he himself condemns. In addition, and I say this with a degree of regret, it requires that we rehash details of particular events that have been inaccurately portrayed in certain quarters in order to undermine Chomsky's Effect. I say "with regret" because in many ways the details of these events are rather ridiculous, and with even a cursory reading of relevant materials this becomes obvious; but they need to be addressed because they have been harnessed to ensure that people have one-line reasons to dismiss what many people consider to be crucial work. The final revisions to this book were undertaken during a year I spent in France, a place where Chomsky is quite literally reviled by many intellectuals who, with a remarkable degree of what could only be described as willful ignorance, continue to equate him with *négationnistes*, those who deny the existence of the Holocaust.[2] One could only conclude that these are people who, out of acts of faith, refuse to read what Chomsky writes,

and out of a sense of misdirected moral outrage, perhaps, ignore the details of the "affairs" that apparently demonstrate Chomsky's approach to the Holocaust. I'll address the approach taken by these people because it, along with, say, the fire-breathing Republicans of the "First Iraq, Next France" bumper sticker type, are the best examples of the resisting and reviling tendency I hope to set forth. In short, to engage and then disagree with a body of work is healthy, provided (and of course this applies to anything in the world) there's a real justification for doing so beyond a kind of belief that has been formed based upon disinformation. So this chapter will cover, with what I hope will be adequate and thorough detail, events that continue to be invoked for counterproductive reasons of eliminating powerful ideas from discussions to which they properly belong.

There is as well an array of reasoned and serious criticisms of Chomsky's work, in all of the fields in which he is engaged, and although I could not possibly touch on all of them, I do wish to offer a reasonably representative sampling thereof. There is no way to agree with all of Chomsky's ideas, if only because his views of things have evolved through the years and because, to put it simply, we are not Noam Chomsky. He has lived a particular life, has read certain books, speaks specific languages and was born with certain traits; so his work needs to be constantly and properly situated—as does our own. One can, however, either support or deride his basic attitudes, his way of thinking about questions, his deeply held values, or his natural instincts. It is in these areas that I myself find the strongest degree of accord, and it's for this reason that I have devoted a good part of my professional and personal life to his work, and I don't blush when I say that my overall conclusion is that he is a person with whom I have very powerful grounds of agreement. For this reason, I want to explain the effect he has had upon my thinking, but I also want to look to the negative effects, to those who resist him, not to lead people to my conclusions, but to their own.

Professional Affiliations

Those with professional proximity to Chomsky for more than half a century were, of course, his colleagues and students in the Linguistics and Philosophy Department at MIT. For them, he is for the most part a tireless and impassioned teacher and scholar whose door is open for long and detailed discussions. But there are some notable caveats. Stephen Pinker, an early admirer of Chomsky's work, was cited in the *Boston Globe Magazine*[3] as saying: "He implies that people who disagree with him are stupid and ignorant. He is a brilliant debater and an out-and-out bully. It's great fun if you're on his side, but not if you're suddenly the target. People storm off and hate his guts for the rest of their lives." David Pesetsky, another MIT colleague, was quoted in the same article as saying that "the most striking fact is how consistently people with anything at all to say about language feel the need to strike some attitude for or against Chomsky's ideas." Chomsky is considered to be the foundational force of the department at MIT that he and Morris Halle founded, and therefore he represents that institution. For that reason, he has been described to me by students and faculty as the prime mover in some strange institutional rivalry and struggle that plays itself out as Chomsky/MIT versus UPenn or Berkeley or Yale or Chicago, complete with spies and espionage expeditions. In that same article Joan Bresnan of Stanford is cited as saying that Chomsky "revolutionized linguistics but did it in a divisive way. . . . He's a polarizer. He's created warring schools." And Nathan Glazer, a professor of sociology at Harvard who was an important young voice in the radical circles of the 1930s and 40s that contained people like Seymour Melman and Irving Howe, commented that "it's an old Marxist style of analysis: a polemic. Everything all hangs together. No matter what happens, it benefits the ruling class. . . . That kind of analysis . . . can be tiresome."

When one reads these kinds of comments, it becomes clear that Noam Chomsky is revered and reviled for similar traits; he refuses to back down once he has taken a position, he defends his linguistics and his politics in ways that even allies sometimes find too stringent, he draws lines that seem to eliminate the possibility of reasonable concessions, and, on the basis of certain of his views or hobbyhorses, he manages to alienate a large compendium of individuals who might otherwise find in his work valuable tools for their own approaches. At the extreme end of this we find people like Paul Postal who writes in the *Anti-Chomsky Reader*:

To us, the two strands of Chomsky's work [linguistic work and sociopolitical ideas] manifest exactly the *same* key properties: a deep disregard and contempt for the truth, a monumental disdain for standards of inquiry, a relentless strain of self-promotion, remarkable descents into incoherence and a penchant for verbally abusing those who disagree with him. There is also a marked similarity in the way he disseminates his linguistic and his political ideas: often in off-the-cuff, independently unsupported remarks in interviews and lectures, or in anecdotal comments embedded in articles, and so forth. This mode of promulgation shares nothing with universally acknowledged requirements of historical or social research, still less with those of a *science*. Indeed, a remarkable feature of Chomsky's linguistic writings is how few of them (the percentage has shrunk to almost zero over time) are professionally refereed works in linguistic journals. This is very significant since the professional review process—which arguably has intervened only marginally in the evaluation of Chomsky's work—is rightly taken to be a hallmark of modern science and a key shield against error, deception and fraud. Finally, like his sociopolitical writings, Chomsky's linguistic output often represents outright invention, unanchored by demonstrable fact. (204)

These dizzying condemnations awaken us to the vociferous nature of Chomsky's foes, but seem remarkably heavy on accusations and light on evidence (the entire linguistic enterprise is challenged by Postal in fewer than thirty pages, which are mostly peppered with the type of prose found in the preceding paragraph).

A more interesting but technical critical work on Chomsky's linguistics is *Chomsky and His Critics*, which contains pointed discussion of Chomsky's scientific work by such figures in the field as Norbert Hornstein and Louise Antony (coeditors of the volume), William G. Lycan (University of North Carolina), Jeffrey Poland (University of Nebraska), Galen Strawson (University of Reading), Frances Egan (Rutgers), Georges Rey (University of Maryland), Peter Ludlow (SUNY), Paul Horwich (Graduate Center), Paul Pietroski (University of Maryland), Ruth Garrett Millikan (University of Connecticut) and Alison Gopnik (Berkeley). This edited collection is directed toward the specialist, and it contains heavily referenced and tightly argued articles which are then commented on by Chomsky at the end of the book. A cursory perusal of his carefully argued reactions to the critiques and assessments challenges the Postal-type accusations, filled as they are with careful discussion and reactions to the critiques, which are prefaced by respectful statements like "before turning to the important issues raised in William

Lycan's essay" (255), "I find myself in close agreement with the main thrust of Jeffrey Poland's 'methodological physicalism'" (263), "I will review the basic framework of Galen Strawson's careful and illuminating paper" (266), "I think that Frances Egan and I agree about basic issues" (268), "Georges Rey covers a good deal of important and often contested ground, and provides a valuable critique of the resort to obscure 'intentional talk' in several domains" (274), "the project that Paul Pietroski outlines and develops seems to me an eminently reasonable one" (304), and so forth. This seems hardly dismissive of contemporary work, even when undertaken by those working in ways that question Chomsky's approach. This is not to say that he can't be a strident opponent to certain individuals, and I myself have read some of his prickly replies to linguists for whose work he has little respect. But given the sheer volume of work in the world, and the multitude of domains to which he contributes, this doesn't seem to me all that surprising. Once again, one of his great attributes—his willingness and ability to reply to so many in such detail—can also become a liability. It would undoubtedly be easier to ignore, rather than criticize, those who don't work in the same paradigm (as many professors do), but this is simply not Chomsky's approach.

Getting the Word Out

Outside of the professional realm of linguistics and language studies, Chomsky is generally considered a marginal figure, which is not to say that he is ignored, or that there is necessarily a concerted collusion among all members of the mainstream media to keep him at bay (although there is some evidence that this does exist in institutional ways), but that he simply does not hold the place that would normally be accorded to someone whose accomplishments are so overtly important as his own. In the 1981 collection *Radical Priorities,* Carlos Otero asked:

How much genuine freedom of expression can the Free Press accommodate? Not very much, it would appear, in the absence of even the bare beginnings of a mass-based movement capable of guaranteeing a measure of evenhandedness. Thus at the peak of active opposition to the Indochina War, Chomsky's writings, which were widely read, "covered interminable pages in the *New York Review of*

Books" (as a new mandarin, unhappy with the situation, put it at the time), and he even had token access to mainstream media. In contrast, today he is often the object of the most outlandish denunciations, and even his letters to the editor responding to innuendo or direct attack fail to find an obscure corner in the Free Press. How low has a culture to fall before it can make a pariah out of its "most important intellectual alive" (arguably)? (14).

Eighteen years later, a January 3, 1999, *Baltimore Sun* article noted that "For the most part, Chomsky has remained off the radar screen of U.S. mass media. With typical discretion, the nightly 'News Hour' program anchored by Jim Lehrer, on national PBS television, has interviewed Chomsky just once in 23 years." Chomsky frequently mentions facts like these, although David Barsamian calls this phenomenon "fitting" because Chomsky is "on the cutting edge—he's pushing the envelope of permissible thought. . . . He's challenging us to examine and re-examine our assumptions. He's like an avant-garde musician, exploring and expanding the boundaries of . . . the way people think." This may sound odd to those who find the whole spectrum of views represented in their news sources, in this era of feel-good criticism of government policy, although I would consider it in line with one of the overall theses of this book, which is that much of Chomsky's work is simply too radical in its implications to be "heard" within the spectrum of what is normally presented. A *Baltimore Sun* interview with Jeff Greenfield, formerly of ABC, seems to confirm this: "Some of that stuff [on media and propaganda] looks to me like it's from Neptune" and Chomsky's "notions about the limits of debate in this country" are "absolutely wacko." And in the same *Baltimore Sun* article, the author notes:

But decision-makers at National Public Radio News—ostensibly devoted to depth and breadth—have avoided Chomsky like the plague. The number of times that he has been on "Morning Edition" or "All Things Considered" during the last quarter-century can be counted on one hand. . . . In a letter to the public-broadcasting newspaper *Current* four years ago, "All Things Considered" host Robert Siegel was remarkably dismissive—sniffing that Chomsky "evidently enjoys a small, avid, and largely academic audience who seem to be persuaded that the tangible world of politics is all the result of delusion, false consciousness and media manipulation." When I asked Siegel for clarification recently, he mentioned that he had interviewed Chomsky on "All Things Considered" once in 1988. "I should assure you that there are people of varied political stripes who believe they should be on NPR and are unfairly excluded," Siegel added. "The editor in chief of the *New Republic*, no political bedfellow of Professor

Chomsky, has expressed himself in this regard." But NPR News programs routinely present views in line with the editorial outlook of the *New Republic*. The airing of political perspectives akin to Chomsky's, however, is rare indeed. That's a key point: Avoidance of Chomsky is significant because it reflects media biases that operate across the board.

Chomsky does have mainstream supporters in the popular press, often in smaller more local newspapers in communities in which people write for their local papers rather than relying upon wire sources; but even in the years during which I worked on this book (1996–2007) I have seen the many ebbs and flows of this support or interest—even on the part of particular journalists. A notable figure in this regard is Christopher Hitchens who concluded an enlightening 1985 article about some of the events and comments that people have invoked to justify their criticisms or slander of Chomsky with the following:

Not even Mills, or Chomsky in his "New Mandarins" essay, could have anticipated the world of the Heritage Foundation, of "Kissinger Associates," of numberless power-worshipping, power-seeking magazines and institutes interlocking across the dissemination of culture, priority, information, and opinion. But Mills did write, in 1942: 'When events move very fast and possible worlds swing around them, something happens to the quality of thinking. Some men repeat formulae; some men become reporters. To time observation with thought so as to mate a decent level of abstraction with crucial happenings is a difficult problem.' Noam Chomsky has attempted, as a volunteer, necessarily imperfectly, to shoulder this responsibility at a time of widespread betrayal of it. And it must be an awed attitude to the new style—a willingness to demonstrate flexibility in the face of so much pelf and so much cant—that allows so many people to join in ridiculing him for doing so. As a philosophical anarchist, Chomsky might dislike to have it said that he had "done the state some service," but he is a useful citizen in ways that his detractors are emphatically not.[4]

Hitchens was criticized in an unsigned article titled "The Chorus and Cassandra: A Response"[5] for taking Chomsky's side in that piece, and providing justifications and explanations for Chomsky's approach. That article then goes on to note how, in light of Chomsky's writings about 9/11, Hitchens changed sides and became a strong Chomsky detractor: "In the wake of the September 11 terrorist attacks, Hitchens and Chomsky parted company. Hitchens criticized what he regarded as Chomsky's attempts to rationalize the attacks.[6] Chomsky, in response, insinuated that Hitchens was a racist for refusing to accept comparisons between the 9/11 attacks and the American bombing of a pharmaceutical factory in Sudan: 'He must be unaware that he is expressing such racist contempt for African victims of a terrorist crime. . . .'"[7] Hitchens responded that "with his pitying tone of condescension, and his insertion of a deniable but particularly objectionable innuendo, I regret to say that Chomsky displays what have lately become his hallmarks."[8] Interestingly, it's on the issue of comparisons that Hitchens "parted ways" with Chomsky, just as it is on the comparison between the massacres in East Timor and those in Cambodia, or on the comparison between U.S. bombings and terrorist attacks, that so many have criticized Chomsky's approach. This is perhaps one of the foundations that people stand upon in their respect or their revilement of his work, either the positive sense that he brings the same set of core values to all of his writings, or that he confuses issues by not realizing the difference between the intentions or objectives of one side versus those of another even when they are committing similar acts, as we will see throughout this chapter.

Discounting Chomsky

In looking through the assaults against Chomsky, it is striking to note how many people find themselves able to dismiss a humanist corpus on the basis of one issue, which is often summed up in one catch-phrase (the Faurisson Affair, or his attacks on the U.S. government's use of propaganda as "rubbish"), which makes one wonder how the author of long tomes on particular issues can defend himself against dismissals and one-liners. Here again, the writings of Christopher Hitchens are revealing:

Whether he is ignored, whether he is libeled, or whether he is subjected to an active campaign of abuse, Chomsky is attacked for things that he is thought to believe, or believed to have said. A lie, it has been written, can travel around the world before truth has even got its shoes on. Merely to list the accusations against Chomsky, whether they are made casually or with deliberation, is a relatively easy task. Showing their unfairness or want of foundation involves expense of ink on a scale which any reader who has got this far will know to his or her cost. Perhaps for this reason, not all the editors who publish matter about Chomsky ever quite get around to publishing his replies. I could write an ancillary article showing this in detail, with his answers either unpublished or unscrupulously abridged. And, of course, a man who writes a lot of letters to the editor soon gets a reputation, like Bellow's Herzog, as a crank, an eccentric, a fanatic. Whereas the absence of a reply is taken as admission of guilt.[9]

The problem is exacerbated on radio shows or television, where it is much easier to pull off the Cheney-style insult, the one-liner, the knock-out punch than it is to create the convincing, complex argument. It has often been noted that Chomsky makes regular direct and indirect appearances in the pages of the popular media in places like the United Kingdom, Sweden, Holland, Israel, and Canada—indeed in most countries of the world he is well known in various quarters, and well respected in most. One reason may be that the media in those places, particularly the popular publicly owned media (CBC in Canada, BBC in the UK, etc.), have a more direct role and are more "popular" than NPR, which is often attacked for being "too liberal" and which plays a more marginal role amid the plethora of private radio channels. Perhaps as a consequence of people outside of the United States being more accustomed to the longer style of discussion, they are more apt to tune into the longer programming, or to watch long and didactic documentaries like *Manufacturing Consent*.

But the most powerful means of discounting Chomsky has for many years now been associated with his critique of Israel, which has caused people who know him both professionally and personally to accuse him of being anti-Zionist or even anti-Semitic.

Man: You've been called a neo-Nazi, your books have been burned, you've been called anti-Israeli—don't you get a bit upset by the ways your views are always distorted by the media and by intellectuals?

NC: No, why should I? I get called anything, I'm accused of everything you can dream of: being a Communist propagandist, a Nazi propagandist, a pawn of freedom of speech, an anti-Semite, liar, whatever you want. Actually, I think that's all a good sign. I mean, if you're a dissident, you're typically ignored. If you can't be ignored, and you can't be answered, you're vilified—that's obvious: no institution is going to help people undermine it. So I would only regard the kinds of things you're talking about as signs of progress.[10]

The irony of these accusations about his being anti-Semitic is quite literally incredible, given that Chomsky grew up in an important Jewish and Zionist family, he attended the Hebrew school in which both of his parents taught, he wrote his master's thesis on the Hebrew language, and, moreover, that he supported the tenets of socialist Zionism to the point of briefly moving with his wife, Carol, to Israel in his youth, with the intention of living on a Kibbutz.[11] What he has opposed about Israel is what many in his circle have derided, which is its militarism, its version of nationalism, and the premise that Israel should differentiate in its treatment of citizens depending upon their religion, or that certain decisions rendered by state representatives should ultimately defer to Judaism on account of the history of persecution of Jewish peoples. An example of the type of rhetoric he uses, in this case comparing in an unfavorable fashion Israeli treatment of Arabs to apartheid, South Africa's treatment of Blacks, gives a sense of what infuriates defenders of Israel:

Again, if Israel has any intelligence, it will really follow the model of the white racists in Apartheid South Africa, who did subsidize the Banustans. Israel doesn't. Israel gives almost no support to the territories it has occupied. In fact, that's a scandal that's happened under Israeli occupation. It's willing to have Europe pump in money to the Palestinian authority, most of it ripped off by Arafat and his friends and stuck in Israeli banks. They're willing to have that, and then they can complain about the corruption and the brutality. But they're not doing anything for the territories. Israeli industrialists have been pointing out for years, even before the Oslo accords, that this is stupid. What they ought to do is set up something like the maquiladoras, or what South Africa did around the Bantustans. Put up industrial parks where you can get super-cheap labor under miserable conditions. You don't have to worry about work standards or anything else. Then you won't get the Palestinians coming into Israel to do the dirty work. They'll be over there. But we'll make huge profits and we'll control the exports—kind of a maquiladora setup. That would make more sense. So far, they have been too racist to do that. But if they move to the standard colonial pattern—like the United States in Central America, or the South African model in the Bantustans—if they elevate themselves to that level, they'll allow for the kind of dependent development in the territories that takes place in Haiti, in northern Mexico, or El Salvador.[12]

This type of comment sends the "Jewish lobby" in the United States and Canada into a frenzy, and contributes to the fact that people like Alfred Kazin write in the *Jerusalem Post* that Chomsky is a "dupe of intellectual pride so overweening that he is incapable of making distinctions between totalitarian and democratic societies, between oppressors and victims."[13]

It should be said at this point that it is to one's peril to criticize Israel in the West, particularly in the United States and Canada, even though many Israeli policies fly in the face of those we apparently advocate, such as providing full rights to minorities, keeping religion distinct from politics or law, enforcing the equal treatment of human rights law for all persons on the territory, allowing for the free circulation of all citizens throughout the country, encouraging movement across national boundaries, and so forth.[14] My own experience with the latter issues has led me to conclude (as Chomsky has on other matters) that the "Jewish lobby" is far more stringently (and blindly) pro-Israel than people in Israel are, even people inside the offices of political power, that is, those who recognize the many contradictions and complexities of a state of Israel on annexed Palestinian territory. I confronted this fact head-on in research I did on the admission of Convention refugees from Israel into Canada, a policy that was attacked by the Canadian Jewish Lobby even as high-ranking members of Israel's government with whom I met in Jerusalem voiced sympathy to these same claimants (mostly former Soviet citizens who had come to Israel thanks to the "Law of Return" and therein found themselves as persecuted for being not Jewish enough as they had been in the former Soviet Union for being too Jewish).[15]

One way that people approach Chomsky on the question of Israel is to challenge him on his Judaism, a link that for some reason even many Jews cannot seem to unravel. For example, a long interview with Hawzheen O. Kareem recorded in Znet[16] casts a strong light upon the idea that he suffers from a form of "Jewish self-hatred": "Some criticize you as the most militant American among those who are opponent to Israel, some say that you, as a Jew, hate yourself. How does it come about that you criticize Israel in such manner?" The answer, clearly well rehearsed in light of the number of times this has been raised, begins with reference to the Biblical past: "The charges are interesting. Those who know the Bible know their origins. The charges trace back to King Ahab, who was the epitome of evil in the Bible. King Ahab condemned the Prophet Elijah as a hater of Israel. The flatterers at King Ahab's court agreed. Elijah was a 'self-hating Jew,' to borrow the terminology of the contemporary flatterers at the court, because he was criticizing the policies of the King and calling for justice and respect for human rights. Similar charges were familiar in the old Soviet Union: dissidents were condemned for hating Russia. And there are other examples in military dictatorships and totalitarian states. Such criticisms reflect deeply held totalitarian values." The answer moves from the accusation to a deeper felt sense of values and also a strongly held disgust Chomsky holds for the "totalitarian values," herein represented by the fear and refusal to criticize authority even in the face of its violation of principles of freedom and concomitant fundamental rights. He then clarifies who is the object of his critique, which, as is often the case, invokes the crimes of the United States, something for which many criticize Chomsky (U.S. hater) but which by invocation includes Israel: "In fact, I do not particularly criticize Israel, but I do strongly criticize the crucial role of the US—my country, after all—in supporting barbaric crimes of its client state, and barring a peaceful political settlement along the lines that have been supported by virtually the entire world since the 1970s. For the totalitarian mentality, this is "hating Israel," or "hating the United States." King Ahab and the flatterers at his court, the Kremlin and its commissars, and others who call for abject submission to power will doubtless agree. Those who treasure freedom, justice, and human rights will follow a different path, as throughout history."

Chomsky's efforts to bring the United States to bear in this discussion ensures that we do not allow ourselves to become innocent, which he accomplishes by insisting that the "over there," where we have interests and where we play a direct role, becomes "over here." This is an anathema to those who consider that the United States generally fights the good fight, and an abomination to those who believe that Israel is also fighting the good fight in a truly inhospitable land of Arab resistance to a Jewish homeland. This perhaps accounts in part for the contrast between how the Israeli question is treated in Canada or the United States and how it is discussed in Israel itself, which points to key differences in the Chomsky Effect across not only disciplines and interest groups, but also on the basis of nationality. I have been amazed to hear people in Jerusalem and Tel Aviv, including government officials, discussing Chomsky's opinions about the Middle East, because they tended to take his views on Arabs, Palestinians, and American involvement in the country more seriously than do many Zionist groups in the United States and Canada, where the line tends to be much more clearly drawn in favor of Israeli policy, be it what it may, simply because criticism of Israel is deemed somehow sacrilegious.

The examples of Jewish lobby–style critique of some of the positions described above abound, and generally they focus on several concerns articulated, for example, in Paul Bogdanor's "Chomsky's War Against Israel."[17] The brunt of the attack is against the deemed preposterous idea that Israel should not exist in its present form. This provides significant fuel to Bogdanor and many others, who avoid looking back to the history of Zionism, pre-1948, which from certain perspectives demonstrates that the idea of a Jewish state in Palestine was imposed largely out of guilt about Western inaction on the Jews' behalf during the second world war.[18] What else could explain the dramatic turnaround that occurred post-1945, when suddenly world powers, including England and the United States, came out in support of a specifically Jewish state as opposed to one of the other options, such as a Swiss-style federation or a binational state, that had been discussed at the time? These discussions were not just marginal babblings, but instead included the likes of David Ben-Gurion and Albert Einstein, who were looking to avoid the kind of violence and animosity that has been borne out of the way things unfolded post-1948.[19]

There is significant evidence for this, and a powerful effort has been made to forget these discussions and debates in favor of some idea about a Jewish state being the logical and desirable outcome of Zionism. A letter from David Ben-Gurion to Louis Brandeis, dated December 6, 1940, sets forth the types of proposals on the table that stood between Jews and Arabs during the war. In discussions with Arab leaders, Ben-Gurion found that "the Arab people as such, and especially those who represent the true national interests of the Arabs, would never willingly agree to hand Palestine to the Jews, or even to share it with the Jews on a basis of equality." Mussa Alami, who was once the attorney general in Palestine and the Arab nationalist leader, suggested to Ben-Gurion that the best solution would be "economic and social cooperation with those Jews already in Palestine" rather than heavy Jewish immigration. Ben-Gurion's preferred solution, which he proposed to Arab officials, was "the idea of a federation—a federation between a Jewish Palestine and neighboring Arab states." The advantages were clear; first, "the Arabs in Palestine, with a Jewish majority, although numerically a minority, would not feel that they were in a foreign state, as they belonged together with the whole of Palestine to a larger unit which would be predominately Arab." Second, "they would have the political and economic help of the Jews in establishing Arab unity and independence in the greatest part of Arab territory." And third, "they would have the benefit of a highly developed Palestine, as a member of the larger Arab federal unit." This idea was "more popular amongst the Arabs," including Auni Abdul Hadi, the head of the Independence Party in Palestine, Readi Sulch, the leader of the National Bloc in Syria, Amir Aslan, the head of the Palestine-Syrian delegation in Geneva, and others. There was resistance even to this compromise, however, on the basis that Jewish Palestine would be independent before Arab unity could occur, the fact that Palestine "is the natural link to all the Arab countries," and, moreover, "a highly developed Palestine, instead of being a source of strength, might become a menace to the neighboring Arab countries." These obstacles did not dissuade Ben-Gurion in his attempt to "get nearer to the Arab leaders," and indeed several leaders, notably in Syria, Lebanon, and Transjordania, were anxious to secure an agreement with the Jews as soon as possible. On the other hand, Ben-Gurion also notes that the position of Jews worsened during the war because, although the Arabs didn't sympathize with Mussolini, there was "wide-spread sympathy for Hitler" because "the Arabs respect and admire strong action." Furthermore, "the Nazi philosophy, in certain respects, is not altogether strange to the philosophy of Islam," and many Arabs believed at the time that a Nazi victory would allow for the establishment of an Arab empire.[20]

The critiques of Noam Chomsky's or, I might add, Edward Said's position on Israel[21] take on a rather different hue in this light, and it is regrettable that the history of the foundation of Israel has been so neglected, or in some cases falsified, and that the warnings, from Ben-Gurion, Einstein, and American Jews such as Seymour Melman and Zellig Harris, are nowhere near the center of debates about Palestine and Israel. This (conscious?) ignorance leads to the statements of strange ahistorical astonishment, such as the following by Paul Bogdanor in his piece titled "Chomsky's War Against Israel":[22] "Central to Chomsky's position is the idea that Israel should cease to exist in its present form. This view is set out in his earliest writings on the subject, where he [Chomsky] proclaims that Israel is 'a state based on the principle of discrimination. There is no other way for a state with non-Jewish citizens to remain a Jewish state. . . .'[23] It does indeed seem obvious that a Jewish state that in

ultimate decisions defers to the protection of the country as a *Jewish*
state will take decisions that will discriminate against non-Jews, but for
Bogdanor this is incomprehensible and indeed, he says, 'Taken literally,
the claim hardly merits debate.' This would seem true, but not for the
reasons he suggests.

Bogdanor's next point of amazement is that anyone would consider
that which was discussed by Zionists less than sixty years ago:

How would Chomsky replace the Jewish state which he is so anxious to abolish?
His proposed alternative is "socialist binationalism." But Chomsky's ideal is far
more objectionable than a Jewish state with non-Jewish citizens: in his scheme
there will be Jewish cantons with Arab inhabitants, and Arab cantons *with no
Jewish inhabitants*. At one point Chomsky does stipulate that any individual
"will be free to live where he wants." But then he abandons this principle in
favor of the binational state which he considers "the most desirable," one in
which "Palestinian Arabs who wish to return to their former homes within the
Jewish-dominated region would have to abandon their hopes," while "Jews who
wish to settle in the Arab-dominated region would be unable to do so." In other
words, Arabs will not become a *majority* in Jewish areas, while Jews will be forbidden even to live as a *minority* in Arab areas. The founders of apartheid would
surely applaud. The details of Chomsky's plans are even more disturbing. His
binational socialist state will be "integrated into a broader federation" and
modeled on the "successful social revolution" in communist Yugoslavia, where
70,000–100,000 people were massacred. It is in fact a "people's democracy" of
the familiar type, which will have to be "integrated" into the Arab world by
force, given that "support for compromising Israeli independence is virtually
non-existent in Israel."

That the details of this historical plan are distorted here is certainly part
of the anti-Chomsky effect, and once again one only needs to return to
the historical documents to understand the idea of, for example, the binational state or the arguments that were put forth pre-1948 for its elaboration. For instance, in *Zionism and the Arabs 1882–1948*, Yosef
Gorny reminds us that the Ihud leaders proposed to the UN Commission of Enquiry that there be a binational state which would represent
"an 'ideal' theoretical model of equilibrium and restraint in the relations
between the two peoples." The principle was based on a sense of "the
historical rights of the Jews and the natural rights of the Arabs as equal
under all conditions," a belief that equality should be a "numerical
balance between the two peoples," and, in the constitutional sphere, "it
was envisaged as equal representation of Jews and Arabs in the future
Palestinian state institutions." This plan, which was rejected by the UN

Commission "for practical reasons," was to establish a "federation under Western protection" to allay "the fascist tendencies of Arab nationalism and the possible Levantinization of the Palestinian state" (288). Many texts recount this history, and many individuals have taken this approach very seriously, but even well-known American Jewish lobbyists such as Alan Dershowitz seem to deny that it comes from anywhere other than Chomsky's imagination:

I first debated Chomsky in 1973, several weeks after the Yom Kippur War. Chomsky's proposal at that time was consistent with the PLO party line. He wanted to abolish the state of Israel, and to substitute a "secular, binational state," based on the model of binational "brotherhood" that then prevailed in Lebanon. Chomsky repeatedly pointed to Lebanon, where Christians and Muslims "lived side by side," sharing power in peace and harmony. This was just a few years before Lebanon imploded in fratricidal disaster. This is what I said about Chomsky's hare-brained scheme in our 1973 debate: "Putting aside the motivations behind such a proposal when it is made by the Palestinian organizations, why do not considerations of self-determination and community control favor two separate states: one Jewish and one Arab? Isn't it better for people of common background to control their own life, culture, and destiny (if they so choose), than to bring together in an artificial way people who have shown no ability to live united in peace. I confess to not understanding the logic of the proposal, even assuming its good will."[24]

The idea that the "logic" of such a proposal is incomprehensible is odd, for reasons already named, and the alternative that seems to be presented here is that removing people (in this case Palestinians) from their homeland through brute force, and then denying them rights in the name of unity is okay because then those with a "common background" will "control their own life, culture, and destiny." But what about the "common background" of the majority, the Palestinians, who occupied Palestine before it became a Jewish State? Even more salient for the present discussion is the ways in which these views come to feed a frenzy of reactions to the gamut of Chomsky's work and then to stir the kinds of knee-jerk reactions such as finding in Chomsky's writings—which always attack totalitarianism, Stalinism, and oppression in all of its forms—apologies for anti-Semitism.

Nor can we forget the unadulterated bile which Chomsky has seen fit to pour upon his fellow American Jews. Explaining why his *Fateful Triangle* was virtually ignored in the American Jewish media, he charged that "[t]he Jewish community here is deeply totalitarian. They do not want democracy, they do not want freedom." Elsewhere he felt compelled to mention New York, with its "huge Jewish population, Jewish-run media, a Jewish mayor, and domination of cultural and economic life." After all, he insists, American Jews are now "a substantial part of the dominant privileged elite groups in every part of the society . . . they're very influential, particularly in the ideological system, lots of writers, editors, etc. and that has an effect." Horrified by this injustice, America's leading "dissident" will bravely endeavor to protect the suffering masses from their Jewish oppressors.

In the United States, however, there is serious discussion and debate that occurs around such views, and the Internet is rife with commentary about Chomsky, from a range of perspectives. There is also a growing awareness of this anti-Chomsky lobby, particularly as it comes to be tied to the various "wars against," which have become fashionable and successful ways of shutting down dissent. One online article by Richard Wall noted this anti-Chomsky move, and commented:

Some of this criticism and commentary is abusive, and has little worth other than to discredit those who convey it or to pander to the prejudices of fellow warmongers. Most of it, however, is couched in terms of the prevailing ideological medium of the new world order: the war on terrorism. It does not take a genius to see the origins and motivations of such dogmas. Unconditional, jingoistic flag-wavers, of the "my country right or wrong" variety, for whom the only freedom of expression permitted is freedom of the kind of speech they like, are among those who take most unkindly to having their mental processes analyzed and their assumptions exposed, whether those assumptions be hypocritical, as they often are, or genuinely well-meaning. Unfortunately, in the latter case, they may be even worse in their effects than the barefaced lies and hypocrisy which are the order of the day in the politics of the war on terrorism.[25]

These polemics make for interesting reading, and make it such that to work through the kinds of hard questions Chomsky forces us to confront, one needs a wide array of sources, beyond newspapers, beyond journals, and way into the Internet's blogs, letters, reviews, commentaries, and rants. It is frankly only in this kind of open territory that all of it—the positive, the negative, the disgusting, the fanciful and the revealing—has the necessary room for exploration.

French Resistance

Just as a lot of the anti-Chomsky rhetoric in this country has ties to Judaism, much of the debate about Chomsky's supposedly hidden alliances often has some connection to Paris, which begs the question of how his work is regarded in the place that he considers the most closed to free and unfettered debate. For those of us who are familiar with France, Chomsky's negative views of the French seem questionable, or at least overstated; anyone who has sat in the cafés of Paris or Marseille knows of the French propensity for good food, good wine, and, moreover, a good debate about political and philosophical issues, which often leads to strongly demarcated lines of dissension, discord, and controversy. There is as well a deeply engaged reading public that feeds on nightly cultural and political debates on television, and in newspapers and magazines such as *Le Monde diplomatique*, *Le Canard Déchaîné*, and *Libération*. And the United States is very close to France in terms of its own Founding Fathers and its foundational constitutional texts, which means that both countries share in the legacies of Descartes, Diderot, Montesquieu, Rousseau, Voltaire, notably the erection of intellectual work based upon rationality and secularism rather than prestige or superstition. But a significant difference between the Parisian intellectual scene and the American one is the role that has come to be played by twentieth-(and twenty-first) century French intellectuals, which is worth discussing in this regard since it turns out to be one of the critical points of disjunction between Chomsky's approach and the French reception thereof. It is not sufficient in my view to think of the oddball reactions to the French exemplified by such inventions as Freedom Fries, or similarly misguided ideas in France that suggest that most "Americans" are in agreement with or could in their attitudes be likened to George W. Bush. The French-American dance of fetishism and animosity has much deeper roots, and a more complex set of motives.

Since some of the differences in approach between Americans and the French are tied to the study of language and culture, we can begin by looking at the status of French linguistic, literary, and cultural theory. Chomsky's work is closely followed throughout the world, notably in the Netherlands (where a significant amount of material about linguistics is published), England, Italy, Germany, and Japan. Despite widespread knowledge of his approach (albeit somewhat dated in most quarters), his work is less the benchmark for linguistics departments in France than is the case in other Western countries, which might at first

blush seem somewhat surprising given its history and its on-going interest in language studies. This can be explained by the unusual status that
linguistics has in France, probably a product of the continued prestige
of French structuralism, the pride in Ferdinand de Saussure, and, moreover, a different definition of linguistics' object domain.

From Chomsky's perspective, there is more to this story. From his
reading, the situation in France with regard to his approach to linguistics began to change in the 1970s, but certainly not to the same degree
as in other countries:

In the 1960s, almost nothing was allowed in France. In the 1970s, things began
to change, by accident. As you may recall, they set up a branch of the university at Vincennes, hoping to banish all the disruptive third world and radical
types there, and the intellectual establishment didn't pay much attention to what
was happening. A student of ours (from the Linguistics and Philosophy Department, Massachusetts Institute of Technology), who is a really brilliant linguist,
took a position there (his French is fluent, and his main work had been on
French) and pretty soon every smart young linguist in Europe was going to study
with him.[26] That spawned modern European linguistics, but France itself kept
the virus pretty much under control. (letter of 9 September, 1997)[27]

This reflects Chomsky's sense that there is a strong measure of control
exerted by organizations like universities, publishing houses, and
research institutes. But there are other factors, notably that key texts by
Chomsky and his disciples are not translated into French in a timely
fashion, if at all (*Lectures on Government and Binding* has never been
translated, not to mention more recent texts like *The Minimalist
Program*), which limits the range of texts available to French linguists.
John Goldsmith does not see this as an issue, because "very little linguistics is translated from English and published in France, and of the
stuff that's translated and published in France, a large part, it seems to
me, is Chomskian. But more to the point, French academics, like Europeans in general, take it for granted that they have to read English. I
cannot imagine a French linguist who cannot read English." Nevertheless, the question remains: why would the French keep this "virus . . .
under control," and why are things different in France than elsewhere?
For this we need to look back, to issues of Judaism and Israel, and
forward, to the Faurisson Affair, which has had extremely complicated
and long-standing effects upon how Chomsky's work is viewed in
France, and beyond, as we will see.

Discussions of Chomsky's broader projects have been revitalized in the last decade, partly with the publication of *Noam Chomsky: Une voix discordante*,[28] and partly on account of the diffusion and discussion of the popular film *Manufacturing Consent*. Denis Slakta's article about the film in *Le Monde* (December 3, 1993), for example, describes the importance of Noam Chomsky as an intellectual and goes on to declare that Chomsky is, "without doubt one of the great linguists of this century. Whether they like it or not, linguists must accommodate themselves in terms of a pre- and a post-Chomsky era; they must explain and situate their work accordingly." And Nancy Dolhem's September 1995 note commenting on *Year 501* for *Le Monde diplomatique* includes the suggestion that "every book written by this great American intellectual, Noam Chomsky, produces in the reader a rare sensation of intellectual jubilation by the sheer rebellious force of this non-conformist author who has been called by some a 'contemporary Voltaire'." Neither opinion is particularly original (although Dolhem's remarks are rather remarkable in their implications); an array of individuals working in fields as diverse as linguistics, philosophy, cognitive sciences, history, and politics would agree on both counts. What is remarkable is that these articles were published in France.

The effort to vitalize, or revitalize Chomsky's work in France is the focus of attention for a small publishing group in Marseilles that gravitates around a press and journal called *Agone*, the role of which is in part to disseminate his (and similar) work in France. Members of the Agone collective have described to me a strong resistance, however, notably among the French intelligentsia, which continues to write Chomsky off as a *négationniste* (Holocaust denier) without, of course, dealing with the facts of his writing. The term *French intelligentsia* is itself a source of confusion for many, so distinctions must be made early on. Generally speaking, it refers to an identifiable group of French intellectuals in Paris who have been associated with particular political beliefs and actions over the years, beginning perhaps with Émile Zola (who sets the positive standard for effective and thoughtful intellectual engagement), through the uneven approach taken by Jean-Paul Sartre, and continuing today with Bernard Henri-Lévi; yet the lines that connect or separate the individuals lumped together under this rubric are not always easily discerned, and alliances exist on various fronts. For instance, an article that was published on March 31, 1999, in *Le Monde* titled "Statement by French intellectuals" was signed by Pierre Bourdieu, Pauline Boutron, Suzanne de Brunhoff, Nolle Burgi-Golub, Jean-Christophe Chaumeron, Thomas Coutrot, Daniel Bensaid, Daniel Durant, Robin Foot, Ana-Maria Galano, Philip Golub, Michel Husson, Paul Jacquin, Marcel-Francis Kahn, Bernard Langlois, Ariane Lantz, Pierre Lantz, Florence Lefresne, Catherine Levy, Jean-Philippe Milesy, Patrick Mony, Aline Pailler, Catherine Samary, Rolande Trempe, and Pierre Vidal-Naquet. This gives some idea of a (1999 vintage) French intellectual elite, but if this list is any indication, there is no clear "party line" that unifies them, even from Chomsky's own perspective (and he does use the idea of the "Paris intellectual" quite frequently). For example, one person on this list stands on the opposite end of Chomsky's spectrum as regards the Faurisson Affair (Pierre Vidal-Naquet), while another (Pierre Bourdieu, also published by the Agone collective) published a book called *Acts of Resistance: Against the Tyranny of the Market*, which received remarkably strong praise from Chomsky, as an endorsement: "Bourdieu once again selects the right targets and, as always, has much to say that is incisive and enlightening." (I might add that Bourdieu's work in both language and politics has been a huge inspiration for me along the way, and I think that his work both defies and completes Chomsky's approach by thinking about how people live and work inside of "marketplaces" of discourse, which, over and above general competency, tend to color, if not determine, the meaning of utterances or texts.) Further, the petition that accompanied the list of names of this French intelligentsia was very much in the spirit, sometimes to the letter, of Chomsky's own opposition to the bombing of Serbia, described in various media, including in a discussion between Patrick Cain and Noam Chomsky in June 1999.

NC: ... When involved in a confrontation, you use your player strong card and try to shift the confrontation to the arena in which you are most powerful. And the strong card of the United States is the use of force. That's perhaps the only realm of international relations where the US has a near monopoly. The consequences of using force in Yugoslavia were more or less anticipated. The NATO Commanding General Wesley Clark stated that it was entirely predictable that the bombing would sharply increase the level of atrocities and expulsion. As indeed it did. The NATO leadership could not have failed to know that the bombing would destroy the quite courageous and promising democracy movement in Serbia—as indeed it did; and cause all sorts of turmoil in surrounding countries—as indeed it has, though still not at the same level of crisis as Turkey or other places. Nevertheless, it was necessary, as the Clinton foreign policy team kept stressing, to preserve the credibility of NATO. Now when they talk about credibility, they are not talking about the credibility of Denmark or France. The Clinton Administration doesn't care about those countries' credibility. What they care about is the credibility of the United States. Credibility means fear: what they are concerned with is maintaining fear of the global enforcer, namely, the US. And that's much more important than the fate of hundreds of thousands of Kosovars, or whatever other consequences are incurred. So the US and NATO have helped to create a humanitarian catastrophe by knowingly escalating an already serious crisis to catastrophic proportions. (www.chomsky.info)

This is in some ways comparable to elements of the preamble to the French intellectuals' perspective, notably in the sense that alternatives other than the US/NATO show of force existed when the bombing began:

Either support the NATO intervention or support the reactionary policies of the Serb authorities in Kosovo? The NATO bombing raids, which made necessary the withdrawal of OSCE personnel from Kosovo, created more favorable conditions for a ground offensive by Serb paramilitary forces, rather than preventing it; they encourage the worst forms of ultra-nationalist Serb desire for revenge against the Kosovar population; they consolidate the dictatorial power of Slobodan Milosevic which has muzzled the independent media and succeeded in uniting around it a national consensus which must, on the contrary, be broken if a path to peaceful and political negotiations on Kosovo is to be opened up. Either accept as the sole possible basis for negotiation the "peace plan" drawn up by the governments of the United States and of the European Union or bomb Serbia? No long-term solution to a major internal political conflict can be imposed from outside by force. It is not true that "every attempt was made" to find a solution and an acceptable framework for negotiations. The Kosovar negotiators were forced to sign a plan which they had initially rejected after they were given reason to believe that NATO would become involved on the ground in defense of their cause. This is a lie which fosters a total illusion: not one of the governments which have supported the NATO air strikes are willing to wage war against the Serb regime to impose independence for Kosovo. The strikes will perhaps weaken part of the Serbian military machine, but they will not weaken the mortars which are being used to destroy Albanian houses, nor the paramilitary forces which are executing UCK (Kosovo Liberation Army) fighters.

Similar on critical points, there is nevertheless a quite different emphasis here between Chomsky (bombing ensures that the U.S. government will achieve personal ends through fear and violence) and the French (bombing cannot possibly solve the problem at hand), even when these two camps are arguing the same point (stop the bombing). Nevertheless, the French-Chomsky split has been considerably wider than simple emphasis in the past, and the evolution of political thinking on both sides is of interest in itself.

But the French-Chomsky relationship deserves investigation beyond these matters because it speaks to the question of how texts by or about Chomsky are read and understood in different contexts, notably in France where the role of the intellectual in society, the nature of the media, and the relationship between the government and its ruling classes is quite different from those of the United States. For example, it is clear from the published documents describing the Faurisson Affair that the whole discussion came to be dominated in the French press by a single, remarkably homogenous voice, and this despite the fact that groups of French anarchists, anti-Bolshevik Communists, as well as a range of individuals variously affiliated with the left in France would find in Chomsky's work significant areas of overlap; and yet Chomsky is seldom mentioned even in these milieus, partly on account of these Affairs. The conclusions that one can draw from this material may also shed light upon certain intellectual milieus, and help clarify the grounds for Chomsky's oft-repeated statement that in France, "the fundamental principles of all discussion—namely, a minimal respect for facts and logic—have been practically abandoned"(verso of *Réponses inédites*). And finally, they may awaken in some a desire to question why Chomsky has had this reception in France, what it suggests about the power of a certain ruling elite over the "official version" and what this might suggest about other historical events in France.

Harnessing Hatred

To examine some of the ways in which a body of dissent is pushed away from the mainstream is important because it shows how misinformation can been used, and used remarkably successfully in certain quarters, to question or discount opposition. An example comes, from the realm of music and popular culture. Chomsky's popularity in the music and youth scene doesn't pass the Chomsky detractors unnoticed, and Stefan Kanfer, in an article titled "America's Dumbest Intellectual," for *City Journal* magazine,[29] notes it all with horror:

Walk onto the popular-music floor of Virgin Records in midtown Manhattan, and you encounter, as you'd expect, kids with shoulder tattoos and pierced body parts, wandering through rows of the latest hip-hop, altrock, and heavy-metal CDs as heavily amplified beats thunder. At the checkout counter, though, is a surprise. A single book is on display: perennial radical Noam Chomsky's latest anti-American screed, *9/11*—an impulse item for the in-your-face slackers of the Third Millennium. Strictly speaking, *9/11* is a non-book, a hastily assembled collection of fawning interviews with Chomsky conducted after the terrorist attack on New York City and the country, in which the author pins the blame for the atrocities on—you guessed it—the U.S. But you'd be wrong to dismiss *9/11* as an inconsequential paperback quickie. More than 115,000 copies of the book are now in print. It has shown up on the *Boston Globe* and the *Washington Post* best-seller lists, and in Canada, it has rocketed to seventh on the best-seller list. And as its prominent display at Virgin Records attests, *9/11* is particularly popular with younger readers; the book is a hot item at campus bookstores nationwide. The striking success of *9/11* makes Chomsky's America-bashing notable, or at least notably deplorable—especially here in New York, which lost so many of its bravest on that horrible day.

Kanfer notes with scorn the fact that "Chomsky has achieved rock-star status among the young and hip. Rock groups like Bad Religion and Pearl Jam proudly quote his writings in interviews and in their music. To the self-styled bohemian coffee-house crowd, observes *Wired* magazine, 'Chomsky is somewhere between Kerouac and Nietzsche—carrying around one of his books is automatic countercultural cachet.'" The problem, apparently, is that Chomsky didn't stay where he belonged, to let the experts take care of the domains he has dared to breech: "With this fame as a base, the professor proceeded to wander far from his area of expertise. Such uses of fame, ironically, are common in the country Chomsky attacks so relentlessly. In America, you come across two kinds of fame: vertical and horizontal. The vertical celebrity owes his renown to one thing—Luciano Pavarotti, for example, is famous for his singing, period. The horizontal celebrity, conversely, merchandises his fame by convincing the public that his mastery of one field is transferable to another. Thus singers Barbra Streisand and Bono give speeches on public policy; thus linguistics professor Chomsky poses as an expert on geopolitics." As is (virtually) always the case, the foray that is most telling for this writer is into issues relating to Israel: "The Chomskian rage hasn't confined itself to his native land. He has long nourished a special contempt for Israel, lone outpost of Western ideals in the Middle East. The hatred has been so intense that Zionists have called him a self-hating

Jew. This is an unfair label. Clearly, Chomsky has no deficit in the self-love department, and his ability to stir up antagonism makes him even more pleased with himself. No doubt that was why he wrote the introduction to a book by French Holocaust-denier Robert Faurisson. *Mémoire en Defense* maintains that Hitler's death camps and gas chambers, even Anne Frank's diary, are fictions, created to serve the cause of American Zionists. That was too much for Harvard law professor Alan Dershowitz, who challenged fellow leftist Chomsky to a debate."

So here it comes, even in a discussion about the sale of a book of his in a music store, the Faurisson Affair is raised, because it has created such a strongly galvanized opposition to his ideas that he is constantly having to defend a point he has always deemed obvious, that his support for an individual's freedom of speech is not the same as supporting that individual's ideas. On the basis of this Faurisson Affair, Chomsky is made out to be anti-Zionist, pro-revisionist (as regards the Holocaust), even négationniste, implying that he denies that the Holocaust ever occurred. This far-fetched view relates to what is sarcastically called in Philip Roth's *Operation Shylock* "Shoah business" (recalling what Martin Jay has called in his *Cultural Semantics* "a particularly distasteful article" from a 1993 magazine article in *Der Spiegel* called "Das Shoah-business"[30]), since it creates a kind of monolith around discussions of the Holocaust and ensures that every word that falls outside of the accepted view is not only discounted, but so too is the other work by those who utter divergent opinions. The Affair has also made him some bedfellows with whom he'd much rather not be associated, including revisionist groups of various stripes who use his support for their freedom to exist as a kind of support for their position. Examples abound, and the whole problem, including the irritation and the affiliations created, is described by the International Secretariat of the Association des Anciens Amateurs de Récits de Guerre et d'Holocauste (AAARGH) a group of revisionist historians:

Whenever Noam Chomsky, an activist involved in the critique of the State, with an anarchistic background, criticizing most of all the U.S. State and its imperialist policies, starts a speech in front of an ever-growing audience, in North America, or in front of the medias, there is always a guy or a small group in the public to complain in a more or less bitter way about Chomsky's involvement with the revisionists, materialized by a text he has written and which has been used as a foreword to the pretrial defense tract issued by Faurisson in 1980, his *Mémoire en défense*. So that, Chomsky, after twenty years, has to repeat, every evening, that the freedom of expression is a whole, cannot be cut into pieces and that Revisionists, whatever their views *that he does not share at all*, have the same right as anybody else to talk freely without being victimized by a stupid repression. This question reappears in each of Chomsky's interventions in the press, TVs and elsewhere. We know how irritating the recurrence of these silly questions can be, launched by the Lobby spokespersons, the supporters of an aggressive Israel and the enemies of freedom. Day after day, in a thousand articles and interventions, Chomsky has to claim again and again his solidarity with our basic rights. We greet his constancy and we know that the bonds of friendship and solidarity which united us before the emergence of the revisionist question maintained themselves unadulterated because they are rooted in the same critique of the State, of its violence and its lies, of the classes and the groups that use its power to impose their private interest over the toiling people who feed them.[31]

The widespread awareness of the Faurisson Affair throughout the world (especially among Jewish groups) is the result of the power of the media to pick up on certain elements (in this case deemed distasteful) of someone's works in order to draw attention away from the rest of his work. For a surprising number of individuals, over one hundred books, a thousand articles, hundreds of talks, all evaporate in the face of this affair. It's true that we only hear of Faurisson because Chomsky signed the petition, but, to counter the arguments from certain quarters, it is the press that made the connection that brought Faurisson to the public eye, not Chomsky. Its effects have spilled over into North America on account of some articles in the popular media and, especially, the single-minded efforts of Alan Dershowitz who, in a number of talks and in his best-selling books about Judaism, has consistently found places to attack Chomsky and his views. I was once asked by administrators of McGill University to write a response to a letter that had been written by a Dershowitz-inspired Jewish professor who abhorred that university's decision to invite Chomsky to speak there, although it clearly wasn't the first time such a thing had happened. The *Washington Post* (A21, June 22, 1985)[32] reported that Cornell University Medical College had chosen Chomsky as the principal speaker at the school's commencement in May 1995. A month before the engagement, "Richard H. Dyckman, president of the Class of 1985 . . . said that the invitation had caused 'considerable dismay' among the graduating class, which 'has expressed the concern that your positions, particularly those regarding Zionism, deeply offend a large portion of students . . . your presence would make a political statement which would disturb what otherwise would have been a very happy occasion.' "

That this is a regular occurrence was confirmed when I myself became embroiled in the controversy that started when Chomsky came to the University of Western Ontario to receive an honorary doctorate. On Tuesday, April 18, 2000, in the course of his Canadian visit during which time he was also awarded an honorary doctorate from the University of Toronto, the *Globe and Mail* published "Noam Chomsky: A Degree Too Far," an attack by a graduate student named Eli Schuster against Chomsky and those institutions that chose to honor him. For Schuster, "Canadians of Cambodian descent—indeed, any Canadians interested in historical truth—ought to be outraged by the decisions of the University of Toronto and the University of Western Ontario to grant Noam Chomsky honorary doctorates this spring." Describing Chomsky as "well known on university campuses, yet obscure among the general public," she suggests (citing David Horowitz) that "his writings often reach paranoid extremes," particularly in the cases of his apologies for Pol Pot and his "support" for Robert Faurisson. She also suggests that "scholarship is supposedly about discovering the truth, yet Prof. Chomsky's writings actually argue for intellectual dishonesty. At one point, he addresses 'American dissidents,' warning them that they are morally responsible for the consequences of their acts, including the inevitable misuse by Washington of even 'accurate critical analysis of authoritarian state socialism in North Vietnam or in Cuba or in countries that the United States is trying to subvert. The consequences of accurate critical analysis will be to buttress these efforts, thus contributing to suffering and oppression.' She suggests a defiant act on the part of participants, turning one's back to the stage" would allow "faculty and convocating students [to] tell Mr. Chomsky what they think of a man who denied the existence of a Cambodian holocaust, and encouraged others to be less than truthful for an evil cause."

That day, I received from Chomsky a comment on that article, which had invoked Pol Pot, upon which we will focus attention shortly, and Chomsky's politics:

Dear Robert,

I'm sure you saw the *Globe & Mail* today, and just want to fill you in a bit about the background. On the article itself, no need to comment. It's straight out of ADL Stalinism, but at an ever higher fever pitch than usual. Carefully written in such a way that response is impossible. Just crazed charges, based on David Horowitz, etc. And in a style that I'll bet the G&M has never before published. The fact that the G&M is offering a platform is interesting and important. They are not a rag, after all. Also, well in advance so that there is plenty of time to organize protests and possibly more (among the Indochinese refugee committee too, which is virtually called upon to protest my alleged claim that Khmer Rouge atrocities were a media fabrication). It started a few weeks ago, aimed at the Windsor conference where I am to be speaking on the 4th. Letter-writing and petition campaigns demanding that I be kept off the program, with all the usual names (Dershowitz, etc.), and with the *Jewish Forward* (the old Yiddish-socialist newspaper, now so far to the jingoist-right one can hardly find it on the spectrum) planning more, and I'm sure plenty of others. I understand the organizers of the Windsor conference told them to get lost, which is probably the reason for this ratcheting up. The G&M lies are pretty brazen. To mention one you may not recognize off-hand, check out David Hawk, who in fact did play a significant role in preventing mobilization of opinion against Pol Pot, as Southeast Asia specialist of Amnesty International, which played down the atrocities throughout. See "Manufacturing Consent," p. 292, for some references. Citing him for the charge that I (meaning Ed and I) had a chilling effect on mobilizing protest (by one review article, the contents of which you know, and a book, which you also know, that went to press after the Vietnamese invasion)—that's pretty much, even by the standards of Pravda in the good old days. Something similar is going on in France, incidentally, with a new wave of hysteria because I don't follow the Party Line on Kosovo—my book just appeared there in French translation, with—to make it worse—a new section reviewing the documentation produced by NATO, the OSCE, State Department, and other Western sources, which is just as unacceptable as US intelligence on Cambodia, because it utterly explodes the stories used to rally the troops for the parade. There was a tantrum in *Libération* (naturally), reprinted in the French press in Switzerland (which will allow me to respond, if I choose; they actually seem pretty sympathetic, but would never have run the review, which is utterly crazed, without a lot of pressure). Anyway, I'd suggest that you prepare, and prepare others, for the worst. They are plainly out for blood and believe, maybe rightly, that they can turn these events into a major campaign to rid themselves at last of enemy No. 1 on their list.

Noam

As the coordinator of the University of Western Ontario event, I received a letter from the public relations department, which was to give me the "heads up," and which suggested I not reply to the *Globe and Mail*, especially since a University of Toronto professor was going to make it clear

that the honorary degree was (for Toronto) to honor Chomsky's work
in linguistics. I responded by saying that "We should certainly not shy
away from replying to such rubbish, in my opinion; the problem is, the
letter is so obviously ill informed, it would be difficult to know where
to begin. I would also think that Noam is and should be honored for his
amazing political contributions, in addition to his linguistics; for the University of Toronto professor to suggest that only the linguistics counts
for the degree is to suggest that the politics are somehow not worthy,
which is nonsense. Anyhow, as I said, I hesitate to wallow in such low
and filthy gutters, which may keep me from wanting to reply." In the
end I did write a long missive, which was edited down and published,
and I received a number of calls blasting me for the piece from people
who referred to themselves as "Zionists." Chomsky replied to the news:

Glad that they printed something. About the calls, it's not hard to believe. For
some reason, the Jewish communities in Canada, Australia, Mexico, and a few
other countries are far more rabid than in the US, which is vastly worse than
Israel. I wonder if the same is true of other ethnic groups (Ukrainians, etc.).
I suppose you heard of their attempt to have Ruth Birn fired after she dared
to show that Goldhagen was a fraud. On publishing something in the G&M, I
doubt that I would be willing to do so, even if I have a text in advance (the university wrote to ask for one, which surprised me). I rarely have a chance to
prepare a text, and I wouldn't want to have anything to do with the G&M,
frankly. No minimally respectable journal would sink to the level of publishing
vicious personal attacks as they did, surely without even trying to impose
minimal conditions of factual accuracy, and I am sure they have never done it
before: in fact, I can hardly think of counterparts, outside of the Stalinist press.
Can you?
Noam (personal correspondence with author, May 6, 2000)

The Faurisson Affair

Given the number of times this Faurisson Affair has been invoked, it's
clear that it needs to be addressed in some depth at this point. This is
remarkable to me, because Chomsky has been categorical enough in his
statements about Faurisson as to suggest that the continued reference to
the issue occurs for some other reason. He has written, for example, that
"Faurisson's conclusions are diametrically opposed to views I hold and
have frequently expressed in print (for example, in my book *Peace in the*

Middle East?, where I describe the holocaust as "the most fantastic outburst of collective insanity in human history"). But it is elementary that freedom of expression (including academic freedom) is not to be restricted to views of which one approves, and that it is precisely in the case of views that are almost universally despised and condemned that this right must be most vigorously defended. It is easy enough to defend those who need no defense or to join in unanimous (and often justified) condemnation of a violation of civil rights by some official enemy."[33] One would think that this should be sufficient. So why do so many people continue to relate some of his ideas to those of Faurisson? Perhaps it is because the people who do so tend to stand on the opposite end of the political spectrum, and they use the popular misconceptions about the Affair to legitimize their refusal to openly engage his ideas. Or perhaps it is the same phenomenon that we saw with the critique of Israel, which would suggest that some subjects are just too sensitive for rational discussion. Whatever the case may be, this type of resistance to Chomsky recurs with surprising frequency, again suggesting reasons for examining the effect that this affair has had upon Chomsky, particularly in his work beyond the university.

Before I begin, let me be clear about my own views. I denounce with disgust the garbage that is Holocaust revisionism, and I recoil in horror reading the falsifications that are spread by the likes of Faurisson. Furthermore, I join Chomsky in condemning those who would for their own selfish reasons make of Faurisson's work a cause célèbre and use it to justify the entirely untenable position that the Holocaust never occurred.

Now to the details.

In the 1970s Robert Faurisson began to make public statements concerning the Holocaust, including the following, from a January 16, 1979 letter to *Le Monde*: "Until 1960 I believed that these gigantic massacres had really occurred in 'gas chambers.' Then, after reading the work of Paul Rassiner, himself a deportee and the author of *Mensonge d'Ulysse*, I began to have my doubts. After fourteen years of personal reflection, and four years of relentless inquiry, I, like twenty other revisionists, have become certain that I am in the face of an historical lie."[34] This proclamation, along with other statements in the same vein, led to a strong backlash against Faurisson. So in the fall of 1979, an acquaintance of

Chomsky's named Serge Thion asked Chomsky to add his name to a petition in favor of the freedom to express opinions without persecution.[35] Thion himself has undergone some scrutiny in the United States and France on account of his conversion to a revisionist position. The petition, which eventually included signatures from five hundred people, was dubbed by the French media as "Chomsky's petition," and from that point on he became inexorably associated with the whole matter. The fact that the other 499 names are seldom mentioned (I've never seen them recalled in any of the literature about this affair) speaks volumes about the relationship between the actual issues and the efforts to challenge or denounce Noam Chomsky. This is not atypical of how media functions, of course, but given the effect that the whole affair has had, one might question the motives of those who insisted upon turning this into a story directly related to an American intellectual who characteristically added his name to a list of people who denounce persecution of those with unpopular views. The actual wording of the petition is as follows:

Dr. Faurisson has served as a respected professor of twentieth-century French literature and document criticism at the University of Lyon 2 in France. Since 1974 he has been conducting extensive independent historical research into the "Holocaust" question. Since he began making his findings public, Professor Faurisson has been subject to a vicious campaign of harassment, intimidation, slander and physical violence in a crude attempt to silence him. Fearful officials have even tried to stop him from further research by denying him access to public libraries and archives. (cited in Vidal-Naquet, *Assassins of Memory*, 285)

Says Chomsky, "I was asked to sign a petition calling on authorities to protect Faurisson's civil rights, and did so. I sign innumerable petitions of this nature, and do not recall ever having refused to sign one. I assumed that the matter would end there. It did not, because a barrage of lies in France, claiming, among other absurdities, that by defending Faurisson's civil rights I was defending his views. I then wrote the statement mentioned before. This and similar comments of mine evoked a new wave of falsification."[36]

Vidal-Naquet[37] has some clarifications to make about the petition: first, he states that contrary to the views of certain persons, Faurisson's civil rights were not violated, and indeed he was never, as some claimed, "prohibited [access to] either libraries or public archives" (286). Despite what Vidal-Naquet calls the "regrettable" conditions that drove

Faurisson from his position in Lyon and into the Centre national de télé-enseignment, his right to freedom of expression as protected in contemporary law was "never endangered. Indeed, on two separate occasions he was able to publish in *Le Monde*" (288). This, as Vidal-Naquet himself notes earlier on and in a footnote to the preceding statement, is not entirely true: "As for the interdiction to which Faurisson was a victim: that the personnel from the Centre de Documentation Juive Contemporaine question Faurisson in his fundamental activities, relating to the memory of the crime, and after long years refused to serve him, seems to me completely normal" (271). So were Robert Faurisson's civil rights compromised? Was he refused access to public archives? It would appear that the answer, whatever Vidal-Naquet thinks about it, is yes. Why? Because, says Vidal-Naquet, the Second World War obviously has a special significance for French citizens who endured it, and the memory thereof obliges them to assume special tasks: "My generation, comprised of men in their fifties [now nineties], is more or less the last for which Hitler's crimes remain a memory. That it is necessary to struggle against the disappearance or, worse, the degradation of this memory seems to me obvious. Neither prescription nor pardon seem to me conceivable. Imagine if Dr. Mengele came to visit the Auschwitz museum or presented his card to the Centre de documentation juive contemporaine? But this memory what are we to do with this memory, which is not common to all persons? The pursuit against the perpetrators of the crime seems to me both necessary and derisory" (270).

This type of reasoning (Faurisson was not denied his civil rights—although he was eventually denied some rights, which is regrettable—but the denial of his rights is justified in light of his activities, and those who denied him his rights were justified in light of the obligation they have as keepers of the memory to ensure that the crimes of the Holocaust are never forgotten) is the type that Chomsky attacks when he suggests that we must struggle hardest to protect those with whom we don't agree. Here is one of the central issues, for many people claim that if Hitler had been stopped before his Nazi Party came to power, we wouldn't have endured the horror of the Second World War. But this reasoning, as Chomsky suggests, could justify the worst atrocities; in fact, if it puts into the hands of some group or another the means, if not the obligation, to deny rights to those deemed to be a threat, then it starts looking like a justification for Stalinist-style purges, for example. And I can easily imagine a lot of incarcerated British, French, or U.S. officials if we were to follow this logic; indeed, the list of those susceptible to do time would likely be as long as the names of current administrations' members!

The other question that Vidal-Naquet raises bears upon the relationship between the ivory tower and the world that exists beyond, for it concerns the quality of Faurisson's research: "Is it or is it not the case that the petition represents Robert Faurisson as a serious historian who is undertaking real historical research?" (286). Others have joined Vidal-Naquet to question the validity of saying that Faurisson is (or was) a *respected* professor of literature, and, moreover, that the research in which he was engaged was "extensive" or "historical." Vidal-Naquet suggests that "Faurisson, with the limited exception of Anne Frank's *Journal*, is in search of falsification, not the truth. Is this a 'detail' that is of no interest to Chomsky? And if we understand that, misinformed, he [Chomsky] signed in full confidence a text that was authentically 'scandalous,' how is it possible to admit today the degree of care he exercises towards a falsifier?" (286). The question of intention is a complicated one, for here the point is that Vidal-Naquet can on the basis of the facts at hand determine that Faurisson was never out to discover the truth about history, but aimed instead to spread malicious lies. But intention is tricky business, as any literary critic (or lawyer) will tell you, and judging the facts thereof based upon one's own reading of the result is of course rather precarious.

Finally, Vidal-Naquet makes another oft-repeated comment concerning Chomsky's single-mindedness: "But it gets better: by considering himself untouchable, impervious to criticism, unaware of what Nazism was in Europe, draped in an imperial pride and an American chauvinism worthy of 'new mandarins' that he once denounced, Chomsky accuses those who are not of his opinion to be enemies of liberty" (286–287). Here a series of issues previously discussed come to the fore; as a promulgator of anarchist ideals, Chomsky is often accused of being blissfully "untouchable" because he never has to explain the details of the society to which he aspires, but instead can comfortably speak of the

need for free and unfettered creativity, whatever the (other) consequences. Further, by speaking in idealistic terms he can afford to ignore
the details of what "Nazism was in Europe," and thus by-pass the difficult obstacles to the elimination thereof for the present generation. The
issue of American "chauvinism" and "imperial pride" are deemed to
underwrite his universalist approach, an approach that demands equal
treatment of all people according to classical liberal principles despite
whatever historical reparations might be due to those who have been
persecuted in the past. This is indeed what Lyotard might call a *dif-
férend*,[38] an inexorable and unresolvable difference based upon wholly
different ideological bases according to which particular arguments are
constructed. This difference between idealism and historical circumstances will dog this affair to the end, as we'll see, and will touch upon
a range of concerns including the relationship between knowledge claims
that are deemed to be useful for certain groups or individuals and knowledge that is deemed to be true.

"A Few Elementary Comments on the Right to Free Expression"

The petition caused a significant uproar, notably in France, which is
described by Chomsky in an article he wrote about it for the *Nation* in
1981.[39] For example, Chomsky recalls an article in the magazine *le
Nouvel Observateur*, in which Claude Roy[40] wrote that "the appeal
launched by Chomsky" supported Faurisson's views. Says Chomsky:
"Roy explained my alleged stand as an attempt to show that the United
States is indistinguishable from Nazi Germany." In response to the
uproar, Chomsky wrote a short memoir on the civil liberties aspects of
the Faurisson case to clarify the distinction between supporting somebody's beliefs and fighting for the right to express them. He then gave
this text, called "Quelques commentaires élémentaires sur le droit à la
liberté d'expression," to Serge Thion with his tacit authorization to use
it as he thought best.[41] Thion gave it to Pierre Guillaume, who published
it as a "préface" to Robert Faurisson's book *Mémoire en défense contre
ceux qui m'accusent de falsifier l'histoire: La question des chambres à
gaz* (1980).[42] In *Réponses inédite*,[43] a collection of unpublished replies
to accusations made against Chomsky in the French media, Chomsky

makes the point once again that "I didn't write this text so that it would serve as the preface for a book that I didn't know existed; that I then demanded that it be withdrawn, but although only a few weeks after I wrote it, it was already too late to stop its publication; at issue here is a series of facts which have provoked a large number of absurd and malevolent comments in the French press that I won't recall here" (40). In short, says Chomsky, it's useful to reconsider "my own engagement with the Faurisson affair: it consisted of a signature at the end of a petition, and then some replies to lies and slander. That's it, that's all!" (43).

Vidal-Naquet then offers a widely cited description of what in his opinion happened next. "We learned (18 December) that Noam Chomsky retracted, by a letter of 6 December addressed to Jean-Pierre Faye, if not the text at least the use that was being made of it as preface to the book by Robert Faurisson. This book was nevertheless printed with the preface in question, which is dated 11 October. Further, independent of its utilization, this text does pose a series of questions to which it is worth responding" (289). Let us examine the substance of this letter-turned-preface, which in its entirety is but a few pages long, so as to judge for ourselves the various versions of this story that have been offered up for public consumption.

From its appearance this "préface" looks like nothing other than a letter, not even an unusually long letter by Chomsky's standards, containing "quelques commentaires élémentaires sur le droit à la liberté d'expression." But since Chomsky begins by saying that "this document contains remarks which are so banal that I must excuse myself before reasonable people who might come to read them," it does seem apparent that Chomsky did envision that the text would be read by more than one person. Whatever the projected audience, however, the principle reason he offers for even writing it in the first place is because his commentaries "shed light upon some remarkable aspects of intellectual life in contemporary France" (ix). This is interesting in light of the ensuing debate since it indicates that from the very beginning the subject of the piece is intellectual life in France, not Faurisson. "Herein I deal with a specific and particular subject, the right to express ideas, conclusions and beliefs. I won't say anything here about the work of Robert Faurisson or about his critics, about which I know very little, or about the subjects that they discuss, upon which I have no particular illumination" (ix). He repeats once again his earlier statements when he adds the second point: "I will have some unsavory (but well-deserved) comments to make about certain sectors of the French intelligentsia who have shown that they have no respect whatsoever for reason, as I've had the occasion to learn at my own expense in circumstances to which I will not return" (ix–x).

The next paragraph consists of Chomsky recounting that he had been asked to sign a petition for Robert Faurisson's right to freedom of expression and, critically, he notes the following: "The petition said absolutely nothing about the character, the quality or the validity of his research, but was confined very explicitly to the defense of elementary rights which are in democratic societies taken for granted; it demanded that the university and other authorities 'do everything possible to guarantee Faurisson's security and the free expression of his legal rights'" (x). He then describes the uproar caused by this petition, notably from "a former Stalinist, who changed his allegiances but not his intellectual style" and who published in *Le nouvel observateur* "a falsified version of the petition's contents, accompanied by a torrent of lies which don't even merit comment" (x). More surprising, for Chomsky, was the response of Pierre Vidal-Naquet who in a 1980 article for *Esprit* described the petition as "scandalous" for one reason; because the petition puts forth "conclusions" by Faurisson "as though they were in fact discoveries" ("comme si elles étaient effectivement des découvertes"). Here, the substance of the clash is in the word "découvertes," which in the original English petition, the one that Chomsky saw and signed, was *findings*. Vidal-Naquet translates this term as "découvertes," something he claims to have corrected prior to publication of the text in *Esprit*. In response, Chomsky recalled once again that the word in the petition was "findings," and suggested that Vidal-Naquet misinterpreted the English term. What is at stake here is that the term "findings" seems to suggest a kind of validity; but if the use of this term were the only problem, then Chomsky could have defused the issue long ago. Indeed there are people, like George Jochnowitz, who wonder why Chomsky never chose to compromise on this: "Did Chomsky have to fight so long and hard about the word "findings"? That is his style, of course, but it suggests a certain sincerity, a loyalty to the cause represented by the petition. It would have been easy—he can still do it!—to admit that "findings" is itself denial, and that a petition including this word is a denial. He could say that he innocently signed a denial and that he now recognizes it as such" (personal correspondence August 7, 1998). Whatever the case, this particular debate is much more of a hair-splitting exercise than what was to come.

Chomsky's reply then leads into the point that even if the person in question for the petition was doing scandalous or even dreadful work, even if the work that the person in question is doing is legitimately judged to be shocking, it does not bear upon the present issue: "We would have to conclude that the individual in question believes that the reason why [Vidal-Naquet] considered the petition scandalous was because Faurisson should indeed be deprived of his normal right to express himself, that he should be thrown out of the university, that he should be tormented and even subjected to physical violence, etc." (xi). This is a very sensitive point since it touches upon a gamut of concerns relating to what is transmitted, in this case through teaching, to future genera-tions. George Jochnowitz offers a range of objections to Chomsky's point when he asks: "Should a professor of history be allowed to teach that the Japanese-Americans were never interned (as distinct from saying they should have been) or that slavery had never existed in the United States? Should a historical linguist be allowed to teach that all languages are descended from Hungarian? Arthur Butz taught engineering. His job wasn't threatened because his subject was not relevant to the issue. The right to advocate murder is different from the right to say genocide didn't happen when your title is Professor of 'document criticism' " (personal correspondence August 7, 1998).

I would imagine that Chomsky would disagree on a number of issues raised in this letter, and in discussions about this he often describes the alternative, that is, the suppression of those opinions that do not accord with our own by an inquisition, or a group of political commissars assigned to the task. But the central point here is that it is much easier to defend the rights of those with whom we agree and much simpler to suppress those who utter things we don't want to hear (in this case for good reason). But to defend only those with whom we agree is for Chomsky relatively meaningless, a view that can be traced back to the

Enlightenment tradition and, moreover, to Voltaire, says Larry Portis. "In this sense, the position taken by Chomsky coincides with that of Voltaire, concerning the defense of the right to express opinions which he considers abominable" (167).[44]

Larry Portis's reference to Voltaire returns us to the very source of the problems between Chomsky and those who feel that he simply goes too far in his defense of those (like Faurisson) we should, in fact, be suppressing for our own good, and for the good of future generations. Voltaire himself was admonished for what could be considered a consistent application of classical liberal principles in public affairs, summed up by his famous dictum, "I disagree with everything you say, but I shall fight to the death for your right to say it."[45] Voltaire and others who have been important influences for Chomsky, such as Bakunin, support the thrust of this utterance and don't take it to mean that this defense necessitates an engagement with the material deemed offensive. The view of many persons with whom I myself have had contact in France, including the editors of the French version of my Chomsky biography, disagree. The latter wrote that Chomsky's views on the application of this principle (especially Faurisson) are so unpopular in France that support thereof could lead people to boycott any text that supports him in this regard. The problem is not related to the signing of the petition, but rather that Chomsky did so without in any way interesting himself in Faurisson's writing. For the French editors, as for many others in France, the defense of freedom of expression of someone whose work you have not read does not obligate you in any substantive way, and that to follow the spirit of Voltaire's approach necessarily presupposes that we not only defend one's right to express his or her view, but that we become interested therein so as to refute it. In other words, this position would demand of Chomsky that he proclaim: "I have read what you've written, I am not in agreement with you for the following reasons, but I will defend with all my might your right to express your opinion."

The effort that one would have to expend in order to follow this precept is monumental, particularly for those like Chomsky who regularly sign this type of petition; on the other hand, Chomsky is quite famous for having read and assimilated such tremendous amounts of material that one just assumes him capable of adding to this volume exponentially. This is itself part of the Chomsky Effect; he leaves us with the impression of having an informed view on most matters, and of being familiar with a remarkable array of materials, in short, of simply having read everything. In popular forums he is as likely to be asked about the proper way to raise a child as he is about the specific details concerning some atrocity committed in the distant or recent past, somewhere in the world. The reality, as he suggests, is that nobody could possibly hope to deal with assessing all works by all those for whom petitions are circulated, and that furthermore it is virtually inconceivable that we'd be in agreement with views expressed by all these people; a huge effort would have to be expended in each case to embark upon the (unrelated) exercise of commenting upon works of people we're trying to defend.

Chomsky's Perception of the French Intellectual Scene

Many of the things that Vidal-Naquet calls in the previous statement "regrettable" go on in other countries besides France, of course, in varying degrees. In Canada, for example, we are led to believe (on account of our being inundated by popular media from the United States) that we have similar rights and freedoms as Americans, whereas in fact we are subject to a more elaborate system of government controls in matters relating to media, freedom of expression, and so on. In his discussions of classical liberalism, which are increasingly frequent, Chomsky often praises aspects of the American judicial system, the Bill of Rights, the Constitution, and the mentality of the Founding Fathers to illustrate the degree to which other countries limit citizens' rights. Once again, we find a point of intersection here with Rudolph Rocker who, in *Pioneers of American Freedom* (1949), and also in his 1933 tome *Nationalism and Culture*, traces the roots of radical thinking in America to the writings of Ralph Waldo Emerson, Thomas Jefferson, Abraham Lincoln, Thomas Paine, Henry David Thoreau, and others. This idea underwrites both men's thinking about the peculiar form of American anarchism; as Mina Graur writes, Rocker's 1949 book's "main purpose was to show that anarchism and libertarian ideas in America had not been imported from Europe, but were a product of the unique social conditions and historical traditions of the country. Indeed, whereas anarchism in Europe proceeded mainly along communist lines, native anarchism in the United States had been almost exclusively individualist. Anarchism, claimed Rocker, had existed in the United States at a time when no indication of similar movements could be found in Europe" (229–230). But Chomsky also criticizes the degree to which American politics deviates from the model upon which it was erected, and to which it nevertheless refers constantly in justifying actions (bombing in the name of democracy, trading with oppressive regimes in the name of human rights, erecting embargoes in the name of free trade, and so forth).

With reference to the Faurisson Affair, Chomsky often notes that he has signed potentially more inflammatory petitions in the United States without the kind of backlash, in either the legal or media realms, as the one he has witnessed in France, and that furthermore the United States has its own versions of Faurisson in the person of Arthur Butz. So why was it such a big issue in France? asks Chomsky: "If it weren't for the extraordinary effort of first French, then American, intellectuals to give the maximal possible publicity to Faurisson, he would have remained in (much deserved) obscurity. That's why you can't get a copy of his 'Mémoire,' to which my statement on freedom of expression was added as an 'avis.' No one cares about what is in it; it has been used rather the way Bosnia has, as a technique of self-aggrandizement by intellectuals who are too ridiculous to discuss. Same with Butz. It was recognized early on that it wouldn't be wise to make a fuss about him; freedom of speech is protected here, unlike France. So he is ignored, and his influence is undetectable. Lessons? Pretty obvious, except maybe to those utterly immersed in the commissar culture" (letter of June 23, 1997). One small aside, relating to the very vocabulary of this remark ("ridiculous," "fuss," "ignored," "obvious"): the Chomsky Effect is in some ways dependent upon a cynical, acerbic, or sarcastic humor that is omnipresent in his political writings. This makes him a darling of some, in particular younger individuals, since his humor forces us to confront standard versions of events with alternative readings; I will return to this point at the end of the book.

"Faurisson Is a Kind of Apolitical Liberal"

Let's return to the infamous final paragraph of this "préface," the one that has been cited most often by those who use the Faurisson Affair as justification for refusing to engage Chomsky's opinions. Here Chomsky takes up the question of Faurisson's anti-Semitism, first by suggesting that even if he were anti-Semitic, he still warranted protection from those who would like to take away his right to research and to work. He then makes a series of statements that don't really accord with the central argument nor with his previous declaration of unconcern about Faurisson's work. "One could really ask oneself if Faurisson really is anti-Semitic or Nazi. As I said, I don't know his works very well. But in light of what I've read, largely on account of the nature of the attacks made against him [by Vidal-Naquet, incidentally, something which he himself later revealed], I see no proof which would support such conclusions. Nor do I find credible proof thereof in the documents that I've read about him, either in published texts or in private correspondence. From what I can tell, Faurisson is a kind of apolitical liberal" (xiv–xv). This of course offers fuel for Vidal-Naquet's flame; referring to Chomsky's opening comments, he writes: "The preface in question emerges from a rather new genre in the Republic of Letters. Noam Chomsky read neither the book for which he wrote the preface, nor previous writings from the author, nor criticisms made thereof, and he is incompetent in the domain to which they apply." Referring to Chomsky's closing comments, about Faurisson's anti-Semitism, Vidal-Naquet remarks that Chomsky has just affirmed that he's not competent to judge the works since he hasn't read them. So, says Vidal-Naquet, "Chomsky-the-double read Faurisson and never read him, read his critics and never read them" (282).[46]

Chomsky's response is that "writing elementary remarks on the right of freedom of expression is not a 'rather new genre in the republic of letters,' and I didn't read the book I 'prefaced' because I didn't 'preface it' or even know that it existed, all of which Vidal-Naquet knows very well." Once again, Chomsky's own remarks send us back to the préface: "I nowhere proclaim my 'competence.' Rather I proclaimed my *in*competence, clearly and explicitly." And concerning Faurisson's anti-Semitism, Chomsky's point remains as it was then: Vidal-Naquet had not at that time provided clear evidence of Faurisson's anti-Semitism, and "if the harshest and most knowledgeable critic of Faurisson can produce nothing but that evidence in support of the charge of anti-Semitism, then the charge must be weakly grounded indeed. That's completely accurate, whatever may have been discovered later" (September 9, 1997).

It is indeed the case, as Vidal-Naquet suggests here, that Chomsky's final paragraph contains speculations concerning Faurisson's allegiances, and so does this last statement. In fact, to even ask the question about Faurisson's political orientation was, as Chomsky himself points out, totally unnecessary in light of the previous discussion. Chomsky responds: "That leaves the matter of whether it is appropriate, in a statement on the right of freedom of expression, to say at the end that the person charged may indeed be an anti-Semite or worse, but if so, that will change nothing about his right of free expression. And furthermore, that such charges are themselves serious, and should be backed by evidence, which, in this case, those who make the charges make clear they cannot provide. I could have—and perhaps should have—elaborated on the little I had seen of Faurisson's writings. In fact, it consisted of several letters to newspapers (refused publication) in which he praised those who fought 'the good fight' against the Nazis and praised the heroism of the Warsaw Ghetto fighters" (September 9, 1997).

Commenting more generally upon the whole affair, Christopher Hitchens draws a few conclusions: "Let us not waste any time on Robert Faurisson. He is an insanitary figure who maintains contact with neo-Nazi circles and whose project is the rehabilitation, in pseudoscholarly form, of the Third Reich. How he came to be appointed in the first place I cannot imagine (from what I have seen his literary criticism is pitiful),[47] but in 1979 he was a teacher in good standing of French literature at the University of Lyons. If, like our own Arthur Butz, who publishes "historical revisionist" garbage from Northwestern University, he had been left to stew in his own style, we might have heard no more of him."[48] And if Chomsky had not speculated on Faurisson's politics, we would probably not have heard as much out of him and his detractors. This is in fact one of the three areas where Hitchens finds fault with Chomsky, the other two being the fact that he gave the document to Serge Thion, "who seems rather a protean and quicksilvery fellow," and "attempting at the last minute, when he discovered too late that he was being bound into the same volume as work he had not read, to have his commentary excised." Hitchens' assessment of Faurisson suggests that he really is a shady character with objectives far outside of reasonable historical evidence, and this view is given further credibility by Lawrence L. Langer in his article "Pre-Empting the Holocaust" (*Atlantic Monthly* November 1998), by which he means "using—and perhaps abusing—its [the Holocaust's] grim details to fortify a prior commitment to ideals of moral reality, community responsibility, or religious belief that leave us with space to retain faith in their pristine value in a post-Holocaust world" (105).

However one views this debate, there is in my opinion nothing to suggest any relationship between Faurisson's hypotheses concerning the Holocaust and Chomsky's defense of the former's right to defend them. As regards the existence of gas chambers, Chomsky has made a number of statements, including the following: "For me, no reasonable evidence exists which puts into doubt the existence of gas chambers." This does not mean that questions thereabout, such as how people could enter the "showers" hours or minutes after prisoners have been gassed to death, should not be posed. According to Chomsky, "the issue here is facts, not religious beliefs. Only religious fanatics would refuse that one inquire about facts" (*Réponses inédites*, 44). Faurisson's work, like the gamut of Holocaust denial, relies upon obvious falsifications, as has been demonstrated widely. Again, though, this is no reason to question the facts as widely accepted; further research tends to clarify the facts, while offering further fuel for challenging revisionist theses.

The other point to examine is the turns that the debate has taken in the last few years. One significant turn, frequently mentioned, is to recall the politics of those involved in the publication of the text. For instance, Manuel Prutschi of the Canadian Jewish Congress writes in a short article called "Holocaust Denial Today"[49] about the various affiliations of those involved. "A number of radical leftists in France are intimately connected to Holocaust denial. They include Serge Thion, who is a defender of both Rassinier and Faurisson. Thion is linked with the once-Marxist publishing house "La Vieille Taupe," founded by Pierre Guillaume. Guillaume is the publisher of many of Faurisson's works and has now associated himself with Henri Roques." And then of course the usual diatribe against Chomsky, including factually incorrect statements such as: "Chomsky has described the Holocaust as 'the most fantastic outburst of collective insanity in human history'. Yet this did not lead him to prevent a piece he had allegedly written purely to uphold the right of free speech from being used as an introduction to one of Faurisson's books. It also did not stop him from giving Guillaume publication rights in France to one of his important books."[50] The reader can judge both assertions on the basis of the facts previously presented. It should be noted, though, that "one of [Chomsky's] most important books" is, in Prutschi's opinion, the collection of unpublished articles that Guillaume prefaced and arranged to have published with Spartacus Press! As for Guillaume's role in this, Chomsky has indicated indifference and noted the link between various publishing houses and unsavory activities, past and present.

Many academics have asked why Chomsky does not look into the question of the Holocaust more seriously, given his interests and given the accusations against him. There have also been suggestions that he could defuse the Faurisson problem with a stronger stand against those revisionists who deny the existence of the murderous Nazi camps. The point about there being this one reference in Chomsky's writings to the Holocaust that is continuously drummed up by Chomsky is in this sense interesting. Once again, the revisionist group AARGH has commented upon this very question extensively (I have made some corrections to the original misspellings):

Chomsky has stated many times that he had expressed once [and] for all his feelings about what some people want to call the "holocaust." He has quoted time and again THE sentence he had written long before the Revisionist affair had broken loose, a sentence he hoped would exonerate him from any lingering suspicion: the sentence is a warrant of his orthodoxy in the acceptance of the official version of the said Holocaust. Let's consider it once again: ". . . savage persecution culminating in the most fantastic outburst of collective insanity in human history. . . ." The reference: *Peace in the Middle East? Reflections on Justice and Nationhood*, [1969], Vintage Books, 1974, 57–58. We should note, first, that it is only a fragment of a sentence, that the whole book is devoted to the Middle East and does not deal with events of WW2. It belongs to a chapter titled "Nationalism and Conflict in Palestine." Reading the whole paragraph indicates the presence of a rhetorical ploy: there are two sets of arguments, he says, one Arabic, the other Jewish; but the other, when he unveils the content, he calls Zionist. And it is in the middle of the Zionist set of arguments that one can find the famous fragment of sentence.

So far so good. However this group is not satisfied to end here, since they find that by reading into the rhetorical strategy presented here they can pull the sheets over to their side of the bed, and bring Chomsky along with them:

If we put it in another way, we see that these considerations about Holocaust are those of the Zionists, anxious to justify their military occupation of Palestine, and certainly not of Chomsky who does not share their views. As a consequence, the extraction of this sentence fragment from its context and its portraying it as a justification of a behavior willing to ignore everything about revisionism, is akin to a *leger-de-main*. The critiques of Chomsky could have realized that, if only they'd read the texts. What conclusions can we draw from this trick? First, Chomsky never expressed the bottom of his mind on the "Holocaust." He never had the opportunity to deal with the historical question, to really deal with what happened to certain Jewish communities in Europe under the Nazi rule. He has consistently evaded the question because he knows that he does not know much on the subject, that he has not done the minimum of research into the subject to obtain at least an educated understanding of the basics of the question. This is a correct attitude for someone who knows what learning is about. (This is the reverse of the Parisian intelligentsia for whom the rule is to always talk about subjects on which you know nothing about.) Chomsky always maintained the possibility of having the revisionist thesis verified by the facts. He repeatedly said the same thing we have been saying all along: even if the gas chambers have not existed, this does not change at all our condemnation of Nazism as a particularly inhumane policy. As he refrained to judge the orthodox thesis on this subject, he also refrains to judge the revisionist thesis. But if, by hypothesis, he would start to work on this question, who can say today to what conclusions he would arrive, what side he would take in the conflict between rationalists and materialist[s] who lead the revisionist crowd and crazy mystics like Elie Wiesel, meandering rabbis like Berenbaum, silent historians like Rousso, mind-consensus readers like Hilberg, document destroyers like Lanzmann, leading the anti-revisionist hordes. We are committed to publish here those who would want to take up the challenge.

What happens here is that the view of the Holocaust becomes akin to a kind of agnosticism, an unwillingness to speak until facts are presented. This is not outside of Chomsky's view, but it does once again deny the fact that revisionism isn't and never has been the subject of Chomsky's own involvement in this affair—freedom of expression is. But one can see how the move can be made to appropriate Chomsky in this case.

On the other hand, Chomsky has made reference to the Holocaust elsewhere, in ways that clearly suggest his belief that the Holocaust is a historical fact. For example, in an open letter distributed by the Preamble Center, Washington, D.C.,[51] "An Appeal from American Jews to the Green Party of Germany," we find the following: "We are Jewish Americans who are deeply concerned that the memory and tragedy of the Holocaust is being invoked in order to justify an unjust bombing campaign against the civilian population of Yugoslavia. Many of us have friends who lost family members in the Holocaust, or have lost relatives ourselves. We are deeply aware of our own history and the need for the world community to intervene in situations where there is a threat of genocide, in order to prevent it. However, this is clearly not what is happening in Yugoslavia today." The point of this plea is to prevent the rendering banal the term and the atrocity to which it refers: "Many supporters of the bombing have drawn analogies to the Holocaust, arguing that the world cannot simply stand by in the face of ethnic cleansing in Kosovo. But the bombing has greatly worsened the situation of the Kosovar Albanians, as is now universally recognized. It has also destroyed the pro-democracy movement within Yugoslavia, and is destabilizing neighboring countries. We urge you to reject these false and exaggerated analogies to the Holocaust and World War II, which are being used to garner support for a bombing campaign that is intensifying the suffering of all nationalities in Yugoslavia. We appeal to the Green Party of Germany to oppose this war, and to support a negotiated solution of the conflict."

The Refusal to Publish Chomsky's Replies

Being a popular academic implies that there exists an audience eager to read Chomsky's views of things, a desire that is satisfied by his tremendous output of books, articles, and talks. As previously mentioned, the principal outlets for his work are not mainstream magazines or newspapers like *The New York Times*, *Time*, or *The New York Review of Books* (any more). Nevertheless, for those in search of his views, there is ample coverage to be found in less popular outlets. In France, however, the situation has been somewhat different. First, although well-known within the public domain, Chomsky does not have the kind of outlet afforded to him in, say, England (and this for reasons beyond language research). The Faurisson Affair has played a role in this too, perhaps as an excuse to marginalize him, and this is at least partly the result of the fact that he was never given a chance to offer his side of the story to magazines and newspapers like *Le Matin de Paris*, *Nouvelles littéraires* and *Libération* despite the fact that they printed inflammatory articles about his views (hence his publication of *Réponses inédites*, the assembly of unpublished replies). In Chomsky's opinion, some of the errors propagated by the French media are so obviously out of sync with his views that they should have been noted immediately. For instance, "I [Chomsky] will mention once again *Le Matin de Paris* which suggests that I consider "even the idea of genocide" as an "imperialist myth," even though the editors could not have not known that I'd described "the massacre of the Jews" as the most fantastic outburst of collective insanity in the history of mankind; and that the book in question (*American Power and the New Mandarins*) is devoted to numerous examples of genocide throughout the world" (*Réponses inédites* 42–43). Is the media really that different in the United States than in France? As preceding discussion suggests, the French media operates with a different series of constraints and expectations. More to the point here, however, is that the functioning and the role that media plays in French society is different, for better or for worse, from the way it works in the United States. Or at least Chomsky believes this to be true, which affects his views of French life, just as preconceptions in Paris about Chomsky are in some ways colored by views that the French have about American life.

The entire debacle moved further beyond the realms of academia with the involvement of PEN club in France. Once again, in *Le Monde*, we find a piece published on December 31, 1980, in which PEN, which struggles for the freedom of imprisoned writers, complained that on account of Chomsky, the Faurisson Affair, which had previously been a kind of folklore, became once again an international controversy. Chomsky replies: "What moved the affair into the public arena was their decision to give it extraordinary publicity: by the *Le Monde* statement, the suspension from teaching, the 'falsification of History' trial (which, interestingly, Vidal-Naquet always seeks to deny or evade), etc. As for its becoming 'international,' the *New York Times* story on a 'tempest in a teapot' is not inaccurate. It became 'international' precisely because of the actions of those who seek to give maximal publicity to Holocaust revisionists" (September 9, 1997). The other point about the role of the media is suggested by Chomsky's own words, that they did create a tempest in newspapers like *Le Monde*, but then failed to fully represent both sides of the debate. Indeed, *Le Monde* "in the last 15 years has exhibited the worst bad faith and the most violent hostility towards Chomsky, guilty of judging the Parisian intelligentsia as mediocre and deeply committed to Stalinism."[52] PEN then concluded that the whole business was all the more deplorable since it occurred during a period of resurgent anti-Semitism and mounting violence. Chomsky of course pointed out that PEN is supposed to be concerned with the defense of free expression for writers, and yet they are the ones who complain about the press's publicity about a book in which an author defends himself from attacks leveled against him on account of his writings (27). In light of PEN's stated objectives, it seems more appropriate for them to take up the issue of an author's inability to argue his own view in the media that was attacking him.

Beyond the Media

The questions of facts regarding these issues spill over into many domains, including books by Pierre Vidal-Naquet and Jean-Claude Milner, discussed by Chomsky in *Réponses inédites*, in various writings by Alan Dershowitz, and in reviews of Chomsky's work by a range of commentators. Chomsky is characteristically forthcoming in his replies; for instance, while referring to one of Vidal-Naquet's (patently untrue) claims (in *Les Juifs . . .*) he suggests that "one must have an unwavering faith in the gullibility of his readers to risk making such flagrant falsifications." Jean-Claude Milner, for example, has written a chapter of a book called "Chomsky et les politiques d'extermination" (Chomsky and the Politics of Extermination),[53] which accuses him of lending an air of credibility to the revisionist thesis, and to Faurisson himself. By means of introduction, Chomsky writes that "in a manner consistent with the methods of the 'Paris intellectuals,' Milner does not consider it necessary to prove that I actually hold these views. It would in fact be quite easy to demonstrate that this is not the case, and that in reality they are pure fabrications. It would also be quite easy to demonstrate that Milner's fantasies in this matter are frequently repeated in Parisian circles, which probably constitutes his source" (*Réponses inédites* 60). He then goes on to make a whole series of corrections to Milner's text regarding how things related to these issues have been reported in Paris. The level of misunderstanding and misreporting in this matter reaches, as we have seen, quite extraordinary heights; but this is more than a matter between a stubborn and tenacious American intellectual and his counterparts in France, because Faurisson's cause became a matter for the courts. There may be something else going on here as well, since the J.-C. Milner who wrote with such vitriol about the Pol Pot affair is the same J.-C. Milner who was writing about generative phonology in the late '60s, and the same Milner who eventually took over the linguistics department at University of Paris 8. In other words, the writer running down Noam Chomsky on Pol Pot was not simply a "disinterested intellectual" (as if such a thing existed) but perhaps someone with other motives.

More recently, in November 2005, we find these issues recurring, this time on American soil,[54] in "Chomsky and Dershowitz debate Middle East peace process at Kennedy School," an article by Rob Meyer, of the Kennedy School Communications. "Those expecting a heated debate between Noam Chomsky and Alan Dershowitz at the Kennedy School of Government Tuesday night (November 29, 2005) were not disappointed as the two venerable Cambridge professors faced off in an event titled "Israel and Palestine After Disengagement: Where Do We Go From Here?" The two scholars—who met in the 1940s at a Hebrew summer camp—have each written extensively on the Arab-Israeli conflict, with Dershowitz an outspoken supporter of Israel and Chomsky an influential critic of U.S. foreign policy, which he described as the "continued dedication to the road to catastrophe" in the Middle East. "The time has come for compromise," Dershowitz, the Felix Frankfurter Professor of Law at Harvard, said in his opening remarks. "This will require the elevation of pragmatism over ideology. It will require that both sides give up rights. . . . I strongly believe that there is a genuine will for peace on both sides now and that the pragmatic differences can and will be resolved." Chomsky said current proposals for a Palestinian state will lead to "the breaking of its organic links to Jerusalem and the disintegration of the remnants of Palestinian society." Dershowitz assailed international scholars who fuel the ideologues on each side and "send a destructive message to those who must make peace on the ground. Many academics around the world are contributing to an atmosphere that makes peace more difficult to achieve," said Dershowitz before a capacity crowd in the Kennedy School forum. "They are encouraging those Palestinians who see the end of Israel as their ultimate goal to persist in their ideological and terrorist campaign. . . . To the Israelis, the message is whatever you do in the name of compromise, you will continue to be attacked and demonized." Chomsky and Dershowitz quarreled on most issues, including the diplomatic history of the dispute, the validity of each other's sources of information, and the details of the current proposals for a two-state solution. An audience member asked Chomsky about the history of violence directed toward Jews, from the Holocaust to today. "That is half of a very important question," Chomsky said. "What is the effect of war and terrorism on the Palestinians? . . . The balance of terror and violence is overwhelmingly against the Palestinians, not surprisingly given the balance of forces. That's true right to the present." Chomsky continued: "In the first month of the Intifada in October 2000, 74 Palestinians were killed, four Israelis were killed. . . . Clinton responded by sending the biggest shipment of military helicopters in a decade. . . . The press responded too, by not publishing it, refusing to publish it." Dershowitz quickly countered: "The idea that there is this vast conspiracy between the American media and both Democrats like Clinton and Republicans like Bush to hide the truth from the American public just does not bear reality . . . Why would newspapers not cover these stories? One reason—they are figments of Chomsky's imagination, and they just never happened."

Beyond the university and into the justice system leads us as well to the "tribunal" that condemned Faurisson, which in turn leads us to considerations of the differences between the American and the French legal systems. When Faurisson was found guilty, Chomsky expressed his astonishment: "The French tribunals have now condemned Faurisson for having, in addition to other villainous acts, been lacking in the "responsibility" and "prudence" of the historian, for having been negligent for not using certain key documents, and for having been "*laissé prendre en charge par autrui (!) son discours dans une intention d'apologie des crimes de guerre ou d'incitation à la haine raciale*" (letting others use his statements as an apology for war crimes, or the incitement to racial hatred). Most surprising was that "the court then claimed that it doesn't restrain the historian's right to express him or herself freely, but does condemn Faurisson for having exercised this right. By this shameful judgment, the state has been accorded the right to determine an official truth (in spite of protests from the judges) and to punish those responsible for 'irresponsibility.' If this decision does not provoke massive protests, this will be a dark day for France" (*Réponses inédites* 43–44). His point of view does not preclude the possibility of speaking out against anti-Semitic, racist, xenophobic, or obviously falsified accounts of the world; it does however refuse the point of view that the State (or any other institution) should be given the right to determine for individuals who has the right to speak or do research. Chomsky draws attention to another point, relating to Vidal-Naquet's early accusations regarding Faurisson's anti-Semitism, in his assessment of this court decision: "Incidentally, when the court condemned Faurisson a few years later, it never charged him with anti-Semitism (at least, according to the excerpts from the judgment published in *Le Monde*). Rather, it charged him with having 'allowed others' to use his work for nefarious ends—a pretty astonishing charge, but indicating, apparently, that they could find no basis for the charge of anti-Semitism, several years later" (September 9, 1997). In the end, the facts of the case seem relatively clear, and the effects upon Chomsky's reputation, profound. But this wasn't the only event of its kind, and the Pol Pot and Cambodia affair require yet another airing, with this same level of attention to detail.

The Pol Pot Affair

Noam Chomsky has on a number of occasions over the last twenty-five years teamed up with Edward S. Herman, who has undertaken intensive research into media analysis. Together, Chomsky and Herman have written, among other works, *Counter-Revolutionary Violence: Blood-baths in Fact and Propaganda* (1973), *The Political Economy of Human Rights* (1979, in two volumes), and *Manufacturing Consent: The Political Economy of the Mass Media* (1988). The two-volume work on human rights has been the subject of some controversy in France for the view promoted therein that the media often finds "newsworthy" stories of brutality or oppression that are promulgated by official enemies, while they find it appropriate to maintain silence when similar events go on in countries to which they are allied. This is a thesis that Chomsky has upheld in a number of circumstances. For instance, in the introduction to chapter the first volume of *The Political Economy of Human Rights* titled "Cambodia: Why the Media Find It More Newsworthy Than Indonesia and East Timor," Chomsky and Herman write: "The way in which the media have latched on to Cambodian violence, as a drowning man seizes a lifebuoy, is an object lesson as to how the U.S. media serve first and foremost to mobilize opinion in the service of state ideology" (21). This is not to suggest that the media shouldn't report examples of violence, repression, and oppression throughout the world, but rather that there is an obvious link between what gets reported and who is doing the reporting.

This second "affair" stems not only from Chomsky's book on human rights but also from work he was doing elsewhere to promote the cause of Timor to a disinterested international community. In an unpublished letter written to *Le Matin de Paris*, dated December 27, 1979, Chomsky states that "In a deposition before the United Nations, I presented a report on the consequences of Indonesian aggression in Timor, which was supported by the West, emphasizing that even though the horror of the situation was comparable to that of Cambodia (which is finally being acknowledged), the West has remained silent, and the facts have been censured for four long years, which has permitted Western powers to furnish the material needs and the diplomatic cover that Indonesia needed in order to pursue the massacre" (*Réponses inédites* 17). In other words, Chomsky (and Herman) note that Western intellectuals tend to concentrate upon crimes for which others are responsible, even as they maintain their silence about other crimes promulgated by their own state. Chomsky offers an example, in this letter to *Le Matin de Paris*: "For example, in September of 1978, the Minister of Foreign Affairs, de Guiringaud, in the course of his visit to Djakarta, set forth the grounds for an accord to furnish the warplanes and other military equipment. Asked about the French attitude to Timor, where these arms were to be used in a manner which had not been concealed any longer, he was quite satisfied to reply that France would not place Indonesia in an embarrassing situation in case the question was to be asked in the United Nations (*Le Monde*, September 14, 1978). I wrote at the time, 'imagine if the great powers had offered arms to the Cambodians to practice repression inside of that country' " (*Réponses inédites* 19). Notable is that Chomsky's deposition is never discussed with regard to this matter, and that the words he has spoken that relate to the Cambodia-Timor comparison remain to this day largely unheard, in France and beyond. Even more notable in terms of Chomsky's own media studies is the date of this debate; few people recall specific views held by anyone twenty-five years ago, on account of the speed of information and the changing nature of popular information fads. And yet Chomsky is still known in France and beyond, by a large number of people simply on account of his supposed views about Pol Pot and Faurisson.

For his views, Chomsky received a reply from Jacques Attali and Bernard-Henri Lévy in the form of an article in a December 17, 1979, issue of *Matin de Paris*. This is an interesting response, since it takes a stance against Chomsky from what sounds to be a left-wing position: "Until when will intellectuals continue making small change out of intervening cadavers? When will it stop, this bloody ballet of words uttered around contemporary mass graves? Does he have any idea what speaking means, this linguist Noam Chomsky, when he sets up an opposition between the 'good' dead persons from Timor and the 'bad' dead persons from Cambodia? What does it mean, this strange rumor that we must choose between progressivist starving persons and 'reactionary' half-starved persons, according to the political stripes of the despot who overwhelms them, in one case being Soviet and in the other Indonesian? In other words, by condemning Western intellectuals for turning a blind eye to a massacre supported by their own state while calling attention to one that is not, Chomsky is suggesting that there are good and bad massacres?" A tribute to the effect that Chomsky's approach can have, even upon those who may claim allegiance to a concern for human rights, Attali and Lévy conclude: "For all of those who are not so deaf to the memory of this century, there is in this type of undertaking an old, very old and very odious sickness of a certain kind of 'left': the tragic accounting of sufferings which nourished the darkest hours of the Stalinist night."

Chomsky's and Herman's work attempt to draw attention to the unequal treatment received by certain oppressed persons in comparison with others, and that the imbalance can generally be linked to the interests of those doing the reporting. Somehow, however, this is lost in translation since it doesn't accord with another tendency present in contemporary society, that of following the basic governmental line as articulated by the government itself. Attali and Lévy thus reverse the very point of the Chomsky-Herman book when they write: "Is it necessary to remind Chomsky, the militant anti-totalitarian, that for the peasant from Timor or the damned from Vietnam, the bombs have no color and neither does the 'publicity' that might save them? Is it necessary to remind Chomsky the well provided for, Chomsky the well-nourished, that among the forty-six countries in which agricultural production has declined for two years we find Iraq, Angola and Cuba, as well as Togo, Jordan and Mali?" Finally, Attali and Lévy condemn the actions of an intellectual who, like Bakunin, insists upon the responsibility of intellectuals to denounce and struggle against oppression and who, moreover, states that they must engage in the very difficult task of criticizing their own government rather than the enemy Other. In this light it is odd to read their concluding remarks: "No Chomsky! The problem is not to come down on one side or the other from our universities, our chapels and our academies in this indecent debate: either Cambodia or Timor. The pressing issue is to finish with these quarrels among clerks, archaic and fearsome, for which the starving are always in the end the victims. From now on, without any delay, Timor and Cambodia." Chomsky's reply to this attack remains unpublished, which certainly speaks to the kind of mis- or nonrepresentation to which Chomsky and Herman refer in their work. Chomsky's letter makes the point quite clearly: "By the prowess of a most remarkable reasoning, they conclude that I propose to choose between 'Cambodia or Timor' and that I fight so that we will only concern ourselves with victims of Indonesian crimes supported by the West, by a kind of reverse neo-Stalinism. As is the rule in this type of commentary, they can offer no proof to support this absurd deduction and, of course, they couldn't have any since none exists" (*Réponses inédites* 19).

Although less well known than the Faurisson Affair, the Pol Pot Affair has had its effect in the Anglo-American world as well, partly on account of Steven Lukes, who has attacked Chomsky in print on a number of occasions. A representative example of Lukes's views is "Chomsky's Betrayal of Truths" in the *Times Higher Education Supplement*[55] in which he begins with the standard criticism: "What, then, is Chomsky doing contributing to deceit and distortion surrounding Pol Pot's regime in Cambodia? Last year he published a book *After the Cataclysm . . .*, with Edward Herman, in which the record of that horrendous regime is subjected to an extraordinary and perverse scrutiny, the conclusions of which are twofold: that the atrocities and number of killings are most probably greatly exaggerated; and that they are, in any case, 'a direct and understandable response to the still more concentrated and extreme savagery of a U.S. assault that may in part have been designed to evoke this very response'." Lukes adopts Chomsky's own traditional role, evident in books such as *The New Mandarins*, and turns it against Chomsky: "What responsible person, let alone intellectual, can doubt that Cambodia between 1975 and 78 suffered a regime of terror . . . of course many deaths resulted . . . from Chomsky's favorite cause, 'peasant revenge'." Lukes seems to suggest that Chomsky's stance is a guidepost for intellectuals, and his approach is the appropriate one, but that he has somehow deviated when it comes to Pol Pot: "It is sad to see Chomsky writing these things. It is ironic, given the U.S Government's present pursuit of its global role in supporting the seating of Pol Pot at the U.N. And it is bizarre, given Chomsky's previous stand for anarchist-libertarian principles. In writing as he does about the Pol Pot regime in Cambodia, Chomsky betrays not only the responsibility of intellectuals, but himself."

The effect of this affair, and this type of criticism of Chomsky, has lingered; in the Billingsley article, for example, we find the following:

As it turned out, the accounts of the Khmer Rouge's genocide Chomsky was attacking came from *Murder of a Gentle Land* by John Barron and Anthony Paul, and *Cambodia: Year Zero* by François Ponchaud. Those accounts understated the magnitude of the cataclysm. This past February, after years of careful study, field workers from Yale University with the Cambodia Genocide Project estimated that as many as two million Cambodians were either directly killed or died as a result of the genocidal class warfare policies of the Khmer Rouge, close to one third of the population. But unlike truly responsible intellectuals like Arthur Koestler, who had also once been men of the left, Chomsky failed to hear the screams. His growing radicalism had made him tone deaf to intellectual as well as literal atrocity.

The point that seems to cause confusion concerns Chomsky's concentrating upon U.S. policy and the representation thereof in the Western media rather than that of the (then) official enemy, the USSR. Indeed, the same point is raised by Paul Thibaud in an article in *Le Monde*, dated December 31, 1980, when he notes that "in the course of the last few years, [Chomsky] has not spoken of either Vietnam or Cambodia, but of the manner by which the Western press speaks of them." In fact, to describe the press's reporting of massacres undertaken by his own country (and others) is consistent with Chomsky's approach, as he himself notes: "Ever since my earliest writings about the war, my central concern has been the politics of the American government and the ideological climate created to support it in the media and by the Universities. In my more recent texts, I conserve this basic approach, and this for two good reasons: First, if I have any particular competence, it is related to the United States, its politics and its institutions. Second, it is these very structures of propaganda and ideology which support it that I hope to modify through my writings or my participation in direct action and resistance" (*Réponses inédites*, 24–25).

All of this is interesting in light of the broader issues raised in this chapter since it speaks not only to the Effect that Chomsky has, but the Effect that he hopes to have in contemporary society. The Effect in this sense is presumably partially the result of the population's coming to know the truth about contemporary events. So there is in Chomsky's model an idea that once we have been shown that our intuitive or commonsense approach is in fact legitimate, we will from that point on read and act differently. In this sense, the "rabble" often have more astute, because more commonsensical, views than do the propagandistic, or propagandized, elite.

As an American living in the United States, Chomsky has a voice that can be heard and can thereby contribute and have an effect in ways that would not be the case in, say, Russia to heightening people's awareness of crimes carried on by the American government and hidden behind walls of silence and propaganda. So there is a broader issue here, notably that, as Chomsky notes in the unpublished interview, "a sensible person will envisage the human consequences of what he or she does. A person truly concerned about these consequences would necessarily concentrate what limited energy available to them to subjects which would permit them to contribute towards the alleviation of human miseries and to extend the rights of mankind" (*Réponses inédites* 49). This speaks directly to the "Pol Pot Affair" since, in Chomsky's view, "the crimes of Pol Pot could very well be denounced, since nobody knows how to bring them to an end. At the same time, we could have put a stop to comparable crimes in Timor if public opinion would have been mobilized since the principle sources of responsibility were the United States and its allies. As a result, it is not surprising to consider that there was a great scandal surrounding Cambodia at the same time as this great silence with regards Timor" (50).

Chomsky receives support from unexpected quarters in the form of an open letter from Serge Thion to reply to an article published by Leopold Labedz in the British journal *Encounter*.[56] Herein, as a "dissident intellectual" who is acquainted with Chomsky's work, and as a self-proclaimed "scholar involved since ten years in research on Cambodia, as co-author, along with Ben Klernan (probably unable to reply quickly to L. Labedz because he is busy doing research in Phnom Penh) of a forthcoming book on Cambodian Communism, as an involved participant in a general discussion in France and abroad on what exactly we mean by historical truth in contemporary politics, as my name has been mentioned by Leopold Labedz in your journal, I feel somewhat qualified to address some comments to his 'Chomsky Revisited'" (*Encounter*, July 1980).[57] Thion begins by recalling Chomsky's overall objective:

It would be fair for Mr. Labedz to disagree with Chomsky on political grounds and support his views by arguments pertaining to the core of the disagreement.

I should not dispute that. Instead, with a fascinating bad faith, notwithstanding the devastating reply he already attracted to his February attack, he conveys this idea that Chomsky is attempting to deny that massacres occurred in Cambodia, thus showing his true nature of supporter of tyranny. There is something really odd in this new image of a writer previously known for his libertarian critique of the US policy, turning suddenly into an adept of the worst authoritarianism. Mr. Labedz is just the last one to join the choir of those who sing on the same false tune. This common error stems from an interesting fact, easy to gather with a cursory glance: CHOMSKY DOES NOT WRITE ON CAMBODIA. He writes on America, or more broadly on the Western intelligentsia and the way it describes the actual sequence of events in Cambodia. He never indulges, as I do, in analyzing them. By using internal evidence, he demonstrates, in my view quite convincingly, that the Western press is guilty of gross manipulations and distortions of its own basic information, that its message is modeled inside a painless ideological framework. It is expected that the press will reject this criticism and deny any guilt. For that reason, Chomsky has been widely and wildly attacked, and Mr. Labedz is rushing with the last straw.[58]

Why isn't this viewpoint better known? Or, better still, why is the clearly skewed version of Chomsky's views so well known in certain influential circles while his critiques of these circles, and his true views, are so successfully repressed? It is clear that the effect of his approach is not foolproof or, to follow his own approach, that certain views simply cannot be "heard" within a particular social discourse. One of the places where the hearing is quite clearly limited is in the world of publication, where we find books like François Ponchaud's *Cambodge, année zéro*, which Chomsky reviewed for *The Nation*. This review was subject to criticism, once again, by Labedz. Thion writes:

It would be too long and fastidious to list all of Mr. Labedz' ultra-selective quotations and their use to escape the main avenues of Chomsky's argument. I have already done that with another "strange revisitor," Parisian style, Claude Roy (1). I shall take one example only of Mr. Labedz' "outlandish" falsehoods: he writes of Chomsky "dismissing such first-hand studies as the book by Father François Ponchaud." Chomsky in his review of the book (*The Nation*, June 25, 1977) does not dismiss it at all but points to some of its weaknesses and recommend its reading. It seems to me a banal reaction to a book and, as a matter of fact, I had the same. I wrote that F. Ponchaud and F. Debré "do not understand much of politics, and particularly of the Indochinese revolutionaries' policy. Condemning a policy should not lead to spare the effort to explain it" (*Libération*, 07 03 1977). Mr. Labedz is so uneasy at the idea of criticizing the good father Ponchaud that he mistakes it for a dismissal; he even believes it is a "first-hand study," which the book could of course not be, due to circumstances.[59]

Thion visited Cambodia (as a press correspondent for *Le Monde*, invited by the guerilla organization, from 26 to 28 April 1972) and recalls in his open letter some contradictions and unanswered questions that bear upon the Labedz article as a means of showing "how difficult it is to only assess the facts. This kind of reporting is almost totally useless because, being unable to incorporate the historical and political context, it cannot formulate the relevant question to be asked today in a Khmer village. If Mr. Labedz really feels satisfied with this kind of 'evidence,' he lives in a Disneyworld."[60]

Chomsky further adds to the intrigue when he notes in *Réponses inédites* that Ponchaud's book was published in two editions—one American, and one international. In the American edition we find an introduction containing glowing statements about Chomsky's "responsible attitude and the precision of his thought" He also notes that Chomsky's writings contain similar compliments toward work by Ponchaud, which Chomsky describes as "serious" and "which are worth reading" (52). In the international edition of the same book, the story is quite different. These same passages are missing and replaced with the affirmation that Chomsky had "severely criticized" his book, denied the existence of massacres in Cambodia, rejected the accounts by refugees, and based his findings upon the "deliberately chosen official declarations" (52). This did not pass unnoticed, says Chomsky: "When Paul Thibaud wrote in *Esprit* that Ponchaud committed an error by taking into account in the American edition 'remarks from Chomsky,' it was a particularly interesting method of conceding that the simultaneous international edition contained glaring lies with regards to these remarks" (53). The story, according to Chomsky, gets worse: "I had some correspondence with Ponchaud, to which he refers, following up on questions about his book that we raised in our review. In each case, it turned out that our questions much understated the problem: there were really serious errors (and important ones; this included every reference to the book that Lacouture made in his remarkable review). In the American edition, all of these are corrected. In the international edition and subsequent translations, all of the errors and falsifications remain. It's hard to avoid the conclusion that Ponchaud realized that in the US, someone would check to see whether he was keeping material that he knew was completely wrong, but that elsewhere he could get away with it, so why not lie?" (September 9, 1997).

A more reliable source, for Thion, is the CIA study, *Kampuchea: A Demographic Catastrophe*,[61] which, although "disputable," offers some "sober" estimates of the massacres. Thion then asks: "Does all this 'fall fully into the terrible category of genocide'? The mention here of a 'category' points to the recent origin of the word (but not the fact), i.e. political rhetorics. If this word means anything, it is the complete destruction of a people. This is not the case of the Cambodians. If 'genocide' is just another word for 'massacre', why then use it, if not for polemical purposes?" Chomsky makes similar points in a Znet posting,[62] in which he remarks that:

The conclusions of the CIA study were "intolerable to the doctrinal system" because it was a whitewash of the Khmer Rouge, claiming that there were killings at the beginning but not too many (they give a low estimate and claim they were mostly military personnel and the like), that peasants didn't suffer all that much, and that by 1978 (when the US was tilting toward China and Pol Pot), things were looking better. The CIA study attributes the mass of the killings to the Vietnamese, after their invasion. That plainly won't fit the picture of the KR as comparable to Hitler and Stalin, a conception desperately needed by the Western intellectual community to provide retrospective justification for the US war, for which the atrocities were used, massively. Similarly, the extraordinary apologetics for Pol Pot by people like Douglas Pike (the leading US government scholar on Indochina, and now the head of the Indochina research center at Berkeley) are completely suppressed, as are the reports from the "Far Eastern Economic Review" (among them, their conclusion in January 1980, which they later attributed to the CIA, that the population had actually RISEN by about a million under Pol Pot), and the reports by their highly respected correspondent Nayan Chanda that high U.S. officials predicted in 1975 that a million would die in Cambodia from the aftereffects of the U.S. bombing. Material of this sort is simply unacceptable, along with much else. One should [not] underestimate the extraordinary doctrinal significance of the KR atrocities for the commissar culture.[63]

The virulence of the remarks against Chomsky, and the very fact that this chapter exists to support or at least attempt to accurately describe his views, are two sides of the Chomsky Effect. He is challenged on a number of grounds: he refuses to back down once he has taken a position, he defends his intellectual work in linguistics in ways that even allies sometimes find too stringent, he draws lines that seem to eliminate the possibility of reasonable concessions, and, on the basis of certain of his views, or hobbyhorses (like Israel), manages to alienate a large compendium of individuals who might otherwise find in his work valuable tools for their own approaches. But the effect he is looking for, outside of his academic research—which is by all reasonable indicators a quest for knowledge—is an anarchist-inspired one: to stimulate the "rabble" to creative action that accords with their own views and experiences. He has at times regrets that his effect is rejected or ignored in popular media, but on other occasions rightly points out that if he were held up as an icon in these corporate-controlled outlets he'd have to question the degree to which his message was appropriately dissenting. David Heap sums it up well when he comments that Noam Chomsky has a vast array of effects that can sometimes lead to complex reactions because "he does not want to be either worshipped or reviled, he just wants to stimulate people to think critically. So his own intention is in fact at odds with the Effect on the public: it is very hard to get people to believe that they can think for themselves when you are either the unwilling object of adulation or the unwilling object of smear campaigns." But he certainly has been a significant source of motivation, and the very diversity of the audiences who come to hear him, year after year, speaks volumes, as does his courage. Even so, Chomsky refuses to consider that he is even responsible for his notoriety], ascribing it instead to a cowardly ruling class: "I happen to belong to a sector of the society where those who have real power are going to want to protect me—I mean, they may hate everything about me and want to see me disappear, but they don't want the state to be powerful enough to go after people like me, because then it could go after people like them."[64] And so he continues to speak out and he is indeed heard, and, in certain quarters, he inspires great work on a whole range of levels. Given the magnitude of his ambition, to help people think for themselves by accepting as legitimate their own approach, this in itself is a great achievement.

3

Effective Precursors: Anarchists, Cartesians, Liberals, and the Radical Left

The currents of anarchist thought that interest me (there are many) have their roots, I think, in the Enlightenment and classical liberalism, and even trace back in interesting ways to the scientific revolution of the 17th century, including aspects that are often considered reactionary, like Cartesian rationalism. There's literature on the topic (historian of ideas Harry Bracken, for one; I've written about it too). Won't try to recapitulate here, except to say that I tend to agree with the important anarchosyndicalist writer and activist Rudolf Rocker that classical liberal ideas were wrecked on the shoals of industrial capitalism, never to recover (I'm referring to Rocker in the 1930s; decades later, he thought differently). The ideas have been reinvented continually; in my opinion, because they reflect real human needs and perceptions. The Spanish Civil War is perhaps the most important case, though we should recall that the anarchist revolution that swept over a good part of Spain in 1936, taking various forms, was not a spontaneous upsurge, but had been prepared in many decades of education, organization, struggle, defeat, and sometimes victories. It was very significant. Sufficiently so as to call down the wrath of every major power system: Stalinism, fascism, western liberalism, most intellectual currents and their doctrinal institutions—all combined to condemn and destroy the anarchist revolution, as they did; a sign of its significance, in my opinion.[1]

Chomsky is an original thinker, but people often overlook that his overall approach is deeply rooted in a series of historical moments, some as old as Western civilization. Recalling Aristotle's *Politics*, for example, Chomsky makes the point that we have digressed in our thinking about democracy from earlier ideas about the role of equality in civil society.

Aristotle's *Politics* is based on the assumption that a democratic system cannot survive, cannot exist, except under conditions of relative equality. He gives good reasons for this. Nothing novel or exotic about this. The same assumption was made by people like Adam Smith. If you read Adam Smith carefully and he was pre-capitalist, remember, and I believe anti-capitalist in spirit, but if you look at

www.PostmodernHaircut.com
The Adventures of...
NOAM CHOMSKY
... and his dog Predicate!
by Jeffrey Weston
OUCH!
Those nasty neighbourhood kids pulled my tail!
This looks like a case of the chickens coming home to roost.
Chickens? What the hell are you talking about?
They probably did it because you bark at them all the time.
I do that because I've been trying to protect our property and our home!
That doesn't matter, they're responding to your oppression.
Is there anything that happens to me that's not my fault then?
Uhh..
I'll get back to you on that.

his argument for markets, it was a kind of a nuanced argument, he wasn't all that much in favor of them, contrary to what's claimed. But when you look at the argument for markets, it was based on a principle: the principle was that under conditions of perfect liberty, markets ought to lead to perfect equality; under somewhat impaired liberty, they'll lead to, somewhat, a degree of inequality. And equality was taken as an obvious desideratum, you know, a good thing. He wasn't thinking about democracies, he was thinking in other terms. These are important ideas. They have to be revived, I think, brought back into our mode of thinking, our cultural tradition, the focus of our activism and the planning for how to change things. And it's no simple business. It wasn't easy to get rid of kings, either.[2]

In thinking about the Effect of Chomsky's work, we have had to dwell upon the reception of Chomsky's work and the perception of Chomsky as a Jew, a linguist, a philosopher, a historian, a gadfly, an icon, and an anarchist. This reception is deeply colored by what is said about Chomsky and his work—he is a hero for the downtrodden, a self-loathing Jew, a model of human integrity, and "the most important intellectual alive. For those familiar with his work there is most likely to be some link between his approach and his effect, but nearly everyone who is interested in his approach chooses his or her points of engagement, without aspiring to look at the range of work undertaken in the plethora of disciplines to which he contributes. Fewer still are aware of the individuals or the references that Chomsky invokes to explain the sources of his ideas, partly because there are so many, and partly because most of his central references are figures who seldom appear in classroom discussion, never mind ordinary conversation. So in order to provide some sense of the crucial references in Chomsky's work, those which he (or I) think should be revived or at least remembered, and, moreover, those that are important but downplayed in studies of his work, I will look into passages like this one to flesh out some of the links between Noam Chomsky's approach and a range of historical influences including the Scottish Enlightenment (especially David Hume and Adam Smith), those he himself refers to as "Cartesian thinkers" (Wilhelm von Humboldt, René Descartes, Jean-Jacques Rousseau), anarchists (Michael Bakunin, Peter Kropotkin, and, especially, Rudolph Rocker), socialist and communist Zionists (associated with the founding of Kibbutz Artzi, with the organization called Avukah, and with some pre–Israeli state ideas such as the struggle for Arab-Jewish Cooperation), and a range of anti-Bolshevik Marxists (Zellig Harris, Paul Mattick, Anton Pannekoek, Bertrand Russell). I wish to emphasize these links, and will continue to mention and expand upon them in later chapters, as a means of both recalling valuable ideas from significant past movements and reinforcing the degree to which Chomsky, who is viewed by many as standing so completely outside of mainstream ideas as to be his own island, is in fact anchored to us by a range of lines connecting his ideas to those of previous eras.

This exercise is useful as a means of contextualizing Chomsky's work, but it is also heartening; for those who support Chomsky's ideals it would be disconcerting to learn that he invented the whole system of thought we associate with him, and then modified it through the years to meet each new circumstance, in part because it would make us all wonder what to do when his voice falls silent. The point is, people shouldn't come to depend upon a single voice, but, rather, upon an approach, as Chomsky himself suggests: "Personally, I have no confidence in my own views about the 'right way,' and am unimpressed with the confident pronouncements of others, including good friends. I feel that far too little is understood to be able to say very much with any confidence. We can try to formulate our long-term visions, our goals, our ideals; and we can (and should) dedicate ourselves to working on issues of human significance. But the gap between the two is often considerable, and I rarely see any way to bridge it except at a very vague and general level."[3] We cannot expect that Chomsky will eternally remain the voice of reason in critical matters relating to contemporary politics for reasons to do with his own mortality, but neither should we necessarily expect that he should play this role for us. In fact, one of his most urgent messages is that we must think for ourselves, and this on the basis of some solid and consistent values.

By situating Chomsky's approach into appropriate historical paradigms, and studying it with regard to specific origins and historical texts, we find ways of productively examining the relationship between Chomsky's ideas and the array of movements and intellectual currents from which he has drawn sustenance. Furthermore, undertaking such a project we come to recognize the degree to which Chomsky's work can be called upon to serve as a gateway into whole domains of still-valuable knowledge, too seldom recalled in this era of historical amnesia (particularly in popular culture) or in this postmodern moment which favors (in certain academic realms) references to fashionable contemporary intellectual trends over historical research. Chomsky constantly reminds us, implicitly and explicitly, that the works by a range of thinkers from different eras are put aside at our own peril.

Chomsky's choice of texts and precursors with whom he seeks affiliation is of course guided by specific criteria. Generally speaking, he has supported and looked for ways to nourish the libertarian and creative character of the human being, and to that end has sought out the theories and the company of those who support such endeavors. He is as well a consistent rational thinker who applies reason to both his political and linguistic research. By considering these two tendencies we can become familiar with the fundamental impulses that guide him in his thinking, and, within limits, predict the approach that he will take to a particular issue, if not the substance of what he might say. These basic impulses and attitudes inform the *values* that guide his approach, which are remarkably consistent, and consistently "radical." A radical approach in this regard makes reference to the etymology of the word *radical*; it goes to the root of the issue, making observations that would be true across the various seasons of growth and decline.

Chomsky's values, and the approach that flows from them, are best understood as a range of anarchist texts, on the one hand, and related Enlightenment and classical liberal texts on the other. The first group of influences, the anarchists, are particularly problematic and misunderstood within much of mainstream thinking. "No one owns the term 'anarchism'," says Chomsky. "It is used for a wide range of different currents of thought and action, varying widely. There are many self-styled anarchists who insist, often with great passion, that theirs is the only right way, and that others do not merit the term (and maybe are criminals of one or another sort). A look at the contemporary anarchist literature, particularly in the West and in intellectual circles (they may not like the term), will quickly show that a large part of it is denunciation of others for their deviations, rather as in the Marxist-Leninist sectarian literature. The ratio of such material to constructive work is depressingly high."[4] One could say similar things, it seems to me, about oft-used terms such as "anarchist," "communist," Marxist, "radical," or even "conservative," "liberal," "right wing," or "left wing."

What makes the whole issue of understanding Chomsky's anarchism (or radicalism) more complex is the links that exist, and the links that he himself has suggested, between his version of anarchism and both French and Scottish Enlightenment thought. Chomsky himself blends Enlightenment thinking from various sources into his work, reminding us along the way that the American small "l" liberal tradition, including the architects of the Constitution and the Bill of Rights, worked very much in a framework that is recognizably inspired by Enlightenment thought, as we shall see beginning with a series of eighteenth-century English, French, Prussian, and Scottish figures.

The Scottish Enlightenment

It is true that with the exception of David Hume and Adam Smith, few thinkers from the eighteenth-century Scottish Enlightenment figure as prominently in Chomsky's work as do Wilhelm von Humboldt, René Descartes, or Rudolph Rocker (for different reasons). Nevertheless, I think there is something typically American in the way that Chomsky appeals to rationalism, common sense, and solid "small c" conservative values, and texts from the Scottish Enlightenment help explain where these intellectual movements meet. An examination of the writings of Benjamin Franklin or Thomas Jefferson or James Madison, all strongly influenced by the Scots, is a way of demonstrating that good ol' American values are at odds with many contemporary policies carried out in their name. Some of the concordances between the United States and Scotland are not coincidental; there was during the period now referred to as the Scottish Enlightenment some fascinating links between Philadelphia and Edinburgh. For instance, contemporaries from both places "aimed to create a society that was modern and progressive, at least in the eyes of significant sections of their controlling elites, rather than provincial and backward."[5] And David Daiches suggests that "there were some common factors in the Scottish and American situations in the eighteenth century that made Americans especially receptive to Scottish concerns with language, and more especially with the language of political persuasion."[6]

There were many occasions for Americans and Scots to exchange ideas. Benjamin Franklin visited Scotland in 1759 and 1771, and in the course of these visits met David Hume, Sir Alexander Dick, William Robertson, Adam Ferguson, Joseph Black, William Cullen, the two Monros (Alexander and John), Adam Smith, Robert Simson, Alexander Wilson, the Foulis brothers (Robert and Andrew), John Anderson, John Millar, David Gregory, and Patrick Baird. Franklin proclaimed that Edinburgh contained "a set of as truly great Men, Professors of the several Branches of Knowledge, as have ever appeared in any Age or Country."[7] Andrew Hook comments that "such a view would soon be commonplace among American intellectuals, but Franklin's position in Philadelphia's intellectual world was so central that his words gain much more than a personal significance: if in Scotland he was a kind of intellectual ambassador for his own country, then he was inevitably a channel of the most significant kind for the conveyance of almost every aspect of the Scottish Enlightenment into Philadelphia's cultural scene." Overall, says Hook, "the pattern of education in Philadelphia owed a specific debt to aspects of the Scottish Enlightenment," (236) the legacy of which can be found in the rationalist, ethical, and commonsensical Noam Chomsky (who was born, coincidentally, in that city).

There was no consistent view of language espoused by those who came to be associated with the Scottish Enlightenment, but some of the texts written by Adam Ferguson, for example, do work with the kinds of assumptions that underwrote works by the "Cartesians," as we'll see. For instance, in *Principles of Moral and Political Science*, Ferguson suggests that

parts of speech, which, in speculation, cost the grammarian so much study, are in practice familiar to the vulgar: The rude tribes, even the idiot and the insane are possessed of them. They are soonest learned in childhood; insomuch, that we must suppose human nature, in its lowest state, competent to the use of them; and, without the intervention of uncommon genius, mankind, in a succession of ages, qualified to accomplish in detail this amazing fabric of language, which, when raised to its height, appears to be much above what could be ascribed to any simultaneous effort of the most sublime and comprehensive abilities.[8]

Finding the roots of useful intellectual or political projects is one motivation for examination of past movements; another is that such research allows us to evaluate assertions made by politicians and others about the grounds upon which they lay their claims to legitimate actions. For example, Chomsky recalls the views of America's Founding Fathers (in particular James Madison, who was deeply influenced by Scottish Enlightenment thought) as a way of identifying central trends of classical liberalism and as a means of dismantling claims made by contemporary American politicians about their fidelity to traditional American values. In a speech delivered at the Progressive Challenge, an educational forum held in Washington, D.C. on January 9, 1997, Chomsky said that "background issues are worth attention, because it's important, I think, to recognize how sharply contemporary ideology has departed from traditions and values which are quite important and significant and which it claims it upholds. That divergence is worth understanding and I think it carries a lot of direct lessons about the current scene."[9] The background issues to which he refers are both factual historical issues and whole approaches, such as the commonsense approach to language and action, itself an important element of Enlightenment thought.

Common Sense and the Common Good

In this postmodern era, when knowledge is deemed to have "claims" rather than validity,[10] and where events are mere "simulacras,"[11] Chomsky ventures into the now-hazardous domains of truth and untruth, and even dares to speculate about the nature of human nature. He further reminds us that those engaged in intellectual work should pay attention to "the real problems of society," and intellectuals themselves should be doing more to promote the values of freedom and liberation. In so doing, he imposes a heavy burden upon those who study or comment upon issues because for him, the deliberate distortion, concealment, or obfuscation of ideas is more than just attempts made at "dressing up" or rendering obscure our language (to impress or to sway); it has the very concrete and nefarious effect of directing our attention away from what is important for our own lives, and for people around us. Chomsky invokes Orwell in this regard, when he recalls in *Radical Priorities* that "Orwell once remarked that political thought, especially on the left, is a sort of a masturbation fantasy in which the world of fact hardly matters" (200). Indeed, Chomsky's whole approach to commonsense ideas put forward with straightforward language recalls Orwell's words on the subject of "Politics and the English Language":

Inflated style is itself a kind of euphemism. A mass of Latin words falls upon the facts like soft snow, blurring the outlines and covering up all the details. The great enemy of clear language is insincerity. When there is a gap between one's real and one's declared aims, one turns as it were instinctively to long words and exhausted idioms, like a cuttlefish squirting out ink. In our age there is no such thing as "keeping out of politics." All issues are political issues, and politics itself is a mass of lies, evasions, folly, hatred and schizophrenia. When the general atmosphere is bad, language must suffer.[12]

An early source for this kind of approach, to which Chomsky refers in his "Roots of Progressive Thought in Antiquity," is Aristotle's *Politics*, in which the main problem is how to achieve "the Common Good of All" in a state deemed to be "a community of equals." Not surprisingly, the Scottish Enlightenment, which emphasizes the practical, social benefits of progress and improvement for the "common good," also drew heavily from Aristotle. Thomas P. Miller remarks that Aristotle's civic humanism underwrote the Scottish approach to political and ethical theory, and that his approach to rhetoric, which "emphasized *phronesis*, practical wisdom or prudence," "led to the foundation of new traditions in rhetoric and moral philosophy."[13] These new principles, according to David Daiches, "informed the political rhetoric of the American Founding Fathers and their offspring for generations to come."[14]

Classical Liberalism in the US of A

The concept of the common good is for Chomsky at the core of classical liberalism and of Enlightenment thinking, and one of its proponents (whose name is most often invoked to uphold contemporary capitalist practices—testament to our ignorance of his work) is Adam Smith. Like Aristotle, Smith understood that upholding the common good requires substantial intervention to assure lasting prosperity of the poor by distribution of public revenues. Common good also requires that we measure the effects of contemporary capitalist practices, including the division of labor, lest we fall prey to its nefarious effects; on this Smith said that the division of labor "will turn working people into objects as stupid and ignorant as it is possible for a human creature to be."[15] The antidote was government action, which should be initiated to overcome devastating market forces.

Adam Smith was a conduit through which classical liberal ideas flowed into the United States, as was James Madison, whose interest in, and connection to, the Scots is well documented. Madison's influence is reflected in his contributions to the American Constitution and in the tenth *Federalist* paper "in which he develops an idea put forward by David Hume in his 'Idea of a Perfect Commonwealth.'"[16] And John Witherspoon in fact educated James Madison, who pursued his studies with him after graduation. Says Thomas Miller, "In his *Federalist* essays Madison not only drew on the political and rhetorical theories he encountered in Witherspoon's teaching but also put them into practice by helping to build an American political consensus based on the idea of balancing competing interests to protect the shared interest" (109). The link goes beyond the role of rhetoric in society because, as Chomsky recalls, "by 1792, shortly after the Constitution was established, he was already expressing deep concerns over the fate of the democratic experiment that he had crafted. He warned that the rising developmental capitalist state was leading to a real domination by the few under an apparent liberty of the many."[17]

In a style more reminiscent of the radical left than the Founding Fathers, to which corporate America sometimes defers for justifying some of its more dubious activities, Madison also deplored "the daring government, bribed by its largesse and overawing it with their powers and combinations, casting over society the shadow that we call politics."[18] Chomsky finds important similarities to the fears that Madison expressed and the approach that was taught by the Scottish, including Adam Smith: "Madison expected the threat of democracy to become more severe over time because he expected an increase in the proportion of those who 'will labour under the hardships of life, and secretly sigh for a more equal distribution of its blessings.'" He was also concerned by "the symptoms of a levelling spirit," recalls Chomsky, "and he warned of the future danger 'if the right to vote were to place power over property in hands without a share in it.'" Needless to say, this is a far cry from the commonly accepted view of the American values that underwrite contemporary politics. Says Chomsky, "Madison, like the rest of classical liberalism, was pre-capitalist and anti-capitalist in spirit. And he [Madison] expected the leadership to be benevolent and enlightened and so on." Chomsky makes similar links in his peculiar sense of Enlightenment figures from France, who he links to Humboldt, to create the category of thinkers he refers to as "Cartesians."[19]

Cartesian Thinkers

In both *Cartesian Linguistics* and *Language and Mind*, Chomsky considers past linguistic contributions as regards contemporary language research and finds that René Descartes, Juan Huarte, the Port Royal grammarians, Wilhelm von Humboldt, and others contributed to a "rationalist theory of language" that offered "a set of simple concepts that provided the basis for some startling successes." Comparative Indo-European studies in the nineteenth century had led to the founding of a new domain that was "largely defined by the techniques that the profession itself has forged in the solution of certain problems," the success of which shifted interest away from classical problems. Regrettably, says Chomsky, these successes were somewhat narrow and "I think we can now see clearly that the disparagement and neglect of a rich tradition proved in the long run to be quite harmful to the study of language" which was "surely unnecessary."[20] The reorientation of the field toward a revitalised interest in deep structures and universal grammar, a product of the interest that Chomsky stimulated with his early work, is testament to the value that this (then forgotten) approach could have for the field. Looking backward is not likely to help us understand contemporary linguistics, but taking into consideration the way that language was considered does help us understand the way that the human mind was deemed to function, a significant indicator for the evaluation of philosophical approaches. Further, the link with the past is not an exercise in academic hermeneutics, but more a recognition of the ways in which past work can be employed, and present work can be bolstered, with reference to particular ideas from a time when people working through them were not tied to the limitations of the current paradigm.

I am not proceeding in the manner of an art historian so much as in that of an art lover, a person who looks for what has value to him in the seventeenth century, for example, that value deriving in large measure from the contemporary perspective with which he approaches these objects. Both types of approach are legitimate. I think it is possible to turn toward earlier stages of scientific knowledge, and by virtue of what we know today, to shed light on the significant contributions of the period in a way in which the most creative geniuses could not, because of the limitations of their time. This was the nature of my interest in Descartes, for example, and in the philosophical tradition that he influenced, and also Humboldt, who would not have considered himself a Cartesian. I was interested in his effort to make sense of the concept of free creativity based on a system of internalised rules, an idea that has certain roots in Cartesian thought, I believe.[21]

The critical text for understanding the link between Chomsky's work on language (and in some ways politics as well) and Cartesian thinking is his book *Cartesian Linguistics,* part of the Studies in Language series he edited with Morris Halle, the aim of which was "to deepen our understanding of the nature of language and the mental processes and structures that underlie its use and acquisition" (ix).

Chomsky begins by suggesting that contemporary linguistics had lost touch with a highly pertinent corpus of work from the European tradition of linguistic studies that he calls Cartesian even though, as he says, it includes some ideas not expressed by Descartes or his followers: "My primary aim is simply to bring to the attention of those involved in the study of generative grammar and its implications of the little-known work which has bearing on their concerns and problems and which often anticipates some of their specific conclusions" (2). Crucially, Chomsky notes that Descartes, in the course of studies concerning the limits of mechanical explanation, came to realize that man has unique abilities that cannot be understood on purely mechanistic grounds, an idea that led him to postulate a theory of human motivation. In the Cartesian view,

a human . . . is only incited and inclined to act in a certain way, not compelled. Humans may tend to act as they are incited and inclined to do, so prediction of behaviour may be possible within a certain range, and a theory of motivation might be within range, but all of these endeavours miss the central point. The person could have chosen to act otherwise, within the limits of physical capacity, even in ways that are harmful or suicidal. Theories of prediction of behaviour or motivation, even if they were successful in their own terms, would not qualify as serious theories of behaviour. Human action is coherent and appropriate, but uncaused, apparently. . . . These considerations lie at the heart of the dualist metaphysics of the Cartesians, which again accords rather well with our common sense understanding.[22]

Crucially, Chomsky does not suggest that the Enlightened thinkers had all the right answers and then pursued their implications; in fact, it was in many cases quite the contrary, even in Descartes's idea described here:

On everything being a machine, surely no scientist should have believed this since Newton refuted the "mechanical philosophy"—that is, the belief that the inorganic world is a machine—outraging the scientific establishment (Huygens, Leibniz, Bernoulli, etc.) and himself as well, since he regarded this conclusion as absurd, and sought (vainly) to refute it for the rest of his life, as did Euler, D'Alembert, and other major figures of the 18th century—and beyond; these efforts underlie the various other theories. But by this century, Newton's demonstration that NOTHING is a machine has been almost universally accepted among scientists. So again, I don't see what the issue is. Or any connection to postmodernism (which, I admit, I don't understand). . . . On Descartes's "ghost in the machine," that notion made sense in the time of Descartes, and was indeed straight, normal science. But the concept collapsed when Newton exorcised the machine (leaving the ghost intact). There's been a lot of confusion about this since, and maybe postmodernism contributes more confusion (not understanding it, I can't say). But the basic facts seem to me clear enough.[23]

Chomsky traces the Cartesian viewpoint through the Enlightenment and the Romantic period, pausing at Humboldt and explaining as regards a whole series of his ideas the ways in which his own work follows up on Humboldt's approach, both political and linguistic. Although this link has been explored in some depth both in Chomsky's writings about Cartesian linguistics and elsewhere,[24] a source for how this can be understood more broadly deserves further discussion. And given the strong debt that Chomsky acknowledges to early French thought, it would be valuable to assess in detail the substance and the legacy of Cartesian and Enlightenment thinkers upon radicals in the United States and beyond. For this reason it is revelatory to read Chomsky alongside of the writings of Montesquieu, Rousseau, Voltaire, and others, because the whole approach they take looks from this distance to be a warning for the future that is, alas, our present world. Ideas of fundamental rights, ensconced in internationally recognized treatises, or universal rule of law, upheld by states abiding by international law, seems in light of unequal distribution and use of military might to be a strange utopia, and those who speak of it are accused of being soft, indecisive, somehow mushy compared to the hard and belligerent doers who bomb first and cover up later.

Wilhelm von Humboldt and the "Limits of State Action"

[Wilhelm Von Humboldt] looks forward to a community of free association without coercion by the state or other authoritarian institutions, in which free men can create and inquire, and achieve the highest development of their powers—far ahead of his time, he presents an anarchist vision that is appropriate, perhaps, to the next stage of industrial society. We can perhaps look forward to a day when these various strands will be brought together within the framework of libertarian socialism, a social form that barely exists today though its elements can be perceived: in the guarantee of individual rights that has achieved its highest form—though still tragically flawed—in the Western democracies; in the Israeli *kibbutzim*; in the experiments with workers councils in Yugoslavia; in the effort to awaken popular consciousness and create a new involvement in the social process which is a fundamental element in the Third World revolutions, coexisting uneasily with indefensible authoritarian practice.[25]

The Limits of State Action was written in 1791–1792, when Wilhelm von Humboldt was only 24 years old, and its partial publication in 1792 (of chapters II, V, VI, VIII, and part of III) in *Berlinische Monatsschrift* and in Friedrich von Schiller's journal *Neue Thallia*, were given particular resonance against a backdrop of revolutionary events in France. As a whole, however this book is much more than a youthful response to political events; indeed, through its amazing breadth and scope it provides a framework for considering some of the most critical issues concerning citizens' relationship with the state, and in so doing offers a blueprint for what has come to be known as the "classical liberal" approach to society to which Chomsky refers so often in his writing.

The most important of Humboldt's writings for our purposes is *The Limits of State Action*[26] which has garnered interest among those justifiably impressed by Humboldt's work as architect of the Prussian educational system, and founder of the University of Berlin (and by extension many ideas that underwrite the modern university). It has also come to be an important work for those who have considered the milieu within which Humboldt lived, peopled by the likes of Matthew Arnold, Georg Forster, Johann Wolfgang Goethe, Friedrich Jacobi, John Stuart Mill, Friedrich Von Schiller, or Mme de Staël. Finally, this text resonates strongly among a certain strain of anarchist thinkers, serving as a kind of starting point for a state built upon tenets of unrestricted freedom and the protection of fundamental rights. Chomsky makes the succinct case that "the principles of people like von Humboldt and Adam Smith and others were that people should be free. They shouldn't be under the control of authoritarian institutions. They shouldn't be subjected to things like division of labor, which destroys them, and wage labor, which is a form of slavery."[27]

Humboldt-inspired work promotes an approach to society that is deeply rooted in the rule of law, the respect of "home," the dangers of nationalism, and the promotion of unfettered creativity. The apparently difficult balancing act of tempering the anarchist resistance to authority with the classical liberal belief in legitimate institutions like the judiciary relies upon the idea that a "Cartesian" approach is not only valid but was in fact a guiding set of values during the popular uprisings in Barcelona of the 1930s, as Chomsky wrote to me:

I haven't convinced anyone, but I think there is an important and detectable "thread" (to borrow your term) that runs from Cartesian rationalism through the romantic period (the more libertarian Rousseau, for example), parts of the enlightenment (some of Kant, etc.), pre-capitalist classical liberalism (notably Humboldt, but also Smith), and on to the partly spontaneous tradition of popular revolt against industrial capitalism and the forms it took in the left-libertarian movements, including the anti-Bolshevik parts of the Marxist tradition. I also disagree with lots of things along the way, and putting all of that material in a lump yields immense internal inconsistencies (even within the writing of a single person, say Humboldt or, notoriously, Rousseau, most of them pretty unsystematic). But I'm speaking here of a thread that can be extricated, and that may have only been dimly perceived (as is standard, even in one's own scientific work, when one thinks it over in retrospect).[28]

For all of the promise of Humboldt's political vision, however, we do well to heed Chomsky's caution about the "immense internal inconsistencies," even in this single text; so although I would hold up much of this text to counteract contemporary challenges to basic rights that were entrenched into the very constitutions that lend legitimacy to our countries, some of the points Humboldt makes about the importance of security could also be employed to challenge the freedom of those outsiders who pose threats to citizens in ways that recall similar violations that have occurred during our own era.

The Right to Be Left Alone

The Limits of State Action begins with two overriding statements from which most of Humboldt's liberating ideas flow. First, "the true end of

Man, or that which is prescribed by the eternal and immutable dictates of reason, and not suggested by vague and transient desires, is the highest and most harmonious development of his powers to a complete and consistent whole. Freedom is the first and indispensable condition which the possibility of such a development presupposes." The second, which plays into Humboldt's lifelong interest in education but which resonates as well with a liberal humanist conception of a "good society," is that "there is besides another essential—intimately connected with freedom it is true—a variety of situations." The type of freedom he's most interested in is suggested in the very title of the book, and is clarified in a simple and commonsensical statement that in its implications would be deemed to be a very radical proposition: "Any State interference in private affairs, where there is no immediate reference to violence done to individual rights, should be absolutely condemned" (16). This is powerful stuff, but not specific to Humboldt; indeed, versions of this view can be found in a number of Humboldt's contemporaries, including Adam Smith, and in those he influenced. This is precisely a point where American constitutional matters meet anarchism, and it marks one of the ways in which historical texts like this one can be called upon in moments of crisis. In other words, when the limits of state action are broadened, lawmakers are not only attacking the freedom of citizens, they are attacking the very basis upon which their society was erected. So for those persons for whom the American way has come to be associated with unfettered imperialism and unobstructed incursions both at home and abroad, we can point to Humboldt to demonstrate that from a legal and properly historical standpoint, America should stand in opposition to both. In other words, unrestrained faith and unconditional support for, say, U.S. government policies is by definition un-American, as is any form of unrestrained, patriotic flag-waving. It is for this reason that a writer such as Allen Ginsberg in poems such as "America" celebrates homosexuality, his having read Karl Marx, his support for Sacco and Vanzetti, his propensity to enjoy illegal barbiturates, his being poor and disenfranchised, his denunciation of corporate propaganda, his ridiculing of political leaders in his own country; in so doing, he is the one who is following in the stated Enlightenment-inspired traditions of his own country:

America I've given you all and now I'm nothing.
America two dollars and twenty-seven cents January 17, 1956.
I can't stand my own mind.
America when will we end the human war?
Go fuck yourself with your atom bomb
I don't feel good don't bother me.
I won't write me poem till I'm in my right mind.
America when will you be angelic?
When will you take off your clothes?
When will you look at yourself through the grave?[29]

The fact of the matter is, and he comes to this very conclusion, Allen Ginsberg is "America" in the same way that those who demand silence, obedience, and prayer in the White House, are not.

I'm addressing you.
Are you going to let our emotional life be run by Time Magazine?
I'm obsessed by Time Magazine.
I read it every week.
Its cover stares at me every time I slink past the corner candystore.
I read it in the basement of the Berkeley Public Library.
It's always telling me about responsibility. Businessmen are serious.
Movie producers are serious. Everybody's serious but me.
It occurs to me that I am America. . . .

Here one can begin to see why it is that the foundational documents of the United States (or France) are classical liberal in their emphases, but they are also anarchistic, in the tradition of Rudolph Rocker, who is very clear about his intellectual antecedents. This seeming impossibility rests upon the fact that Rocker himself writes with great admiration for Humboldt, who "wanted to see the activity of the state restricted to the actually indispensable and to entrust to it only those fields that were concerned with the personal safety of the individual and of society as a whole. Whatever went beyond this seemed to him evil and forcible invasions of the rights of the personality, which could only work out injuriously."[30] Humboldt knew the meaning of state incursion in Prussia for, as Rocker recalls, "in no other country had state guardianship assumed such monstrous forms as there, where under the arbitrary dominion of soulless despots the scepter had become a corporal's baton in civil affairs." Part of what made Humboldt pertinent for Rocker was that he knew such incursions as well in Nazi Germany of 1933: "The same spirit which saw in the abject debasement of man to a lifeless machine the highest wisdom of all statecraft and lauded the blindest dead obedience as the highest virtue, celebrates in Germany today its shameless resurrection, poisoning the heart of youth, deadening its conscience and throwing to the dogs its humanity."[31] It doesn't take the incursion of Friedrich Wilhelm's despotic rule in the 1850s, or Nazism in 1933, to bring on an attack against the fundamental freedoms a state is supposed to guarantee; as we are seeing today, using the rhetoric of protecting citizens against "terrorism" or "drugs" through constant "warfare," states that defer to the rule of law for their very legitimacy defy very principles they are apparently trying to uphold or spread.

The judicial recourse offered to Americans to resist attacks upon fundamental freedoms is much stronger, and it has been regularly tested in U.S. courts; but even with the strength of its protections, the United States has a history of attacking its own standards of classical liberal-inspired laws, leading state practice further and further afield from Founding Fathers intentions. A number of examples could be cited in this regard, but a particularly pertinent one for a discussion of Humboldt is offered by the landmark 1928 Supreme Court decision in *Olmstead v. United States*, a case that addressed the limits of individuals' right to privacy.[32] In a major blow to individual freedoms, which is by now familiar to all of us in light of current wiretapping debates, the court upheld the FBI's right to wiretap private residences, thereby crossing the line of "legitimate" state action, as described by Humboldt. This is made clear in the blunt and lucid view of Justice Louis Brandeis, who wrote for the dissenting side.

The makers of our Constitution undertook to secure conditions favorable to the pursuit of happiness. They recognized the significance of man's spiritual nature, of his feelings and of his intellect. They knew that only a part of the pain, pleasure and satisfactions of life are to be found in material things. They sought to protect Americans in their beliefs, their thoughts, their emotions and their sensations. They conferred, as against the government, the right to be let alone—the most comprehensive of rights and the right most valued by civilized men. To protect that right, every unjustifiable intrusion by the government upon the privacy of the individual, whatever the means employed, must be deemed a violation of the Fourth amendment. . . . The greatest dangers to liberty lurk in insidious encroachment by men of zeal, well-meaning but without understanding. (cited in Mitgang 20–21)[33]

So according to *The Limits of State Action*, the State should exist to "promote happiness," both by leaving people alone and by encouraging personal initiative, a project best realized in a program for society that "most faithfully resemble the operations of the natural world" (5), an idea that comes to nourish Humboldt's ideas about education.

Nourishing Seeds of Freedom and Possibility

The sense that reason, rationality and diversity (of opportunity and action) are "natural," and that limitations upon this growth and nourishment tend to be imposed by illegitimate authority, are components of Humboldt's work that are found not only in Chomsky's approach but also in that of his teacher, Zellig Harris, and one of his personal inspirations, Bertrand Russell. Humboldt sets the tone for this when he suggests in *The Limits of State Action* that "the seed, for example, which drops into the awaiting soil, unseen and unheeded, brings a richer and more blessed growth than the violent eruption of a volcano" (5). This idea has crucial implications for those interested in the relationship between templates for society and their imposition, and had the twentieth century refused the range of "ism" solutions we might have avoided the calamities Humboldt most certainly feared: "We should never attempt to transfer purely theoretical principles into reality, before the latter offers no further obstacles to achieving results to which the principles would always lead in the absence of outside interference." Instead, "in order to bring about the transition from present circumstances to those which have been planned, every reform should be allowed to proceed as much as possible from men's minds and thoughts" (142). The model he prefers comes from "the vegetable world," wherein "the simple and less graceful form seems to prefigure the more perfect bloom and symmetry of the flower which it precedes, and into which it gradually expands. Everything hastens towards the moment of blossoming. What first springs from the seed is not nearly so attractive. The full thick trunk, the broad leaves rapidly detaching themselves from each other, seem to require some fuller development; as the eye glances up the ascending stem, it marks the grades of this development; more tender leaves seem longing to unite themselves, and draw closer and closer together, until the central calyx of the flower seems to satisfy this desire." We begin our lives at the first point, according to Humboldt, because "whatever man receives externally is only like the seed. It is his own active energy alone that can turn the most promising seed into a full and precious blessing for himself. It is beneficial only to the extent that it is full of vital power and essentially individual." For this reason, the highest idea "of the co-existence of human beings seems to me to consist in a union in which each strives to develop himself from his own inmost nature, and for his own sake" (13). To be simultaneously left alone and nourished is, therefore, at the heart of Humboldt's state project and his pedagogical approach, and we see its echoes in a number of classically liberal-inspired thinkers.

Terrorism, Security, and Expanded State Action

If read in bad faith, Humboldt's work could also have an antirevolutionary or even prostate action side, which reflects his interest in the positive welfare of the citizen and its relation to state security. I say bad faith, because the principle impulse of his work is to uphold liberty and attack illegitimate authority; as such, I would suggest that his approach to criminality and security must be read as protections that a state must erect in order to promote freedom, as opposed to justifying incursions into people's lives on the basis of protecting them. Humboldt begins his reflection on state security with the observation that in addition to promoting happiness (through freedom, education, creativity), the state must also "prevent evil," whether in the form of "natural enemies" or that which springs from man himself" (16). He specifies early on, however, that "the state is to abstain from all solicitude for the positive welfare of the citizens, and not to proceed a step further than is necessary for their mutual security and protection against foreign enemies; for with no other object should it impose restrictions on freedom" (33). The question is, what constitutes security, and, moreover, what justifies acting against those who potentially threaten it? Humboldt suggests that citizens of a State are increasingly secure, given the power of constitutions and the diminishing number of attacks against individuals across state lines. The measure of this security is when, "living together in the full enjoyment of their due rights of person and property, they are out of the reach of any external disturbance from the encroachments of others," that is, when they have "legal freedom" (84). When this security is threatened, then the State should keep a "vigilant eye" (89) and act accordingly, but within limits:

In order to provide for the security of its citizens, the State must prohibit or restrict such actions, relating directly to the agents only, as imply in their consequences the infringement of others' rights, or encroach on their freedom or property without their consent or against their will; and further, it must forbid or restrict these actions when the probability of such consequences is to be feared—a probability in which it must necessarily consider the extent of the injury feared, and on the other hand the consequences of the restriction on freedom implied in the law contemplated. Beyond this, every limitation of personal freedom lies outside the limits of state action. (91)

So in fact, despite his upholding of State rights and his strong views on crime and criminal behavior, Humboldt is careful to delimit the range within which state authority can function. As regards such efforts as preemptive strikes, or the limiting of individual rights in the name of possible actions in the future, he is very clear: although the state should uphold "the strictest surveillance of every transgression of the law, either already committed or only planned," nevertheless there must be clear limits of police powers. "I think I may safely assert that the prevention of criminal actions is wholly outside the State's proper sphere of activity" (123). Recall, however, that laws for him cannot be arbitrary or illegitimate, but must, like their concomitant punishments, be "good and well-matured" (123). This demands a constant and rigorous supervision of institutions set up to prevent, investigate, and punish crimes, lest they transgress the fundamental precepts of this approach.

Of Love, Faith, and the Opposite Sex

The far-reaching aspects of this text bring Humboldt to discuss institutions and customs, including those that regulate the relations between men and women. Naturally reticent about institutions, but nevertheless involved in their foundation (for educational purposes), Humboldt offers much that precedes and compliments work by such authors as the French sociologist Pierre Bourdieu (a contemporary of Chomsky who shared a number of basic insights on the workings of institutions). On the whole, Humboldt's work is a precursor to Pierre Bourdieu's texts such as *Language and Symbolic Power*, and it offers some interesting observations pertinent to the establishment or the critique of institutions such as government offices: "Anyone who has an opportunity of occupying himself with the higher departments of State administration must certainly feel conscious from experience how few political measures have really an immediate and absolute necessity, and how many, on the contrary, have only a relative and indirect importance, and simply follow from previous measures." This has nefarious effects, not only upon good governance, but upon the individuals involved, because "the administration of political affairs itself becomes in time so full of complications that it requires an incredible number of persons to devote their time to its supervision, in order that it may not fall into utter confusion." Furthermore, "by far the greater portion of these have to deal with the mere symbols and formulas of things; and thus, not only are men of first-rate capacity withdrawn from anything which gives scope for thinking, and useful hands are diverted from real work, but their intellectual powers themselves suffer from this partly empty, partly narrow employment" (29–30). As a consequence, in most states as the number of public officials increases, "the liberty of the subject proportionately declines" (30), an added woe to the problem of state incursion into ever-broader spheres of citizens' lives.

Humboldt even wallows into the murky waters of matrimony through his discussions of institutions, suggesting that marriage is of tantamount importance in society because it brings out or accentuates active principles in peoples' natures. For this reason, Humboldt thinks that "as it is a union so closely related to the very nature of the respective individuals, it must have the most harmful consequences when the State attempts to regulate it by law, or through the force of its institutions to make it rest on anything but simple inclination." Indeed, this is an area from which the state should "withdraw its active care," and "leave it wholly to the free choice of the individuals" (26). This modern approach to human relations is echoed as well in his views of woman, who is "nearer to the ideal human nature than man;" the "woman's careful hand draws the salutary inner limits within which alone the fullness of strength can be refined to proper ends; and she defines the limits with more delicate precision, in that she grasps more deeply the inner nature of humanity, and sees more clearly through the intricate confusion of human relations, for all her senses are alert, and she avoids the sophistications which so often obscure truth" (25). In matters of sensual relations between the woman and the man, Humboldt strives for a kind of balance and restraint, since people in the throes of incontinence and immoderate behavior are more likely to "infringe upon the rights of others."

Similarities between this moderate approach and his overall project are present as well in Humboldt's take on religion, which advocates adherence to principles of ethical and moral behavior rather than to dogma and blind faith. Nevertheless, he finds that "even comparatively unenlightened conceptions of religion often influence a large part of the people in a nobler fashion," partly because "being an object of loving care to an all-wise and perfect being gives them new dignity," and partly because "the trust in eternity leads them to a higher point of view," bringing "order and purpose to their actions." However, he warns, "for religion to have these effects it must permeate the mind and sensibility, which is not possible where the spirit of free inquiry is hampered." So yet again, we find this consistency of approach, which leads him in this short text to consider the relationship between action and authority, and individual behavior and the collective good which, for him, is subsumed under the banner of freedom and development. As we rubber-stamp laws limiting individual freedoms, attacking fundamental rights, and ripping asunder the classical liberal documents upon which our societies have been erected, we are indeed challenging those principles that may indeed make our societies worth preserving.

Rudolph Rocker, that "Anarchist Rabbi"

Perhaps Chomsky's work would resonate more clearly if more attention were paid to the likes of Wilhelm von Humboldt or, I might add, Rudolph Rocker, alongside the whole canon of other figures who make up the so-called liberal arts curriculum. There may be many reasons why this is not the case, why we study, say, Marx, Lenin, and Stalin but not

Bakunin, Kropotkin, and Rocker, but it is tempting to suggest that this suppression follows conscious attempts in a range of quarters to harp on weak alternatives to the present-day capitalist societies so as to avoid the serious issues raised by more valuable criticisms and proposals. Sound dubious? How many courses in political science include anarchists? How many people who have heard of anarchy have only heard the Bakunin dictum about the creativity of violence? Why do we read Lenin, Mao and Stalin, or at least about them, but seldom about Karl Korsch, Rosa Luxemburg, or Anton Pannekoek? Is it simply that we encounter texts by those who actually held or hold power? What I am suggesting is not some vast conspiracy, but, instead, that those who uphold the status quo find unquestionable legitimation when they compare their actions to those whose work can be more easily dismissed. In response to a question about anarchy's utopianism, Chomsky wrote: "I tend to agree that anarchism is formless and utopian, though hardly more so than the inane doctrines of neo-liberalism, Marxism-Leninism, and other ideologies that have appealed to the powerful and their intellectual servants over the years, for reasons that are all too easy to explain."[34] It was of course particularly fortuitous that Lenin, Stalin and the whole Bolshevik Party came to bear the label of "Marxist" or "communist," despite the fact that their actions bore virtually no resemblance to the societies envisioned by Marx or by the supporters of communism.

The stronger versions of either Marxism or communism, such as the anti-Bolshevik variety or the Council Communists, are seldom discussed in terms of our contemporary world. As Chomsky points out, "the [anti-Bolshevik, or anarchist] point of view itself offers no power and prestige to intellectuals, unlike Bolshevism, which is basically a justification for the rule of Bakunin's "red bureaucracy"—very appealing to the intellectuals."[35] This relates to some of Bakunin's most interesting and forward-thinking theses about the rise of the intellectual as the "new class" who would solidify its power base by controlling technical knowledge. Says Chomsky, "In a series of analyses and predictions that may be among the most remarkable within the social sciences, Bakunin warned that the 'new class' will attempt to convert their access to knowledge into power over economic and social life. They will try to create 'the reign of scientific intelligence,' the most aristocratic, despotic, arrogant and elitist of all regimes. There will be a new class, a new hierarchy of real and counterfeit scientists and scholars, and the world will be divided into a minority ruling in the name of knowledge, and an immense ignorant majority. And then, woe unto the mass of ignorant ones."[36]

I think that the Chomsky-Bakunin relation is in some ways critical, notably in the latter's sense of community and his appeal to spontaneous and profoundly humanist social structures tied to collective habits formed around individual needs. Murray Bookchin writes:

Beneath the surface of Bakunin's theories lies the more basic revolt of the community principle against the state principle, of the social principle against the political principle. Bakunism, in this respect, can be traced back to those subterranean currents in humanity that have tried at all times to restore community as the structural unit of social life. Bakunin deeply admired the traditional collectivistic aspects of the Russian village, not out of any atavistic illusions about the past, but because he wished to see industrial society pervaded by its atmosphere of mutual aid and solidarity. Like virtually all the intellectuals of his day, he acknowledged the importance of science as a means of promoting eventual human betterment; hence the embattled atheism and anticlericalism that pervades all his writings. By the same token, he demanded that the scientific and technological resources of society be mobilised in support of social co-operation, freedom, and community, instead of being abused for profit, competitive advantage and war. In this respect, Mikhail Bakunin was not behind his times, but a century or more ahead of them.[37]

In *Anarchism and Anarcho-Syndicalism* Rudolph Rocker adds to this a description of Bakunin's economic approach when he writes that Bakunin "based his ideas upon the teachings of Proudhon, but extended them on the economic side when he, along with the federalist wing of the First International, advocated collective ownership of the land and all other means of production, and wished to restrict the right of private property only to the product of individual labour" (14). Both visions are more accurate portrayals of the Bakunin approach than the joyful rule-breaking to which he is reduced in most texts that refer to Bakunin (i.e., the idea of "creative violence). It is true that Bakunin, Rocker, and most other anarchists are against the arbitrary or self-serving use of power, but this does not forestall the possibility of free associations. To examine but one concrete historical example, of the anarchy that existed in mountain *pueblos* in Spain after the 1870s, is to glimpse the degree to which being antiauthoritarian can also imply a need for forming social units on the basis of clearly-defined values and goals. I quote at length from Murray Bookchin's *The Spanish Anarchists* to give a taste of an anarchist existence:

The solidarity, reinforced by a harsh environment of sparse means and a common destiny of hard work, produces a fierce egalitarianism. The preferred form of transaction between peasants and labourers is *aperceria*, or partnership, rather than wages. Although they own the land and work as hard as the labourers, the peasants may give as much as half the crop to their temporary "partners." This type of relationship is preferred not only because it is wiser to share what one has in hand rather than to speculate on monetary returns, but also owing to a rich sense of fraternity and a disdain for possessive values. In the life of the *pueblo*, poverty confers absolutely no inferiority; wealth, unless it is spent in behalf of the community, confers absolutely no prestige. The rich who own property in or near the *pueblo* are generally regarded as a wicked breed whose power and ambitions corrupt society. Not only is the *pueblo* immune to their influence, but in reaction, tends to organise its values around the dignity of work and the importance of moral and spiritual goals. (80–81)

This last statement is the key because it indicates the relationship between being antiauthoritarian and "adopting all the personal standards of the Anarchists in the cities," standards that in some cases were consistently libertarian but not necessarily random, violent or uncontrolled. "A man did not smoke, drink, or go to prostitutes, but lived a sober, exemplary life in a stable free union with a *compañera*. The church and state were anathema, to be shunned completely. Children were to be raised and educated by libertarian standards and dealt with respectfully as sovereign human beings" (81). The key to this form of anarchism, which eventually gave way to a more anarcho-syndicalist approach as proletarian anarchism drifted increasingly towards syndicalism, particularly in the cities, was not this kind of chaotic breaking of rules for its own sake but living "in a stable free union with *compañera*" (81).

Despite the overlap with Bakunin, I believe that Rudolph Rocker deserves a special place in this chapter because he is one, if not the most important, of Chomsky's formative influences. This is especially true in my opinion of *Nationalism and Culture*, originally published in 1935,[38] and, to a lesser degree *Anarchism and Anarchosyndicalism*,[39] published in 1937. Chomsky has frequently suggested that *Anarchosyndicalism* was for him the most compelling of Rocker's writings; but I find in

Nationalism and Culture a wide-ranging overview of Rocker's thinking, from language to history to politics, which allows the reader a privileged space from which to contemplate Rocker's overall approach and, by extension, that of Noam Chomsky. Study of *Nationalism and Culture* demonstrates that similarities between these two thinkers occur on a vast range of levels which, when taken together, confirm an approach to society that I have come to know as the "good society."

A word about Rudolph Rocker. He was born in 1873 in Mainz, in the German Rhineland, and died just as Noam Chomsky was beginning to be recognized for his achievements in linguistics, in 1958. An early supporter of socialism, he moved in his late teens toward anarchism, a movement we can trace in Chomsky's teenage years as well. Rocker, unlike Chomsky, was a Gentile but he became involved in the Jewish anarchist movement, learned Yiddish, lived in the Jewish community, and both lectured and wrote in Yiddish for a variety of groups. Nicolas Walter notes that "in 1898 he edited *Dos Fraye Vort* (The Free Word), a new Yiddish weekly paper in Leeds, for a couple of months, and then became editor or *Der Arbeter Fraint* (The Workers' Friend), a revived Yiddish weekly paper in London, and in 1900 also of *Germinal*, a new Yiddish monthly.[40] Chomsky's exposure to anarchism was through his readings and contacts with family members in New York City and, as we've seen, his early readings in this area included whatever works by Rudolph Rocker he could procure, and their impact is apparent in each of the domains to which he contributes.

Language and Preexisting Knowledge

We can begin in the unlikely area of language studies. Some of what came to be known as Chomsky's previously mentioned Cartesian approach to language is present in Rocker's writings. Interestingly, while Rocker claims an overt debt to the rationalist and classical liberal tradition for his understanding of matters relating to language studies, Chomsky asserts that this approach simply confirmed what he had learned himself. "In a reasonable world," writes Chomsky, "it would have been true that I had a debt to the 'Cartesian' approach.' In this world, the debt was (unfortunately) zero. It's a tribute to the arrogance of the prevailing intellectual culture that none of this—even much more obvious things—was known at the time I was working on these topics. I found out about the history after I'd reached the conclusions and done the basic work. There was no influence and no debt. Too bad, but true" (September 9, 1997). So the Cartesians did confirm (from a world long past) many of the observations that Chomsky proposed early on in his writings and research or, to think about Chomsky's sense of innate propensities, the Cartesian approach was already somehow present in the attitudes with which Chomsky was born.

Rocker found in the Cartesians support for a number of claims that he makes about language in *Nationalism in Culture,* such as the idea that language in the broad sense does not have a national origin. Rather, says Rocker, human beings are endowed with the ability to "articulate language which permits of concepts and so enables man's thoughts to achieve higher results, which distinguish man in this respect from other species" (284). Rocker's objective in discussing language is to undermine notions of racial purity, upheld by the Nazis at the time when he was writing his book. It is true that his description of the principles that underlie human language and the parameters within which it functions is different from Chomsky's in many respects, but certain assumptions are applicable to both. In another passage describing the regimentation of the French life in the seventeenth century, Rocker gives the example of the establishment of the French Academy in 1629, commenting that such an act was passed in order "to subordinate language and poetry to the authoritarian ambition of absolutism" (429). The effect was that the French language was "given a strict guardian that endeavored with all its power to eliminate from it popular expressions and figures of speech. This was called 'refining the language.' In reality, it deprived it of originality and bent it under the yoke of an unnatural despotism from which it was later obliged forcibly to free itself" (287).

Chomsky would repeat this statement almost fifty years later, virtually verbatim, in response to a question posed to him in Barcelona about the virtues of establishing an Academy for the Catalan language.[41] And even as he spoke of the undesirability of institutions of authority like academies, he did so speaking as a rational individual and not as a linguist, because, in his opinion, the study of linguistics would have nothing to say about these kinds of issues. This kind of disclaimer is not unusual for Chomsky; indeed anyone who has ever attended a linguistics talk given by him would be struck by the combination of intellectual ambition and modesty, his far-reaching hypotheses proposed amidst constant reiterations of the fact that at our present level of knowledge we can say very little about the language faculty, and his constant appeal for input from those present for discussion about matters presented. Even in this attribute we find similarities with Rudolph Rocker; for instance, at the end of a chapter on the relationship between language and nationalism, Rocker states that "the origin and formation of the different languages is wrapped in such impenetrable darkness that we can only feel our way forward with the help of uncertain hypotheses. All the more is caution commanded [sic] where we can so easily go hopelessly astray" (294).

Of course Chomsky the linguist has tried to penetrate this darkness, while Rocker was simply trying to make the point that nationalist claims about language are built upon fallacious assumptions: "The idea that every language is the original creation of a particular people or a particular nation and has consequently a purely national character lacks any foundation and is only one of those countless illusions which in the age of race theories and nationalism have become so unpleasantly conspicuous" (294). Here the differences in historical circumstances surrounding both individuals become clear; nevertheless, the overlap in approach remains convincing.

Liberalism

When we look to the major hypotheses proposed in Rocker's work, the similarities with Chomsky's approach are all the more evident. An interesting case in point is Rocker's views of liberalism. We are by now familiar with Chomsky's frequent references to the writings of Karl Wilhelm von Humboldt, and his oft-repeated statement that there exists a red thread linking what he calls classical liberalism to certain strains of anarchism. This link, says Chomsky, was suggested to him early on in the course of his reading works by Rudolph Rocker. In *Powers and Prospects*, he says: "My personal visions are fairly traditional anarchist ones, with origins in the Enlightenment and classical liberalism." This version of classical liberalism, previously described, is what Chomsky calls "the original, before it was broken on the rocks of rising industrial capitalism, as Rudolph Rocker put it in his work on anarchosyndicalism 60 years ago" (71).

To put it simply, Rocker shared with upholders of liberalism a belief that "the continuous guardianship of the state was just as detrimental to the fruitful development of all creative forces in society as the guardianship of the Church had been in previous centuries" (*Nationalism and Culture* 135). Absolute freedom from all sources of oppression and power—the Church in earlier eras and the state today—is a recurrent theme because "only in freedom does there arise in man the consciousness of responsibility for his acts and regard for the rights of others; only in freedom can there unfold in its full strength that most precious social instinct: man's sympathy for the joys and sorrows of his fellow man and the resultant impulse toward mutual aid in which are rooted all social ethics, all ideas of social justice" (148). This implies that for Rocker (and for Chomsky) we need to legislate on the basis of freedom, rather than upon our sense that we all carry within us "innate evil," a concept that is frequently employed to justify the worst kinds of oppression. This is not to say that evil as well as good tendencies are not innately rooted; indeed we all comprise various mixtures of both. But this is not a valid reason to justify oppression to quash the presence of the former (or, indeed, the latter).

The examples of liberal thought serve Chomsky well in his analysis of the contemporary American political scene. He, again like Rocker, frequently refers to statements by America's founding fathers and other notable American figures who made warnings that would in light of contemporary government practices sound both dire and, in light of the rhetoric employed by politicians to justify their actions, rather surprising. For instance, it was George Washington who warned that "Government is not reason, it is not eloquence—it is force! Like fire it is a dangerous servant and a fearful master; never for a moment should it be left to irresponsible action"; and Thomas Jefferson who bluntly asserted that "that government is best which governs least"; and Benjamin Franklin who suggested that "they that can give up essential liberty to obtain a little temporary safety deserve neither liberty nor safety"; and Abraham

Lincoln who cautioned that "If there is anything that is the duty of the people never to entrust to any hands but their own, that thing is the preservation and perpetuity of their own liberty and institutions."[42]

That the State should not interfere with the lives of individuals is, of course, only half the story; the other half is the exploration of individual and collective human potential through this freedom. And indeed one half can become a measure for the other, as is illustrated in Rocker's reference to the "ancient wisdom of Protagoras," which he uses to bolster his own support for liberalism. Rocker finds in Protagoras's doctrine an evaluation of the social environment based upon an assessment of whether "it furthers the natural development of the individual or is a hindrance to his personal freedom and independence. Its conceptions of society are those of an organic process resulting from man's natural necessities and leading to free associations, which exist as long as they fulfill their purpose, and dissolve again when this purpose has become meaningless" (161). This is a critical passage in Rocker's book and, by extension, it is an extremely useful one if we hope to understand Chomsky's work because it makes an important link between anarchism's refusal of all forms of authority, and liberalism's belief that "government in certain matters cannot be entirely dispensed with" (162). This sounds like a contradiction until we note, with Rocker, that this form of liberalism upholds a belief that the state "had a right to exist only as long as its functionaries strove merely to protect the personal safety of its citizens against forcible attacks" (ibid.).

In *Powers and Prospects*, and in articles for *Z Magazine*, Chomsky emphasizes the importance of defending and even strengthening certain elements of State authority in the short term even though, as he himself suggests, "the anarchist vision, in almost every variety, has looked forward to the dismantling of state power." Although Chomsky does "share this vision," he also considers that "it offers weak protection to some aspects of that vision" because "unlike the private tyrannies, the institutions of state power and authority offer to the despised public an opportunity to play some role, however limited, in managing their own affairs."[43] He then goes on to suggest that: "In today's world, I think, the goals of a committed anarchist should be to defend some state institutions from the attack against them, while trying at the same time to pry them open to more meaningful public participation—and ultimately, to dismantle them in a much more free society, if the appropriate circumstances can be achieved" (75).

It is interesting, finally, to consider that this kind of approach, which favors loose social organizations of individuals toward common ends, is characteristic as well of some forms of socialism. The translator of *Nationalism and Culture*, Ray E. Chase, has a precautionary passage in his preface. "Here it will perhaps not be out of place to remind the English-speaking public, accustomed to a much narrower meaning, that in general Rocker uses the word *socialism* in the broad sense which it commonly has on the continent, to cover all proposals for a society in which production and distribution are carried on and controlled for the benefit of all."[44] This kind of cautionary note regarding terminology could in fact be applied to most of the keywords associated with Rocker (and Chomsky), notably liberalism, socialism, radicalism, and, of course, anarchism.

Anarchism

This leads us to the heart of Rocker's and Chomsky's work on anarchism, and to the assumptions that lie behind it. The first step is to question blind allegiance to national interests because, as Rocker states in *Nationalism and Culture*, "behind everything 'national' stands the will to power of small minorities and the special interests of the caste and class in the state" (202). For Rocker, "all nationalism is reactionary in nature, for it strives to enforce on the separate parts of the great human family a definite character according to a preconceived idea. In this respect, too, it shows the interrelationship of nationalistic ideology with the creed of every revealed religion" (213). Indeed, says Rocker, "national states are political Church organizations, the so-called national consciousness is not born in man, but trained into him. It is a religious concept; one is a German, a Frenchman, an Italian, just as one is a Catholic, a Protestant, or a Jew" (202). Notice that the urgency of Rocker's political context had him writing specifically of the dangers of nationalism. Chomsky, as was evident in his discussion of the state, speaks to quite a different world when he describes the "manufacture of consent" because it is a different kind of nationalism, perhaps one more strongly linked to corporatism, that he describes in his work. Nevertheless, the link is there. I might add, this whole discussion clarifies, and is at the origin of, Chomsky's views of sports, where someone comes to associate him or herself with a team, as though this is or should be the key factor in identity politics. I have seldom encountered this form of allegiance among my students in Canada, and even less so in Quebec; but in the United States, when I ask people in my classes who they are, they are as likely to describe the sports teams with which they feel allegiance as the countries from which their parents come or the houses of worship to which they feel spiritual adherence.

But how without a state does one form the kind of communities, the loose affiliations of workers and people, which Chomsky and Rocker favor in their discussions of anarchism? And, on a more emotive level, what does one do with the human being's natural, and indeed healthy, attachment to home, to family, to friends, and to the immediate community (which, some might argue, include sports teams)? Rocker makes here a critical distinction, seldom discussed or even raised in discussions of nationalism, between "home" and "state," which helps clarify this while providing further applicability to the program he is describing. Rocker claims that "home sentiment," an "attachment to that spot of land on which a man has spent the years of his youth is deeply intergrown with his profoundest feeling." Indeed early impressions of home are "most permanent and have the most lasting impression on his soul;" they can even bring "in later years some yearning after a past long buried under ruins "and offer the romantic" the means "to look so deeply within." This is not to be confused with the flag-waving, jingo-chanting, and sentimentality-invoking undertaken by the state to further the interests of its elite. Indeed, says Rocker in a truly stunning passage, "the attempt to replace man's natural attachment to the home by a dutiful love of the state—a structure which owes its creation to all sorts of actions and in which, with brutal force, elements have been welded together that have no necessary connection—is one of the most grotesque phenomena of our time." This state fanaticism, which has come to replace religious fanaticism, has indeed become, according to Rocker, "the greatest obstacle to cultural development" (214).

The kind of "cultural development" to which Rocker refers in this assertion includes creative production in the broadest sense. An upshot of unfettering human beings is that their creative abilities will thereby flourish. Under State-directed oppression, human relationships are perverted: "The shocking inequality of human conditions and, above all, the state, which bred the monopoly whose festering, cancerous growth has destroyed the fine cellular tissue of social relationships" (246). This attempt to depict human interaction as organic falls into line with Chomsky's sense of how precious human relationships are, and how important it is to cultivate them in a spirit of goodwill, liberty, and freedom. The anarchist society hereby imagined would allow all persons to explore the innate qualities with which each person is endowed, the innate qualities that are the object of Chomsky's own linguistic search.

Artificial Intelligence and the Behavioral Sciences

Chomsky's questioning of the so-called behavioral sciences is logical in light of his discussions of innate qualities. Any program that pretends to regularize or systematize or render predictable human behavior for purposes of controlling people is abhorrent, and using behavioral sciences as a justification is tantamount to resorting to fraudulent theories to do so, as he has indicated elsewhere (notably in his critiques of Skinner's work). So the question becomes, why would anyone even propose such a program? For him, such efforts are part and parcel of a larger effort aimed at exploiting unfounded research agendas deemed scientific as a justification for oppression, and thereby disposing of personal needs of individuals and stifling their powers and abilities. To what end? Rocker, again from his own perspective as an anarchist writing in Hitler's Germany, sees it as a State-promoted idea because the easier it is to dispose of "the personal needs of the citizens," the easier it is for the State "to dissolve society into its separate parts and incorporate them as lifeless accessories into the gears of the political machine" (247). For Chomsky, attempts to atomize individuals through isolating activities such as watching television, and interfering in the lives of citizens under the guise of patriotism, are attempts at disrupting spontaneous gatherings and discussions among people. Why is such disruption necessary?

Because "*people are dangerous* when they get together, because together they can voice common concerns, take account of their situations, and find solutions to their problems that lie outside of the predictably narrow range of possibilities presented within the status quo" [emphasis mine].

So what is an appropriate social model for the type of society that the ruling elites require, that is, one that has its majority acting as "lifeless accessories in the gears of the political machine?" Rocker defines this concoction as the "mechanical man," "autonomous in human form" who "gives the illusion of calculated human action." In Rocker's day, it was "social engineering" like Fordism or Taylorism, for which he spares no wrath: "Just as they calculate the marvelous mechanism [the machine] to the tiniest fraction, they also calculate the muscle and nerve force of the living producers by definite scientific methods and will not realize that they thereby rob him [the worker] of his soul and most deeply defile his humanity. We have come more and more under the dominance of mechanics and sacrificed living humanity to the dead rhythm of the machine without most of us even being conscious of the monstrosity of the procedure. Hence we frequently deal with such matters with indifference and in cold blood, as if we handled dead things and not the destinies of men" (247).

These automatons have their equivalent in contemporary society in the form of a majority that is forced or condemned by necessity to obey corporate or state masters. "The modern 'mass man,' this uprooted fellow traveler of modern technology in the age of capitalism, who is almost completely controlled by external forces and whirled up and down by every mood of the moment—because his soul is atrophied and he has lost that inner balance which can maintain itself only in true communion—already comes dangerously close to the mechanical man" (247). This depiction of man, "controlled by external forces" falls right into line with the behaviorist model proposed by Skinner, and perhaps the virulence of Chomsky's attack on Skinner in his famous December 30, 1971, *New York Review of Books* article[45] is given fuller explanation in light of Rocker's comments. All of this leads us back to Chomsky's own sense that what is interesting about behaviorism is not the program itself—which is in his opinion obviously fraudulent—but its acceptance. The optimism that Chomsky and Rocker display flows from their belief that the stifling of creative powers and energies cannot be carried on indefinitely. Rocker even expressed optimism in the dark of days of Hitler when he wrote that "we are firmly convinced that even today mankind carries within it a multitude of hidden forces and creative impulses which will enable it victoriously to surmount the calamitous crises now threatening all human culture" (247–248). So once again, why promote an anarchist society? Because "such an upsurge can occur only under the sign of freedom and social union, for only out of these can grow that deepest and purest yearning for social justice which finds its expression in the social collaboration of men and smooth the way for a new community" (248). The enemies of this upsurge were in Rocker's day the fascists and the nationalists. The emphasis today would be placed more heavily upon nationalism through patriotism, and the corporation, and hence Chomsky's insistence thereupon (and his frequent description of the corporate structure as fascistic and totalitarian). The movement across time, from Rocker to Chomsky, is a movement from religion to nationalism to corporatism and, in the United States at least, back to rising religious fanaticism.

Why Not Marxism?

There are significant points of overlap between anti-Bolshevik Marxism and anarchism, but overall one should find in Rocker's and Chomsky's writing a profound distrust of what has come to be known as Marxism and, of course, the so-called state Marxism of the Bolsheviks. One of my principal contentions is that anarchism of the type favored by Rocker or Chomsky has been discredited through rhetorical tactics, such as equating anarchism and chaos, or with "utopianism" or "idealism," which, rather ironically, have become dirty words in our society. Incidentally, it was condemned in Rocker's society as well, on different grounds: "Communism is to be taken as merely a name for the present Russian system of government which is as far removed from the original meaning of communism as a social system of economic equality as is every other system of government" (532).

In fact, anarchism is a much more serious alternative to contemporary society than any of the Marxisms in my opinion, for reasons that were apparent seventy years ago to Rudolph Rocker. An examination of his views of Marx, Marxism, and Bolshevism provide another useful means of understanding Chomsky's own writings on these matters. The principle concern elucidated by Rocker in *Nationalism and Culture* is predictable in light of previous discussions: a "dictatorship of the proletarian," one of the cornerstones of the *Manifesto*, is still a dictatorship. A Marxist state is still a state. And a Bolshevik party, despite their claims, is composed of elites whose interests were in maintaining a totalitarian hold over the vast majority of those in the U.S.S.R. and its satellite states. But Rocker's critique goes still further, sometimes into the writings of Marx himself rather than his interpreters such as Lenin and Stalin. Citing Marx's famous line, "the philosophers have variously interpreted the world, but it is necessary to change it," Rocker comments that Marx did nothing during his whole life that followed this precept except to reinterpret the world and its history. "He analyzed capitalistic society in his way, and showed a great deal of intellect and enormous learning in doing so, but Proudhon's creative power was denied him. He was, and remained, the analyst—a brilliant and learned analyst, but nothing else" (235). This has been frequently observed—that Marx was but a powerful theorist of capitalism—but Rocker finds in his work something nefarious and limiting, suggesting that Marx "enmeshed the minds of his followers in the fine network of a cunning dialectic which sees in history hardly anything but economics and obstructs every deeper insight into the world of social events" (235). This is a stunning condemnation, which in fact has its many equivalents in Marx's work; for the moment, though, it is worth recalling Chomsky's distrust of the cult of Marxism or any other ideologically driven (over) theorization of the social world.

At the heart of Rocker's condemnation of Marx was, as well, a sense that the "transformation of capitalist society" would not occur as Marx had predicted. This transformation stage is a critical one, seldom theorized beyond general statements.[46] For Marx, it would begin with a dictatorship of the proletariat, a notion deemed "idle" by Rocker: "History knows no such transitions. There exist solely more primitive and more complicated forms in the various evolutionary phases of social progress" (237). Furthermore, the effort to inflict a transformation upon a people in the name of Marxist idealism was for Rocker a tyranny like any other:

"If the Russian example taught us anything it is only the fact that social-ism without political, social and spiritual freedom is inconceivable, and must lead to unlimited despotism, uninfluenced in its crass callousness by any ethical restraints. This was clearly recognized by Proudhon when, almost one hundred years ago, he said that an alliance of socialism with Absolutism would produce the worst tyranny of all times" (546).

The anarchist program favored by Rocker has been described in various of his writings, but perhaps the clearest text is the short book called *Anarchism and Anarcho-Syndicalism* in which he advocates the "abolition of economic monopolies and of all political and social coer-cive institutions within society" (7). In their place Rocker suggests that there should exist "a free association of all productive forces based upon co-operative labor, which would have for its sole purpose the satisfying of the necessary requirements of every member of society." With his hatred for nationalism he needs to find an alternative to state power: "In place of the present national states with their lifeless machinery of polit-ical and bureaucratic institutions, anarchists desire a federation of free communities which shall be bound to one another by their common eco-nomic and social interests and arrange their affairs by mutual agreement and free contract" (7). It is of critical importance to note, however, that for Chomsky the present political situation requires a *defense* of the state as a means of staving off other forces of oppression, at least in the short term. This may, as was pointed out earlier, come as a surprise in light of his *anarchist* label; but he offers further graphic illustration of his approach in criticizing the notion that we must *begin with* the disman-tling of state power as a means of initiating the transformation of capitalist society, discussed by Zellig Harris, for example. "There are circumstances (we live in them, in fact) in which state power, however illegitimate, offers vulnerable people at least some protection against even worse forces; to dismantle the defense and leave the vulnerable prey to these is outrageous. Suppose we are in a cage and a saber-tooth tiger is roaming about outside. The cage should be dismantled, but to say that the first step must be to get rid of the cage is madness."[47] This indicates the distance in time and space between Rocker's writings and those of Noam Chomsky, but the overall approach of both remains similar, and the lessons of both are and remain applicable to a contemporary world seldom presented with truly emancipatory possibilities for radical change.

Zellig Harris

It would be remiss to consider the effective precursors, particularly in the area of Marxism/anarchism, without thinking about the role that Zellig Harris played, from very early on, in Chomsky's life.[48] Chomsky was nineteen years younger than Harris, but since his parents, William and Elsie Chomsky, were friendly with the Harrises, Noam had visited the Harris family home in Philadelphia. Years later, Chomsky met Zellig Harris, the Benjamin Franklin Professor of Linguistics, at the University of Pennsylvania. The young Chomsky was poised to become not only Harris's most powerful student but also, according to some versions of the many stories about this relationship, his most formidable adversary. From the beginning, this was no ordinary teacher-student relationship: "The primary teacher of Noam was Zellig Harris," says Dr. Henry Hiz, emeritus professor of linguistics, who also taught Chomsky at Penn. "It's very difficult to describe the profound influence Harris had on him—and on me, too." "Zellig Harris was a primary influence on Noam, perhaps *the* primary influence back then," agrees Carol Chomsky, who went by Carol Schatz until she and Noam were married in 1949. "Noam admired him enormously, and I think it's fair to say that Zellig Harris was responsible, in so many different ways, for the direction that Noam's intellectual life took then and later."[49] Harris himself was no ordinary teacher, and Noam, no ordinary student, would become a key assistant and then interlocutor for Harris's ideas. Noam was also one of the small number of students who entered Harris's world through the very intense and personal courses he gave, in what would today seem like an unusual and remarkably un-institutional fashion. He never used textbooks, favoring instead a more open-ended style of teaching that would begin with a few suggestions and ideas, and then take on a life of its own. Many of these "classes" were in fact conducted in his apartment in New York, or else in diners, and some of the students who were part of this select group came to be very well known in their own right, especially Nathan Glazer, Frank Lukoff, and Seymour Melman. But it was the importance of

Chomsky's work, and the ways in which he diverged from Harris's framework, that has generated historical interest. Indeed, a sense of how Harris's political approach intersects with, and diverges from, the political views of Noam Chomsky help shed light on both thinkers and upon the radical movements with which their work can be associated.

The subject of the Harris-Chomsky relationship is of considerable interest when investigating the development of both of these thinkers. The problem is, because of the eventual importance of both linguistics frameworks, and because of a well-publicized "rift" between the two of them, there are camps that exist to describe, criticize, attack, challenge, or belittle one side or the other. The other problem is that Zellig Harris's work is largely unknown, except to a small group of intellectuals, mostly academic linguists, which suggests that somewhat more detail will be needed in order to make the point about there being important overlaps and influences. I will begin with what seems to me an obvious assertion on this issue: the claim, made by certain linguists, that Chomsky has simply lifted Harris's ideas and dressed them up for a larger public consumption, is inaccurate at its very base and even a cursory comparison of their output (linguistic and political), makes this obvious. It is true, however, that some of the questions they ask, about underlying structures, the possibility of addressing certain questions, and the ways in which language is generated, are at times similar. And the considerable overlap between respective milieus means that there is bound to be a series of shared assumptions about what constitutes linguistic methods and scientific research. Furthermore, there are crucial overlaps in the ways that these two radical Jewish linguists from Philadelphia think about political issues, and there are very important convergences of the fundamental value systems that guide their respective approaches to society. Here again, however, the differences between the two political paradigms are as important as those between, say, Harris's work on self-governed production and Noam Chomsky's anarchism.

One way to begin this comparison is to look to critical precursors; key influences for Harris include Albert Einstein, Erich Fromm, and Paul Mattick, while Noam Chomsky frequently refers to Michael Bakunin, Rudolph Rocker, and Bertrand Russell. Even here, however, there are crucial differences. While Harris finds much that is valuable in the work of his friend Paul Mattick, he is a long way from this style of ideological writing, and while Chomsky uses some of the categories that Bakunin elaborated in his discussions of teaching, he has nothing in common with the latter's ideas about violence. In short, a thorough assessment of these two figures requires some very measured and careful analysis, and therein I find no place for the mudslinging, professional jealousies and holier-than-thou views that cause complex issues to be reduced to the oddly incongruous formation of camps, a tendency that at times sullies the field of linguistics.[50]

Zellig Harris deserves significant attention here because it was as a result of his influence that Chomsky abandoned his plans to drop out of college to work on one of the kibbutz Artzis, in Israel. "[His] was a very powerful personality, and he was very interested in encouraging young people to do things." Along with teaching him a "tremendous amount" about political matters, Chomsky recalls, Harris "just kind of suggested that I might want to sit in on some of his courses. I did, and I got excited about that." So much for dropping out. "In retrospect, I'm pretty sure he was trying to encourage me to get back in," says Chomsky.[51] Harris encouraged the kind of unstructured, lively, and creative debate that had been characteristic of Chomsky's early education (at a Deweyite elementary school), and upon which he had thrived in the company of his uncle, who worked at a newsstand in New York City. "I suppose Harris had in mind to influence me to return to college, though I don't recall talking about it particularly, and it all seemed to happen without much planning."[52] Harris was a good mentor for Noam Chomsky for several reasons, one being that he shunned formal relationships and scholarly hierarchies in favor of informal gatherings, broad-based discussions, and intellectual exchange. The University of Pennsylvania's linguistics department was at that time a very small and rather closed group composed of graduate students who shared an interest not only in linguistics but in politics as well. Harris encouraged these students but not through traditional "academic" work, as Chomsky recalls: "There used to be a Horn & Hardart's right past 34th Street on Woodland Avenue . . . and we'd often meet in the upstairs, or in his apartment in Princeton. His wife was a mathematician; she was working with Einstein." Despite the linguistics courses, most of which were with Harris, Chomsky says he "never studied linguistics in a conventional or formal manner" at Penn. . . . "Chomsky's education reflected Harris's interests closely," writes Randy Harris in *The Linguistic Wars*. "It involved work in philosophy, logic, and mathematics well beyond the normal training for a linguist. He read more deeply in epistemology, an area where speculation about the great Bloomfieldian taboo, mental structure, is not only legitimate, but inescapable."[53]

The discussions ranged over many areas of work throughout entire days, and were described by Chomsky as being "intellectually exciting as well as personally very meaningful experiences."[54] Chomsky recalls Harris as "a person of unusual brilliance and originality," who encouraged him to take graduate courses in philosophy, with Nelson Goodman and Morton White, and mathematics, with Nathan Fine. He also studied Arabic with Giorgio Levi Della Vida, whom he described as an "antifascist exile from Italy who was a marvelous person as well as an outstanding scholar."[55]

Despite his interest in language studies, what really drew Chomsky to Harris was the politics, in part because "in the late 1940s, Harris, like most structural linguists, had concluded that the field was essentially finished, that linguistics was finished. They had already done everything. They had solved all the problems. You maybe had to dot a couple of i's or something but essentially the field was over."[56] This project that was supposed to end the field was Zellig Harris's long-standing dream of elaborating a scientific basis for the study of language, which culminated with the completion, in 1947, of *Methods in Structural Linguistics*, the first and most important step toward a large-scale interest in structuralism, discourse analysis, studies of information representation, mathematics-inspired theories of language, the attempt to derive formulas of science information from science reports and the attempt at discovering the linear distributional relations of phonemes and morphemes. This work flowed into a general optimism about using mathematical formulations for basic processes, about which Chomsky comments in *Language and Mind*:

For those who sought a more mathematical formulation for the basic processes, there was the newly developed mathematical theory of communication, which, it was widely believed in the early 1950's, had provided a fundamental concept— the concept of "information"—that would unify the social and behavioral sciences and permit the development of a solid and satisfactory mathematical theory of human behavior on a probabilistic base. About the same time, the theory of automata developed as an independent study, making use of closely related mathematical notions. And it was linked at once, and quite properly, to earlier explorations of the theory of neural nets. There were those—John von Neumann, for example—who felt that the entire development was dubious and shaky at best, and probably quite misconceived, but such qualms did not go far to dispel the feeling that mathematics, technology and behavioristic linguistics and psychology were converging on a point of view that was very simple, very clear, and fully adequate to provide a basic understanding of what tradition had left shrouded in mystery.[57]

Through the course of his work with Harris and others, Chomsky ultimately received an unconventional B.A. from the University of Pennsylvania, which turned around his interests in linguistics, philosophy, and logic. His B.A. honor's thesis, which set the stage for some of his later work and which is taken to be the first example of modern generative grammar, was completed in 1949 when he was twenty years old. Harris himself, then chair of the department, signed the note to the dean, indicating on June 3, 1949, that "Mr. Noam Chomsky has successfully fulfilled all the requirements for an honors major in the Linguistics Department." He would later add, in a March 14, 1950, memo to the dean, that "In giving you the departmental report on the application for scholarships in Linguistics I neglected to add that the department recommended Mr. Chomsky very strongly and considers that he is exceptionally deserving of a scholarship." A few months later, in response to an application from Chomsky to candidacy for the degree of master of arts in linguistics, Harris signed a December 18 memo admitting Mr. A[vam] N[oam] Chomsky to candidacy for the degree of master of arts, the only M.A. (or PhD) degree offered that semester in linguistics. This degree was actually delayed, following a memo from Noam Chomsky: "I've decided to wait for the five credits till the fall, and try to get my degree in February, on the theory that this may keep me out of the army for another year. I hope my tardy decisions haven't caused you too much extra trouble" (n.d.). Noam Chomsky recalls: "I was 1-A. . . . I was going to be drafted right away. I figured I'd try to get myself a six-week deferment until the middle of June, so I applied for a PhD. I asked Harris and Goodman, who were still at Penn, if they would mind if I reregistered—I hadn't been registered at Penn in four years. I just handed in a chapter of what I was working on for a thesis, and they sent me some questions via mail, which I wrote inadequate answers to—that was my exams. I got a six-week deferment, and I got my PhD."[58]

Inspired by people like Harris, and increasingly concerned intellectually by the kind of work that he had undertaken for the B.A. thesis, Chomsky decided to extend his studies into graduate school, once again at the University of Pennsylvania. He began in the fall semester of 1949, and within a short period of time wrote a master's thesis (degree granted in 1951), which was a 1951 revision of his B.A. thesis, and which was edited further in 1951 and again in 1979, when it was published as *Morphophonemics of Modern Hebrew* [MMH]. It is interesting to note that Harris wrote to Bernard Bloch of the Yale Linguistics Department on December 19, 1950, with the following question: "A student of mine, A. N. Chomsky has been doing a great deal of work in formulation of linguistic procedures and has also done considerable work with Goodman and Martin. Last year I [gave] him the morphological and morphophonemic material which I had here. He added to it a great deal by means of informant work and turned out a rigorous detailed morphophonemic which I am sending you under separate cover. I thought you would be interested in it for its own sake. In addition I wonder whether you think there would be any point in publishing it and if so, in what form." On the same day, Zellig Harris wrote as well to Dr. Charles Hockett of Cornell, using exactly the same first paragraph, and then adding: "In addition, I remember that you once asked me about doing a general analysis of Hebrew for a volume on European languages. Is that volume still being considered? If we do any work that would include Chomsky's morphophonemics, that would be included in such a volume."

Harris also wrote to the graduate school dean to solicit further support for his promising young student on February 28, 1951: "I wish to write in support of Mr. A. N. Chomsky's application for a University Scholarship in Linguistics. Mr. Chomsky has just received his M.A. in this department and is continuing his work toward the Ph.D. He is one of the best students we have ever had and is highly regarded by men in various departments with whom he has worked, in particular, by Professors Goodman and Martin of the Philosophy Department. He has taken a considerable amount of work in logic and mathematics and has come to the attention of the Rockefeller Foundation as a possible key man in interdisciplinary research between linguistics and mathematical logic." Further support for this request was found in the person of Henry Hoenigswald, who considered that "in spite of his youth it has already become clear that he [Chomsky] will develop into an original worker in our field" (March 9, 1951).

Chomsky's own description of that work, and how it related to contemporary studies in the field, is described in an interview with Mitsou Ronat, for *Language and Responsibility*: "As an undergraduate at the University of Pennsylvania in the late 1940s I did an undergraduate thesis called 'Morphophonomenics of Modern Hebrew,' later expanded to a master's thesis with the same title in 1951. That work, which has not been published, was a 'generative grammar' in the contemporary sense; its primary focus was what is now called 'generative phonology,' but there was also a rudimentary generative syntax. I suppose one might say that it was the first generative grammar in the contemporary sense of the term. Of course there were classical precedents: Panini's grammar of Sanskrit is the most famous and important case, and at the level of morphology and phonology, there's Bloomfield's *Menomini Morphophonemics*, published only a few years earlier, though I did not know about it at the time." The goal of this work was "an attempt to demonstrate in painstaking detail that the generative grammar I presented was the simplest possible grammar in a well-defined technical sense: namely, given a certain framework for the formulation of rules and a precise definition of 'simplicity,' the grammar was 'locally optimal' in the sense that any interchange of order of rules would lead to a less simple grammar" (112).

During this period his friendship with Harris grew, taking on what could now be described as mythic proportions. Noam Chomsky seemed to have been elected to follow up on and expand Harris's work, and Harris represented for Noam Chomsky an inspiration with whom, and ultimately against whom, he could measure his own achievement. In terms of linguistics, Chomsky considers that Harris "thought of linguistics as a set of procedures for organizing texts, and was strongly opposed to the idea that there might be anything real to discover. He did think that the methods of linguistic analysis could be used for analysis of ideology, and most of my actual graduate courses were devoted to that; you can see some of the fruits in his articles on discourse analysis in *Language* in the early '50s, though he kind of downplayed the political side that was everyone's main interest."[59] Chomsky's early work in linguistics was in his words concentrated around "trying to make his [Zellig Harris's] methods work" (ibid.), the early fruit of which was Chomsky's first published article, in *The Journal of Symbolic Logic*. Chomsky described these efforts to Mitsou Ronat: "For a long time I thought that the discovery procedures appearing in the literature were correct in the essentials, that is, that the methods employed by structural linguists like Zellig Harris . . . were in principle correct, and that only some refinements were necessary to make them work. I spent quite a lot of time and energy, for about five or six years, I guess, trying to overcome some obvious defects of these procedures so that they would be able to produce a correct grammar with infinite descriptive scope from a finite corpus of the language; that, evidently, is the proper formulation of the task, if we think of these procedures as in effect a 'learning theory' for human language" (115).

Chomsky's undergraduate thesis also applied some of Harris's ideas, but according to Chomsky, he had by then totally abandoned all of Harris's methods by taking a "completely non-procedural, holistic (in that the evaluation measure proposed was a measure applied to the whole system), and realist' approach" (March 31, 1995):

Phrase structure rules can generate representations of syntactic structure quite successfully . . . for quite a range of expressions, and were introduced for this purpose in the earliest work on generative grammar. It was at once apparent, however, that phrase structure rules . . . are insufficient in themselves to account properly for the variety of sentence structures. The earliest approach to this problem, which has a number of subsequent and current variants, was to enrich the system of rules by introducing complex categories with features that can "percolate down" to the categories contained within them, expressing global dependencies not captured in a simple system of phrase structure rules. . . . I adopted this approach in an undergraduate thesis of 1949, modifying ideas of Zellig Harris from a somewhat different framework.[60]

So even at this early point, Chomsky was already pursuing an approach that diverged fundamentally from what Harris had been interested in elaborating, even though letters to Bloch and Hockett suggest that Harris recognized the importance of Chomsky's work. For

Chomsky, though, his own work was "radically at odds with everything in structural linguistics, to my knowledge, which is why it was published only 30 years later." MMH was, in other words, "as different from structural linguistics as anything could be"; in fact, according to Chomsky, MMH remains "the only text in existence, to my knowledge, that seeks to apply an evaluation measure in anything remotely like that detail" (March 31, 1995). We see here the building up of a complex teacher-student relationship that has provoked speculation, particularly among Harris's friends and other adepts. Harris's involvement in and knowledge of Chomsky's political and linguistic work, and the proximity between Harris's and Chomsky's approaches, lead to discussions about influence, authority, and power struggles, just as speculation about the relationship between Chomsky and his own students (in particular the so-called schismatics) led to discussion and even controversy in later years. A number of texts have been published that explore the proximity of Chomsky's linguistic theories to those of Harris, including "The Fall and Rise of Empiricism," in *An Integrated Theory of Linguistic Ability* by Jerrold J. Katz and Thomas G. Bever: "[C]ontrary to popular belief, transformations come into modern linguistics, not with Chomsky, but with Zellig Harris's rules relating sentence forms. These are genuine transformations, since they are structure-dependent mappings of phrase markers onto phrase markers. That this is so can be seen from the examples of transformations Zellig Harris gives."[61] Even the *New Encyclopedia Britannica* (1986, 5:721) has something to say about this relationship: "Since [Zellig] Harris was Noam Chomsky's teacher, some linguists have questioned whether Chomsky's transformational grammar is as revolutionary as it has been taken to be, but the two scholars developed their ideas of transformation in different contexts and for different purposes. For Harris, a transformation relates surface structure sentence forms and is not a device to transform a deep structure into a surface structure, as it is in transformational grammar." Chomsky assesses his own relation to this work in *Language and Responsibility*: "That grammar [in his *Morphophonomics of Modern Hebrew*] did . . . contain a rudimentary generative syntax. The grammar associated phonetic representation with what we would now call 'base-generated' syntactic structure. Parenthetically, this was a pre-transformational grammar.

Harris's early work on transformations was then under way and as a student of his I was familiar with it, but I did not see then how this work could be recast within the framework of generative grammar that I was trying to work out. In place of transformations, the grammar had a complex system of indices assigned to syntactic categories, which indicated syntactic relations inexpressible within the framework of segmentation and classification that was later constructed, in somewhat different terms, as the theory of phrase structure grammar" (112).

Harris's colleagues view the transformation work in laudatory terms, and link it to Chomsky's efforts in their department. Henry Hoenigswald suggests that Harris's

linguistic achievement has no equal. The discovery of syntactic "transformations" by him and then by his pupil Noam Chomsky in the 50's of the century was profound in a way for which there are few parallels in any discipline. Transformations—the basis of generative grammar—were new concepts in the sense in which the great discoveries in the history of science were "new." They made things that had been known after a fashion, as well as things that had hardly been known at all, fall into place in dazzling fashion. To be sure, he disdained to talk descriptively *about* them, leaving it to those who would study his work to develop it or attack it as they saw fit. In that he wasn't always lucky, but such was his temperament.[62]

In Henry Hiz's "Linguistics at the University of Pennsylvania," a clear distinction is made between distributional description and transformational theory, such that "the first characterizes each linguistic entity as a class of some lower-level entities, whereas the latter derives a sentence from another sentence or sentences, thereby deriving a sentence from entities of the same level." Pursuing his history of the Penn department (and the field), Hiz notes that "in 1952 Harris introduced procedures of sentence transformation into discourse analysis, as a method of regularizing a text and of finding equivalences between its segments." Soon afterward, recalls Hiz, "transformational theory was divorced from discourse analysis and became an autonomous part of linguistics." For him, "Noam Chomsky's dissertation connected to many things. Sentences are related and their relations are to be studied by a grammar. It may be done without much semantics when transformations are only sentence-preserving."

Chomsky as student continued to pursue his attempt "to make sense of Harris's *Methods* and procedural approaches to language altogether in the operationalist style of the day"[63] while continuing his own work on generative transformational grammar as a kind of hobby. I use the word *hobby* just as Chomsky does when speaking of the interests that he was cultivating on the side during his years as a graduate student. He remained at Penn largely because of Harris and the new-found stimulation of political and philosophical discussion. But even as a student, he strongly believed that the things he really cared about, libertarian politics and a divergent opinion concerning the entire field of language studies as construed within the academy, were valuable but essentially personal interests.

The Political Influence of Zellig Harris upon Noam Chomsky

In short, Chomsky claims Harris as an "early influence" in terms of his linguistic work but recalls that: "we'd essentially parted ways by about 1950 or so, definitively after I abandoned the *Methods* program a few years later." What remained was regular meetings between the two; they "remained good friends, but kept to politics."[64] So why then am I insisting upon the importance of Harris's influence upon Chomsky? Chomsky notes, again in personal correspondence, that "Harris was a very impressive person, and his intellectual impact was enormous. My picture of the world, as a teenager, was certainly shaped very strongly by his influence, which in fact fit in very well to commitments I'd already developed elsewhere (anarchist and left anti-Bolshevik and anti-Marxist sources, particularly)."[65] Hilary Putnam, in his preface to *The Form of Information in Science*, recalls that a graduate course he took called Linguistic Analysis at Penn, along with only one other undergraduate—Noam Chomsky—was difficult and filled with technicalities, "but the powerful intellect and personality of Zellig Harris drew me like a lodestone, and, although I majored in Philosophy, I took every course there was to take in Linguistic Analysis from then until my graduation" (xi). The reason for Putnam's persistence bears upon both his experience as a freshman and as a commentator on Harris's much later work on mathematics: "the idea that informs [*The Form of Information in Science*] is, like all of Harris's central ideas, breathtaking in its combination of simplicity and daring: to take a subfield of a particular scientific discipline and compare the structures of the texts in that subfield before and after a particular 'scientific revolution' in the subfield. The details look formidable at first blush—just as the papers on the grammars of various languages that I encountered as a freshman in Harris's notation looked formidable at first blush. But the reader who is serious about wanting to know if such a thing as 'structural analysis of discourse' is possible and who is willing to do a little work will find that the presentation is not as hard to follow as it looks, and that the payoff is large" (xiii). Putnam, now a professor at Harvard, had been a friend of Chomsky's since high school; however he does not appear to have been part of the "Harris circle," certainly not when Chomsky was there. Nevertheless, his observations coincide with those made by all of the people with whom I spoke who knew Harris). Seymour Melman also spoke of Zellig Harris's generosity and its relationship to Chomsky's own approach. Said Melman: "Harris was also very unassuming; to many people that may have seemed to be almost reclusive. For example; he would rarely sign things. He was more interested in the intrinsic ideas, and in getting the cooperation of the whole group in thinking through political issues, and social issues broadly understood. It doesn't require a giant leap of imagination to see how many of these characteristics are mirrored in Noam Chomsky. Something else: he clearly stood for democratic dealings among people, and was never a friend of authoritarianism of any kind" (July 26, 1994). Henry Hoenigswald's vivid message sums up these tendencies beautifully: "He spent all his time with students; more and more, as time went on, with small groups of very advanced students. This was his way of hammering out his theoretical linguistic position. Of course, he had a firm political position, too, though I was often surprised by his amazing tolerance on some issues. I'm sure there is a connection, though I don't quite know what it was; the connection is much clearer in Chomsky's case because Chomsky is so articulate about overt philosophy and politics as he sees them."[66]

The way Melman describes Harris resonates upon my sense of Chomsky and, I might add, upon others who had been taught or influenced by him and with whom I have been in contact, such as Herman, Melman, Otero, and so forth. Indeed Harris's attitude concerning the importance of the movement, rather than individual achievement, is indicative of the kind of attitude that makes Chomsky reluctant about biographical studies. The spirit of left libertarianism, reflected in Harris's teaching style and his commitment to encouraging rather than stifling individual creativity reflect back upon Chomsky's own descriptions of pedagogy, group relations, and appropriate political frameworks. Whether Chomsky inherited these traits from Harris, or whether this was another way in which Chomsky felt that Harris's values fit into his own is irrelevant beyond the point that there is an important overlap on these matters. But Chomsky himself (uncharacteristically) recalled the power of Harris's personality in the context of our correspondence, suggesting that "he was a much greater influence than is recognized, extending to all sorts of people. The first time I met Nathan Glazer, for example, after a few minutes I asked him whether he knew Harris. He said yes, he'd studied with him 25 years earlier. I didn't tell Glazer why I'd asked. The reason was that he was mimicking all sorts of idiosyncratic Harris gestures. Not the only case" (December 13, 1994).

In retrospect we realize that Chomsky's early association with the university and with its various levels of bureaucracies and administrative apparatus is very unusual, particularly in the present-day world of formal academic requirements and strict regulations; indeed, he describes the scene at the University of Pennsylvania during his education there as "strange" and "complex." In his words, however, "People who were at the University of Pennsylvania from the late 1950s could describe what things were like there. It was a very strange scene, and a complex one. However, none of that has anything to do with me, except that I was a figure in many people's fantasy lives. It has to do with a biography of Harris, which could be quite interesting.[67] He was a complex and curious person."[68] This unique atmosphere has led to some rather odd suggestions concerning rivalry between MIT and UPenn, and even some cloak-and-dagger attempts by students from the other institution to infiltrate or spy on the respective departments. This seems absurd, and Chomsky himself disregards it, suggesting that it "gives paranoia a bad name."

Conclusions

I have focused on a particular group of individuals in my thinking about logical precursors to the Chomsky approach, in particular the Cartesians, Harris, Humboldt, Rocker, and Russell. My point is that Chomsky is both an original thinker and also someone who gladly points us in interesting historical directions for the sources of his ideas. It is crucial that we look back to these texts, in my opinion, and in particular that we recall the powerful role played by the now virtually forgotten anarchists. In his December 23, 1996, response to "Tom"[69] Chomsky sums up his views:

Anarchism, in my view, is an expression of the idea that the burden of proof is always on those who argue that authority and domination are necessary. They have to demonstrate, with powerful argument, that that conclusion is correct. If they cannot, then the institutions they defend should be considered illegitimate. How one should react to illegitimate authority depends on circumstances and conditions: there are no formulas. In the present period, the issues arise across the board, as they commonly do: from personal relations in the family and elsewhere, to the international political/economic order. And anarchist ideas—challenging authority and insisting that it justify itself—are appropriate at all levels.

It is not just the sense that antiauthority is always better than authority, but that this idea is in accord with our essence, with Chomsky's hope (which is the best we can do at the moment, given our lack of knowledge) that core elements of human nature include sentiments of solidarity, mutual support, sympathy, concern for others, and so on. Would people work less in an egalitarian society? "Yes," says Chomsky, "insofar as they are driven to work by the need for survival; or by material reward, a kind of pathology, I believe, like the kind of pathology that leads some to take pleasure from torturing others. Those who find reasonable the classical liberal doctrine that the impulse to engage in creative work is at the core of human nature—something we see constantly, I think, from children to the elderly, when circumstances allow—will be very suspicious of these doctrines, which are highly serviceable to power and authority, but seem to have no other merits." Would an absence of government allow the strong to dominate the weak? "We don't know. If so, then forms of social organization would have to be constructed—there are many possibilities—to overcome this crime. What would be the consequences of democratic decision-making? The answers are unknown. We would have to learn by trial. Let's try it and find out" (ibid.). Chomsky makes this point repeatedly in his work.

About a future society, I . . . may be repeating myself, but it's something I've been concerned with every since I was a kid. I recall, about 1940, reading Diego Abad de Santillan's interesting book After the Revolution, criticizing his anarchist comrades and sketching in some detail how an anarchosyndicalist Spain would work (these are 50 year old memories, so don't take it too literally). My feeling then was that it looked good, but do we understand enough to answer questions about a society in such detail? Over the years, naturally I've learned more, but it has only deepened my skepticism about whether we understand enough. In recent years, I've discussed this a good deal with Mike Albert, who has been encouraging me to spell out in detail how I think society should work, or at least react to his "participatory democracy" conception. I've backed off, in both cases, for the same reasons. It seems to me that answers to most such questions have to be learned by experiment. Take markets (to the extent that they could function in any viable society—limited, if the historical record is any guide, not to speak of logic). I understand well enough what's wrong with them, but that's not sufficient to demonstrate that a system that eliminates market operations is preferable; simply a point of logic, and I don't think we know the answer. Same with everything else.[70]

So after filling in some of the noticeable gaps in the pantheon of valuable references, we are left with a stronger sense of the origins and critical references for Chomsky's thought, but we are also left to the resources of the people who make up a given compendium and not to the great dictates of the past. Armed with this material, the struggle to understand and confront critical issues in daily life seems both more possible and more open ended.

II
Milieus

4

Just Effects: Chomsky on Law, Ethics, and Human Rights

Many of those people vaguely familiar with Noam Chomsky's political stance, notably his anarchy, would find it difficult to imagine what relationship might exist between Noam Chomsky and the law.[1] The reasons for this reflect popular (and academic) misconceptions about anarchy, which lead people to associate it quite narrowly with lawlessness, chaos, violence, destruction, and illegal challenges to authority (including the police and other representatives of state order). Evidence for this misconception can be traced through popular use of the term *anarchy*, as we've seen variously, but also in the literature describing its relationship to law. Chhatrapati Singh writes in *Law From Anarchy to Utopia*,[2] which he subtitles "an exposition of the logical, epistemological and ontological foundations of the idea of law, by an inquiry into the nature of legal propositions and the basis of legal authority," that:

anarchy is not merely a state in which law and order break down. This is a misleading way of putting things, and not without reason. Order can be achieved in many ways: through compulsion, brainwashing, conditioning, deception or religious conviction. Only one sort of order is a legal order. Hence there can be order even in the absence of law. But all such non-legal orders which are not based in human rationality and co-operation will be pathological, because they will deprive people of freedom and retard natural growth. . . . Anarchy, thus, is not merely a question of disorder but also of orders which are pathological. If people are not allowed to develop socially, culturally, economically, scientifically or otherwise, and if order is maintained through coercion or deception, greater disorder results when people realize their deprivation. Pathological orders, whether they are maintained through colonialism, imperialism, dictatorship or straightforward repression, are as much conditions of anarchy as are acts of terrorism or guerrilla warfare. (xiii)

There is much that is inaccurate in this description, beginning with the fact that much of what is deemed positive in this apparently antianarchist ideal, such as rationality and cooperation, are the true objectives of anarchists and indeed the very raison d'être for their approach. Anarchy is not some unattainable utopia that exists beyond or outside of the realm of law, as many people believe, including Richard Taylor who asserts, in *Freedom, Anarchy, and the Law: An Introduction to Political Philosophy*,[3] that "if freedom is an unqualified good, then the ideal societal state can be nothing but an anarchical one—a state of men living together without any conventional coercion whatever. Such an ideal societal state would be quite literally one of lawlessness, and the ideality of it is, of course, that only in such a state can men enjoy the unqualified goodness of freedom. The introduction of a single rule or law into such a state is the beginning of its corruption, for such a law can only serve to restrain someone from doing what he might otherwise want to do and can therefore only serve to divest him of an unqualified good, that is, of his freedom" (42). In fact, Bakunin, Goldman, Kropotkin, and Rocker all have descriptions of law's role in their good societies, and Chomsky has taken from each, notably when a link is created in their works between Enlightenment thinking, classical liberal ideas, and an appropriately anarchist society.

Most of Chomsky's political lectures contain references, generally positive, to international law, rule of law, and to charters, treaties and declarations such as the Bill of Rights, the U.S. Constitution, the Declaration of Rights and Freedoms, and to certain United Nations resolutions. This may seem to some surprising, since he appears to be in agreement with our own government's "reverence for certain symbols of the modern rule of law: the Magna Carta, which set forth what are men's rights as against the kind; the American Constitution, which is supposed to limit the powers of government and provide a Bill of Rights; the Napoleonic Code, which introduced uniformity into the French legal system."[4] What's confusing here is if the link is made, as it often is, between anarchy and lawlessness, then Chomsky's ideas become an enigma. Even people sympathetic to his view might consider that his approach, which sometimes speaks favorably of institutions such as law courts, international tribunals, or the United Nations, overlooks the conservative and elite nature of most legal institutions. Then, of course, there are the personal anecdotes about Chomsky, including those that emanate from widely reproduced articles such as "Noam Is An Island," by Jay Parini (*Mother Jones* October 1988), in which Parini expresses his surprise at the care that Chomsky takes in crossing the street, and his respect for traffic laws generally, which again seems to suggest some divergence from what people generally consider anarchist behavior.

One of the objectives of this chapter is to demonstrate that individuals working in a classical liberal framework find important areas of overlap with anarchism through the study of law. Such an effort is a bit of a tightrope walk at times, because Chomsky does not consistently support international law or the institutions set up to enforce it; instead, he can be either critical or supportive, depending upon how the laws are constituted or employed. For example, he suggests that "the United Nations is 'functional' today because it is (more or less) doing what Washington wants, a fact that has virtually nothing to do with the end of the Cold War, the Russians, or Third World maladies. The 'shrill, anti-Western rhetoric' of the Third World has, very often, been a call for observance of international law. For once, the U.S. and its allies happen to be opposed to acts of aggression, annexation, and human rights violations. Therefore the U.N. is able to act in its peacekeeping role. These truths being unacceptable, they do not exist. They belong to the domain of 'abuse of reality' (actual history), not reality itself (what we prefer to believe)."[5] Nonetheless, despite limitations that are for the most part related to the role that the United Nations plays in a capitalist global economy, it does have certain mechanisms that, if followed, would cut down on some of the misery of the world. Unfortunately, the United Nations, like the international law upon which it is based, can be just another way of pursuing contemporary politics, and as such it often mimics existing political realities and power relations rather than acting to fulfill a more fundamental mandate to ease oppression and support justice. It is interesting to look back in light of the second intervention in Iraq to some of the things that Chomsky has written about the role of force in earlier texts on Iraq, for instance: "Choice of policy is determined by the goals that are sought. [For example,] if the goal had been to secure Iraq's withdrawal from Kuwait, settle regional issues, and move towards a more decent world, then Washington would have followed the peaceful means prescribed by international law: sanctions and diplomacy. The goal is to firm up the mercenary-enforcer role and establish the rule of force."[6] This "rule of force" is a constant refrain, and much of Chomsky's work in this area is aimed specifically at showing that this is in fact the dominant ideology. For instance, in an interview with David Barsamian on Israel and the United States, we find the following exchange:

DB: The conditions of the US-Israel alliance have changed, but have there been any structural changes?

NC: International law transcends state law, but Israel says these resolutions are not applicable. How are they not applicable? Just as international law isn't applicable to the United States, which has even been condemned by the World Court. States do what they feel like—though of course small states have to obey.

DB: I remember talking to Mona Rishmawi, a lawyer for the human rights organization Al Haq in Ramallah on the West Bank. She told me that when she would go to court, she wouldn't know whether the Israeli prosecutor would prosecute her clients under British mandate emergency law, Jordanian law, Israeli law or Ottoman law.

NC: Or their own laws. There are administrative regulations, some of which are never published. As any Palestinian lawyer will tell you, the legal system in the territories is a joke. There's no law—just pure authority.[7]

The difference between UN-supported politics and power politics, and the reason Chomsky sometimes supports the former but almost never the latter, is that the actions of the former are at least theoretically rooted in legitimate values, rather than in the arbitrary exercise of power through force (one has only to read the Charter of the United Nations,[8] or its mission statements, to see this). As Chomsky constantly reminds his (American) public, the reigning American dogma holds that the United States stands rightly and justly above the law, and should be free to use violence as it pleases. This is where international organizations like the United Nations can at least theoretically intervene, and thus fulfill its self-appointed role as a forum of international appeal against the aggressive imperialism of the great powers. On the other hand, given the United Nations dependence upon great power support and the often nonbinding nature of international conventions, treaties, charters and accords, international laws can turn out to be declarations of intention or ideal behavior that serve as a measure of the distance we have to travel if we hope for some kind of equitable justice. As Chomsky notes, "the World Trade Organization has no authority to compel the U.S. to change its laws, just as the World Court has no authority to compel the U.S. to terminate its international terrorism and illegal economic warfare. Free trade and international law are like democracy: fine ideas, but to be judged by outcome, not process."[9] The very mention of the W.T.O. is a sign of the imperfection of particular organizations and treaties, and the actions of the police and troops who have been called in during the various W.T.O meetings is a sure sign of how force is used above rational action as a criteria to determine who wins and who loses.

This is where the positive side of international law comes to bear upon Chomsky's argument, for here he speaks to its potential for decent action according to fundamental principles. When international law is invoked for these ends, it is rejected by the elites, from which emanates Chomsky's sense of the hypocrisy of the current system:

The U.S. has been radically opposed to international law since its modern foundations were established under U.S. initiative in 1945. In the early days, that was kept to internal (now declassified) documents, such as the first Memorandum of the newly-formed National Security Council (NSC 1/3), calling for military action in Italy if the left won the election. . . . With the Kennedy Administration, disdain for international law became quite public, in particular, in speeches by senior Kennedy adviser Dean Acheson. The main innovation of the Clinton/Reagan years is that it has become entirely open. In fact, the US is the only country to have vetoed a Security Council resolution calling on all states to observe international law—mentioning no one, but everyone understood who was meant. . . . It's entirely obvious why the powerful should have contempt for international law, and why the weak (particularly the former colonies) should generally favor it. The powerful do what they want anyway; treaties and systems of world order don't offer them any protection. They do, however, offer at least some limited protection for the weak. That is why the real "international community" is quite commonly opposed to the resort to violence by the US/UK (and now their NATO partners). In the U.S. the term "international community" is used to refer to NATO, but we can surely dispense with that racist/imperialist jargon ourselves.[10]

For Chomsky, the positive sides of international law are undercut by U.S. "disdain" and disregard; but if this is the case, what guides the policies they promote? Here Chomsky looks to the relationship between law and force, a critical issue for contemporary policies of preemption, terrorism and security:

Q: If undermining international law is part of U.S. policy, what about maintaining U.S. credibility as a violent international actor?

NC: It seems to me that undermining international law and maintaining "credibility" go hand in hand. For similar reasons, in its major study of "post–Cold War deterrence," Clinton's Strategic Command advised that "it hurts to portray ourselves as too fully rational and cool-headed. . . . That the U.S. may become irrational and vindictive if its vital interests are attacked should be a part of the national persona we project." It is "beneficial" for our strategic posture if "some elements may appear to be potentially 'out of control'." Actual policy conforms reasonably well to prescriptions in internal documents, and it's easy to trace the story far back—not only in the U.S. of course; there are many precedents. These are quite natural attributes of overwhelming power.[11]

To situate these various distinctions and discussions, one must once again look back in time to those who have theorized the rule and the role of law in existing and imagined social organizations.

Against Hypocrisy through Appeal to a Rational Past

Chomsky reconciles a conservative or, better still, a classical liberal conception of law with his anarchist vision by looking to historically grounded antecedents and connections. For example, he repeatedly insists that we look back to the actual documents upon which the legitimacy of our society is founded, and to recall the blood that has been shed in the past to provide us with the relative freedoms we have come to enjoy.[12] The effectiveness of the state-corporate propaganda system is illustrated by the fate of May Day, a workers' holiday throughout the world that originated in response to the judicial murder of several anarchists after the Haymarket affair of May 1886, in a campaign of international solidarity with U.S. workers struggling for an eight-hour day. In the United States, all that has been forgotten. May Day has become "Law Day," a jingoist celebration of our

"200–year-old partnership between law and liberty" as Ronald Reagan declared while designating May 1 as Law Day 1984, adding that without law there can be only "chaos and disorder." The day before, he had announced that the United States would disregard the proceedings of the International Court of Justice that later condemned the U.S. government for its "unlawful use of force" and violation of treaties in its attack against Nicaragua. "Law Day" also served as the occasion for Reagan's declaration of May 1, 1985, announcing an embargo against Nicaragua "in response to the emergency situation created by the

Nicaraguan Government's aggressive activities in Central America," actually declaring a "national emergency," since renewed annually, because "the policies and actions of the Government of Nicaragua constitute an unusual and extraordinary threat to the national security and foreign policy of the United States"— all with the approbation of Congress, the media, and the intellectual community generally; or, in some circles, embarrassed silence.[13]

He then compares the rhetoric with the action in order to demonstrate, over and over again, that the United States is in constant violation of its own ruling "principles," but acts in perfect accord instead with the "rule of force."[14] This rule of force is upheld as though it were a legitimate way to protect "state interests," a dubious idea in itself if we look to the fundamental legal documents of our society.

In the U.S. Constitution and its Amendments, one can find nothing that authorizes the grant of human rights (speech, freedom from search and seizure, the right to buy elections, etc.) to what legal historians call "collectivist legal entities," organic entities that have the rights of "immortal persons"—rights far beyond those of real persons, when we take into account their power. One will search the U.N. Charter in vain to discover the basis for the authority claimed by Washington to use force and violence to achieve "the national interest," as defined by the immortal persons who cast over society the shadow called "politics," in John Dewey's evocative phrase. The U.S. Code defines "terrorism" with great clarity, and U.S. law provides severe penalties for the crime. But one will find no wording that exempts "the architects of power" from punishment for their exercises of state terror, not to speak of their monstrous clients (as long as they enjoy Washington's good graces): Suharto, Saddam Hussein, Mobutu, Noriega, and others great and small. As the leading Human Rights organizations point out year after year, virtually all U.S. foreign aid is illegal, from the leading recipient on down the list, because the law bars aid to countries that engage in "systematic torture." That may be law, but is it the meaning of the law?"[15]

One way of understanding this distinction, between law and the meaning of law, is to consider the crucially important distinction between legitimate and illegitimate laws. For instance,

Defenders of American actions frequently argue that questions of law are too complex for the layman and should be left to experts. However, in this case, a careful reading of the arguments, pro and con, reveals little divergence over questions of law. The issues debated are factual and historical: specifically, is the U.S. engaged in collective self-defense against armed attack from North Vietnam? This is an issue concerning which the layman is in a position to make a judgment, and the responsible citizen will not be frightened away from doing so by the claim that the matter is too esoteric for him to comprehend. Extensive documentation is available, and, I believe, it shows clearly that the American war [in Vietnam] criminal, even in the narrowest technical sense."[16]

Howard Zinn suggests similar ideas, but in terms of the difference between law and justice, which he describes as follows: "the great artists and writers of the world, from Sophocles in the fifth century B.C. to Tolstoy in the modern era, have understood the difference between law and justice. They have known that, just as imagination is necessary to go outside the traditional boundaries to find and to create beauty and to touch human sensibility, so it is necessary to go outside the rules and regulations of the state to achieve happiness for oneself and others."[17] This is the important point, to go beyond state rules and regulations, and into the realm of universal justice, which sometimes leads us into clear defiance of authority and its enforcers: "What kind of person can we admire, can we ask young people of the next generation to emulate—the strict follower of law or the dissident who struggles, sometimes within, sometimes outside, sometimes against the law, but always for justice? What life is best worth living—the life of the proper, obedient, dutiful follower of law and order or the life of the independent thinker, the rebel?"[18] Zinn draws support for this idea from American icons such as Thomas Jefferson ("the spirit of resistance to government is so valuable on certain occasions that I wish it to be always kept alive. It will often be exercised when wrong, but better so than not to be exercised at all"), Henry David Thoreau ("A common and natural result of an undue respect for law is, that you may see a file of soldiers, colonels, captains, corporals, privates, powder-monkeys, and all, marching in admirable order over hill and dale to the wards, against their wills, nay, against their common sense and consciences, which makes it very steep marching indeed, and produces a palpitation of the heart").[19]

A similar point is raised by Chomsky in his discussion with Michel Foucault (moderated by Fons Elders),[20] which is worth citing here at length:

Elders: Well, perhaps it would be interesting to delve a little deeper into this problem of strategy. I suppose that what you call civil disobedience is probably the same as what we call extraparliamentary action?

Chomsky: No, I think it goes beyond that. Extraparliamentary action would include, let's say, a mass legal demonstration, but civil disobedience is narrower than all extraparliamentary action, in that it means direct defiance of what is alleged, incorrectly in my view, by the state to be law.

Elders: So, for example, in the case of Holland, we had something like a population census. One was obliged to answer questions on official forms. You would call it civil disobedience if one refused to fill in the forms?

Chomsky: Right. I would be a little bit careful about that, because, going back to a very important point that Mr. Foucault made, one does not necessarily allow the state to define what is legal. Now the state has the power to enforce a certain concept of what is legal, but power doesn't imply justice or even correctness; so that the state may define something as civil disobedience and may be wrong in doing so. For example, in the United States the state defines it as civil disobedience to, let's say, derail an ammunition train that's going to Vietnam; and the state is wrong in defining that as civil disobedience, because it's legal and proper and should be done. It's proper to carry out actions that will prevent the criminal acts of the state, just as it is proper to violate a traffic ordinance in order to prevent a murder. If I had stopped my car in front of a traffic light which was red, and then I drove through the red traffic light to prevent somebody from, let's say, machine-gunning a group of people, of course that's not an illegal act, it's an appropriate and proper action; no sane judge would convict you for such an action. Similarly, a good deal of what the state authorities define as civil disobedience is not really civil disobedience: in fact, it's legal, obligatory behavior in violation of the commands of the state, which may or may not be legal commands. So one has to be rather careful about calling things illegal, I think.

Foucault: Yes, but I would like to ask you a question. When, in the United States, you commit an illegal act, do you justify it in terms of justice or of a superior legality, or do you justify it by the necessity of the class struggle, which is at the present time essential for the proletariat in their struggle against the ruling class?

Chomsky: Well, here I would like to take the point of view which is taken by the American Supreme Court and probably other courts in such circumstances; that is, to try to settle the issue in the narrowest possible grounds. I would think that ultimately it would make very good sense, in many cases, to act against the legal institutions of a given society, if in so doing you're striking at the sources of power and oppression in that society.[21]

This is the critical point, whether or not deferral to justice strikes at sources of power, notably sources of illegitimate power, that is, power that does not act in the interest of the persons affected by it, but rather in the interest of some other objective like profits or nationalism. To make this point clear, we have to consider what elements of the American legal system Chomsky admires and what he rejects, that is, the link between Cartesian thinking of the type that Chomsky has long upheld and the anarchist society to which he aspires.

American-Style Resistance to Authority

How should one decide which laws should be challenged? What criteria should be applied to determine the legitimacy of laws? Noam Chomsky, like Rudolph Rocker, believes that legitimate laws are natural out-growths of individuals living in society, they are the habits that are formed after generations to ensure the survival of individuals and groups. For instance, in the course of a discussion about free speech, Chomsky reminds us that: "[F]reedom of speech is by no means a deeply entrenched tradition even in the United States, which by comparative standards is quite advanced in this regard." To make his point Chomsky cites Rudolf Rocker's observation that "political rights do not originate in parliaments; they are rather forced upon them from without. And even their enactment into law has for a long time been no guarantee of their security. They do not exist because they have been legally set down on a piece of paper, but only when they have become the ingrown habit of a people, and when any attempt to impair them will meet with the violent resistance of the populace." So legal protections and rights offered in documents such as the U.S. Constitution need to be supported, but also updated and improved if society is to advance. Says Chomsky: "History provides ample warrant for this conclusion. As is well known, even the right to vote was achieved in the United States only through constant struggle. Women were disenfranchised for 130 years, and those whom the American Constitution designated as only three-fifths human were largely denied this right until the popular movements of the past generation changed the cultural and political climate."[22]

There is hope as well in legal institutions, when they act in accordance with legitimate law, and when they act with the support of those who can enforce their rulings; oftentimes the United Nations or the World Court act in accordance with the former, but without support needed for the enforcements of their own rulings or decisions:

Nicaragua in the 1980s was subjected to violent assault by the US. Tens of thousands of people died. The country was substantially destroyed; it may never recover. The international terrorist attack was accompanied by a devastating economic war, which a small country isolated by a vengeful and cruel superpower could scarcely sustain, as the leading historians of Nicaragua, Thomas Walker for one, have reviewed in detail. The effects on the country are much more severe even than the tragedies in New York the other day. They didn't respond by setting off bombs in Washington. They went to the World Court, which ruled in their favor, ordering the US to desist and pay substantial reparations. The US dismissed the court judgment with contempt, responding with an immediate escalation of the attack. So Nicaragua then went to the Security Council, which considered a resolution calling on states to observe international law. The US alone vetoed it. They went to the General Assembly, where they got a similar resolution that passed with the US and Israel opposed two years in a row (joined once by El Salvador). That's the way a state should proceed.[23]

They should proceed this way because it ensures that civilizations don't fall into hubris, the endless cycle of violence and counterviolence, as we're seeing today in Iraq. So "surely no 'civilized world' would plunge the world into a major war instead of following the means prescribed by international law, following ample precedents."[24] In this rather strange culture that surrounds us, statements about such things are likely to come from unlikely sources, so we find for example Brittany Spears being questioned about her views of government leaders, to which she responded that we need to just trust them because they are charged with ruling the country. In a sense, perhaps many people would like to entrust credibility to authority, they would like to believe that decisions made by rulers deserve our support rather than our questioning or our legal challenges. Says Chomsky on this point, "Of course, there will be those who demand silent obedience. We expect that from the ultra-right, and anyone with a little familiarity with history will expect it from some left intellectuals as well, perhaps in an even more virulent form. But it is important not to be intimidated by hysterical ranting and lies and to keep as closely as one can to the course of truth and honesty and concern for the human consequences of what one does, or fails to do. All truisms, but worth bearing in mind."[25] Considering the question of local involvement in government decisions offers another perspective on recent legislation concerning wiretapping, torture, *huis clos*[26] hearings, and keeping evidence from persons accused of involvement in terrorism in the interest of "national security." It is hard to denounce "lies our government tells us" when the substance of these lies is never revealed for public scrutiny!

So part of the objective of an anarchist, surprisingly perhaps, is to challenge authority by supporting legitimate laws, those which incline in the direction of the oppressed against their oppressors, those which cordon off law from other means of enforcing state will, notably force. But struggle for a higher level of justice must not come to an end, it must build from previous gains and from continued activism against attacks upon codified advancements in international law. For example, in 1988

Chomsky noted that "Secretary of State George Shultz informed the OAS that the U.S. would persist in the unlawful use of force by its "resistance fighters" until a "free Nicaragua" is established by Washington standards, thus consigning the accords to oblivion, along with international law."[27] This is but a representative example of Chomsky's insistence upon maintaining classical liberal ideals and institutions against nationalist or imperialist will as a backdrop to his discussions of the United States' abuses of international law, and to its condoning of similar abuses when effected by its allies. A principal offender here is Israel, mentioned frequently by Chomsky in this regard, from early on in his work. For example,

there is an intriguing sidelight to the US-Israeli insistence that the political representatives of the Palestinians be excluded from negotiations. The official reason is that the PLO is a terrorist organization. Under Israeli law, anyone who has any dealings with it is subject to criminal penalties under the Law for the Prevention of Terror. The prime targets are Palestinians, but the law has also been used to punish Jews for contacts with the PLO, most recently, the courageous Abie Nathan, jailed once again. The background for the law was reviewed by one of Israel's leading legal commentators, Moshe Negbi, discussing a recent academic study of Lehi (the "Stern gang"), published on its 50th anniversary. Negbi's article is entitled "The Law to Prevent Meetings with the Head of State." As he explains, the Law for the Prevention of Terror was instituted on the initiative of Prime Minister David Ben-Gurion six days after the assassination of UN Ambassador Folke Bernadotte. Ben-Gurion's goal was to break up Lehi, known at once to be responsible for the assassination. One of the three commanders of Lehi was Yitzhak Shamir. The law not only barred any contact with Shamir, but was also applied against Menahem Begin's terrorist Irgun Zvai Leumi (Etsel), impelling Begin to dismantle his Jerusalem organization. It was also used to jail religious extremists, including Rabbi Mordechai Eliyahu, currently chief Rabbi. It was bitterly denounced as a "Nazi law, dictatorial, immoral" and hence illegal, by Menahem Begin and other civil libertarians. Despite efforts to have it modified under Labor governments, it remained in force, formally directed against Shamir and his Lehi associates, until 1977, when Begin was elected Prime Minister. Today the "Nazi law" still remains in force, but only to bar contacts with the PLO and to justify the US-Israeli refusal to permit Palestinians to select their own representatives for negotiations.[28]

And once again: "The occupation [of Palestinian occupied territories] is in violation of UN Security Council resolution 425 of March 1978, calling on Israel to withdraw immediately and unconditionally from Lebanon. The government of Lebanon has reiterated this demand, notably in February 1991 during the Gulf conflict; apart from odd corners like this journal, the request was drowned out by the self-congratulatory oratory about the wondrous new order of law and justice. Israel is free to ignore such minor annoyances as the Security Council and international law thanks to the stance of its superpower patron, which is powerful enough to reduce the UN to an instrument of its foreign policy and to shape international law as it chooses, as was seen once again in the ludicrous legal arguments put forth to justify Clinton's bombing of Iraq in June."[29]

One of the areas for which Chomsky is most frequently criticized relates to his denunciation of the United States on issues of international law even though most other countries are guilty of similar or worse offences. For Chomsky, the United States claims to be its strongest advocate: "The second question is rarely raised explicitly, except in the course of complaints about our faint-hearted and money-grubbing allies, who lack the courage, integrity and sturdy national character of the Anglo-American duo. The general question, however, suffers from no shortage of answers, including impressive phrases about the sanctity of international law and the U.N. Charter, and our historic mission to punish anyone who dares to violate these sacred principles by resorting to force. President Bush declared that "America stands where it always has, against aggression, against those who would use force to replace the rule of law." While some questioned his tactical judgment, there was widespread admiration for the President's honorable stand, and his forthright renewal of our traditional dedication to nonviolence, the rule of law, and the duty of protecting the weak and oppressed. Scholarship weighed in, adding historical and cross-cultural depth. A noted Cambridge University professor of political science wrote in the *Times Literary Supplement* (London) that "Our traditions, fortunately, prove to have at their core universal values, while theirs are sometimes hard to distinguish with the naked eye from rampant (and heavily armed) nihilism. In the Persian Gulf today, President Bush could hardly put it more bluntly. . . ."[30] Says Chomsky, "Others too basked in self-adulation, though it was conceded that we had not always applied our traditional values with complete consistency, failures that we are sure to rectify as soon as we have finished with the business at hand."[31]

Even democracy, our most sacred of principles, the very raison d'être for so much foreign and domestic policy, is but a label employed to legitimize specifically undemocratic actions.

Without proceeding in detail, if you look through these things, here's what you discover. Decision-making on major issues is now vested in international institutions which are so remote from public influence, that the public has no idea what's going on. I mean, in the case of NAFTA, incidentally the Labor Advisory Committee report was never reported in the press, right, I'd be surprised if any of you know about it, here's a case where the government radically violated the law, demonstrated utter contempt for the democratic process, rammed through a secret executive agreement of enormous influence, wouldn't even let the one popular group that is supposed to see it by law, the labor-based group, even look at it, they write the report, and then the press censors it. All right, here we have the ultimate in the destruction of democracy, the ideal that everybody's been dreaming of. Not only is the rabble excluded, they don't influence policy, but they don't know what's in policy, and finally they don't know that they don't know. Virtually nobody knows that they don't know what is going on. Well, you know, now we've reached the ultimate. That's the ultimate possibility in the destruction of democracy.[32]

Chomsky also insists that the whole charade of U.S. politics, that it speaks of democracy and the rule of law even as it acts against the precepts of both, is upheld by an obedient rather than critical media.

The first, and one of the most revealing, is Nicaragua. Recall that just as the Wall fell, the White House and Congress announced with great clarity that unless Nicaraguans voted as we told them, the terrorist war and the embargo that was strangling the country would continue. Washington also voted (alone with Israel) against a UN General Assembly resolution calling on it once again to observe international law and call off these illegal actions; unthinkable of course, so the press continued to observe its vow of silence. When Nicaraguans met their obligations a few months later, joy was unrestrained. At the dissident extreme, Anthony Lewis hailed Washington's "experiment in peace and democracy," which gives "fresh testimony to the power of Jefferson's idea: government with the consent of the governed. . . . To say so seems romantic, but then we live in a romantic age." Across the spectrum there was rejoicing over the latest of the "happy series of democratic surprises," as *Time* magazine expressed the uniform view while outlining the methods used to achieve our Jeffersonian ideals: to "wreck the economy and prosecute a long and deadly proxy war until the exhausted natives overthrow the unwanted government themselves," with a cost to us that is "minimal," leaving the victim "with wrecked bridges, sabotaged power stations, and ruined farms," and providing Washington's candidate with "a winning issue," ending the "impoverishment of the people of Nicaragua."[33]

The lesson is clear; if you are a powerful state, you resort to international law when it best serves some higher purpose, like profits, and you ignore it when your objectives are better served through force. This of course gives the world's superpowers obvious advantages in dictating the shape of contemporary policies around the world, over and above the force that they have solely on the basis of their own financial and military resources. There are systems of restraint, even against superpowers, such as the World Court; but they do not necessarily meet up to the challenges of the powerful, as history has demonstrated:

The World Court did not take up the charge of aggression in the Nicaragua case. The reasons are instructive, and of quite considerable contemporary relevance. Nicaragua's case was presented by the distinguished Harvard University law professor Abram Chayes, former legal adviser to the State Department. The Court rejected a large part of his case on the grounds that in accepting World Court jurisdiction in 1946, the US had entered a reservation excluding itself from prosecution under multilateral treaties, including the UN Charter. The Court therefore restricted its deliberations to customary international law and a bilateral US-Nicaragua treaty, so that the more serious charges were excluded. Even on these very narrow grounds, the Court charged Washington with "unlawful use of force"—in lay language, international terrorism—and ordered it to terminate the crimes and pay substantial reparations. The Reaganites reacted by escalating the war, also officially endorsing attacks by their terrorist forces against "soft targets," undefended civilian targets. The terrorist war left the country in ruins, with a death toll equivalent to 2.25 million in US per capita terms, more than the total of all wartime casualties in US history combined. After the shattered country fell back under US control, it declined to further misery. It is now the second poorest country in Latin America after Haiti—and by accident, also second after Haiti in intensity of US intervention in the past century. The standard way to lament these tragedies is to say that Haiti and Nicaragua are "battered by storms of their own making," to quote the *Boston Globe*, at the liberal extreme of American journalism. Guatemala ranks third both in misery and intervention, more storms of their own making.[34]

This condemnation by the World Court is frequently recalled by Chomsky as an archetypical example of how the United States spins stories about its role and functioning on the international legal scene:

Amy Goodman: Noam Chomsky, you have written about the U.S. as being the only country in the world to be convicted in the World Court of terrorism. And this had to do with the bombing of the Nicaraguan harbor, which took place under Reagan. Can you talk about that?

Noam Chomsky: Yeah. That, too, is a little misleading. Nicaragua was hoping to end the confrontation through legal means, through diplomatic means.

Amy Goodman: I mean the mining of the harbor.

Noam Chomsky: Yes, the mining of the harbors. They decided to—they asked a legal team headed by a very distinguished American international lawyer, A. Chayes, professor of law at Harvard who had long government service, and that legal team decided to construct an extremely narrow case. So, they kept to matters that were totally uncontroversial, as the U.S. conceded like the mining of the harbors, but it was only a toothpick on a mountain. They picked the narrowest point in the hope that they could get a judgment from the World Court, which would lead the United States to back off from the whole international terrorist campaign, and they did win a judgment from the court, which ordered the U.S. to terminate any actions, any violent actions against Nicaragua, which went way beyond mining of the harbors. That was the least of it. So, yes, that was the narrow content of the court decision, although, if you read the decision, the court decision that goes well beyond, they're all conscious of the much wider terrorist campaign, but the Harvard—the Chayes run legal team didn't bring it up for good reasons. Because they didn't want any controversy at the court hearings about the facts. There was no controversy about that, since it was conceded. However, it should be read as a much broader indictment, and a very important one. I mean, the term that was used by the court was "unlawful use of force," which is the technical term for the informal notion, international terrorism. There's no legal definition of international terrorism in the international domain. So I bet it was in effect a condemnation of international terrorism over a much broader domain. However, we should bear in mind, it's important for us, that horrible as the Nicaragua war was, it wasn't the worst. Guatemala and El Salvador were worse. I suggest that in Nicaragua, the reason was that in Nicaragua, the population at least had an army to defend it. In El Salvador and Guatemala, the terrorist forces attacking the population were the army and the other security forces. There was no one to bring a case to the World Court that can be brought by governments, not by peasants being slaughtered.[35]

To return to Rocker's view, these laws invoked by the World Court are ingrained within the classical liberal conception of law as put forth by the likes of Rousseau or Humboldt, and then upheld in later periods by those who have combated the rise of arbitrary, discretionary, administrative, and totalitarian law. It is interesting that prevailing opinions about anarchy exclude the possibility that it could have a legalistic side, just as prevailing opinions suggest that an anarchist society would be necessarily technologically retrograde. This is the type of status quo opinion that accompanies other great proclamations, like the so-called end of history, a convenient motto for supporters of capitalism in its present form:

If we take the trouble to distinguish doctrine from reality, we find that the political and economic principles that have prevailed are remote from those that are proclaimed. One may also be skeptical about the prediction that they are "the wave of the future," bringing history to a happy end. The same "end of history" has confidently been proclaimed many times in the past, always wrongly. And with all the sordid continuities, an optimistic soul can discern slow progress, realistically I think. In the advanced industrial countries, and often elsewhere, popular struggles today can start from a higher plane and with greater expectations than those of the past. And international solidarity can take new and more constructive forms as the great majority of the people of the world come to understand that their interests are pretty much the same and can be advanced by working together. There is no more reason now than there has ever been to believe that we are constrained by mysterious and unknown social laws, not simply decisions made within institutions that are subject to human will—human institutions, which have to face the test of legitimacy, and if they do not meet it, can be replaced by others that are more free and more just, as often in the past.[36]

Is this naive? Is this utopian? There are concrete examples that suggest that significant moves forward can be made, and that the capacity for populations of being "defooled"[37] is great: "Skeptics who dismiss such thoughts as utopian and naive have only to cast their eyes on what has happened right here in the last few years, an inspiring tribute to what the human spirit can achieve, and its limitless prospects—lessons that the world desperately needs to learn, and that should guide the next steps in the continuing struggle for justice and freedom here too, as the people [for example] of South Africa, fresh from one great victory, turn to the still more difficult tasks that lie ahead."[38]

Law's Rational and Moral Authority

One way to think about these ideas relates to Chomsky's desire to appeal to a "higher authority" in the determination of appropriate legal decisions. This authority is rational, humanistic, and is roughly in line with what classical legal thinkers describe when they talk about law. To the degree that international law is an example of this type of law, then it is legitimate, and worth defending, says Chomsky. The point, once again, is that we must distinguish between the international law that simply reflects the power of those who write and pass it and the international law that is in accord with some higher values, that is, classical liberal principles. The Michel Foucault–Noam Chomsky debate is a source for clarifying this distinction:

Foucault: Are you committing this act in virtue of an ideal justice, or because the class struggle makes it useful and necessary? Do you refer to ideal justice, that's my problem.

Chomsky: Again, very often when I do something which the state regards as illegal, I regard it as legal: that is, I regard the state as criminal. But in some instances that's not true. Let me be quite concrete about it and move from the area of class war to imperialist war, where the situation is somewhat clearer and easier. Take international law, a very weak instrument as we know, but nevertheless one that incorporates some very interesting principles. Well, international law is, in many respects, the instrument of the powerful: it is a creation of states and their representatives. In developing the presently existing body of international law, there was no participation by mass movements of peasants. The structure of international law reflects that fact; that is, international law permits much too wide a range of forceful intervention in support of existing power structures that define themselves as states against the interests of masses of people who happen to be organized in opposition to states. Now that's a fundamental defect of international law and I think one is justified in opposing that aspect of international law as having no validity, as having no more validity than the divine right of kings. It's simply an instrument of the powerful to retain their power.

But, in fact, international law is not solely of that kind. And in fact there are interesting elements of international law, for example, embedded in the Nuremberg principles and the United Nations Charter, which permit, in fact, I believe, require the citizen to act against his own state in ways which the state will falsely regard as criminal. Nevertheless, he's acting legally, because international law also happens to prohibit the threat or use of force in international affairs, except under some very narrow circumstances, of which, for example, the war in Vietnam is not one. This means that in the particular case of the Vietnam War, which interests me most, the American state is acting in a criminal capacity. And the people have the right to stop criminals from committing murder. Just because the criminal happens to call your action illegal when you try to stop him, it doesn't mean it is illegal. A perfectly clear case of that is the present case of the Pentagon Papers in the United States, which, I suppose, you know about. Reduced to its essentials and forgetting legalisms, what is happening is that the state is trying to prosecute people for exposing its crimes. That's what it amounts to. Now, obviously that's absurd, and one must pay no attention whatsoever to that distortion of any reasonable judicial process. Furthermore, I think that the existing system of law even explains why it is absurd. But if it didn't, we would then have to oppose that system of law.

So Chomsky measures U.S. government (or other government) action against the "higher authority" of international law.

This central feature of the accords is redundant, since such actions are barred by a higher authority, by international law and treaty, hence by the supreme law of the land under the U.S. Constitution, which we are enjoined to celebrate this year. The fact was underscored by the World Court in June 1986 as it condemned the United States for its "unlawful use of force" against Nicaragua and called upon it to desist from these crimes. Congress responded by voting $100 million of aid and freeing the CIA to direct the attack and to use its own funds on an unknown scale. The U.S. vetoed a UN Security Council resolution calling on all

states to observe international law and voted against a General Assembly resolution to the same effect, joined by Israel and El Salvador. On November 12,
1987, the General Assembly again called for "full and immediate compliance"
with the World Court decision. This time only Israel joined with the U.S. in
opposing adherence to international law, another blow to the Central American
accords, unreported by the national press as usual.[39]

This higher authority is also a moral authority, something worth fighting for but something that is easily cast aside in favor of self-interest. A
more recent example comes from Chomsky's 1999 assessment of the U.S.
government bombing of Iraq, described in *Frontline: India's National
Magazine.*[40]

Although I agree that Saddam Hussein remains a serious threat to peace, there
happens to be a way to deal with that question, one that has been established
under international law. That procedure is the foundation of international law
and international order and is also the supreme law of the land in the United
States. If a country, say the United States, feels that a threat is posed to peace,
it is to approach the Security Council, which has the sole authority to react to
that threat. The Security Council is required to pursue all peaceful means to deal
with the threat to peace, and if it determines that all such means have failed, it
may then specifically authorize the use of force. Nothing else is permitted under
international law, except with regard to the question, here irrelevant, of self-
defense. The U.S. and Britain have simply announced, very clearly and loudly,
that they are violent criminal states that are intent on destroying totally the fabric
of international law, a fabric that has been built up laboriously over many years.
They have announced that they will do as they please and will use violence as
they please, independently of what anyone else thinks. In my view, that is the
sole significance of the bombing and is probably the reason for it.

This is true in terms of national interests, but it is also true of individual behavior; you abide by the law when it is in your favor, you ignore
it and "throw dirt" when it isn't, as is clear from his discussion of the
Harvard Law Professor Alan Dershowitz's approach:

Turning to Dershowitz, there's partly the same story. Again, he knows that he
can't respond to what I say. He doesn't have the knowledge or the competence
to deal with the issues. Therefore, the idea is to try to shut it up by throwing as
much slime as you can. There's a famous story attributed to Sam Ervin, a conservative Senator, who once said that as a young lawyer he had learned that if
the law is against you, concentrate on the facts. If the facts are against you, concentrate on the law. And if both the facts and the law are against you, denounce
your opposing counsel. Dershowitz is not very bright, but he understands that
much. If you can't answer on the facts and if you can't answer on the principles,
you better throw dirt. In his case there happens to also be a personal reason.

He's been on a personal jihad for the last twenty years, ever since I exposed him for lying outright in a vicious personal attack on a leading Israeli civil libertarian. Despite pretenses, he's strongly opposed to civil liberties. Using his position as a Harvard law professor, he referred to what the Israeli courts had determined. But he was just lying flat outright. This was in the *Boston Globe* (April 29, 1973). I wrote a short letter refuting it (May 17). He then came back (on May 25) accusing everybody of lying and challenging me to quote from the court records. He never believed I had them, but of course I did. I quoted the court records in response (June 5). He then tried to brazen it out again. It finally ended up with my sending the transcript of the court records to the *Globe* ombudsman, who didn't know what to do any more with people just taking opposite positions. I translated them for him, and suggested that he pick his own expert to check the translations. The ombudsman finally told Dershowitz they wouldn't publish anymore letters of his because he had been caught flat out lying about it. Ever since then he's been trying to get even, so there's just one hysterical outburst after another. That's not surprising, either. He's basically a clown. In that case there's a personal issue overlaying the political issue, which is much more interesting. This personal stuff is not interesting. But if you look at the Anti-Defamation League or the Berkeley professors, and there are plenty of others, it's the Sam Ervin story. You know you can't deal with the material. Either you ignore it, or if you can't ignore it, then defame the speaker. That's the only way you can deal with it if you don't have the brains or the knowledge or you just know your position can't be defended. I think that's understandable, and in a sense you can appreciate it. That's just the hallmark of the commissar.[41]

In the way that Dershowitz's actions are described here, law becomes a tool, generally of the powerful, which is to be invoked or ignored as best seems fit for the case at hand, a sign of the arbitrariness against which anarchist law as I am describing it here struggles.

Natural versus Positive Law

Rocker's approach to anarchism and law relies very strongly upon another distinction, also present in Chomsky's work but less overtly, between "natural law" and "positive law," the former being those laws that are in line with the fundamental needs of a given society, as demonstrated over a prolonged period of time, and the latter being law established by government authority and therefore more clearly linked to class and power interests in society. As we have seen, consecutive U.S. administrations have invoked or used both, as a matter of convenience. For example, "the [U.S.] media had dismissed the World Court as a 'hostile forum' whose decisions are irrelevant, while liberal advocates of world order explained that the U.S. must disregard the Court decision. With this reaction, U.S. elites clearly articulate their self-image: the United States is a lawless terrorist state, which stands above the law and is entitled to undertake violence, as it chooses, in support of its objectives. The reaction to the 'indispensable element' of the Central American accords merely reiterated that conviction."[42]

Positive law is supported when history is forgotten, maligned, or misinterpreted, which occurs with amazing regularity in the popular media:

In its new-found zeal for international law and the United Nations, the *New York Times* repeatedly turned to one heroic figure: Daniel Patrick Moynihan. He was brought forth as an expert witness on "the new spirit of unanimity at the United Nations," explaining that there were "some pretty egregious violations of international law in the past," but now "the major powers have convergent interests and the mechanism of the U.N. is there waiting to be used." His "firm espousal of international law" was lauded in a review of his study *The Law of Nations*. The reviewer took note of his "sardonic, righteous anger," which recalls "the impassioned professor who suspects no one's listening" while he is "clearly fuming that an idea as morally impeccable as international law is routinely disregarded as disposable and naive." In a *Times Magazine* story, we learn further that Moynihan is "taking particular delight" in being proven right in his long struggle to promote international law and the United Nations system, "abstractions" that "matter dearly" to him. At last, everybody is "riding Moynihan's hobbyhorse" instead of ignoring the principles he has upheld with such conviction for so many years. No longer need Moynihan "revel in his martyrdom." Now "history has caught up with him." Omitted from these accolades was a review of Moynihan's record as U.N. Ambassador, when he had the opportunity to put his principles into practice. In a cablegram to Henry Kissinger on January 23, 1976, he reported the "considerable progress" that had been made by his arm-twisting tactics at the U.N. "toward a basic foreign policy goal, that of breaking up the massive blocs of nations, mostly new nations, which for so long have been arrayed against us in international forums and in diplomatic encounters generally." Moynihan cited two relevant cases: his success in undermining a U.N. reaction to the Indonesian invasion of East Timor and to Moroccan aggression in the Sahara, both supported by the U.S., the former with particular vigor. He had more to say about these matters in his memoir of his years at the United Nations, where he describes frankly his role as Indonesia invaded East Timor in December, 1975: "The United States wished things to turn out as they did, and worked to bring this about. The Department of State desired that the United Nations prove utterly ineffective in whatever measures it undertook. This task was given to me, and I carried it forward with no inconsiderable success." He adds that within a few weeks some 60,000 people had been killed, "10 percent of the population, almost the proportion of casualties experienced by the Soviet Union during the Second World War."[43]

Recording facts of history is critical here, as is clear from "Chomsky Answers Some Queries About Moral Principals and International Law."[44] This is a highly pertinent piece for this discussion because it speaks to questions of what we are protecting when we are acting in the interest of human rights, for here Chomsky appeals to discussions of immanent qualities and "moral truisms" which hold for "any person," in this case X. "The first truism is that X is primarily responsible for the likely consequences of his/her own actions, or inaction. The second is that X's concern for moral issues (crimes, etc.) should vary in accordance with X's ability to have an effect (though that is of course not the only factor). The two principles tend to correlate, even coincide, in the conclusions that X will draw—that is, if X is a moral agent, someone worth paying attention to." This is crucial and links up to Chomsky's appeal to rational thinking and what is known in postmodern circles, usually for derogatory reasons, as the Cartesian subject—that is, the fixed, consistent subject who transcends time and circumstance.

Chomsky distinguishes here between different actions according to their "moral significance"; for instance, "it is highly worthwhile to attend to U.S.-backed atrocities (say, in Turkey, or Colombia, or East Timor, or Iraq, or many other places), because we are responsible for the crimes and can do a lot about them—very easily; namely, by withdrawing our (often decisive) support. But attention to [say] Pol Pot's crimes, while a worthy enterprise (if done honestly, which was rarely the case), had little if any moral significance because there was no hint of a proposal as to what to do about them—and when they were terminated, the US was infuriated and severely punished the criminals (the Vietnamese) who carried out the clearest case of 'humanitarian intervention' since World War II." This leads to the point in his work about the inconsistency of the American "moral stance," which leads to the following: "We understand these truisms very well when we are thinking of others. Thus no one in the U.S. was impressed when Soviet commissars railed about U.S. crimes; we were much impressed, however, when dissidents in the USSR condemned Soviet crimes. The reasons were the two moral truisms just mentioned (which, as is commonly the case, coincided in their implications)." This is why Chomsky focuses upon American policy, and comes out against, for example, *The Black Book of Communism*, which catalogued crimes of Bolshevik and Maoist regimes; first, people who had paid attention to critiques by (yet again) Rocker in the 1930s, or Pannekoek, or Luxemburg, or so many others who recognized the actual power issues of the Soviet Union or, later on, of Maoism, knew very well the atrocities of these powers. More important, though, is his second point, which is that "one of the hardest things to do is to look into the mirror. It is also often the most important thing to do, because of the moral truisms. And there are very powerful institutions (the entire doctrinal system, in all of its aspects) that seek to protect people from engaging in this difficult and crucially important task. Every society has its dissidents and its commissars, and it's close to a historical law that the commissars are highly praised and the dissidents bitterly condemned—within the society, that is; on the other hand for official enemies the situation is reversed."

The other point that he has raised frequently, and also relates to a book like *The Black Book of Communism*,[45] which does, after all, condemn atrocities, is that "focusing attention on the crimes of others often gives us a nice warm feeling of being 'good people,' so different from those 'bad people.' That's particularly true when there is nothing much we can do about the crimes of others except to help make them far worse, from a distance. Then we can simply wail without cost to ourselves. Looking at our own crimes is much harder, and for those willing to do it, often carries costs, sometimes very severe costs." As we've seen, Chomsky has himself paid some of these debts when he has defended this principle in both the Faurisson and the Pol Pot Affairs.

Rule of Law versus Exceptions in Law

The statements Chomsky makes about classical liberalism are often challenged in the current postmodern setting, in which subjectivity, the possibility of communication, and a sense of common values are called into question on the basis of the indeterminate and unstable subject. The idea that "mutual agreements" could exist between "free and equal" individuals, necessarily constituted as stable subjects with consistent and knowable needs and desires, and upheld by international organs such as international law, has been everywhere upset by postmodern and poststructuralist thought. This is not an area into which I will venture at any length, but instead would suggest that the reader refer to the debate between those who, from a postmodern perspective, uphold the idea that we need ample discretion in law[46] and those who consider such a heavily discretion-based system as a menace to fundamental rights and freedoms,[47] and thus consider that it was no accident that the early advocate of this approach, Karl Schmitt, was the architect of Nazi law.

In line with this anti-postmodern idea that we need stable, consistent, and founded laws that would be applied in a formal fashion across time and space, William Scheuerman suggests in *Between the Norm and the Exception: The Frankfurt School and the Rule of Law*[48] that the tendency in most Western states is to move away from a classical liberal notion of rule of law, with its insistence upon consistent and universal legal norms, and toward a form of law that "takes an increasingly amorphous and indeterminate structure as vague legal standards like 'in good faith' or 'in the public interest,' proliferate" (1). Scheuerman claims that Franz Neumann and Otto Kirchheimer, who were both associated with the Frankfurt Institute for Social Research in the late 1930s and 1940s, saw in this trend a danger that was confirmed in the reliance of the Nazi state upon the work of scholars such as Carl Schmitt and Friedrich Hayek for the elaboration of a legal system appropriate for Nazi Germany. Schmitt's idea was to infuse huge state or legal discretion into cases as a way of combating formal law, an idea that has been revitalized of late by the left (especially Paul Piccone and G. L. Ulman in *Telos*), the right (William Buckley and Paul Gottfried in the *National Review*), by various postmodern historians and writers, and by mainstream writers including Joseph Bendersky and George Schwab. Scheuerman's book has implications beyond either a social history of Germany or a more adequate appraisal of the Frankfurt School, because he discusses the inherent dangers of a legal system that relies upon situation-specific administrative decrees, or upon interpretations of claims that depend upon notions such as custom, indwelling right, morality, fairness, or discretion. The danger of "extensive state intervention in an unprecedented variety of spheres of social and economic activity" is that the division between state and society is undermined, reducing the degree to which government action can be deemed predictable or, to use Rocker's conception, legitimate.

The link to Chomsky is found in Scheuerman's concern that state action is directed toward solidifying its power and expanding its influence, and that the classical liberal conception of law is one of the only consistent and reliable counterweights to this move. This suggests that the state's desire to dismantle formal mechanisms of law is not in the interest of fairness, or even postmodern recognition of unstable subjects, but, logically and obviously, in the interests of consolidating illegitimate authority, upheld by force. Some historically disadvantaged groups, such as feminists, disagree and argue that the demise of formal law allows a space for the development of an egalitarian legal alternative that would be based upon some form of "indwelling right" or custom. Neumann and Kirchheimer supported the rule of law and opposed the Schmitt (now postmodern) viewpoint because they upheld a belief that "state action must be based on cogent general rules." In their view, which is supported by Scheuerman, "only clear general norms restrain and bind the activities of the state apparatus, provide a minimum of legal security, and counteract the dangers of a 'creeping authoritarianism'" (2).

As Scheuerman recalls, rather than relying upon legislators or bureaucrats to right the wrongs of modern society, Neumann and Kirchheimer supported a law that would regulate such wrongs because "a genuinely democratic society requires a high degree of legal regularity and predictability to achieve autonomous and uncoerced political deliberation and action" (3). This predictability is for Neumann especially strongly linked to the idea of a legal norm that overrides all other decisions, and also, to invoke Chomsky, precludes the use of force to overturn norm-based legal decisions. Neumann defines this norm as "a rule which does not mention particular cases or individual persons but which is issued in advance to apply to all cases and all persons in the abstract; and . . . as specific as possible in its general formulation."[49] Scheuerman is very sympathetic to this approach, although wary of some of its implications for the present welfare state when he writes: "Neumann concedes that this model can have only limited applicability in a setting necessitating extensive governmental action, and that cogent formal law today is necessarily replaced by vague legal standards and various forms of equity law and bargaining seemingly essential to the contemporary welfare state and its reliance on unprecedented forms of state intervention. Complex state activity requires equally complex (nonformal) modes of law" (207). So even if it could be put into play, the rule of law, according to Scheuerman "can never be rendered perfect, and legal gaps, exceptions, and irregularities are unavoidable side-effects of a social setting having particularistic power concentrations necessarily regulated by clandestine individual measure and administrative commands" (207–208). What Scheuerman does consider a realizable goal is that irregular law be exercised in a rational fashion. This of course is another problem both for the advocates of a postmodern approach to law and those who question Chomsky's own appeals to Enlightenment thinking, Cartesian subjects, rationality, and legal norms such as freedom or responsibility.

Freedom and Responsibility

The fact is—and this is the link back to Rudolph Rocker and his conception of the anarchist society—freedom also creates the responsibilities that come naturally paired with liberation. Thus, for Rocker, "Godwin's work became at the same time the epilogue of that great intellectual movement which had inscribed on its banner the greatest possible limitation of the power of the state, and the starting point for the development of the ideas of libertarian socialism" (148). Reason and responsibility become the bases for individual decision making, not authority and power. And for this conception of law Rocker draws upon various sources, including Richard Hooker, who "maintained that it is unworthy of a man to submit blindly, like a beast, to the compulsion of any kind of authority without consulting his own reason" (140);[50] John Locke, who maintained "that common and binding relationships existed between primitive men, emanating from their social disposition and from considerations of reason" (142); and to others who "aimed to set limits to hereditary power and to widen the individual's sphere of independence," including Lord Shaftesbury, Bernard de Mandeville, William Temple, Baron de Montesquieu, John Bolingbroke, Francois-Marie Voltaire, George-Luis Buffon, David Hume, Henry Linguet, and Adam Smith. Most of them, writes Rocker, "inspired by biological and related science, had abandoned the concept of an original social contract" and "recognised the state as the political instrument of privileged minorities in society for the rulership of the great masses" (142). Classical liberalism upholds individual rights against the privileged, partly on account of the world from which it comes, says Chomsky:

One may argue, as some historians do, that these principles lost their force as the national territory was conquered and settled, the native population driven out or exterminated. Whatever one's assessment of those years, by the late 19th century the founding doctrines took on a new and much more oppressive form. When Madison spoke of "rights of persons," he meant humans. But the growth of the industrial economy, and the rise of corporate forms of economic enterprise, led to a completely new meaning of the term. In a current official document, " 'Person' is broadly defined to include any individual, branch, partnership, associated group, association, estate, trust, corporation or other organization (whether or not organized under the laws of any State), or any government entity," a concept that doubtless would have shocked Madison and others with intellectual roots in the Enlightenment and classical liberalism—pre-capitalist, and anti-capitalist in spirit. These radical changes in the conception of human rights and democracy were not introduced primarily by legislation, but by judicial decisions and intellectual commentary. Corporations, which previously had been considered artificial entities with no rights, were accorded all the rights of persons, and far more, since they are "immortal persons," and "persons" of extraordinary wealth and power. Furthermore, they were no longer bound to the specific purposes designated by State charter, but could act as they chose, with few constraints. The intellectual backgrounds for granting such extraordinary rights to "collectivist legal entities" lie in neo-Hegelian doctrines that also underlie Bolshevism and fascism: the idea that organic entities have rights over and above those of persons. Conservative legal scholars bitterly opposed these innovations, recognizing that they undermine the traditional idea that rights inhere in individuals, and undermine market principles as well. But the new forms of authoritarian rule were institutionalized, and along with them, the legitimation of wage labor, which was considered hardly better than slavery in mainstream American thought through much of the 19th century, not only by the rising labor movement but also by such figures as Abraham Lincoln, the Republican Party, and the establishment media.[51]

Rocker and Chomsky emphasize individuality and creativity, both of which will flourish in the antiauthoritarian societies described. But so too will a higher conception of responsibility and ethics for, as Rocker writes, "all schemes having their roots in natural rights are based on the desire to free man from bondage to social institutions of compulsion in order that he may attain to consciousness of his humanity and no longer bow before any authority which would deprive him of the right to his own thoughts and actions" (143). So, like Chomsky, Rocker is animated by a sense that great popular movements should look to overthrow institutions of power and authority in favor of free associations in which the seeds of freedom, and everything that grows along with them, will germinate vigorously. This is not simply a political objective but a personal one as well, for, as Rocker (like Godwin, Warren, Proudhon, and Bakunin) recognized, "one cannot be free either politically or personally so long as one is in the economic servitude of another and cannot escape from this condition" (167).

The anarchist conception does not accept that people should be compelled to act, even if toward desirable ends; compulsion no matter what the goal is a power relation that will ultimately separate people. Compulsion, says Rocker, "lacks the inner drive of all social unions—the understanding which recognises the facts and the sympathy which comprehends the feeling of the fellow man because it feels itself related to him. By subjecting men to a common compulsion one does not bring them closer to one another, rather one creates estrangements between them and breeds impulses of selfishness and separation. Social ties have permanence and completely fulfil their purpose only when they are based on good will and spring from the needs of men. Only under such conditions is a relationship possible where social union and the freedom of the individual are so closely intergrown that they can no longer be recognised as separate entities" (246). So what we have here is the anarchist conception, the freedom to act, create, and to enter into relationships of love, compassion, and responsibility based upon shared and common concerns and mediated by independent judicial norms, rather than the ability to act only in accordance with existing power structures. So the next question is, how does one learn to be free? What type of education is appropriate for a society in which ideals of interrelationship based upon free associations are to be the norm rather than the exception? How can we find common customs that could serve not only as the basis of our natural law but also as the impetus for our conceiving of ethical behavior in an antiauthoritarian world? And even if we do promulgate such norms and natural laws, how do we convey to all individuals their rights and obligations therein? In other words, is there a way to undertake effective teaching, which inspires the knowledge and freedom we have described here? It is to these questions that we shall now turn, as we consider ideas of inspiring people to be creative and free.

5

Effective Teaching: From Catalyst to Institute Professor

If I think back about my experience, there's a dark spot there. That's what school-ing generally is, I suppose. It's a period of regimentation and control, part of which involves direct indoctrination, providing a system of false beliefs. But more importantly, I think, is the manner and style of preventing and blocking inde-pendent and creative thinking and imposing hierarchies and competitiveness and the need to excel, not in the sense of doing as well as you can, but doing better than the next person. Schools vary, of course, but I think that those features are commonplace. I know that they're not necessary, because, for example, the school I went to as a child wasn't like that at all. I think schools could be run quite differently. That would be very important, but I really don't think that any society based on authoritarian hierarchic institutions would tolerate such a school system for long. (From an interview with James Peck in *The Chomsky Reader*, p. 6)

I'm really not interested in persuading people. What I like to do is help people persuade themselves.[1]

Discussions about the good society lead naturally to questions about education: What role should education play as a catalyst for social change? What kind of education is appropriate given the present socio-historical conditions? What form should education take if we ever make significant advances toward the erection of a good society? Are there uni-versal principles that should apply across time and space to the domain of pedagogy? What do we know about human nature that can inspire within us appropriate methods to stimulate learning?

These questions are especially problematic for anyone sympathetic to the ideals of anarchy, which in virtually all of their manifestations, real or imagined, have been consistently opposed to the exercise of arbi-trary or illegitimate authority. The problem is, authority in theory and

www.PostmodernHaircut.com
The Adventures of...
NOAM CHOMSKY
... and his dog Predicate!
By Jeffrey Weston
So, what are you doing?
I'm finishing up some notes for my next university lecture.
Prepping for another Yawn-Fest, eh?
No. The message makes what I have to say interesting, not the medium.
Is that why I can play your audio CD's on shuffle and they still makes sense?
Well, maybe I could spice things up a bit..
I could use an overhead. Oh! Oh! And I could have a break and everyone can help themselves to some free water.
OK, replace "overhead" with "DJ", "water" with "beer" and "break" with "dance party".
I don't think that's really my style.
Too late. I've already started mixing the delicious beats.
This Tuesday at the University Auditorium...
M.I.T. Professor
Noam Chomsky
with
Dj Predicate
AND HIS FUNKY-PINK
FORIEGN POLICY -BEATS
NOAM CHOMSKY
with
and his
Funky-Pink-Robo-Beats

practice has always been an integral part of most teacher-student relationships, to varying degrees, if only because one party to the relationship is charged with transmitting some form of knowledge to another
who thereby finds him or herself in a more passive or receptive mode or
in a subjugated position relative to the other. The other factor is the
nature of what has been taught, which tends to revolve around obedience, duty, nationalism, and respect for the status quo. The questions I
pose here are: How have anarchists and others from the milieu we have
described construed the issue of education, and how does their work bear
upon what Chomsky considers an appropriate approach to education in
contemporary society?

Education As Catalyst

I suggest that we consider the idea that anarchist education has historically been considered as a catalyst rather than an outright exchange or
infusion of new ideas, and that many contemporary anarchists hold this
idea up as a kind of ideal in their own pedagogical practices. My favorite,
indeed archetypical, example of this idea of the anarchist as catalyst can
be found in the form of a story told about Giuseppe Fanelli in the pro-
logue to Murray Bookchin's 1977 landmark book *The Spanish Anarchists: The Heroic Years 1868–1936*.[2] Indeed, Bookchin seems to have
liked the story so much that he repeats it variously, in "Looking Back at
Spain," the introduction to Sam Dolgoff's *The Anarchist Collectives*,[3]
and probably elsewhere as well.

   Bookchin recalls that Gerald Brenan tells this very same "almost
legendary" story "with great relish" in his 1964 book *The Spanish
Labyrinth*, and I've found references to it in Brian Morris's study of
Bakunin, Sam Dolgoff's chapter on "The Rural Collectivist Tradition"
in *The Anarchist Collectives*, Juan Gomez Casas's *Anarchist Organization*,[4] and beyond. Why have so many anarchists latched onto this story
over and above its obvious historical significance, and why indeed does
Bookchin, who considers that "the revolution of 1936 marked the cul-
mination of more than sixty years of anarchist agitation and activity in
Spain" (58), use 1868, the date given to the events described in this story,
as the moment from which all ideals of the revolution emanate? And

why am I suggesting that it is some kind of key to our understanding of the anarchist-education relationship?

The answer lies in the details. In late October 1868, a tall, bearded Giuseppe Fanelli came to Barcelona after a long voyage by train from Geneva. He arrived, and eventually departed from the city "without incident," and indeed "there was nothing in his appearance that would have distinguished him from any other visiting Italian, except perhaps for his height and his intense prepossessing demeanor." Further, Fanelli was poor, and was traveling "on a shoestring" as a kind of emissary for the ideas of Mikhail Bakunin; in short, the visit "should have been a complete fiasco."[5]

It wasn't a fiasco; instead, it marked the beginning of the idea for which so many fought and died through the years leading up to the Spanish Civil War and beyond. This is not because this idea had been clearly conveyed by Fanelli; indeed, he hardly knew a word of Spanish, and he neglected to bring along an interpreter for his talks, so when he did finally address a small group of young workers of the *Fomento de las Artes* [Promotion of the Arts] in Madrid, he resorted to a "freewheeling mixture of French and Italian," through which he successfully communicated his ideas. In fact, "once the tall, lean Italian began to speak, his rapport with the audience was so complete that all barriers of language were quickly swept away. Using a wealth of Latin gestures and tonal expressions, Fanelli managed to convey with electric effect the richness of his libertarian visions and the bitterness of his anger toward human suffering and exploitation. The workers, accustomed to the moderate expressions of Spanish liberals, were stunned" (Bookchin 12). Anselmo Lorenzo, who was present for the talk, recalled that Fanelli's "voice had a metallic tone and was susceptible to all the inflections appropriate to what he was saying, passing rapidly from accents of anger and menace against tyrants and exploiters to take on those of suffering, regret, and consolation, when he spoke of the pains of the exploited, either as one who without suffering them himself understands them, or as one who through his altruistic feelings delights in presenting an ultrarevolutionary ideal of peace and fraternity" (cited in Bookchin 12).

Considered in its detail, this episode tells so much about the ideals of anarchy and about the nature of an anarchist education: Fanelli, poor and unpretentious, committed to decent human values (Bakunin's anarchy), arrives in a place that is to him entirely foreign. He cannot even speak the language of those to whom he is to address his ideas. He speaks to a small group of ordinary working people, who immediately recognize that antiauthoritarian tone and understand the implications of the ideas that are kind-of conveyed as appropriate to their situation. They discuss among themselves, pledge support for the International, and then they use the idea as a catalyst for "what was not only the most widespread workers' and peasants' movement in modern Spain, but the largest Anarchist movement in modern Europe." Fanelli doesn't dictate to them, he doesn't provide intimate details of what form a revolution should take, he doesn't address himself to leaders, and he doesn't tell them that he is going to stick around to lead the people to the new utopia. He speaks as best he can, conveys his commitment, and then goes back home to Italy.

A number of caveats could be added here of course. First, it seems likely that the crowd of workers could understand at least some of what he was saying, given the similarities between Romance languages, notably Spanish and Italian. Second, there's something here that is quite like the stories that date back at least as far as the Middle Ages, when charismatic priests would travel around Europe and inspire worshippers to revelation without speaking their language. But these corollaries do not detract from the story told, for he is after all addressing himself to a very Catholic audience, suggesting that there may be something in their very tradition that made this event not wholly unlikely. But the point is something else; this is a powerful example of anarchist ideals making sense to a crowd of oppressed people looking for alternatives, as though they were sparks in a volatile vial. And this is the impression that Bookchin himself provides when reminiscing, a century later, about this event.

Education against Authority

This is but one side of the picture, however, because the catalyst for new ideas does not meet all the needs of society. Here the story is more complex because it seems that many anarchists are better at saying what education should not be than what it should be. Examples from pivotal historical figures are crucial if we are to understand both alternatives and obstacles to anarchist education and the types of information that an anarchist education should convey. The principle issue relates to the idea of fostering innate abilities and of respect for the classical liberal idea (proposed by Wilhelm von Humboldt among others) that creative work freely undertaken in association with others is the core value of a human life. Conditions must therefore be created to promote this value.

Then there is the issue of earning what is necessary to ensure a high standard of living, the elimination of useless work, and the assurance that all people can be provided for. Mikhail Bakunin, like Peter Kropotkin and Rudolf Rocker (and more recently Noam Chomsky), believe that the teaching of science and technology would be essential to their versions of the good society, because society organized according to the needs of the populace requires the benefits of science and technology. This idea was put into practice by anarchists in Spain who, "with inexpensive, simply written brochures, who brought the French enlightenment and modern scientific theory to the peasantry, not the arrogant liberals or the disdainful Socialists. Together with pamphlets on Bakunin and Kropotkin, the anarchist press published simple accounts of the theories of natural and social evolution and elementary introductions to the secular culture of Europe"[6] (Bookchin 1994). But this teaching was not to come at any price; life has to come first, as Bakunin advocated in his "revolt of life against science, or rather against government by science, not the destruction of science, for that would be a high crime against humanity—but the putting of science in its rightful place" (Bakunin 1973).

Science from this perspective is not to be used to dominate or subvert; instead it is to be brought to the people, so that neither it nor those who practice it are given the chance to rule over society. This idea of bringing education to all persons to better society and further individual needs and abilities rather than controlling them is everywhere present in the writings of anarchists. Being antiauthoritarian, anarchists fear the uses made of education by the ruling classes; Emma Goldman, herself a catalyst for generations of anarchists and feminists, believed that "constitutionalism and democracy are the modern forms of that alleged consent [to the State]; the consent being inoculated and indoctrinated by what is called 'education.' "[7] This indoctrination is everywhere present in contemporary educational institutions, notably the elite schools that train the "commissar" class to assume its role, in many cases against the original intentions of the students plans:

NC: Let me tell you [Michael Albert] a story I once heard from a black civil rights activist who came up to Harvard Law School and was there for a while. This must have been twenty years ago. He once gave a talk and said that kids were coming in to Harvard Law School with long hair and backpacks and social ideals and they were all going to go into public service, law and change the world. That's the first year. He said around April the recruiters come for the summer jobs, the Wall Street firms. Get a cushy summer job and make a ton of money. So the students figure, What the heck? I can put on a tie and jacket and shave for one day, because I need that money and why shouldn't I have it? So they put on a tie and a jacket for that one day and they get the job for the summer. Then they go off for the summer and when they come back in the fall, it's ties and jackets and obedience and a shift of ideology. . . . Sometimes it takes two years; that's overdrawing the point. But those factors are very influential. I've fought it all my life. It's extremely easy to be sucked into the dominant culture. It's very appealing. And the people don't look like bad people. You don't want to sit there and insult them. You try to be friends, and you are. You begin to conform, to adapt, to smooth off the harsher edges. Education at a place like Harvard is in fact largely geared to that, to a remarkable extent.[8]

So it is a question of whom education serves; if it serves the ruling powers or industry or the State, then it must be attacked or challenged, as Paul Goodman advocated in his 1957 classic *Growing Up Absurd* (although Goodman's conclusion that children should not attend schools does not accord with the positive sides of education described further on). A humorous example of what is deserving of our scorn and attacks comes from Chomsky in one of his more provocative moments: "Take the question of pornography: I mean, undoubtedly women suffer from pornography, but in terms of people suffering from speech in the world, that's hardly even a speck. People suffer a lot more from the teaching of free-trade economics in colleges—huge numbers of people in the Third World are dying because of the stuff that's taught in American economics departments, I'm talking about tens of millions. That's harm. Should we therefore pass a law that says that the government ought to decide what you teach in economics departments? Absolutely not, then it would just get worse. They'd force everyone to teach this stuff" [!][9]

If, on the other hand, education helps individuals meet their needs, encourages learning-by-doing with real problems, and fosters creative growth and understanding, then it is, or at least could be, legitimate. And, of course, education must be made accessible to all children, one advance that was dramatically made in the early years of the Spanish anarchist groups.

The other thread that links various anarchist thinkers with regard to useful forms of education is the belief in rationality and common sense—partly to counteract theology, idealist metaphysics, superstition, and the dangers of idealized nationalist accounts of society's evolution, and partly to place the power of education into the hands of the people rather than into some vanguard or authoritarian figure. Generally speaking, we should be wary of authority figures because they tend to promote particular interests, their own; as Kropotkin wrote in *Mutual Aid*: "Were not the teachings of men of science, and even of a notable portion of the clergy, up to a quite recent time, teachings of distrust, spite and almost hatred towards the poorer classes? Did not science teach us that since serfdom has been abolished, no one need be poor unless for his own vices? And how few in the Church had the courage to blame the children-killers, while the great numbers taught that the sufferings of the poor, and even the slavery of the Negroes, were part of the Divine Plan!" (290).[10]

As such, and consistent with contemporary progressive thinkers like Murray Bookchin, Noam Chomsky, or Howard Zinn, or precursors such as Peter Kropotkin, Mikhail Bakunin, Emma Goldman, or Rudolph Rocker, there is in most anarchist discussions concerning education an implicit belief in rationalism, which suggests that we can use our reason in a consistent fashion, and that we can come to recognize through the application of our reason to given situations the strengths or weaknesses of a given position. This brings us back to Fanelli, for it speaks to the power of words as catalysts for social change and amelioration, not with reference to higher authority, but with regard to our own understanding of the world. It is with these kinds of assumptions that Chomsky's approach is herein described, which leads to the important questions of anarchy and education in the contemporary world.

The Midwives of Social Change

An anarchist education, therefore, is an antiauthoritarian education that works to promote the interests of individuals and collectives by giving them the confidence to believe in themselves, and the tools to act upon their creative spirit and their impulses toward mutual aid. As Bakunin states, the youth should "leave this dying world" of "universities, academies and schools in which you are now locked, and where you are permanently separated from the people. Go to the people. This is your field, your life, your science. Learn from the people how best to serve their cause!" For Bakunin, as for Fanelli, "educated youth must be neither the teacher, the paternalistic benefactor, nor the dictatorial leader of the people, but only the midwife[11] for the self-liberation, inspiring them to increase their power by acting together and coordinating their efforts" (388).

The problem is, we in 2007 are hardly in the position that Fanelli was in, in 1868, even though the objective conditions continue to cry out for social change along the lines of what was being discussed during that period. Why not? To look at Noam Chomsky's writings in light of this question I think provides some useful insight into what he sees as impeding valuable unrest, and what he thinks an educator could or should be doing in the era of ample information, high levels of technology, and possibilities for significant exchange. By looking at what he is doing, and what he is taking for granted when he does it, may also shed some light on the nature of his anarchy, just as looking at Bookchin's Fanelli helped to shed light upon his conception of education as catalyst.

There are many elements of Chomsky's demeanor that resemble that of Fanelli as described by Bookchin. Noam Chomsky is a humble, decent person who speaks in a language that is informal and recognizable to most people, even when the subject matter is complex. He doesn't flaunt his knowledge but applies it to real issues and questions. He doesn't dress in fancy clothing, or drive a luxury car, or live in an uppity neighborhood. In his political talks, he arrives looking like anyone else, and he respectfully listens, respectfully suggests, but never offers to lead or to guide or to dictate terms. Further, whenever he gives a talk, he follows up with question periods, which he is willing to sustain until the last person in the room has had a chance to speak. I have been witness to him being almost dragged off by his host so as to ensure that he is on time for the next event (since he invariably gives several talks each day he is traveling). And then he leaves, back to Lexington, from where he corresponds with multitudes of people on the substance of things he has put forward in the course of his visit. In short, he educates in a manner consistent with what Fanelli did, or Bakunin, Rocker, or Goldman advocated, and he works within the system when it seems appropriate (as Goldman did with her promotion of birth control or Kropotkin did with his scientific work) and outside of the system when necessary. In this light it is amazing to read the short and unbelievably misleading interview with Chomsky in the *New York Times Magazine*, which paints him in a light so odd relative to the way he lives his life as to deserve special comment from him in a message sent to me by Edward S. Herman:

Message: don't have interviews with the NYT. The questions were mostly pointless and inappropriate for an interview, but the interviewer was a nice and perfectly serious person, and after a lot of discussion—went on for about an hour and a half—seemed to get the point. The fact checker then called and went over a few "quotes" they were going to use, which I corrected, and she got the corrections straight—but I see they left at least some of them uncorrected. The "quotes" are phrases extracted from long answers to the questions, mostly explaining (politely) why they are the wrong questions so I cannot answer them, and we should be talking about something different (sometimes discussed). It's interesting to compare this with interviews in journals everywhere in the world, as far as I know, outside of the US mainstream; even in very poor countries, even dictatorships. Radio and TV too, everywhere. It is simply inconceivable that questions like these would be asked in an interview. Rather, questions about serious issues. There are plenty of forms of craziness, but this pathology is, to my knowledge, specific to US liberal intellectual elite culture. Even the photo tells you something about the newspaper trade here. The photographer, also a nice person, asked for a few shots without my glasses after 1/2 hour of very elaborate photography (came all the way to Gainesville for it, where I was giving talks). I said OK, but it's not me. That's the one they used. Why not just put a photo of some other person? What matters is not truth, but making it look a certain a way—in this case, a childish and silly way. Trivial, but symbolic. It's a remarkable divide between US elites and the rest of the world.

I suppose by US standards it's not bad.

—Noam Chomsky

Some radicals with whom I have had conversations bemoan Chomsky's comments about popular media outlets (like the *New York*

Times) or his occasional forays into what the White House should have done in some circumstance or another because for them this engagement with the "status quo" is incongruous with the work of a "radical. In this sense, he seems very unlike Fanelli, very unlike most historical figures associated with anarchy, in fact, although it's clear that Fanelli's ideas *worked* in Spain because they spoke to very specific issues of that time about which perhaps he himself was not aware. In my opinion, Chomsky is quite conscious of the distinction between his observations about the status quo and his overall approach, but he engages issues relating to pedagogy from different fronts to answer to contemporary problems and obstacles, for reasons that are related to the practice of "de-fooling" the populace, a prime objective of his, and of his precursor, Zellig Harris (who employed the term). This practice, like his media analysis or his recounting of contemporary political events, is but a beginning of what needs to be done to transform society in the direction he would like to see it go toward. In other words, Chomsky addresses problems of education on a whole range of fronts; he is a professor at MIT, he is a catalyst for oppressed peoples, he informs us about what is going on, he offers facts and details to counter those with which we are constantly bombarded in the media. But behind it all lurks an approach that aims not to dictate but to encourage individual contemplation of matters that concern people.

I think you learn by doing. I'm a Deweyite from way back, from childhood experience and reading. You learn by doing, and you figure out how to do things by watching other people do them. That's the way you learn to be a good carpenter, for example, and the way you learn to be a good physicist. Nobody can train you on how to do physics. You don't teach methodology courses in the natural sciences. You may in the social sciences. In any field that has significant intellectual content, you don't teach methodology. You just watch people doing it and participate with them in doing it. So a typical, say, graduate seminar in a science course would be just people working together, not all that different from an artisan picking up a craft and working with someone who's supposedly good at it. I think the same is true of these things. I don't try to persuade people, at least not consciously. Maybe I do. If so, it's a mistake.

This leads to a crucial insight into the workings of the Chomsky approach, which relates to the idea of using notions, facts, interactions, and encouragement as a form of catalyst.

The right way to do things is not to try to persuade people you're right but to challenge them to think it through for themselves. There's nothing in human affairs of which we can speak with very great confidence, even in the hard natural sciences that's largely true. In complicated areas, like human affairs, we don't have an extremely high level of confidence, and often a very low level. In the case of human affairs, international affairs, family relations, whatever it may be, you can compile evidence and you can put things together and look at them from a certain way. The right approach, putting aside what one or another person does, is simply to encourage people to do that.

All of this requires hard work on the part of the person interested in the subject at hand, for it is not a passive ingestion of ideas, but rather an active cooperative dialogue that moves both parties to the work into higher levels of understanding about the questions posed.

The way you do it is by trying to do it yourself, and in particular trying to show, although it's not all that difficult, the chasm that separates standard versions of what goes on in the world from what the evidence of the senses and people's inquiries will show them as soon as they start to look at it. A common response that I get, even on things like chat networks, is, "I can't believe anything you're saying. It's totally in conflict with what I've learned and always believed, and I don't have time to look up all those footnotes. How do I know what you're saying is true?" That's a plausible reaction. I tell people it's the right reaction. You shouldn't believe what I say is true. The footnotes are there, so you can find out if you feel like it, but if you don't want to bother, nothing can be done. Nobody is going to pour truth into your brain. It's something you have to find out for yourself.[12]

This speaks once again to the idea of authority, for it is not through the authority of one's teacher that one becomes an authority, nor is it with reference to credentials, institutions, or names that one can root ideas; it is through direct and conscious exploration. This has to be the onus placed upon anyone interested in solving or addressing any question.

Methods of Dissemination

Unlike Fanelli, Chomsky has many outlets for professing ideas or serving to catalyze others. There is much discussion about his letter writing, for instance, including the oft-cited fact that he spends twenty hours per week doing correspondence. Since coming into contact with seriously engaged intellectuals and political figures, I have discovered that Chomsky is not alone in this regard, and indeed writing a popular book about a well-known figure meant that for a period of time even I ended up sending hundreds of e-mail messages a week in response to issues raised from a variety of perspectives. What is fascinating about Chomsky, though, is the way that he sets the standard for such work, over a life-time; he, like so many well-known figures, could simply grant a few precious interviews, write his books, and retire. Instead, he takes other people's questions seriously and uses his remarkable typing skills (his letters are devoid of typos, and this despite what has been described to me as the incredible speed of his typing), phenomenal memory, and extraordinary generosity to respond to people, to the very limits of human ability, and for more than half a century now. He also writes traditional letters, and in fact for a long time refused (except on rare occasions) to use e-mail, for obvious reasons. When he is at MIT, his office door is often open, so people (students, representatives of radical groups, media,—and one day I was there just after the departure of some members of Pearl Jam) could be given access to one-on-one talks with him. And then of course there is the Internet, about which he has not had very much to say, but which he employs on a regular basis thanks in large part to the heroic work that Michael Albert has undertaken with Znet.

The ChomskyChat forum, for example, is a kind of public e-mail response to questions fielded in a whole number of domains, and from this medium we learn a lot about Chomsky's idea of education. The setup is nonauthoritarian, public, and informal. The questions are sometimes long, sometimes short, about linguistics, philosophy, or history, and often political. A good sense of Chomsky's letter-writing techniques flows from the way he engages the questions posed, because we can see how seriously Chomsky takes others' ideas, the pleasure he derives from answering questions, and the way in which he spins questions, at times, to bring them into domains of interest to him. Not surprisingly, Chomsky has things to say in this forum about the forum itself, and of course about pedagogy and the role of the teacher, which I recall here. Chomsky has played an important role as well as a supporter and contributor to the Z enterprise, which includes a summer school, the ZNet's Instructionals (a selection of online instructionals free for all ZNet users), and of course a plethora of online resources.

Chomsky as Teacher

Chomsky's approach in his teaching is always generous, even when he is on the opposite side of an issue. For instance, he begins to answer questions for the forum on pedagogy[13] with the type of line that, from the mouth of Chomsky, is bound to provide impetus for future work: "Good questions, and like most good questions, there are no good answers. At least, that I know." He then describes, in a manner consistent with the Fanelli example, how he hopes he is coming across: "Whether I've in fact 'managed to encourage truly creative productivity and learning' is not for me to say. I hope so, but others have to judge that." Now this for Chomsky isn't, or shouldn't be, unusual because people are naturally curious and ready to learn, and good teaching institutions, such as MIT, bring out this natural ability: "Actually, in graduate programs in a place like MIT, it isn't really hard. In fact, it's normal." Then comes an interesting distinction, still in the same answer; Chomsky makes reference in many discussions of universities to the differences between science and social science orientations, suggesting that sciences don't need heavy ideological indoctrination because they are about something else, about the next scientific question and the search for a satisfactory answer. Since this answer is presumably out there, what MIT students need to do is think through the problem, in whatever way, and perhaps preferably in an unorthodox way, so as to come at the problem from an appropriately original perspective. Part of this is thinking through problems with others, an idea familiar to anarchists through their promotion of free association based upon common concerns. In response to a question concerning Ross Perot's idea of an electronic town hall, which Chomsky considers as just another attack on democracy since it is yet another way to isolate people, Chomsky adds the following comparison: "It's very few people who do scientific work by sitting alone in their office all their lives. You talk to graduate students, you hear what they have to say, you bounce ideas off your colleagues. That's the way you get ideas, that's the way you figure out what you think. That's the way, and in political life or social life, it's exactly the same thing."[14] As such, for Chomsky, "in the sciences, higher education is quite participatory and non-authoritarian." Authority would not make sense if people are all trying to find the answers to a common set of knowable questions. On the other hand, and this question frequently comes up, children pose different types of questions about education. As Chomsky relates, "I've also taught children, years ago. There it takes more imagination and effort. I'm sure it can be done. My own childhood educational experience was an example."[15]

Chomsky offers a further glimpse of how he approaches education in "Democracy and Education," the Mellon Lecture given at Loyola University in 1994.[16] He describes himself as working in the left libertarian tradition, very much along the lines of what has been portrayed to this point, but which for him includes as well "progressive liberals of the John Dewey variety, independent socialists like Bertrand Russell, the leading elements of the Marxist mainstream, mostly anti-Bolshevik, and of course libertarian socialists of various anarchist movements, not to speak of major parts of the labor movement and other popular sectors." Similarly, in a Znet posting he writes: "My feeling, based in part on personal experience in this case, is that a decent education should seek to provide a thread along which a person will travel in his or her own way; good teaching is more a matter of providing water for a plant, to enable it to grow under its own powers, than of filling a vessel with water (highly unoriginal thoughts I should add, paraphrased from writings of the Enlightenment and classical liberalism). These are general principles, which I think are generally valid. How they apply in particular circumstances has to be evaluated case by case, with due humility, and recognition of how little we really understand."[17] He makes a link, therefore, between the anarchists and other humanist or classical liberal movements with regard to the issue of education, for reasons that become clear once we have looked into some of the specific claims from those areas. Furthermore, and this is critical, Chomsky, like Dewey, considers that reforms in early education can be levers for social change; he also believes that universities, despite pressures to the contrary, can also be spaces in which radical alternatives, as well as useful knowledge, can be discussed and proliferated.

Studying Obedience

Anyone who has had any dealings with children knows that they're curious and creative. They want to explore things and figure out what's happening. A good bit of schooling is an effort to drive this out of them and to fit them into a mold, make them behave, stop thinking, not cause any trouble. It goes right from kindergarten up to what Huntington was talking about, namely, keep the rabble out of their hair. People are supposed to be obedient producers, do what they're told, and the rest of your life is supposed to be passive consuming. Don't think about things. Don't know about things. Don't bother your head with things like the MAI or international affairs. Just do what you're told, pay attention to something else and maximize your consumption. That's the role of the public.[18]

Many consider that the university may not be the best place for discussion of critical concerns, that students are out of touch or overly regulated; indeed, given the growing collusion between universities and big business, described by the likes of David Noble, one might ask if institutions of higher learning can in fact be places of useful learning. Chomsky comments:

When you're in university, especially for a student, this is the freest time of your lives. If you think of before and after, this is the time when you've got a lot of opportunities, a lot of choices with relatively little coercion. There are disciplinary effects, including the pressure of obedience . . . but compared with most human beings, you're remarkably free. You can use the freedom, and people often have, and have done very important things. Furthermore, universities have an internal contradiction to them: On the one hand—and that's an important one—they're not just corporations who are just out to make money and increase profits, gain power and so on. But a university has multiple functions, even within an institutional structure. One of them is to induce obedience and subordination. The other is to stimulate creativity and discovery and you have to have both. For example, if you don't have the creativity and discovery, the sciences and technology are going to die. And the corporations won't be interested. Beyond that, there's a kind of commitment to professional integrity which is there at some level, no matter how much obedience and subordination there is. These things lead to internal conflicts and openings and opportunities and so on and so forth—the powers trade place. The same is true of the media. So there are endless numbers of things that you can do. Push too hard, you'll get pushed back. Power does not like to be undermined. But the range is very substantial and I don't think there is any particular limit to it. As the universities "free-up" over the years, the range of opportunity increases. It's very different now than it was 35 or 40 years ago because there's a lot more opportunity. The more universities become free, the more they'll be under external constraints, but the struggle goes on.[19]

Although they are not ideal, universities remain sanctuaries for reflection and action, spaces in which the classical liberal ideal, set forth most clearly by Wilhelm Von Humboldt, is still possible, as we see in this interview with David Barsamian.

DB: Much of the educational system is built around a system of rewards based on grades, beating other students in tests, and then coming to the front of the classroom and being praised by the teacher.

NC: It is, and that's a particular kind of training. It's training in extremely anti-social behavior that is also very harmful to the person. It's certainly not necessary for education.

DB: In what way is it harmful to a person?

NC: It turns them into the kind of people who do not enjoy the achievements of others but want to see others beaten down and suppressed. It's as if I see a great violinist and instead of enjoying the fact that he's a great violinist and I'm not, I try to figure out a way I can break his violin. It's turning people into monsters. This is certainly not necessary for education. I think it's harmful to it. I have my own personal experiences with this, but I think they generalize.[20]

The entire premise upon which Humboldt's approach to society is erected relates to this point and is set out in "Of The Individual Man, and the Highest Ends of His Existence"[21] in which he states that:

The true end of Man, or that which is prescribed by the eternal and immutable dictates of reason, and not suggested by vague and transient desires, is the highest and most harmonious development of his powers to a complete and consistent whole. Freedom is the first and indispensable condition which the possibility of such a development presupposes; but there is besides another essential— intimately connected with freedom, it is true—a variety of situations.[22] Even the most free and self-reliant of men is hindered in his development, when set in a monotonous situation. But as it is evident, on the one hand, that such a diversity is a constant result of freedom, and on the other hand, that there is a species of oppression which, without imposing restrictions on man himself, gives a peculiar impress of its own to surrounding circumstances; these two conditions, of freedom and variety of situation, may be regarded, in a certain sense, as one and the same. (16)

Humboldt's conception of the role of education flows logically from this starting point and sets a kind of standard to which Chomsky refers constantly in his own work and which informs, if not directly at least by inference, much of the other work described further on in this chapter, notably that of Bertrand Russell. For instance, Chomsky recalls in "Toward a Humanistic Conception of Education,"[23] that "Russell had quite a number of things to say on educational topics that are no less important today than when he first discussed them. He regularly took up—not only discussed but also tried to carry out—very interesting and provocative ideas in the field of educational theory and practice" (204). The principal idea that Chomsky takes from Russell is that "the primary goal of education is to elicit and fortify whatever creative impulse a man may possess" (204). Russell joins with Humboldt when he suggests that education should exist to give a sense of the value of things other than domination, to help create wise citizens of a free community, to encourage a combination of citizenship with liberty, individual creativeness, a humanistic conception, "which regards a child as a gardener regards a young tree, as something with an intrinsic nature which will develop into an admirable form given proper soil and air and light" (204). This organic and yet cultivated metaphor is drawn directly from Russell who suggested that "the soil and the freedom required for a man's growth are immeasurably more difficult to discover and to obtain. . . . And the full growth which may be hoped for cannot be defined or demonstrated; it is subtle and complex, it can only be felt by a delicate intuition and dimly apprehended by imagination and respect." What is clear from these descriptions is that the child is perceived to possess a human nature that is characterized by its individuality, its creativity, and its preciousness, which means that it is incumbent upon the educator to foster and protect, to revere and nourish, to put forth possibilities, and to respect. Chomsky sums it up nicely: "the goal of education should be to provide the soil and the freedom required for the growth of this creative impulse; to provide, in other words, a complex and challenging environment that the child can imaginatively explore and, in this way, quicken his intrinsic creative impulse and so enrich his life that may be quite varied and unique" (205).

Russell is important as well as an example of an activist teacher, who suffered for his political views, as Chomsky notes:

Take Bertrand Russell, who by any standard is one of the leading intellectual figures of the twentieth century. He was one of the few leading intellectuals who opposed World War I. He was vilified, and in fact ended up in jail, like his counterparts in Germany. From the 1950s, particularly in the United States, he was bitterly denounced and attacked as a crazy old man who was anti-American. Why? Because he was standing up for the principles that other intellectuals also accepted, but he was doing something about it. For example, Bertrand Russell and Albert Einstein, to take another leading intellectual, essentially agreed on things like nuclear weapons. They thought nuclear weapons might well destroy the species. They signed similar statements, I think even joint statements. But then they reacted differently. Einstein went back to his office in the Institute for Advanced Studies in Princeton and worked on unified field theories. Russell, on the other hand, went out in the streets. He was part of the demonstrations against nuclear weapons. He became quite active in opposing the Vietnam War early on, at a time when there was virtually no public opposition. He also tried to do something about that, including demonstrations and organizing a tribunal. So he was bitterly denounced. On the other hand, Einstein was essentially a saintly figure. They essentially had the same positions, but Einstein didn't rattle too many cages. That's pretty common. Russell was viciously attacked in the *New York Times* and by Secretary of State Dean Rusk and others in the 1960s. He wasn't counted as a public intellectual, just a crazy old man. (166–167)[24]

Similar links can be found in other thinkers to whom Chomsky refers in his work on education, including those that exist between John Dewey the liberal pragmatist and John Dewey the theorist of education.

These are hardly radical ideas. They were articulated clearly, for example, by the leading 20th century social philosopher in the U.S., John Dewey, who pointed out that until "industrial feudalism" is replaced by "industrial democracy," politics will remain "the shadow cast by big business over society." Dewey was as "American as apple pie," in the familiar phrase. He was in fact drawing from a long tradition of thought and action that had developed independently in working class culture from the origins of the industrial revolution. Such ideas remain just below the surface and can become a living part of our societies, cultures, and institutions. But like other victories for justice and freedom over the centuries, that will not happen by itself. One of the clearest lessons of history, including recent history, is that rights are not granted; they are won. The rest is up to us.[25]

In fact, says Chomsky, "much as they disagreed on many other things, as they did, Dewey and Russell were perhaps the two leading thinkers of the twentieth century in the West, in my opinion. They did agree on what Russell called this humanistic conception, with its roots in the Enlightenment, the idea that education is not to be viewed as something like filling a vessel with water, but rather assisting a flower to grow in its own way. It's an eighteenth-century view which they revived, in other words providing the circumstances in which the normal creative patterns will flourish." This idea, like much of what we find in Humboldt, has what Chomsky calls "a revolutionary character," such that "if implemented, these ideas could produce free human beings whose values were not accumulation and domination but rather free association in terms of equality and sharing and cooperation, participating on equal terms to achieve common goals which were democratically conceived."[26]

Chomsky's sense is that Wilhelm Von Humboldt is an extremely important and neglected thinker who rooted discussions about educational practices within a conception of human nature that Chomsky shares. The importance of Humboldt extends into the institution of learning as well because "he was one of the founders of the modern university system and at the same time he was a great libertarian social thinker who directly inspired and in many ways anticipated John Stuart Mill," notably the ideas proposed in *On Liberty*. Chomsky goes on to say in "Toward a humanistic conception of education" that Humboldt's "rationalistic conception of human nature, emphasizing free creative action as the essence of that nature, was developed further in the libertarian social thought of the industrial period, specifically in nineteenth-century libertarian socialist and anarchist social theory and their accompanying doctrines concerning educational practice" (208–209). In these regards, Chomsky's intellectual debt to Humboldt, in terms of both approach and the actual projects relating to pedagogy, is immense. Further, Humboldt is one of the critical links between Chomsky and Rocker, as we have seen, for Rocker refers with great admiration to Humboldt's approach (to both the study of language and to the approach to society), notably in *Nationalism and Culture*. Referring to this same essay on the limits of state action, which Rocker calls "ingenious," he notes that "Humboldt attacked first of all the baseless idea that state could give to men anything which it had not first received from men. Especially repugnant to him was the idea that the state was called to uplift the moral qualities of man, a delusion which later, under the influence of Hegel, befogged the best minds in Germany" (Rocker 156). Citing this same passage referred to above, Rocker offers a critical conception of the state from his own perspective, which reflects so much of what has been said to date: "Humboldt wanted to see the activity of the state restricted to the actually indispensable and to entrust to it only those fields that were concerned with the personal safety of the individual and of society as a whole. Whatever went beyond this seemed to him evil and a forcible invasion of the rights of the personality, which could only work out injuriously."[27]

Even the language of Humboldt's texts seems familiar to those who have read Chomsky or Rocker discussing similar issues; for instance, one passage that Chomsky recalls variously is from "Positive Welfare of the Citizen" (in *The Limits of State Action*), in which Humboldt asserts that "whatever does not spring from a man's free choice, or is only the result of instruction and guidance, does not enter into his very being, but still remains alien to his true nature; he does not perform it with truly human energies, but merely with mechanical exactness" (28). This type of thinking underwrites as well the whole Summerhill approach, described later on, and is echoed in John Stuart Mill's sense that "one whose desires and impulses are not his own, has no character, no more than a steam-engine has a character."[28] The idea of free choice also suggests that a national education policy is inappropriate since it promotes "a definite form of development"; instead, Humboldt favors spontaneous and creative decisions of the individual and hence supports educational approaches that promote "the freest development of human nature, directed as little as possible to citizenship" (*The Limits of State Action* 51). The result is not chaos or the lack of free associations with people, quite the contrary.

[I]f education is only to develop a man's faculties, without regard to giving human nature any special civic character, there is not need of the State's interference. Among men who are really free, every form of industry becomes more rapidly improved—all the arts flourish more gracefully—all the sciences extend their range. In such a community, too, family ties become closer; parents are more eagerly devoted to the care of their children, and in a state of greater well-being, are better able to carry out their wishes with regard to them. Among such men emulation naturally arises; and tutors educate themselves better when their fortunes depend upon their own efforts, than when their chances of promotion rest on what they are led to expect from the State. (*The Limits of State Action* 53)

As is clear from virtually all of Chomsky's works in all fields to which he contributes, the idea that creativity is at the basis of our human nature, so clearly articulated by Humboldt in *The Limits of State Action*, is the foundation of his approach to the world. In Humboldt's words: "to inquire and to create—these are the centers around which all human pursuits more or less directly revolve. Before inquiry can get to the root of things, or to the limits of reason, it presupposes, in addition to profundity, a rich diversity and an inner warmth of soul—the harmonious exertion of all the human faculties combined" (76).

Education and the Workplace

Many of these insights, on education and diversity of experience, apply to the workplace as well, and were discussed by both Dewey and Humboldt:

In a free and democratic society, Dewey held, workers should be the masters of their own industrial fate, not tools rented by employers. He agreed on fundamental issues with the founders of classical liberalism and with the democratic and libertarian sentiments that animated the popular working class movements from the early Industrial Revolution, until they were finally beaten down by a combination of violence and propaganda. In the field of education, therefore, Dewey held that it is "illiberal and immoral" to train children to work "not freely and intelligently, but for the sake of the work earned, "in which case their activity "is not free because not freely participated in." Again the conception of classical liberalism and the workers' movements. Therefore, Dewey held, industry must also change "from a feudalistic to a democratic social order" based on control by working people and free association, again, traditional anarchist ideals with their source in classical liberalism and the Enlightenment.[29]

According to Chomsky, Dewey believed that "the ultimate aim of production is not production of goods but the production of free human beings associated with one another on terms of equality."[30] Picking up on this idea, Chomsky suggests that Dewey and Humboldt, despite their differences, shared a vision with classical liberal thinkers that has been previously described in terms of the "humanistic conception."[31] This point is further elaborated in Chomsky's "Mellon Lecture":

This basic commitment, which runs through all of Dewey's work and thought, is profoundly at odds with the two leading currents of modern social intellectual life, one, strong in his day—he was writing in the 1920s and 1930s about these things—is associated with the command economies in Eastern Europe in that day, the systems created by Lenin and Trotsky and turned into an even greater monstrosity by Stalin. The other, the state capitalist industrial society being constructed in the U.S. and much of the West, with the effective rule of private power. These two systems are actually similar in fundamental ways, including ideologically. Both were, and one of them remains, deeply authoritarian in fundamental commitment, and both were very sharply and dramatically opposed to another tradition, the left libertarian tradition, with roots in Enlightenment values, a tradition that included progressive liberals of the John Dewey variety, independent socialists like Bertrand Russell, the leading elements of the Marxist mainstream, mostly anti-Bolshevik, and of course libertarian socialists of various anarchist movements, not to speak of major parts of the labor movement and other popular sectors.

As we have seen, this humanist conception describes the value of things other than domination to favor individual creativity and individual control over one's own fate. Citing John Dewey, Chomsky suggests that "illegitimate structures of coercion must be unraveled," especially domination by "business for private profit through private control of banking, land, industry, reinforced by command of the press, press agents and other means of publicity and propaganda."[32] If this is not done, then discussions of democracy are moot and, once again citing Dewey, "Politics will remain the shadow cast on society by big business, [and] the attenuation of the shadow will not change the substance."[33]

Readers interested in pursuing this line of thinking (and, in my opinion, following the threads that lead to Chomsky's work is an endlessly fascinating endeavor) can look to the hundreds of books and articles that Dewey produced; for those looking for a synopsis, a representative sampling of his ideas can be found in a brief text called "My Pedagogic Creed."[34] Herein, Dewey suggests that "all education proceeds by the participation of the individual in the social consciousness of the race," and "through this unconscious education the individual gradually comes to share in the intellectual and moral resources which humanity has succeeded in getting together." This form of education "comes through the stimulation of the child's powers by the demands of the social situations in which he finds himself," and "the only possible adjustment which we can give to the child under existing conditions, is that which arises through putting him in complete possession of all his powers." This involves the task of teaching children how to learn, rather than focusing upon very specific tasks as the benchmark against which success is measured. This is for the obvious reason that "with the advent of democracy and modern industrial conditions it is impossible to foretell definitely just what civilization will be twenty years from now. Hence it is impossible to prepare the child for any precise set of conditions. To prepare him for the future life means to give him command of himself; it means so to train him that he will have the full and ready use of all his capacities."

These ideas, for Chomsky, "retain their revolutionary character; in education, the workplace, and every other sphere of life." It is incumbent upon us to recall this work, and to put its insights to work for the good society because

if implemented, they would help clear the way to the free development of human beings whose values are not accumulation and domination, but independence of mind and action, free association on terms of equality, and cooperation to achieve common goals. Such people [Dewey and Russell] would share Adam Smith's contempt for the "mean" and "sordid pursuits" of "the masters of mankind" and their "vile maxim": "All for ourselves, and nothing for other people", the guiding principles we are taught to admire and revere, as traditional values are eroded under unremitting attack. . . . The "humanistic conception" that was expressed by Russell and Dewey in a more civilized period, and that is familiar to the libertarian left, is radically at odds with the leading currents of contemporary thought: the guiding ideas of the totalitarian order crafted by Lenin and Trotsky, and of the state capitalist industrial societies of the West. One of these systems has fortunately collapsed, but the other is on a march backwards to what could be a very ugly future.[35]

Of course, there are points of Dewey's "creed" that reflect the problems and approach of his time period, and others which are in disaccord with some of the ideals put forth by Chomsky, notably his sense of the reasons for which people should be trained, and the kingdom of God to which one should aspire in such efforts. Nevertheless, Dewey does set out a group of workable principles that both articulate some of the ideas previously presented and also serve as the basis for work eventually undertaken in such places as Summerhill.

Summerhill

Chomsky does not specifically mention Summerhill in his writings, or in interviews in which the question of education is raised; nevertheless, there are some important points of overlap between what A. S. Neill describes and what Chomsky considers an appropriate approach to child rearing. Furthermore, the fundamental text describing the insights of the Summerhill approach, Neill's *Summerhill: A Radical Approach to Child Rearing*,[36] has a foreword written by Erich Fromm, who is a critical, though indirect precursor to some of Chomsky's ideas (via, in particular, Fromm's influence upon Zellig Harris and, in turn, Harris's influence upon Chomsky). Fromm's own description of those who advocated progressive education is a nice overview of some of the points raised thus far: "The basic principle of such self-determination was the replacement of authority by freedom, to teach the child *without the use of force* by appealing to his curiosity and spontaneous needs, and thus to get him interested in the world around him. This attitude marked the beginning of progressive education and was an important step in human development" (ix). This conception of education without fear is in great contrast to the efforts undertaken in the world inhabited by Fromm (and even more today), wherein people are managed (by giant enterprises and an education system increasingly geared to their interests) and manipulated (by giant media designed to whet the individual's appetite for new commodities and to direct these appetites toward areas most profitable for industry). In the society Fromm described, "parents and teachers have confused true nonauthoritarian education with *education by means of persuasion and hidden coercion*" (xi, author's emphasis) so that Neill's (and other progressive educators') ideas and objectives have become perverted.

Neill's work, in terms of both the writings and the actual pedagogical practices, are summarized by Fromm. First, there is the belief in the essential goodness of the child, that she or he is born filled with potential and interest in life. Second, education should flow from this insight, so children should be involved with joyfully working to find happiness. This suggests the third point, that education should include both intellectual and emotional development. Fourth, education should be geared to and in accord with the needs and abilities of the child. Fifth, "discipline, dogmatically imposed, and punishment create fear; and fear creates hostility." Neill's experience is devoid of the types of confrontations most people consider normal in the raising of children, because he respects the child, places her upon equal footing, responds to her interests and needs, and provides the opportunities (but without the coercion) to develop inherent abilities. This suggests the sixth point, that there must be mutual respect in a teaching relationship so that the child is not given the right to intrude upon the adult, just as the adult is not given the right to use force upon the child; as such, seventh, sincerity must underwrite the relationship between the teacher and the student. Eighth, the student should be encouraged to develop, to face the world, as an individual; she must learn to recognize and employ her powers "rather than to find security through submission or domination." Ninth, the teacher-child relationship cannot be based upon guilt, any more than it can rely upon fear or coercion, because each creates a sense of hostility and alienation deemed inappropriate. Finally, to quote Neill, there is no religious education at Summerhill because "the battle is not between believers in theology and nonbelievers in theology; it is between believers in human freedom and believers in the suppression of human freedom" (xii–xiv); it is the former impulse that, most often repressed, is developed and nourished at Summerhill. Neill doesn't make specific references to the precursors deemed appropriate to understanding Chomsky's approach, and there are elements that deviate from the principal concerns as described here; but in terms of its program and basic impulse there is much overlap between the radical approach to education and child rearing that has actually been put to the test of time by Neill, and ideas by, for example, Dewey and Russell.

The Science of Education: Project MIND

As we have seen, Chomsky links his interest in the social setting appropriate to developing individual creativity and potential with the science that might teach us something about the mind. Recently he has pursued this work through his participation in an interdisciplinary project at MIT, aimed at studying the processes that underwrite human cognitive abilities. This, like much else, follows directly from his earliest propositions about human nature and relates to education in the sense that understanding learning requires that we understand something about the workings of the human mind. As he stated in his discussion of the power of Bertrand Russell's approach, "the humanistic conception of education clearly involves some factual assumptions about the intrinsic nature of man, and, in particular, about the centrality to that intrinsic nature of a creative impulse. If these assumptions, when spelled out properly, prove to be incorrect, then these particular conclusions with regard to educational theory and practice will not have been demonstrated" ("Toward a humanistic conception of education" 205). On the basis of current work these assumptions seem to be true. But how is it possible to learn something about the "intrinsic nature" of the mind from a scientific perspective? This is the question that has guided Chomsky's linguistics research and underwrote efforts by a group research project in the late 1990s called MIND which he participated in at MIT with Wayne O'Neil, (Department of Linguistics and Philosophy), Robert C. Berwick, (Department of Brain and Cognitive Sciences and Department of Electrical Engineering and Computer Science), Suzanne Flynn, (Department of Foreign Languages and Literatures and Department of Linguistics and Philosophy), Edward Gibson, (Department of Brain and Cognitive Sciences), Morris Halle, (Department of Linguistics and Philosophy), Alec Marantz, (Department of Linguistics and Philosophy), Shigeru Miyagawa, (Department of Foreign Languages and Literatures and Department of Linguistics and Philosophy), David Pesetsky, (Department of Linguistics and Philosophy), Steven Pinker, (Department of Brain and Cognitive Sciences) and Kenneth Wexler (Department of Brain and Cognitive Sciences).[37]

The MIND group was interested in the philosophical and scientific problem of how human cognitive abilities such as language and thought "are organized into a unity of mind and how the biological organ of mind—the brain—supports these abilities." The problem, according to the MIND project description in a pamphlet from the group, is that cognitive scientists (who use interdisciplinary methods that include experimental studies, linguistic theory, and computational modeling to characterize the origin, acquisition, and processing of knowledge) have approached the first question while neuroscientists (who study the brain) the second one, so MIND's specific objective was to "provide a new framework for unifying these approaches to language and thought." The ability to make such a link and move forward in such complex terrain was the result of new technologies (notably echo-planar magnetic resonance imaging, EP-MRI, as well as MEG, magnetoencephalography), which allow for the measurement of human brain activities as well as "to observe parallel activation of functional brain modules in humans engaged in various mental tasks."

This combined interdisciplinary effort asks "how parallel activation of brain modules is able to construct the unity of mind and to provide the physical substrate of computations with complex representations. The cognitive science groups will develop and exploit the solid methodological basis for such imaging experiments, vision and imagery being the most active and fruitful domains for the study of neuronal systems at different hierarchical levels of organization. The neuroscience and cognitive science approaches to mind/brain meet directly in research on reading, which involves visual recognition as well as linguistic processing." This is of course the area of most interest to Chomsky, who notes the limitations of cognitive sciences and who inquires into the question of how the biological study of language can be applied to brain research. "At the moment . . . there are two major hurdles to the merging of brain science and linguistics. The first is that cognitive scientists, relying on standard behavioral experimentation, often appear to have a more vivid understanding of the thinking brain than neuroscientists. Second, linguists have not thought about their theories of representation and computation in terms of the brain and what the brain must be doing. They need to explore different reshaping of linguistic theory to make it responsible to the sorts of data we might expect to get from looking at the brain."

To address these issues, Chomsky worked alongside of other project participants to study the neuronal mechanisms of brain module dynamics ("the hierarchical modular organizations of cerebral association cortices and the dynamic interactions of modules in cognition"), cognitive processes and activation of brain modules ("how the brain can compute at all by revealing, in certain specific domains, how the brain computes with language"), and brain modules of language and thought ("the possibility of articulating mind/brain by exploiting the empirical results and theoretical advances from the work on neuronal mechanisms and cognitive processes"). The hope is that "these studies will provide detailed knowledge about the hierarchically organized modular structures of cognitive processing in the brain. Although the research is limited to vision, memory and language, the mechanisms of dynamic inter-modular interactions presumably underlie all cognitive activity. Answers here should provide a general understanding of how the brain serves the mind and thus how thinking is possible. Practically, this understanding should help us in the diagnosis and treatment of various mental disorders and genetically determined cognitive deficits. More importantly, we hope to provide a deeper understanding of that which makes Homo Sapiens human beings."

Given this scientific approach, which focuses so clearly upon neural activity and cognitive processes, why does Chomsky spend so much time on media analysis, descriptions of the status quo, discrediting widely held beliefs, and attacking well-known intellectual commentators? Why does he not simply remain, say, in the laboratory, or alongside of colleagues working in brain studies? Because, in my opinion, to ignore the social side of language is to avoid the question of what impedes the "Fanelli" in all of us from speaking out; so for Chomsky, education must draw from scientific insights, must be undertaken in a nurturing environment, must be a catalyst to awaken that which is existent in the human brain, and must be a midwife for creativity. But it must also counteract the multitude of attempts to miseducate us for other agendas, particularly today, when this effort is so pervasive and so well funded. Otherwise, those who have learned useful knowledge in their lives and now wish to make Fanelli-like journeys to communities of people in search of new approaches might otherwise be distracted or misled by the omnipresent and all-powerful corporate agenda or by the temptations of consumer culture. This and other matters relating to Chomsky's work on language and propaganda will be raised in the next chapter.

6

Obfuscating the Chomsky Effect: Media, Propaganda, and Postmodern Language Studies

There are people who are simply addicted to the Web. They spend time surfing the Web. People who wouldn't care where France is are getting the latest newspapers from Tibet. It is an addiction which could be harmful. . . .

The interconnection among people that the Internet establishes is very positive in many ways, for organizing and just for human life. But it has its downside too. I've spoken to friends whose teenage children go up to their rooms after dinner and start their social life with virtual characters, chat friends, and who make up fake personas and maybe are living in some other country. This is their social circle. They are with their friends on-line who are pretending to be such-and-such and they're pretending to be so-and-so. The psychic effect of this is something I wouldn't like to think about.

We're human beings. Face-to-face contact means a lot. Not having an affair with some sixty-year-old guy who's pretending to be a fourteen-year-old girl in some other country. There's an awful lot of this stuff going on. It's extremely hard to say what the net effect of the whole thing is.[1]

This is not the place to recall Chomsky's work, over half a century, in the complex domain of linguistics.[2] Instead, I will provide a general sense of Chomsky's overall approach to the study of human language—notably, which questions he asks in his professional linguistics work and what he hopes to someday achieve in that field, and then examine what relation exists between this general program and other approaches to language research and observation, particularly in the domain of literary theory. In a sense the comparison between linguistics and literary theory is entirely unfair because the distance between literary or most "language studies" or "discourse theory" and what Chomsky considers to be linguistics is vast, and also because most of what is done in language studies, particularly in a postmodern framework, is so different from what Chomsky considers either workable or, in most cases,

valuable. On the other hand—and this is the very point of this chapter—although many of the references to Chomsky in language studies are inappropriate, there are ways in which Chomsky's approach to media studies, propaganda, and even literature, could be usefully applied to contemporary work in language studies more broadly conceived. And since this book is focused upon the effect of Chomsky's work in a marketplace of arguments, debates, opinions, analyses, and descriptions, we will also pause to reflect upon the relationship between media and public opinion as regards Chomsky's own work, variously conceived.

Chomsky revolutionized the study of linguistics with his approach to the field in the 1950s and has remained on the cutting edge ever since. Robert B. Lee's 1957 review of Chomsky's first monograph, *Syntactic Structures* already provided some sense of the effect that the Chomsky approach was going to have in the field:

In the reviewer's opinion, Chomsky's book on syntactic structures is one of the first serious attempts on the part of a linguist to construct within the tradition of scientific theory-construction a comprehensive theory of language which may be understood in the same sense that a chemical, biological theory is ordinarily understood by experts in those fields. It is not a mere reorganization of the data into a new kind of library catalog, nor another speculative philosophy about the nature of Man and Language, but rather a rigorous explication of our intuitions about our language in terms of an overt axiom system, the theorems derivable from it, explicit results which may be compared with new data and other intuitions, all based plainly on an overt theory of the internal structure of languages; and it may well provide an opportunity for the application of explicit measures of simplicity to decided preference of one form over another form of grammar.[3]

Chomsky's incredible success at overturning paradigms and challenging dominant views in the field of linguistics has been the foundation of many commentaries and reviews ever since, of course, and has provoked the usual animosities, turf wars, and eventually acerbic comments by people within and outside of the field. This is itself a measure of the "Chomsky Effect" as it applies to language, and in some cases following the debates within the field (i.e., "the linguistics wars") could be a way of evaluating how research projects can get transformed, subsumed, or appropriated by dominant paradigms, or, from another standpoint, how academic resentment can transform the study of words into the war of words. This is an area in and of itself, and those interested should consult the array of claims and counterclaims in the literature.[4]

What is intriguing about this Chomsky Effect is the way that this type of debate has been transmitted into forums outside the field of linguistics; for example, the following quote represents various standpoints from within the field but speaks to a nonprofessional audience and is indicative of how these types of things get reported in a popular forum:

Chomsky has a history of making wild changes in his approaches to syntax every seven years," says James D. McCawley, professor of linguistics at the University of Chicago, whose thesis adviser at MIT was Noam Chomsky. For McCawley, Chomsky seems to be trying to replicate his original linguistic breakthrough to no avail. Salikoko Mufwene, Chairman of the linguistics department at the University of Chicago, says that Chomsky is still the biggest name in the field, but that there are more and more dissenters on such issues as the role of universal grammar and syntactic systems. There are strong challengers such as George Lakoff at UC Berkeley, who takes an approach that is more cognitive and less reliant on biology than Chomsky's, and Stanford's Joan Bresnan, who is working on lexical functional grammar, and Gerald Sadock of the University of Chicago who pursues alternative theories including autolexical syntax, different kinds of syntax within words. In academe, if you snooze, you lose. Now, in one of those peculiar ironies that characterize the careers of American intellectuals, Chomsky is judged primarily on the subject for which he forsook linguistic theory—radical politics. The notion that his contributions in one field make him the intellectual heavyweight champion of the world in the other would find few partisans among serious historians and intellectuals.[5]

The debate reproduced here relates not only to professional struggles but also to the overlap between linguistics and politics, which seems to be interesting to everyone other than Chomsky. In one sense there's no good reason why we should pursue this question, unless perhaps to suggest that Chomsky's success as an activist and dissenter has in part stemmed from his fame as a language researcher and, of course, his position as a professor at MIT. Or, one could take the far less prevalent (and in my opinion less credible) view that Chomsky has somehow forsaken linguistics for politics, although no reasonable criteria could be applied to uphold such a view given Chomsky's output and continued importance in the field. Or, one could simply follow Chomsky's own suggestion, given in response to a question posed following a panel discussion at the University of Wyoming, about the idea that Chomsky is "suspect as a social critic because [he] is a linguist":

You shouldn't pay any attention to what I say as a linguist or as anything else. You should ask whether it makes any sense. You could just as well say I'm suspect as a linguist because I have no training in linguistics, which is in fact true. I don't have any professional background in linguistics. I didn't take the standard courses. That's why I'm teaching at MIT. I couldn't have gotten a job at a bona fide university. That's no joke, actually. You know, I didn't have professional qualifications in the field. At MIT they didn't care. They just cared whether it was right or wrong. It's a scientific university. They don't care what's written on your degree. My own personal career happens to be very odd. I have no professional qualifications in anything. And my work has spread all over the place. It's a very strange question. It's as if there's some sort of a profession, "Social Critic," and only if you sort of pass the prerequisites in that profession then somehow you're allowed to be a social critic.[6]

It is also possible to consider Chomsky as two people, or perhaps ten people, or even more, given the amount of work he has done, and then to consider each of them as regards their contributions to linguistics and politics. But this is equally unsatisfactory because, despite the fact that Chomsky keeps politics out of his classroom and linguistics out of his activism, this is the same person who has investments, as I have shown, in certain traditions, notably anarchism and Cartesian thought, which in some ways guide the questions he considers important and the approaches he finds worth pursuing across the vast spectrum of intellectual endeavors. And there are times when he does find overlap, but in unusual quarters:

Man: Have you ever had your linguistics work censored or impeded in publication because of your politics?

NC: Never in the United States—but in the rest of the world, sure. For instance, I'll never forget one week, it must have been around 1979 or so, when I was sent two newspapers: one from Argentina and one from the Soviet Union. Argentina was then under the rule of these neo-Nazi generals, and I was sent *La Prensa* from Buenos Aires, the big newspaper in Argentina—there was a big article saying, "you can't read this guy's linguistics work because it's Marxist and subversive." The same week I got an article from *Izvestia* in the Soviet Union which said, "you can't read this guy's linguistics work because he's idealist and counter-revolutionary." I thought that was pretty nice.[7]

Further, in language and politics Chomsky applies equal doses of debunking, defooling, and even-handed consistency that stems from a solid center, which I have called his values, creating vistas of possibilities but, necessarily, closing down certain types of inquiry as well. Some of the inquiry he rejects has been appropriated variously by postmodern language researchers, so I think it is interesting to consider how this is done and in what ways it speaks to the appropriation, and the mis-appropriation, of ideas from one field to another. Before going in that direction, however, I will consider its diametrical opposite—that is, how work is done from a purely computational standpoint.

Chomsky and Computer Sciences

There have been some attempts to consider the implications of Chomsky's approach to the study of language for computer research and machine applications, because of work he was doing early in his career. The system of generative grammars he developed, particularly in his work on the late 1950s and early 1960s, has had an important original influence in both cognitive science and the development of computer programming languages. Refining ideas from his PhD work (published as *Syntactic Structures and Logical Structure of Linguistic Theory*), and in articles in *IRE Transactions on Information Theory* (published in 1956), and *Information and Control* (published in 1959), Chomsky examined different abstract forms that rules can take and related each of these forms to the kinds of processing required to analyze sentences. The key idea was that a sentence can be viewed as a string of symbols generated using a particular computational mechanism with well-defined properties and of restricted power. According to Chomsky's approach, the mind has a filtering mechanism, an algebraic generator of an infinite set of sentences based upon an abstract set of rules and a matching computational mechanism. To represent the computational complexity of human language mathematically, Chomsky characterized a range of computational mechanisms for generating languages (i.e., sets of strings), organizing them into a hierarchy of classes, each requiring a more powerful processor than the previous class, and which are still referred to as Chomsky Type 0, Chomsky Type 1, and so forth, classes. He then characterized certain mathematical properties of real human languages that sufficed to show that human languages cannot be characterized by the mechanisms at the lowest end of this hierarchy, the so-called finite state (Chomsky Type 2) or context-free (Chomsky Type 3) classes. He then hypothesized a particular mechanism of Type 1 power, which he called Transformational Generative Grammar, or TGG, which he claimed provided a mathematical characterization of all human languages. Under this view, different languages differ in the particular set of rules, here called transformations, that they employ, but all use the identical computational mechanism.

This work has had a seminal impact both on our understanding of the human mind and on the development of computer science. The core notion of cognitive science is that mental processes can be usefully characterized as a set of interacting, formally described computational mechanisms, and Chomsky's work demonstrated that mental processes could possibly be formally and precisely modeled as computational processes. The mathematical understanding of languages as infinite sets of strings generated by limited computational means was also central to the development of modern programming languages beginning with ALGOL. Chomsky Type 2 languages provided a formal basis for defining the grammars of programming languages and, simultaneously, the computational means for both automatically analyzing the programs themselves and for compiling these programs into machine code for particular machines. Crucially, the Type 2 languages are rich enough to allow recursively embedded structures of the kind needed to express parenthesized arithmetic expressions yet guarantee that strings in these languages can be analyzed quite efficiently. By restricting the grammars of programming languages to a formally definable and quite natural subset of Type 2 languages, it can be guaranteed that the strings can be analyzed in time strictly proportional to the length of the strings. It also turned out that the derivation structures that these grammars produce mathematically allow the very efficient generation of assembler code from programs in the source language. If one simply writes a local translation rule for each rule in the grammar to generate assembler code for each instance of the rule's use, then a simple recursive mechanism based on these rules is capable of compiling entire programs. This realization has allowed even undergraduates to develop simple compilers, and indeed, generative grammars and the Chomsky hierarchy are taught within multiple academic disciplines, are mandatory courses for studies in the theory of computation, and the use of these grammars for compiler design forms the core of all computer science compiler design courses, courses in artificial intelligence, and, especially, to their application to computational natural language processing.[8] This is one field Chomsky eventually abandoned, but media studies, about which he has nothing to say in terms of the linguistics, has remained a constant concern, as we'll see.

Media and Propaganda

It is of course the case that Chomsky has things to say about the issues that the field of language studies considers within its own realm, that is, areas such as media studies or work on propaganda. The latter has been analyzed at great length, so much so that it seems hardly worth recalling much beyond the basic insights, and then recommend that the reader go to some of the excellent sources, either in Chomsky's work in this area, sometimes with Edward S. Herman (like *Manufacturing Consent*) or in Achbar and Wintonick's film (and then in the book that Achbar edited based upon the film) by the same name. One quote from the latter gives a sense of the project:

It's not the case, as the naïve might think, that indoctrination is inconsistent with democracy. Rather, as this whole line of thinkers observes, it's the essence of democracy. The point is that in a military State or a feudal State or what we would nowadays call a totalitarian State, it doesn't much matter what people think because you've got a bludgeon over their head and you can control what they do. But when the State loses the bludgeon, when you can't control people by force and when the voice of the people can be heard, you have this problem. It may make people so curious and so arrogant that they don't have the humility to submit to a civil rule and therefore you have to control what people think. And the standard way to do this is to resort to what in more honest days used to be called propaganda. Manufacture of consent. Creation of necessary illusions. Various ways of either marginalizing the general public or reducing them to apathy in some fashion.[9]

On the other hand, there has been less consideration of how Chomsky's work on the media applies more generally to the production of propaganda. Indeed, Chomsky's notions of how a text is understood by a particular community is in some ways linked to what is known in media or literary studies as "reception theory." Does this suggest some overlap between what I have been calling "language studies" and what Chomsky calls "linguistics"? In one ZNet posting Chomsky comments on a range of issues raised thus far and along the way sets the record of his own views straight: "On JW's comments. I don't agree that a linguist is in any better position to interpret propaganda than anyone else. The professional discipline has a lot of achievements to its credit, but it doesn't help with this. Whatever I do personally in interpreting propaganda is independent of any professional qualifications I may have—and, in fact, is pretty simple-minded; there are no complicated theories about these matters, though I realize there are those who hold otherwise."[10] This of course makes sense, and is easily confirmed by comparing Chomsky's linguistic writings with his political ones; on the other hand, one could suggest that the idea of transmitting knowledge through language is unproblematic in his linguistics work, which means that when he writes the ideas down in language and those trained in the field employ them, there is as it were a simple and direct transmission of knowledge between experts in a given field. This is at odds with his consideration of language in the media or in the political realm, where simple utterances are in fact part of a broader project to conceal actual interests, stakes, or constraints, as we see in this example referring to reporting of what was happening in Kosovo in the late 1990s:

A rare exception was the *Wall Street Journal*, which devoted its lead story on December 31st to an in-depth analysis of what had taken place. The headline reads: "War in Kosovo was cruel, Bitter, Savage; Genocide It Wasn't." The conclusion contrasts rather sharply with wartime propaganda. A database search of references to "genocide" in Kosovo for the first week of bombing alone was interrupted when it reached its limit of 1,000 documents. Hysterical exaggeration of the enemy's unfathomable evil is a classic feature of propaganda, particularly when it is recognized, at some level of awareness, that the case for resort to force is weak. The device is familiar in totalitarian states, but was pioneered in democracies, where the need to mobilize popular support is greater.[11]

This clear line, between rational, straightforward language used in the employment of the diffusion of knowledge and seemingly rational and straightforward language that is used in the employment of, say, exaggerating or hyping-up some event for particular political ends, is indeed worth considering. Presumably it is a question of interests; scientists have an interest in diffusing knowledge to move onto the next question, as Chomsky himself suggests, whereas power elites wish to consolidate and expand their power base, which makes them use their knowledge not to inform, but to obscure. This is another area where John Goldsmith challenges Chomsky's view, however, on the grounds that one should check the use of the term *propaganda* in the 1930s. I would not be surprised at all if it had the use in English that it has in the other European languages, which is much more neutral, more like *advertising* in current English. This would have an impact on the interpretation of Lasswell, writing in 1934, cited by Chomsky. But the more important point is this: can one make a serious case that this media control is important, in the sense that the electorate would have a significant effect on American policy without that media control? At one point the phrase is used, "the majority, who in fact threaten it at every turn." I doubt that, and a few anecdotal remarks are thoroughly inadequate as a means to defend it.[12]

How does one study this effort at obfuscation, and how does one draw the line between purposeful hoodwinking and the spread of information? Chomsky's perspective on propaganda is articulated through discussions of how ruling-class ideology filters out unwanted static (i.e., dissension) by *consciously* blocking thought and understanding, a notion that lends a conspiratorial air to the idea of a discourse marketplace as defined by, for example, Pierre Bourdieu in his book *Language and Symbolic Power*. This is natural, since the examples that Chomsky uses tend to emphasize the level of conscious collusion between powerful groups acting within given discursive realms—say, the media and the ruling elites. In an interview with David Barsamian, reprinted in *Language and Politics*, Chomsky makes some general remarks in response to a question of whether individual words can have specific *power*, or if concepts are able to convey meaning beyond their words. His response is that such observations are "obvious to the point of banality," and he then goes on to make comments that help clarify how marginal discourses function in society. "Terms like 'the free world' and 'the national interest' and so on are mere terms of propaganda. One shouldn't take them seriously for a moment. They are designed, often very consciously, in order to try to block thought and understanding. For example, about the 1940s there was a decision, probably a conscious decision, made in public-relations circles to introduce terms like 'free enterprise' and 'free world' and so on, instead of the conventional descriptive terms like 'capitalism.' Part of the reason was to insinuate somehow that the systems of control and domination and aggression to which those with power were committed here was in fact a kind of freedom. That's just vulgar propaganda exercises" (617). Vulgar as they are, these practices are very effective, to the point where hegemonic discourse can block our perceptions and our understanding of reality. Thus our reading of particular texts can be influenced by the ruling class's attempts to manipulate our understanding of particular concepts. Chomsky's example of how this phenomenon works demonstrates how, when political discourse is reduced to technical meanings, words can become divorced from their traditional references and meanings.

The term "national interest" is commonly used as if it's something good for us, and the people of the country are supposed to understand that. So if a political leader says that "I'm doing this in the national interest," you're supposed to feel good because that's for me. However if you look closely, it turns out that the national interest is not defined as what's in the interest of the entire population; it's what's in the interests of small, dominant elites who happen to be able to command the resources that enable them to control the state—basically, corporate-based elites. That's what's called the "national interest." And, correspondingly, the term "special interests" is used in a very interesting related way to refer to the population. The population are called the "special interest" and the corporation elite are called the "national interests"; so you're supposed to be in favour of the national interests and against the special interests. (*Language and Politics* 662)

Ruling elites can hide behind technical jargon and, through their control of the media and manipulation of a well-indoctrinated American populace, they can get away with passing off, say, mass murder (Vietnam, Laos, Dominican Republic, El Salvador, Libya, Iraq) in the name of some socially acceptable quest, like "pacification." "[Pacification] is used for mass murder; thus we carried out 'pacification' in Vietnam. If you look at what the pacification programs were, they were literally programs of mass murder to try to suppress and destroy a resisting civilization population. Orwell wrote long before Vietnam, but he already noted that pacification was being used that way, by now it's an industry. Orwell had pointed out early examples of this kind of usage" (*Language and Politics* 663). This is one form of manipulation. However the effects thereof are, in Chomsky's view, extremely important if one wishes to understand how discursive practice is *filtered* by a well-indoctrinated society. This filtering process is crucial in the political work of Chomsky, and it plays a role in his later discussions of literary texts because literature is a potential source of revelation for an indoctrinated society. One representative example of how the filtering system works comes out of a discussion of Nicaragua's plan to purchase MIG airplanes from the Russians to defend themselves from aggressors.

They're planning to get MIGs and if they do, of course, we'll have to blast them into the sea. Everybody agrees on that, incidentally, the doves, the hawks, the liberals, everyone, they can't be allowed to get MIGs. Well what does that mean? What are the MIGs for? Of course everyone knows what they're for. Why do they want MIGs? Why don't they want French Mirages? In fact they do want French Mirages, but we won't let them get them. We want them to have MIGs because once they have MIGs they become a Soviet threat. If they just get French Mirages, what are you going to say? Therefore the United States stops them from getting Mirages. Nobody in the press will ever report this. Are they lying? Not really, no. They've already been sufficiently socialized and they suppress it. So when Steven Kinzer of *The New York Times* has an interview with some *commandant* and the guy says, "look, we'd be glad to get Mirages," the words don't penetrate his mind. The parser [perception system] turns off at that point. It doesn't go through. . . . He's not lying outright, he just doesn't hear it because it doesn't fit the ideological structure. (*Language and Politics* 726)

So the hegemony in fact has the power to go beyond its own social discourse-imposed limitations and indoctrinate people in a society, like the United States, so that they will voluntarily go along with ideas that are against their own best interests (not to mention the interests of those against whom the U.S. government is acting abroad). This, in Chomsky's opinion, is beyond Orwell's version of "Newspeak"; in fact, this is a level of indoctrination without parallel in history. The ruling elites have conspired to manipulate teaching curricula, media, and political discourse to reinforce their own power and reassert their own interests. Language, therefore, is in the contemporary society "abused, tortured, distorted, in a way, to enforce ideological goals" (*Language and Politics* 615). These efforts have a long history, as Chomsky points out in the Mellon lecture:

In the presidential address to the American Political Science Association in 1934, William Shepard argued that government should be in the hands of "an aristocracy of intellect and power," while the "ignorant, the uninformed and the anti-social elements" must not be permitted to control elections, as he mistakenly believed they had done in the past. One of the founders of modern political science, Harold Lasswell, one of the founders of the field of communications, in fact, wrote in the *Encyclopedia of Social Sciences* in 1933 or 1934 that modern techniques of propaganda, which had been impressively refined by Wilsonian liberals, provided the way to keep the public in line. Lasswell described Wilson as "the great generalissimo on the propaganda front." Wilson's World War I achievements in propaganda impressed others, including Adolf Hitler. You can read about it in *Mein Kampf*. But crucially they impressed the American business community. That led to a huge expansion of the public relations industry which was dedicated to controlling the public mind, as advocates used to put it in more honest days, just as writing in the *Encyclopedia of Social Sciences* in 1934, Lasswell described what he was talking about as propaganda. We don't use that term. We're more sophisticated. As a political scientist, Lasswell advocated more sophisticated use of this new technique of control of the general pubic that was provided by modern propaganda. That would, he said, enable the intelligent men of the community, the natural rulers, to overcome the threat of the great beast who may undermine order because of, in Lasswell's terms, the ignorance and superstition of the masses. We should not succumb to "democratic dogmatisms about men being the best judges of their own interests." The best judges are the elites, who must be ensured the means to impose their will for the common good.[13]

These elites have a great interest in propaganda, therefore, to uphold their vision of the world, and Lippman and Lasswell imagine that the majority can be relegated to a kind of spectator role; as such, the majority of the population will have access to decisions, but only after they have already been made. But there is another end on this long spectrum, "mislabeled conservatives in contemporary Newspeak" whose ambitions even exceed those described thus far:

So the Reaganite statist reactionaries thought that the public, the beast, shouldn't even have the spectator role. That explains their fascination with clandestine terror operations, which were not secret to anybody except the American public, certainly not to their victims. Clandestine terror operations were designed to leave the domestic population ignorant. They also advocated absolutely unprecedented measures of censorship and agitprop and other measures to ensure that the powerful and interventionist state that they fostered would serve as a welfare state for the rich and not troubled by the rabble. The huge increase in business propaganda in recent years, the recent assault on the universities by right-wing foundations, and other tendencies of the current period are other manifestations of the same concerns. These concerns were awakened by what liberal elites had called the "crisis of democracy," that developed in the 1960s, when previously marginalized and apathetic sectors of the population, like women and young people and old people and working people and so on, sought to enter the public arena, where they have no right to be, as all right-thinking aristocrats understand.[14]

The implications of this approach are seldom studied, which is regrettable, since there are some interesting insights here and also some problematic issue. For instance, it strikes me that once people have heard

Chomsky speak on a given issue—say, the propaganda of ruling elites as regards some military intervention or another—there should, or at least, could be an immediate reaction, a kind of intellectual realization. And in fact, many people do leave auditoriums after hearing Chomsky speak and rush out to buy other books by him, which they then devour and enjoy. But the link between this new knowledge and new actions that flow from it is tenuous, sometimes even nonexistent, such that even some of the most reactionary people I have ever met take a certain pleasure in reading Chomsky and in agreeing with him, whatever (in those cases) that means. And yet they continue to work for the military, turn down refugee claimants, refuse bank loans to honest but poor people, discount the value of personal engagement with environmental issues or local ecology, and so forth. The awakening that is part of the Chomsky Effect does not, in other words, necessarily translate into new approaches to the world. This is a problem, not related to Chomsky's work in my opinion but to the sense of powerlessness we are made to feel in light of a remarkably homogenous ruling elite that works, through propaganda, policing, monetary punishment and so forth, to consolidate and sustain their power. It also reminds us of the often unbridgeable gap between individual desires or "rights" (to consume, pollute, acquire wealth) and social responsibility.

From Language Studies beyond Linguistics to Postmodern Language Studies

Instead of studying these issues, theorists from a range of domains referred to variously as literary theory, cultural studies, critical theory, or even philosophy (in a certain sense) appropriate Chomsky's language theory as they understand it for their own work. As we will see, this language theory tends to flow from linguistics as opposed to, say, media or propaganda studies, and the programs derived from this evolution of theories have a concomitant disconnection to Chomsky's approach to either field. An excellent example is in the aforementioned work of Pierre Bourdieu, as described by John Thompson in his introduction to *Language and Symbolic Power*:

If linguistic theories have tended to neglect the social-historical conditions under-lying the formation of the language which they take, in an idealized form, as their object domain, so too have they tended to analyze linguistic expressions in isolation from the specific social conditions in which they are used. In the work of Saussure and Chomsky, the isolation of linguistic analysis from the social conditions of use is closely linked to the distinctions drawn between *langue* and *parole*, competence and performance, and hence Bourdieu presses his critique further by asking whether these distinctions do justice to what is involved in the activity of speaking. In the first place, it seems clear that speaking cannot be thought of, in the manner suggested by Saussure, as the mere realization or "execution" of a pre-existing linguistic system: speaking is a much more complex and creative activity than this rather mechanical model would suggest. In the case of Chomsky's theory, however, the issues are more complicated, precisely because Chomsky sought to take account of creativity by conceptualizing competence as a system of generative processes.[15]

Bourdieu's objection to this aspect of Chomsky's theory is that the notion of competence, understood as the capacity (and even the propensity) of an ideal speaker to generate an unlimited sequence of grammatically well-formed sentences, is simply too abstract. The kind of competence that *actual* speakers possess not only allows them to generate an unlimited array of grammatically well-formed sentences, it also gives them the amazing ability to produce expressions that are appropriate for specific situations, that is, a capacity to produce expressions apropos. Bourdieu's argument does not require him to deny that competent speakers possess the capacity to generate grammatical sentences; his main point is that this capacity is *insufficient* as a means of characterizing the kind of competence possessed by actual speakers.

This is a beautiful summary of what occurs in most postmodern language approaches; there is a beginning point, generally Saussure and or Chomsky, and then some argument about the insufficiency of both to explain the phenomenon of language. In some cases, such as Julia Kristeva, this serves as a launching point for a discussion of language not in the social but in the psychoanalytic realm:

Despite their variations, all modern linguistic theories consider language a strictly "formal" object—one that involves syntax or mathematicization. Within this perspective, such theories generally accept the following notion of language. For Zellig Harris, language is defined by: 1) the arbitrary relation between signifier and signified, 2) the acceptance of the sign as a substitute for the extralinguistic, 3) its discrete elements, and 4) its denumerable, or even finite, nature. But with the development of Chomskyan generative grammar and the logico-semantic research that was articulated around and in response to it, problems arose that were generally believed to fall within the province of "semantics" or even "pragmatics," and raised the awkward question of the *extralinguistic*.[16]

Kristeva suggests as a remedy to this lacuna that one consider the "motivated" nature of the signifier-signified relation by looking into the "Freudian notion of the unconscious insofar as the theories of drives [pulsions] and primary processes (displacement and condensation), and the way that they can "connect 'empty signifiers' to psychosomatic functionings, or can at least link them in a sequence of metaphors and metonymies" (ibid. 33). And, secondly, she considers another trend in this vein, which "introduces within theory's own formalism a 'layer' of *semiosis*, which had been strictly relegated to pragmatics and semantics." Her own approach, which considers both of these trends, takes off from Chomsky's failure, in her eyes, to consider what else is going on at the sign-signified level of relations. In some ways, this recalls the language-politics rift that people try to overcome, in this case by filling in what's missing between competence and performance.

Examples of this phenomenon abound, since most language theories outside of linguistics begin with Chomsky, but where they land up is often oceans away from his work, and this is particularly true in studies deemed postmodern. As such, I think it critical to briefly define this problematic term, and then assess what Chomsky has to say about work undertaken within its framework, both in terms of its epistemology and also in terms of its misappropriation of scientific knowledge.

Postmodernity is derived from the etymologically baffling combination of "post" (after) and "modo" (just now), and with attributes that can be traced through the history of modern thought but which take present shape after World War II, postmodernity now loosely encompasses or relates to a series of movements, sometimes incompatible, that emerged in affluent countries in the West in art, architecture, dance, literature, music, the social sciences, and the humanities. Postmodern approaches, or descriptions of the "postmodern condition,"[17] which describe our current knowledge state, emerge in the face of the modernist search for authority, progress, universalization, rationalization, systematization, and a consistent criteria for the evaluation of knowledge claims. As such, postmodernity involves a radical questioning of the grounds upon which knowledge claims are made and is thereby linked to a sense of liberation from earlier limiting practices. Its rise has spawned whole new approaches such as cultural studies, feminist studies, women's studies, gay and lesbian studies, gender studies, queer theory, science studies, and postcolonial theory, although it has now become the dominant paradigm that is itself being questioned for its limiting practices. Andreas Huyssen suggests that postmodernity emerges from a schism between two modernist enterprises, the consciously exclusionary "high" modernism, and the historical avant-garde, which, like postmodernity, questioned the aesthetic notions that underwrite the idea that high culture is self-sufficient. Postmodernity is one of the many "post" movements, including postcolonial studies and postmarxism, and it is often confounded with postmodernism, which is more a period label ascribed to cultural products (especially literary) that manifest or display reflexivity, irony, or the sometimes playful mixture of high and low elements. Postmodernity has affinities as well to poststructuralism, which undertook a radical critique of structuralists (Greimas, Goldmann, Kristeva, Todorov), narratologists (Bal, Genette), and semioticians (Barthes, Eco), who, in the 1960s and 1970s, described linguistic structures as ostensibly stable and able to mirror the movement of the mind.

Postmodernity is strongly defended by those who find within it a more reflexive approach to the rigid morals and norms that are the legacy of modernity's more totalizing approaches to politics, philosophy, law, psychology, sociology, and theology. Among those who have become associated with the postmodern project include notably Jacques Attali, Jean Baudrillard, Hélène Cixous, Gilles Deleuze, Jacques Derrida, Michel Foucault, Félix Guattari, Luce Irigaray, Fredric Jameson, Charles Jencks, Julia Kristeva, Jacques Lacan, Jean-François Lyotard, and Robert Venturi. Most of these theorists claim as intellectual forefathers the likes of Friedrich Nietzsche and Martin Heidegger (while invoking much the tradition of continental philosophy), whose relations to specific characteristics of postmodernity are tenuous and variously described. It is interesting to note that these precursors are German thinkers, most of them associated with philosophy, while those ideas against which a significant portion of the postmodern movement is directed can be linked to Chomsky's own approach via French or Scottish Enlightenment thought and classical liberalism. The number of French intellectuals represented on the list of contemporary postmodern theorists gives grounds for further pause, because their work was originally directed to quite a specific paradigm occupied by elite French intellectuals in postwar Paris. Figures like Althusser or Derrida, whose stars were falling (for different reasons) in the 1980s in France, were subsequently appropriated and elevated to a high level of star status on account of an American academy, which, since the 1970s, has recruited and promoted their work as antidotes to the New Critical and formalist approaches that had dominated the American scene since the 1940s. As a result, postmodern texts are read out of context and in translations (sometimes of unreliable quality), which has created considerable difficulties for scholars and students.

Most theorists and practitioners would reject or debate the postmodern label, and clear overlaps between respective projects of different people working with the postmodern paradigm would be difficult to pinpoint. Nevertheless, by virtue of association between these theorists and a range of ideas and practices, they can be broadly classified as representatives of one of two approaches. The first emphasizes the fragmented, unstable, indeterminate, discontinuous, migratory, or hyperreal nature of existence, which leads them to propose various versions of non- or anti-totalizing transgressive or disruptive practices. This makes their work resistant to, and incredulous of, "meta" or "grand" narratives, systematic and organized approaches in theory or practics, or coherence in art or interpretation. The second approach speaks from Fredric Jameson's Marxist economic perspective and emphasizes a crisis of representation, an increasingly monolithic late-capitalism dominated by an ever-smaller group of multinationals, and the valuation of utility and marketability rather than ethics in the domain of knowledge. From this standpoint, postmodernity is a historical period, a stage of capitalism, even a mode of production. Culture offers some terrain for the exploration of this phenomenon, a space for tracing out the evidence for this shift, and the study of its conspicuous characteristics, often described against a backdrop of globalization, capitalist universalization, or the end of history.

The one theorist most cited for the problem of definitions in postmodernity is François Lyotard who, in one of the oft-cited but internally contradictory passages that characterize his *Postmodern Condition: A Report on Knowledge* wrote:

The postmodern would be that which, in the modern, puts forward the unpresentable in presentation itself; that which denies itself the solace of good forms, the consensus of a taste which would make it possible to share collectively the nostalgia for the unattainable; that which searches for new presentations, not in order to enjoy them but in order to impart a stronger sense of the unpresentable. A postmodern artist or writer is in the position of a philosopher: the text he writes, the work he produces are not in principle governed by pre-established rules, and they cannot be judged according to a determining judgment, by applying familiar categories to the text or the work. Those rules and categories are what the work of art itself is looking for. The artist and the writer, then, are working without rules in order to formulate the rules of what will have been done. Hence the fact that work and text have the characters of an event; hence also, they always come too late for their author, or, what amounts to the same thing, their being put into work, their realization always begins too soon. Postmodern would have to be understood according to the paradox of the future anterior. (124)

Paradox indeed; this passage seems to situate postmodernity within and outside of history, it seems to periodize as it confounds such a possibility, it locates postmodernism in the present, and in a period that long precedes it.

The sociologist Zygmunt Bauman discusses postmodernity's "institutionalized pluralism, variety, contingency and ambivalence," which were unwanted by-products of the modernist quest for "universality, homogeneity, monotony, and clarity." "Postmodernity," says Bauman, "may be interpreted as fully developed modernity; as modernity that acknowledged the effects it was producing throughout its history, yet producing inadvertently, by default rather than design, as *unanticipated consequences*, by-products often perceived as waste; as modernity conscious of its true nature—*modernity for itself*." Postmodernity is "modernity emancipated from false consciousness," the institutionalization of the characteristics deemed during the modern period as unfortunate upshots of failed efforts at modernist objectives."[18] This "false consciousness" was presumably undermined by recognition of the murderous legacy of twentieth-century totalitarianism in the guise of Leninism, Stalinism, Bolshevism, Maoism, and the lingering oppression of capitalism. Although the politics of postmodernity are conspicuously inconsistent and ill defined, there is a postmodern suspicion about totalizing social programs, attempts at solving all of society's ills with an overriding ideology or agenda. The most significant myth for the shift toward post-modernity in the all-important domain of French philosophy surrounds events in 1956, notably Khrushchev's secret speech to the Twentieth Party Conference in Moscow in November, and the suppression of the Hungarian revolt. According to Mark Lilla,[19] these events

brought an end to many illusions: about Sartre, about communism, about history, about philosophy, and about the term 'humanism'." It also established a break between the generation of French thinkers reared in the 1930s, who had seen the war as adults, and students who felt alien to those experiences and wished to escape the suffocating atmosphere of the cold war. The latter there-fore turned from the existential political engagement recommended by Sartre toward a new social science called structuralism. And (the story ends) after this turn there would develop a new approach to philosophy, of which Michel Foucault and Jacques Derrida are perhaps the most distinguished representatives.

Lilla questions the degree to which illusions about communism shifted at this point, but he does echo the belief that structuralism altered the terms in which political matters were henceforth discussed, a point that leads into the critical area of language studies.

Language theories figure prominently in the project of postmodernity, through studies of nonreferentiality, the expressive peculiarities of post-modernity's language, as well as problems relating to intention, recep-tion, and representation. For poststructuralists, informed by Derrida's work on deconstruction, all discourse is bricolage, literally tinkering or puttering around, the only activity possible because there is no center, no point of origin and (therefore) no stable meaning. This has implica-tions for all disciplines, notably in the social sciences and humanities, both in its emphasis upon heterogeneity and multidirectedness, and in its insistence upon the central role of language and discourse. There are those who claim that this in itself does not make poststructuralism into an exclusively postmodern phenomenon, despite certain points of overlap; in fact, far from being a radical rupture and discontinuity, Huyssen describes poststructuralism as "a discourse of and about mod-ernism, and . . . if we are to locate the postmodern in poststructuralism it will have to be found in the ways various forms of poststructuralism have opened up new problematics in modernism and have reinscribed modernism in the discourse formations of our own time" (207). There are many disciplines affected by the postmodern conception of, and approach to, the study of language. Psychology and psychoanalysis rely heavily upon Jacques Lacan's work, notably his elaboration of an approach based upon the precept that the unconscious is structured like a language. The postmodern shift in approach to the mind is palpable in that it rebuts the formalist or behaviorist dreams of systematic and predictable results, in favor of a lack of center, "deterritorialization" and connections through "rhizomes." These terms are explored in the complex work of Gilles Deleuze and Felix Guattari, who, for example, celebrate schizophrenia (schizoanalysis) for its inventiveness and its refusal of totalizing approaches.

In the field of law, the emphasis is not so much upon postmodernity in terms of language theory, though there are examples of deconstructionist law, but upon a reorientation of the field in favor of exceptions over norms in decision making. In the domain of literature, we find literary theorists, including Harry Levin, Irving Howe, Leslie Fiedler, Frank Kermode, and Ihab Hassan, who used the term *postmodern* in the 1960s as a way of distinguishing post–WWII works by Samuel Beckett, Jorge Luis Borges, John Barth, Donald Barthelme, and Thomas Pynchon. Debate has raged about pre–WWII literary experimenters who appear to have worked in a framework that seems postmodern *avant la lettre*, that is, before the term postmodern was coined, notably Laurence Sterne, James Joyce, Virginia Woolf, Dorothy Richardson, not to mention the dadaists. Postmodern literature is also a rebellion against values distant from the disenfranchised who in the 1950s formed literary movements, including the Beats, the Angry Young Men, and a range of writers who sought to liberate the creative individual from the straightjacket of the moderns, and rebellion continues through experimentation in form, function, and mediums—notably cybertexts—in the literary domain and in literary criticism.

From architecture comes the earliest reference to "post-modern," which was first used by Joseph Hudnut, who titled his 1945 article "The Post-Modern House." Postmodernity is in evidence in the historical citations found on facades of buildings by Philip Johnson and Michael Graves. Architectural postmodernity appears following the realization that the modernist ideals of the Congress of International Modern Architects (CIMA), based upon rationalism, behaviorism, and pragmatism, are, as Charles Jencks suggests, "as irrational as the philosophies themselves" (470–471). In his text *What Is Post-Modernism*"[20] Jencks dates the death of modernism in architecture as July 15, 1972, when the 1951 Pruitt-Igoe scheme in St. Louis Missouri, the archetypal example of CIMA ideas in practice, was dynamited. Post-modernism, he says, is a "double coding: the combination of Modern techniques with something else (usually traditional building) in order for architecture to communicate with the public and a concerned minority, usually other architects" (472).

Other realms integrate or comment upon the postmodern condition by integrating particular elements deemed postmodern into works or performances. For instance, modern dance challenged traditional categories of dance (such as ballet) by exploring—in new ways and through different means—the body's relationship to time and space, and modern dancers formalized specific (atraditional and traditional) movements. Postmodern dance expanded these efforts by challenging accepted divisions between what we call "dance" and what might be considered pedestrian movement, such as standing up, walking, or lying down. Postmodern dance also questions the spatial divisions of dancer and spectator, removing not only the footlights as separator between proscenium and public but also the very idea of the performer as somehow other than the observer by sometimes using the observer as participant.[21]

Resistance to the Postmodern Approach

Postmodernity is pervasive and ever-present in the academy, and mostly ignored beyond the ivy-covered gates, however this has not stopped theorists from finding ways of making it fit most tendencies in the artistic and political trends in contemporary society. This all-encompassing quality means as well that icons of postmodernity can seem to have used up their cultural capital, and hence the current decline in its stock, and in the stock of approaches that are deemed to flow from, or contribute to, its (il)logic, notably deconstruction. This process arguably began in earnest in 1987 when, first, Victor Farías published a book on Martin Heidegger's involvement with Nazism and its alleged roots in his philosophy, and, second, when it was revealed that Derrida's friend and collaborator Paul De Man had published collaborationist and anti-Semitic articles in two Belgian newspapers in the early 1940s. Derrida and others sympathetic to DeMan, notably colleagues in Yale's prestigious literature department, tried to explain away the offending passages, confirming many people's worst fears about deconstruction's nefarious dark side: its politics. "No wonder a tour through the post-modernist section of any American bookshop is such a disconcerting experience," writes Mark Lilla. "The most illiberal, anti-enlightenment notions are put forward with a smile and the assurance that, followed out to their logical conclusion, they could only lead us into the democratic promised land, where all God's children will join hands in singing the national anthem. It is an uplifting vision and Americans believe in uplift. That so many of them seem to have found it in the dark and forbidding works of Jacques Derrida attests to the strength of Americans' self-confidence and their awesome capacity to think well of anyone and any idea. Not for nothing do the French still call us les grands enfants."[22] The problem may run even deeper, though, and in some cases into the shear nonsense that has been promulgated in the postmodern realm, even by those whose names are most clearly associated with the ideas, including Lyotard himself. In a shocking 1985 interview Lyotard said "I told stories in the book *[The Postmodern Condition]*, I referred to a quantity of books I'd never read. Apparently it impressed people, it's all a bit of a parody. . . . I remember an Italian architect who bawled me out because he said the whole thing could have been done more simply. . . . I wanted to say first that it's the worst of my books, they're almost all bad, but that one's the worst . . . really that book relates to a specific circumstance, it belongs to the satirical genre."[23] Regrettably, an awful lot of students, particularly hapless graduate students enticed by trendy and almost intoxicating theories or theorist professors, have been the intellectual victims of the more dubious versions of this kind of work.

Postmodernity's ir- or anti-rationalism had already been noted variously by Jürgen Habermas and received an extended battering in the hands of Christopher Norris. In *Uncritical Theory,* Norris attacked Jean Baudrillard's "The Gulf War Has Not Taken Place" as a symptom of a larger (postmodern) phenomenon that creates "a half-baked mixture of ideas picked up from the latest fashionable sources, or a series of slogans to the general effect that 'truth' and 'reality' are obsolete ideas, that knowledge is always and everywhere a function of the epistemic will-to-power, and that history is nothing but a fictive construct out of the various 'discourses' that jostle for supremacy from one period to the next" (31). Taking his cue from Norris, Noam Chomsky takes aim at postmodernity's purposeful obfuscation undertaken from careerist purposes ("I await some indication that there is something here beyond trivialities or self-serving nonsense"), undue intellectualization ("I can perceive certain grains of truth hidden in the vast structure of verbiage, but those are simple indeed"), and, most poignantly, the politically stifling quality of postmodern practices ("the fact that it absorbs elements that consider themselves 'on the left'—the kind of people who years earlier would have been organizing and teaching in worker schools").[24]

A range of these points are at issue in the Levitt and Gross book *Higher Superstition* and, more recently, in the "[Alan] Sokal Hoax," the publication in *Social Text* by a physicist of an article containing purposeful inaccuracies, both of which focused attention upon the misappropriation by postmodern theorists of scientific theories, with the suggestion that to the obscurity is added the problem of inaccuracy, a lack of rigor, and a generalized misinformed tomfoolery. One might expect that Chomsky would strongly support the Sokal enterprise, notably to attack the misappropriation of scientific knowledge by a realm of specialists of language studies. But there are important differences between Chomsky's views of postmodernity and those that have eventually emerged from the Sokal debate that deserve clarification as a means of better understanding the Chomsky approach.

Sokal's Hoax and the Illegitimacy of Postmodernity

This is not really the place to yet again trot out the details of the Sokal hoax or the plethora of stances assumed by the range of critics who have made pronouncements on the topic. Any good search engine will lead the curious reader to dozens of sites on the Internet devoted to the affair, and even a quick look at the tables of contents for journals in all sorts of fields will confirm the popularity of the event and the effect that it has had upon public perception of postmodernity. Ever since the truth about

"Transforming the Boundaries: Towards a Transformative Hermeneutics of Quantum Gravity" (*Social Text* 46/47) was revealed in *Lingua Franca*, there has been an explosion of in-depth articles and debates involving scientists (including a Nobel Prize recipient), internationally known scholars in the humanities and social sciences, writers, editors, and students in a range of fields. From the perspective of a book about Chomsky, however, a number of concerns should be considered, notably: What could possibly be at stake here, over and above serious issues of sloppy adjudicating, weak scholarship, strange interdisciplinarity, bizarre French-U.S. relations in the academy, and the ever-problematic cult of personalities? What is there about this hoax that could justify prominent articles in pages of eminent organs of information dissemination such as the *New York Review of Books,* the *New York Times, Le Monde, Dissent,* and the *Times Literary Supplement*? Why have we heard so much about roundtables at Yale, Princeton, Duke, the University of Michigan, and New York University, news conferences in various locales, and angry crowds outside of a conference in New York City fighting their way in to see Sokal? It is not because of Alan Sokal himself, who has persistently commented, in the book *Impostures intellectuelles* and in all the articles he has written in various media outlets, upon misuse of science by certain French theorists, all the while giving the impression of refusing to pass overt judgments upon whole fields or even specific authors. Nor is it related to Jean Bricmont, the coauthor of the book (but not of the original hoax), who has faced those who claim that there is something anti-French, anti-Francophone, or anti-European in the book—an issue that he, as a Belgian, is well placed to discuss, even as he tries to impose some degree of conformity with his own ideas of what useful academic research ought to look like. It is something else or, as I suggest by setting out some possibilities, it is a range of things that make this hoax important for our understanding of the postmodern era and for our sense of how Chomsky's work fits within it.

The discussion that has filled the pages of journals and newspapers suggests a few reasons for the strange popularity of this event and some of the intrigues that lie behind it. First, there is the question of useful and legitimate scholarship, which relates to one of Chomsky's earliest concerns, discussed in articles for the *New York Review of Books*, on the social responsibility of the intellectual in the contemporary world. In a vein that is similar to some of the conclusions one might draw from the Sokal hoax, Chomsky suggested in an interview with Michael Albertt that although there is some "important and insightful" work done in the frameworks of literary and cultural theory, it is nevertheless "hard to figure out" because one has to "labor to try to tease the simple, interesting points out." This in his opinion is a consequence of the simple fact that "it's extremely hard to have good ideas. There are very few of them around. If you're in the sciences, you know you can sometimes come up with something that's pretty startling and it's usually something that's small in comparison with what's known and you're really excited about it. Outside the natural sciences it's extremely hard to do even that. There just isn't that much that's complicated that's at all understood outside of pretty much the core natural sciences. Everything else is either too hard for us to understand or pretty easy." This of course makes life rather complicated for academics in the humanities or social sciences because "you've got to have a reason for your existence. The result is that simple ideas are dressed up in extremely complex terminology and frameworks. In part, it's just careerism, or maybe an effort to build self-respect. Take, say, what's called 'literary theory.' I don't think there's any such thing as literary theory, any more than there's cultural theory." This is not to say, says Chomsky, that you don't read and talk about books, it means that you don't have a "theory" in his sense. But this apparently creates a certain amount of anxiety for literary critics because "if you [the literary critic] want to be in the same room with that physicist over there who's talking about quarks, you'd better have a complicated theory, too, that nobody can understand. He has a theory that nobody can understand, so why shouldn't I have a theory that nobody can understand?"[25]

This is a great example, and it is echoed elsewhere in Chomsky interviews and letters. For example, a Znet response to a series of questions[26] contains the following: "On postmodernism, I don't know anything about the Web, and don't know what you saw of mine on postmodernism, so it's a little hard to comment. But just keeping to what you wrote, I suspect we may be talking about different things. . . ." This in itself is important—that there's some variance between what Chomsky considers postmodernity and postmodern theory and what others consider it to be or, more specifically, what others claim it can accomplish. For instance, "On theory, I don't object to the fact that postmodernism has no theories (i.e., nothing that could sustain a non-trivial argument). No one else does either, when we turn to human affairs or the kinds of things they are discussing. What I object to is that they proudly claim otherwise. Their productions are put forth as 'grand theory,' too deep for ordinary mortals to understand—at least for me: I don't understand it, and am skeptical about whether there is any 'theory' to understand. That's a great technique for enhancing one's own privilege while marginalizing the slobs. Does it serve any other function? If so, what? Am I missing some of the great achievements? If so, what?"[27]

I am not citing Chomsky as though to suggest that decent criticism of cultural and literary criticism is only to be found outside of the field; indeed it was Chomsky himself who first turned me on to Christopher Norris, who has done an excellent job saving Derrida from the doubtful while trashing Baudrillard for the unbelieving. I might add that Jonathan Culler has (in books such as *Structuralist Poetics*) carefully clarified structuralism and deconstruction for an American academic audience, Terry Eagleton has kept his public honest by showing them the political implications of their theory choices, and reams of scholars have done similar things by pointing out areas of misunderstanding about psychoanalysis, history, politics, and so forth. All of this suggests a second point, that the "impostures" mentioned in the title of Sokal's book *Intellectual Impostures*[28] might not really be about postmodern theory, despite widespread belief to the contrary, because the range of people involved should not all be categorized as "postmodern," "poststructuralist," or indeed "post" anything else, just as the people who critique the postmoderns aren't necessarily outside of that domain. So a foray into the Sokal waters suggests that the hoax is of interest because it serves as a corrective among many others to a prevalent trend in the social sciences and humanities, and it further suggests that we can learn from the hoax and improve our work while doing so. The hoax is of further interest in this regard because it shows how little each side understands of the other's positions; if it is true that social scientists do not understand nuclear physics, it is just as true that scientists do not understand deconstruction, and the hoax has not gone a long way to resolving either problem.

Another approach might suggest that there are important power issues here, which relate on the one hand to funding and on the other to a growing schism that has emerged between the sciences and the social sciences, possibly on account of the neoliberal agenda that has been rammed down our collective throats. Chomsky speaks often of the natural or pure sciences as opposed to the social sciences, generally in terms of knowledge claims on both sides and types of intellectual possibilities open to practitioners of each. The Sokal hoax has brought another comparison to bear, which may relate to power and research dollars rather than epistemology. The most important article in this regard is Steven Weinberg's piece in the *New York Review of Books*, on August 8, 1996,[29] which led to the conclusion that "we will need to confirm and strengthen the vision of a rationally understandable world if we are to protect ourselves from the irrational tendencies that still beset humanity" (14). This turns out to be rather fortuitous for Weinberg because we learn along the way that, as a representative (and a Nobel Prize recipient) of what seems from the article to be the most rational of all domains, physics, he considers himself as a kind of model for rational tendencies. So, he says, "those who seek extrascientific messages [notably pertaining to culture, politics, or philosophy] in what they think they understand about modern physics are digging dry wells." In a response to this article, part of a discussion in the *New York Review of Books* titled "Sokal's Hoax: An Exchange,"[30] Michael Holquist (Professor of Comparative Literature, Yale, now emeritus) and Robert Shulman (Sterling Professor of Molecular Biophysics and Biochemistry, Yale) expressed concern about the eventual tenor and claims of a debate that began as a rather clever and quite humorous enterprise, but which "is beginning to bring out the worst in respondents." They are here referring not only to Weinberg, but also to a broadening range of individuals who serve up the argument that "insofar as it is universal and extrahistorical, science is qualitatively distinct from the rest of culture: science *is* nature, and therefore the very opposite of culture."[31] There is a clear danger in this new polarization of culture and science, say Holquist and Shulman, and "if we are to preserve a more holistic view of nature and our own place in it, we must resist not only those extremists who exclude formal knowledge in the name of a homogenizing concept of culture, but those as well who make equally privative claims for an immaculate conception of science."[32] Looking backward we might recall that it was Weinberg who lobbied congress for a multibillion-dollar particle accelerator and almost won. But in this particular debate the scale of luminaries involved is heavy on both sides, even though the tangible costs are largely symbolic (or so it seems). Recall that on the *Social Text* side we have a range of highly respected and high-powered humanities and social sciences scholars, including Stanley Aranowitz (who along with Fredric Jameson and John Brenkman cofounded *Social Text*, was cited several times in the *Social Text* article, and who offered a reply to Sokal in *Dissent*), Julia Kristeva (who granted an interview on the subject for a French daily), Andrew Ross and Bruce Robbins (coeditors of *Social Text*), and Stanley Fish, the executive director of the Duke University Press, which publishes *Social Text* (purportedly the person upon whom David Lodge modeled his character *Morris Zapp*, and who wields enough symbolic power in his fields—literature and law—to inspire the name of a new building at Duke University). This is not to suggest that this is solely a power struggle, or that it is solely a funding issue; but the mystery that lies behind the public fascination may be fuelled in part by the range of well-known characters, and the presence of these well-known characters may be related to the interests that they perceive are at stake. Given the way that this debate has played out, the obsessive repetition of Sokal's actual goals become obscured, which gives the impression, true or false, that his honesty blinds him, even now, to the stakes, constraints, and dollars involved. For some this makes Sokal into a rationalist hero who should have left the fray after making his point, so as to avoid any suggestion of collusion with one side, or one stake, or another. But this picture is far too black and white, for indeed all debates on these types of issues include claims to decency, respectability, useful political action, or honest endeavor even when there seems to be something else going on. This is particularly true here, given that both sides suggest, in various ways, that they are aspiring to leftist ideals, even though many of those who espouse these views are quite obviously pleased with a Republican status quo.

The third approach, relating to the Left, serves to link the two sides of this debate since it speaks to the desires of all parties involved to promulgate useful political action. This of course did not have to be an issue here; people in the hard sciences rarely pretend that their discoveries are ideological, one way or the other, suggesting instead that they are simply "pure" science. Indeed Chomsky himself has sometimes made this very point when discussing the nature of the science researchers at MIT. But Sokal isn't doing science when he's doing the hoax; from his standpoint, he's also trying to better the human condition. He begins this quest with a few farcical statements about his left-wing agenda in the *Social Text* article, including the idea that "the fundamental goal of any emancipatory movement must be to demystify and democratize the production of scientific knowledge, to break down the artificial barriers that separate 'scientists' from 'the public'." He also suggests that "catastrophe theory, with its dialectical emphases on smoothness/discontinuity and metamorphosis/unfolding, will undoubtedly play a major role in the future of mathematics; but much theoretical work remains to be done before this approach can become a concrete tool of progressive praxis." He subsequently confessed that the ideas in the original *Social Text* article were far-fetched, but that the hoax itself was designed to advance progressive social movements when he wrote, in the afterword to the Fall 1996 *Dissent*, that "I am an unabashed Old Leftist who never quite understood how deconstruction was supposed to help the working class. And I'm a stodgy old scientist who believes, naively, that there exists an external world, that there exist objective truths about that world, and that my job is to discover some of them." This is all well and good, but here Sokal is going beyond the project of debunking the misuse of science in postmodern work, which wasn't designed to help the working classes any more than catastrophe theory was; it's a philosophical project that attempts to provide a better description of language functioning than other existing models.

Nor does he stop there. Sokal suggests in the *Lingua Franca* article that "Politically, I'm angered because most (though not all) of this silliness is emanating from the self-proclaimed Left. We're witnessing here a profound historical volte-face. For most of the past two centuries, the Left isn't bothering to trifle with the small caveat, which is that deconstruction has been identified with science and against obscurantism; we have believed that rational thought and the fearless analysis of objective reality (both natural and social) are incisive tools for combating the mystifications promoted by the powerful—not to mention being desirable human ends in their own right." David Bell suggests that such comments by Sokal are revealing, for if he really does believe that "the Left has been identified with science and against obscurantism," then, in Bell's words, "he just doesn't know much about the intellectual history of Europe, and the whole discussion hasn't induced him to take a very hard look, either. If he had, maybe he would have encountered things like the First World War and the doubts about science that it instilled in some of the best thinkers, things like phenomenology, which was an obvious ploy to separate philosophy from the philosophy of science and in some sense signaled the end of positivism (positivism really appears to be the philosophy that Sokal espouses, by the way), things like the economic modernization movement in France in the 30's, whose proponents preached tirelessly for science and efficiency—and implicitly for the modern and efficient economy of fascism as well" (personal correspondence, September 1998). So much for pure science; but Sokal goes further, into issues of pure Leftism.

Although it was not necessary, the debate that ended up swirling around the hoax threw up a lot of holier-than-thou rhetoric that often looked like a struggle to sit in the chair furthest to the left. For example, Stanley Aranowitz, arguing on behalf of *Social Text*, suggests that "what is at issue is whether our knowledge of [the material world] can possibly be free of social and cultural presuppositions," and suggests that "*Social Text* was founded, and remains within, the Marxist project—which, as everyone knows, is profoundly materialist." Andrew Ross was quoted by the *New York Times* on May 18, 1996, that "scientific knowledge is affected by social and cultural conditions and is not a version of some universal truth that is the same in all times and places," which could presumably offer consolation to a left-wing social sciences approach to the hard sciences. According to this approach, therefore, the issue here is not sloppy scholarship, nor funding, nor science versus nonscience, but is in fact a heavily ideological one concerning the advancement of the human condition. It is a tough point to argue, given the subject of the hoax article, and it only works well if we accept to tie it to what Boghossian calls "the pernicious consequences and internal contradictions of 'postmodern' relativism."[33] This is interesting, since it ascribes to scholarly articles in the social sciences more value and impact than they usually expect, and it flies in the face of the point of view that underwrites many Sokal supporters, which is that literary or cultural critics are really doing very little, except pretending to be legitimate by invoking complex theories.

Finally, there is the issue of the relationship between the hoax itself, that is, of Sokal and Bricmont as left-wingers, versus the material to which they refer and the question of whether it is leftist. These are two very different issues, and if Sokal and Bricmont wish to wade into the waters of the latter point, then they are passing judgments of the sort they seem to want to avoid because they are no longer speaking of the erroneous uses made of science by social sciences, they are telling us whether or not Derrida is useful for a leftist project. Hints that they are doing just this appear in Sokal's and Bricmont's writings in which they cite with great approbation the views of Alan Ryan, who writes that: "It is, for instance, pretty suicidal for embattled minorities to embrace Michel Foucault, let alone Jacques Derrida. The minority view was always that power could be undermined by truth. . . . Once you read Foucault as saying that truth is simply an effect of power, you've had it. . . . But American departments of literature, history and sociology contain large numbers of self-described leftists who have confused radical doubts about objectivity with political radicalism and are in a mess."[34] Bricmont seems much more willing than Sokal to condemn the whole postmodern practice, suggesting that the objectives of this project are somewhat less than modest. For instance, Bricmont writes in an article for *Free Inquiry*[35] that "We believe that we have uncovered an extreme form of intellectual abuse—namely, academics trying to impress a nonscientific audience with abstruse scientific jargon that the academics themselves do not understand very well. Our goal was to show that, in some sense, the 'emperor is naked' and that generations of students who had to struggle in order to understand obscure texts were sometimes right to suspect that they were wasting their time" (23). Who is he to say? Again, if he sticks to the science, that is one thing; but here he seems to be venturing outward, "uncovering" and "showing" that students have been wasting their time, that they should have been doing what he thinks they should have been doing. This idea is associated with unsavory elements of the left rather than to valuable left-wing approaches that would condemn this authoritarianism.

This is where the link to Chomsky's work is interesting, because both Bricmont and Sokal seem at times to refer, directly or indirectly, to the types of things that Chomsky says. But notice how different Chomsky's tone is in the following passage from *Year 501*, a text that Bricmont himself cites in his *Free Inquiry* article:

Left intellectuals took an active part in the lively working class culture. Some sought to compensate for the class character of the cultural institutions through programs of workers' education, or by writing best-selling books on mathematics, science, and other topics for the general public. Remarkably, their left counterparts today often seek to deprive working people of these tools of emancipation, informing us that the "project of the Enlightenment" is dead, that we must abandon the "illusions" of science and rationality—a message that will gladden the hearts of the powerful, delighted to monopolize these instruments for their own use.[36]

The point here relates to empowering people, not to appropriating the power presently in the hands of the social scientists for use by the scientists. This is a serious issue for Chomsky:

I'm deploring the fact that while people who considered themselves left intellectuals 60 years ago were devoting themselves to the needs and interests of the great mass of the population (for example, by introducing them to modern science and mathematics), many of those who call themselves "left intellectuals" today prefer to feather their own nests while telling the general public that they should not pay attention to what human intelligence and creativity has achieved, but should leave all of this to the powerful and privileged and join the postmodernists in what (to me, at least) is incomprehensible jargon. All of this is a marvelous gift to power, and much to be deplored, in my opinion. I could well be wrong. I'm quite open-minded about this. I'll be convinced as soon as someone explains to me some of the new insights that have been achieved. So far, what I read in these domains seems to me either near truism, long accepted, or absurd, incomprehensible, or "obfuscatory" (to borrow your term). Good for careers, and a real service to power. But I don't see any other function.[37]

It is clear in the comparison between Bricmont's and Chomsky's approach that Bricmont is missing some of Chomsky's principle points concerning the uses and misuses of knowledge, and by doing so is in my sense maligning those very interests of the left that he apparently wishes to support. Furthermore, both Sokal and Bricmont miss the oft-stated point that what the postmoderns say is in many cases *obvious*, rather than wrong, says Chomsky:

On the problems of science, as actually practiced, doubtless there are many, but I don't see that we gain any understanding of these matters from these sources. Rather, just mountains of confusion and misunderstanding. Not that everything is wrong. What little I understand is often true: e.g., the anti-foundationalism, not only true, but truism, and for hundreds of years. That seems to me the problem: either truism, or unintelligible. To be fair, I'm exaggerating. When one peels away the polysyllabic rhetoric, there are often some good ideas, which could be stated quite simply, I think. If so, why not? Merits thought, it seems to me.[38]

Next, and this relates to issues raised during the Faurisson Affair discussion as well, there's a whole lot here that is lost in translation, both literally and figuratively. One has only to compare original writing in French to the English translation of texts by, for example, Derrida, to recognize the problems of explaining deconstruction to uncertain graduate students in central Iowa. Not only is there a problem of the quality of translation, which there is indeed, but there is also a question of context; students in France are taught in a system that is very different from the American one, and the reader of *Le Monde*, never mind a book of philosophy, expects something quite different than the reader of *The New York Times*, if only in terms of emphasis and knowledge that is taken for granted.[39] This brings us to a critical point regarding the France—United States issue, which itself has received considerable coverage, although the French commentators (such as Denis Duclos, Pierre Guerlain, Bruno Latour, Natalie Levisalles) have been more attentive to it than the Americans. Much of the discussion in the Sokal hoax centered on remarks by Julia Kristeva, who suggested to *Le Nouvel observateur* that the Sokal business was in fact part of a growing anti-French politico-economic campaign. Bricmont and Sokal were particularly upset by this remark, as is evident from their piece in the *TLS*. I doubt that she considered it all that radical to suggest that the American academy was attempting to carry out a cultural agenda that was as consciously imperialist as the New (Economic) World Order. Her view did not surprise those who know of her long experience with high-level and highly politicized intellectual worlds, of which she has long been a well-recognized participant. Further, we have enough knowledge, thanks especially to a slew of books dealing with twentieth-century French history, of what has been called the authoritarian side of certain French intellectual elites. This is a specific use of the term *authoritarian*, relating to ties between the intellectuals and the State, for example, in ties between the supporters of the Parti Communiste Français (many of whom were intellectuals) and the Bolsheviks and later, when the worst atrocities were finally revealed in France, between the French Left and the Maoists. In short Kristeva, who herself followed those trends, is well placed to recognize links between academies and power, and justifiably considered that the Sokal business was ideological as well as corrective. But all this is reasonably well known, both to the French and to the Americans. Besides, as many people have aptly pointed out, those people cited by Sokal (including Kristeva) have been canonized by the Americans far more insistently than by the French, for whom people like Lyotard or Baudrillard could well have been blips on a well-populated philosophy screen. Further, French intellectuals may not have been led to write as they have about wars not taking place, or postmodern conditions, had the audience been either differently construed or, to be more cynical, a little bit less trained to listen in a particular fashion to the intellectual leaders of the era. Baudrillard's articles in French newspapers, later transformed into Indiana University Press books about the Gulf War, look and feel quite different in English than in their original form in French. It does not make this text any less pernicious (or ridiculous), but it does make it better understood by those with knowledge of both the French and the American worlds. Furthermore, Sokal forgets with his remarks that there are intellectual traditions, and that the French have for a very long time engaged in pastiches and literary mystifications, and that this hoax fits nicely into this genre.

So we are back to the beginning: why all the fuss? Because it seems that this hoax is a conduit that connects to a range of sensitive points in the contemporary intellectual world. It forced scientists who would normally have little reason to discuss their science beyond their own specific domains to engage literary theorists, and social scientists to present the nature and consequences of their approach; maybe this is a good thing. But it also shows us the nefarious side of purposeful misunderstanding, of intellectual imperialism, and of power relations among the disciplines. If as Holquist seems to suggest the hoax had stopped with the original punch line, then the overall upshot may have been more uplifting. Reading the views of Bricmont, Weinberg, and others does indeed suggest that not only does the emperor have no clothing, but that there's a coup in the palace, and lots of interested parties are out for the spoils. Further, if we rest at the space that Sokal has opened for us, that is, at the idea that social scientists misunderstand sciences and promulgate their misunderstanding through misinformed articles, then we have not said much. Even if this leads to the suggestion that close reading of certain books in the domain of cultural or literary criticism is likely to reveal contradictions and mistakes, we have but reiterated what serious literary and cultural critics have been saying for years. If on the other hand the hoax has greater significance, then an overview of the positions elucidated serves to demonstrate that larger objectives tend to be nefarious and in many cases power related.

Most regrettable is that so few people on either side of this debate have been able to laugh and learn. Some have been able to laugh without learning, like the scientists who have only managed to criticize the weakest sides of the postmodern world. Some have been able to learn without laughing, which makes me wonder what they've learned. But for the most part the sides are probably as far apart as ever—if not further. It does not follow that just because social scientists have misunderstood, or even misused, the ideas from pure sciences that we should therefore leave the sciences alone to pursue whichever kind of breakthrough scientists think most compelling, or most pure. People do have ideas about what is in their own best interests, and the approach that Chomsky, for example, suggests is to open up discussion, not close it down, to recognize real interests of real human beings, not determine that scientists are the victors because not all social scientists know how to properly use complex scientific ideas. Proper utilization of scientific theories does provide answers to some questions, just as it provides the know-how to annihilate our planet. These are not pure issues, and perhaps it is a general wariness that has led people from all domains to consider carefully the implications of scientific debates, from the viability of multibillion-dollar particle accelerators and space stations to the continued logic of relying upon nuclear power in an era when we seem quite clearly incapable of preventing potentially devastating accidents or even discarding of the wastes that the process produces. Sokal and Bricmont do not render any services when they tell us to keep out because we are too stupid to understand what is going on, and they not support the Left by telling people what to think or how to interpret the world, and in both of these tendencies they betray their dear Left cause. It is useful to engage in self-mockery and self-criticism because it can raise intellectual standards; what we do not need is another academic mandarin to dictate policy.

Language Studies and Anarchy

Beyond the Chomsky studies of media and propaganda, beyond the differences between Chomsky's overall objectives and those of postmodern language theorists, beyond the appropriation of Chomsky for perhaps self-interested attacks against postmodern language studies, is it possible to tease out a link between the Chomsky approach to social issues and his studies of language? We've seen the Enlightenment influence in Chomsky's writings, of course, but in my opinion we could go even further and find in the ways that Chomsky poses questions about language some overlap with certain anarchist ideas. For example, consistent with what Chomsky calls the Cartesian approach to language, previously described, Rudolph Rocker claims in *Nationalism and Culture* that "language itself does not have a national origin. Rather, human beings are endowed with the ability to articulate language which permits of concepts and so enables man's thoughts to achieve higher results, which distinguish man in this respect from other species" (284). Rocker's objective in discussing language is to undermine notions of racial purity upheld by the Nazis at the time when he was writing his book (the 1930s). More important, though, is his sense that discourse is like a living entity inasmuch as it constantly evolves and adapts, taking in new expressions and terms from various strata of society or from different cultures or groups. This dynamic never-fixed status of language threatens authority and is therefore itself subjected to various attempts on the part of authoritarian institutions, like governments, to control its functioning, something described by both Rocker and Mikhaïl Bakhtin. In a passage describing the regimentation of the French life in the seventeenth century, Rocker gives the example of the establishment of the French Academy in 1629, commenting that "such an act was passed in order to subordinate language and poetry to the authoritarian ambition of absolutism" (429). The effect was that authorities tried to render the French language unitary by imposing upon it "a strict guardian that endeavoured with all its power to eliminate from it popular expressions and figures of speech. This was called 'refining the language.' In reality, it deprived it of originality and bent it under the yoke of an unnatural despotism from which it was later obliged forcibly to free itself" (287). Furthermore, "every higher form of culture, if it is not too greatly hindered in its natural development by political obstructions, strives constantly to renew its creative urge to construct" (83). And the sense that people left to their own devices will lazily let the sands of time slip between their inactive fingers is, for Rocker, but a poor scare tactic: "Always and everywhere the same creative urge is hungry for action; only the mode of expression differs and is adapted to the environment" (346).

The whole project of studying language from Rocker's perspective is, therefore, intimately related not to the science-nonscience split so often described in the difference between Chomskian linguistics and language studies, or postmodern studies and real work on language, but to the political agendas of those who would approach languages in certain ways. When *Nationalism and Culture* was written—the early 1930s in Germany—was a time when language was put to the use of nationalism, which explains some of his comments:

Language is not the invention of individual men. In its creation and development the community has worked and continues to work as long as the language has life in it. Hence, language appeared to the advocates of the national idea as the purest product of national creativeness and became for them the clearest symbol of national unity. Yet this concept, no matter how fascinating and irrefutable it may appear to most, rests on a totally arbitrary assumption. Among the present existing languages there is not one which has developed from a definite people. It is very probable that there were once homogeneous languages, but that time is long past, lost in the greyest antiquity of history. The individuality of language disappears the moment reciprocal relations arise between different hordes, tribes and peoples. The more numerous and various these relations become in the course of the millenniums, the larger borrowings does every language make from other languages, every culture from other cultures. (277)

These relations nourish the natural propensity of languages to evolve, just like an organism that lives in a state of constant flux: "Not only does it make the most diversified borrowings from other languages, a phenomenon due to the countless influences and points of contact in cultural life, but it also possesses a stock of words that is continually changing. Quite gradually and unnoticeably the shadings and gradations of the concepts which find their expression in words alter, so that it often happens that a word means today exactly the opposite of what men originally expressed by it" (277).

To study language is therefore to recognize its contextual richness, including the infusion of other languages into a single language for, as Rocker points out, "there exists no cultural language which does not contain a great mass of foreign material, and the attempt to free it from these foreign intruders would lead to a complete dissolution of the language—that is, if such a purification could be achieved at all. Every European language contains a mass of foreign elements with which, often, whole dictionaries could be filled" (277). This tendency is described by Mikhail Bakhtin, a philosopher of language working in roughly the same time period in the Soviet Union, in terms of "polyglossia," "the simultaneous presence of two or more national languages interacting within a single cultural system"[40] and also "heteroglossia," which refers to the various strata of languages that occurs through the various points of contact between different types of language practice—even within a given national language. For Bakhtin, "at any given moment of its historical existence, language is heteroglot from top to bottom: it represents the co-existence of socio-ideological contradictions between the present and the past, between differing epochs of the past, between different socio-ideological groups in the present, between tendencies, schools, circles and so forth, all given a bodily form. These 'languages' of heteroglossia intersect each other in a variety of ways, forming new socially typifying 'languages'" (291).

For Rocker this very same phenomenon can be threatened, and when it is, the very essence of society is put into danger: "For the development of every language the acceptance of foreign elements is essential. No people lives for itself. Every enduring intercourse with other peoples results in the borrowing of words from their language; this is quite indispensable to reciprocal cultural fecundation. The countless points of contact which culture daily creates between people leave their traces in

language. New objects, ideas, concepts—religious, political and generally social—lead to new expression and word formations. In this, the
older and more developed cultures naturally have a strong influence on
less developed folk-groups and furnish these with new ideas which find
their expression in language" (278).

Rocker even enters into the specifics of this phenomenon, noting that
in some cases the foreign expression for a particular idea is not adopted,
even though the idea is, something that he refers to as "loan translation." In this case, "we translate the newly acquired concept into our
own language by creating from the material at hand a word structure
not previously used. Here the stranger confronts us, so to speak, in the
mask of our own language (*halbinsel* from peninsula, *halbwelt* from
demi-monde, etc.). These have an actually revolutionary effect on the
course of development of the language, and show us most of all the un-
reality of the view which maintains that in every language the spirit of
a particular people lives and works. In reality every loan-translation is
but a proof of the continuous penetration of foreign cultural elements
within our own cultural circle—insofar as a people can speak of 'its own
culture'" (282). Chomsky seldom talks about cultural production, and
he is not much interested in his linguistic work in the heteroglossia of
languages; nevertheless, I would venture to say that there is a way by
which one could consider cultural activity from an anarchist perspective,
which recalls some of Chomsky's own insights.

For Rudolph Rocker, cultural matters are foremost, since the stimulation of people through artistic means is related to his sense of the formation and maintenance of communities. "Cultural reconstructions and
social stimulation always occur when different peoples and races come
into closer union. Every new culture is begun by such a fusion of different folk elements and takes its special shape from this" (346). Notice
that he refers in a statement like this one to both foreign elements (polyglossia) and to different strata of culture (heteroglossia). And notice as
well that attempts to seal off cultures leads to a retrograde "inbreeding":
"All experience indicates rather that . . . inbreeding would lead inevitably
to a general stunting, to a slow extinction of culture. In this respect it is
with peoples as it is with persons. How poorly that man would fare who
in his cultural development had to rely on the creations of his own

people!" (346). Communities, like relationships, must be nourished and continuously revitalized with diverse influences, an idea that hearkens back to the previous chapter on education, notably the ideas therein that relate to Bertrand Russell's approach. Says Rocker, in one of his more purple passages: "New life arises only from the union of man with woman. Just so a culture is born or fertilised only by the circulation of fresh blood in the veins of its representatives. Just as the child results from the mating so new culture forms arise from the mutual fertilisation of different peoples and their spiritual sympathy with foreign achievements and capacities" (346). And in a passage that recalls the whole project of this book, and of course much of what Chomsky says about discovery procedures, Rocker writes: "We are always dependent upon our predecessors, and for this reason the notion of a 'national culture' is misleading and inconsistent. We are never in a position to draw a line between what we have acquired by our own powers and what we have received from others. Every idea, whether it be of a religious, an ethical, a philosophic, a scientific or an artistic nature, had its forerunners and pioneers, without which it would be inconceivable; and it is usually quite impossible to go back to its first beginnings. Almost invariably thinkers of all countries and peoples have contributed to its development" (453).

This is an argument for the promotion of unfettered associations of peoples across all cultural and linguistic lines. Says Rocker, "The inner culture of a man grows just in the measure that he develops an ability to appropriate the achievements of other peoples and enrich his mind with them. The more easily he is able to do this the better it is for his mental culture, the greater right he has to the title, man of culture. He immerses himself in the gentle wisdom of Lao-tse and rejoices in the beauty of the Vedic poems. Before his mind unfold the wonder-tales of the *Thousand and One Nights*, and with inner rapture he drinks in the sayings of the wine loving Omar Khayyam or the majestic strophes of Firdusi. . . . In one word, he is everywhere at home, and therefore knows better how to value the charm of his own homeland. With unprejudiced eye he searches the cultural possessions of all peoples and so perceives more clearly the strong unity of all mental processes. And of these possessions no one can rob him; they are outside the jurisdiction of the government and are not subject to the will of the mighty ones of the earth. The legislator may be in a position to close the gates of his country to the stranger, but he cannot keep him from making his demands upon the treasure of the people, its mental culture, with the same assurance as any native" (347).

According to this scenario, the artist is of special interest since he or she is the one who promulgates the "mental culture" of a given place and time by setting down in a unique fashion the currents of existing heteroglossia, not by inventing something that stands outside of contemporary experience.

Of course, the artist does not stand outside of space and time; he, too, is but a man, like the least of his contemporaries. His ego is no abstract image, but living entity, in which every side of his social being is mirrored and action and reaction are at work. He, too, is bound to the men of his time by a thousand ties; in their sorrows and their joys he has his personal share; and in his heart their ambitions, hopes and wishes find an echo. As a social being he is endowed with the same social instinct; in his person is reflected the whole environment in which he lives and works and which, of necessity, finds its expression in his productions. But how this expression will manifest itself, in what particular manner the soul of the artist will react to the impressions that he receives from his surroundings, is in the final outcome decided by his own temperament, his special endowment of character—in a word, his personality. (474)

But no matter how ingrained the author is, no matter how in tune to currents of discourse or to contemporary trends or the general "social discourse" of a society, she or he is also subjected to the limitations imposed by the ruling classes and the form of social organization. The anarchist conception refuses arbitrary power because it considers that compulsion is a power relation that will ultimately separate people. Compulsion, says Rocker, "lacks the inner drive of all social unions— the understanding which recognises the facts and the sympathy which comprehends the feeling of the fellow man because it feels itself related to him. By subjecting men to a common compulsion one does not bring them closer to one another, rather one creates estrangements between them and breeds impulses of selfishness and separation. Social ties have permanence and completely fulfil their purpose only when they are based on good will and spring from the needs of men. Only under such conditions is a relationship possible where social union and the freedom of the individual are so closely intergrown that they can no longer be recognised as separate entities" (246).

Artistic production, being for the most part disinterested (unless tied to financial or state interests, as with socialist realism or prowar propaganda literature, for example), is an interesting example of spontaneous work. Literature is often considered in this fashion, particularly when one approaches it from the Romantic standpoint, as a "spontaneous overflowing of powerful feelings" that dwells outside of the normal economic relations in society. Given that literature can be this overflowing, and given that it is language based, perhaps a brief foray into the area of Chomsky and literary studies per se might produce some interesting insights and points of departure for future work.

7

Literature, Humor, and the Effects of Creative Discourses

He had heard these things so many times that they no longer held any interest for him. Emma resembled all his old mistresses, and the charm of novelty, falling away little by little like articles of clothing, revealed in all its nakedness the eternal monotony of passion, which always assumes the same forms and speaks the same language. This man, who was so experienced in love, could not distinguish the dissimilarity in the emotions behind the similarity of expressions. He couldn't really accept Emma's lack of guile, having heard similar sentences from the mouths of venal and immoral women. One should be able to tone down, he thought, those exaggerated speeches that mask lack of feeling—as if the fullness of the soul did not sometimes overflow into the emptiest of metaphors. No one can ever express the exact measure of his needs, or conceptions, or sorrows. The human language is like a cracked kettle on which we beat out a tune for a dancing bear, when we hope with our music to move the stars.

—Flaubert, *Madame Bovary*

Sigmund Freud made frequent reference to literature in his writings on the assumption that the stories which are told, and retold, often contain archetypes of human behavior. As such, themes that recur in the canon illustrate the ability of many authors to tap into deeper psychic processes and dramatize them in fiction, which is one reason why one might be interested in the types of knowledge one can learn from canonical literary texts. Freud also made much of the jokes we tell one another, and the "slips" that embarrass us, because they tend to offer deeper insights into the tensions and pressures that exist between various forces buried below the level of the conscious self. This would suggest that creative discourse has a privileged role to play, and indeed for many theorists who aim to understand a given social phenomenon, including those for whom literature is not a specific focus of study, literature tends to come

up by way of example, juxtaposition, or explanation. Using unlike references or surprising juxtapositions can also provide comic relief and a
sense of possible alternatives, even when the subject is horrible, so I have
chosen in this chapter to talk about Chomsky's approach to literature and
creative discourse, on the one hand, but also to make reference to his
powerful and omnipresent sense of humor and the role that it plays in
opening up other possibilities for those interested in his work. If literature
allows us to experience worlds to which we would not otherwise have
access, which is a distinct feeling I have when reading, say, a realist novel
by Balzac or Dickens, then laughter has a way of unsettling the world
that I think I inhabit. Literature and laughter, therefore, can offer alternatives to the status quo, and by thinking about Chomsky's work as it
relates to both–and with reference to others who have thought about literature, creativity, and laughter—another side of the Chomsky approach
will I hope be illuminated.

In order to properly situate some of Chomsky's ideas about creative
language, especially in literature, and his own use of humor and laughter to unsettle accepted notions about the world, I will expand upon
earlier discussions of some previously invoked theorists whose work may
be less well known to general readers, notably Marc Angenot, a Belgian-
born philologist and historian, Mikhail Bakhtin,[1] a Russian-born
philosopher of language, and Pierre Bourdieu, the French-born sociologist who made considerable contributions to our understanding of the
relationship between language and power. As has been the case throughout, I am hopeful that these juxtapositions will help broaden our understanding of Chomsky's work—in this case his literary comments and
the way in which he can provoke uplifting, unsettling, and sometimes
salubrious peals of laughter.

The "Creative" Uses of Language

Chomsky's work on language studies has not brought him to apply his
linguistics insights to the domain of literary studies because the questions
asked in the two domains are, at least when posed by Chomsky, incompatible. But he has made statements in the course of his career about
literature, and about the nature of literary knowledge, in many of his

works, including *New Horizons in the Study of Language and the Mind*: "Plainly, a naturalistic approach does not exclude other ways of trying to comprehend the world. Someone committed to it can consistently believe (I do) that we learn much more of human interest about how people think and feel and act by reading novels or studying history or the activities of ordinary life than from all of naturalistic psychology, and perhaps always will; similarly, the arts may offer appreciation of the heavens to which astrophysics does not aspire. We are speaking here of theoretical understanding, a particular mode of comprehension. In this domain, any departure from this approach carries a burden of justification. Perhaps one can be given, but I know of none" (77). This age-old question about the status of literary knowledge has led to significant conjecture about the definition of literature, about its role in our study of human nature and society, and about the special knowledge that authors can bring to bear through their writings. I would like to think about this question with regard to those who have thought about discourse studies in a historical, political, and contextual fashion, since this seems the most appropriate approach for any discussion of literature from a Chomskian paradigm. I therefore suggest that we look into "sociocriticism," an area of literary research that has been advanced by the likes of Marc Angenot, Régine Robin, Claude Duchet, and others, who have asked what literature knows that other kinds of texts do not, or cannot know, and what literature accomplishes in what Pierre Bourdieu has called the "marketplace of competing discursive practices." Sociocriticism is important for our discussion as well because it is hyperconscious of the relationship between the text and its surroundings, which is certainly one of the ways that Chomsky employs his literary references. Many sociocritical studies therefore dwell upon the unique and privileged position of the novel within the traffic of ideas, images, forms, stereotypes, and discursive configurations.[2]

The novel is a locus upon or through which the fluid memory and imagination, and that great mass of social discourse, become crystallized, and it is notable that people like Chomsky, who are wont to invoke literature for discussions of attitudes, histories, or politics, most often make references to the novel, as opposed to poetry or even drama. It seems that the effect upon the imagination of this crystallization gives strong impetus for studying the social aspects of the novel, and the role of the novel as purveyor of images. Régine Robin claims, for example, that characters from novels occupy our imaginations as strongly as our own memories of actual persons, scenes, images, or places. The novel in this sense is a reservoir of images, words, phrases, and situations. For Robin, this reservoir is, by nature of its *socialité* (social nature), subject to changes across time, whereby the text produces new meanings and transforms, inscribes, and displaces meanings. The novel knows a lot about ambiguity, construction, transformation, and transmission through language, and as such knows about discursive genres and the reality they attempt to portray. The novel also has the remarkable ability of rejuvenating communities by differently representing reality and, by emphasizing the thoroughly socialized nature of any text, sociocriticism contributes to a study of the communal nature of language. An interesting sociocritical figure in this regard is Marc Angenot, the founding father of social discourse theory (and practice) who is especially appropriate here because he also happens to be a historian of the radical Left. Sociocriticism, especially as described by Angenot, helps to defetishize literature while situating it into a properly social realm. From this standpoint, it is interesting to examine Angenot's sense that literature does not know the world any better than any other kind of discursive practice, but is nevertheless able to show that those who think they know it are in fact fooling themselves, a viewpoint that suggests the modesty of our understanding and the limitation of any single vision. We need others to fill in for us, for their regard allows for a more complete vision than a single, monologic, perspective, which is the part of sociocriticism that privileges the transgression, the production of meaning through discourse, the innovation, and the internal tensions or mystification of discursive practices. Sociocriticism specifies the nature of the impact that literature has upon the reader by pointing out its paradoxical roles, as on the one hand that which proliferates variously constituted fragments of social discourse (by virtue of its intertextual nature), and on the other that which challenges the broader compendium of social discourse through its ability to juxtapose and articulate contradictory, uncomplimentary, or unrelated fragments of a whole, either in the present or in some undetermined future.

I will integrate thoughts on similar issues from some of Chomsky's political and linguistic writings, in part because he—in, for example, his studies of media—attempts to circumscribe literary knowledge within much larger social projects that center around thinking about the role of language in prevailing sociopolitical structures. This may seem at first an odd juxtaposition. Marc Angenot is a historian, albeit situated in a literature department, who denies literature any particular role or even definition, suggesting instead that it is a realm of discursive praxis that may, like any other realm, have some interesting things to say, or some interesting ways to retell stories told in the overall mass of things said in society. Noam Chomsky is hardly someone who has a strong ear tuned to the aesthetic, the literary, the artistic. And yet, in an interview with David Barsamian, he turns out some surprising insights into propaganda and discourse practices with reference to work by literary figures, usually novelists, such as Fyodor Dostoyevsky:

DB: In your writings you rarely refer to literature. There is one major exception. In *Necessary Illusions* you cite "The Grand Inquisitor" chapter in the *Brothers Karamazov*. What was Dostoyevsky writing about that caught your attention?

NC: That's a particularly striking passage. He's talking about manufacture of consent. It's a very dramatic and accurate presentation of the way mystery, ceremony, fear, and even joy are manipulated so as to make people feel that they must be subordinate to others. It's a denunciation of Christ, because Christ was trying to give people freedom from these constraints. Christ didn't understand that this was what people wanted. They need to be subordinated to mystery and magic and control. So Christ is really a criminal. That's the burden of the argument.

DB: And that the Church must correct the evil work of Christ, as it were. You understood that to be the state.

NC: For Dostoyevsky it just meant power. He was writing in Russia, remember. So it's a combination of the church and the czar, both very closely related.

DB: You say, "[F]ew reach the level of sophistication of the Grand Inquisitor."

NC: The Grand Inquisitor is articulating the view that freedom is dangerous and people need, and indeed at some level even want, subordination, mystery, authority, and so on. That's a sophisticated version of manufacture of consent.[3]

Barsamian is noticeably surprised in this interview because Chomsky the linguist seldom speaks of literature per se and, perhaps not surprisingly, Chomsky the political activist and social thinker also has little or nothing to say about literary texts (which is in itself telling, as we'll see later on). In fact, the issue of discourse as action is seldom raised in his work beyond the study of propaganda, and despite the prodding of various interviewers, Chomsky has never made any substantial remarks concerning the role of literary discourse in society. He does use it on occasion in the way that Karl Marx was wont to use it, or as Marc Angenot uses it, as a set of free and unfettered texts from which we can draw as another way of doing history or doing social observations that can be keener, or better put, than in the history books. Surprisingly, Chomsky has provided over the years enough commentary to allow us to develop an implicit sense of how creative discourse can act upon dominant ideology, and concentrating upon literary knowledge will allow us, as it were, to assemble all of these comments and derive a sense of the system of discursive relations, and some answers to some key questions about creativity in language and beyond. Questions such as: What can art do in a society? Has it the same features as the propaganda system, which could make it a tool to reinforce the power of the ruling class? Is art one of many ways in which the social discourse speaks out through the pen of a single individual? Is literature more susceptible to manipulation because of its linguistic character? What is the status of literary knowledge?

To ask questions like this of Chomsky is problematic; there are slim pickings of Chomsky on literature despite the fact that he has written a number of texts with potentially related titles, such as *Language and Responsibility*, *Language and Politics*, and *Problems of Language and Freedom*.[4] One reason for this is that Chomsky is a linguist and not a literary theoretician, and though his political work could have inspired work on literary texts (social approaches to literature, literature as a reflection of contradictions in society and so forth), he has concentrated on comments about the prevailing political and economic system. The challenge for someone looking to study his views concerning the epistemology of literature is that he does not perceive any clear relationship between his work in linguistics and his libertarian politics. As such, he does not want to impose a relationship whereby one field of his interests is forced to coincide with another, so if his scientific (linguistic) ideas could merge with politics, independently, "that is fine," according to

Chomsky. "But they should not be made to converge at the cost of distortion and suppression, or anything like that" Chomsky admits that there are moments in his linguistic work where heavy emphasis is laid upon "freedom," "creativity," "competence," "spontaneity," and other notions that are used in similar ways as in his political work. But he denies all but a "tenuous connection," that "anyone's political ideas or their ideas of social organization must be rooted ultimately in some concept of human nature and human needs" (*Language and Politics* 143). This leads us to one of the rare discussions concerning art and its relationship to creativity in Chomsky's work.

My own feeling is that the fundamental human capacity is the capacity and the need for creative self-expression, for free control of all aspects of one's life and thought. One particularly crucial realization of this capacity is the creative use of language as a free instrument of thought and expression. Now having this view of human nature and human needs, one tries to think about the modes of social organization that would permit the freest and fullest development of the individual, of each individual's potentialities in whatever direction they might take, that would permit him to be fully human in the sense of having the greatest possible scope for his freedom and initiative. (*Language and Politics* 144)

The first question raised by this quotation relates to the definition of terms, notably the "creative use of language," which comes up frequently in his work. On Chomsky's use of this category in the linguistic realm, John Goldsmith comments:

There is a deep and difficult point that would require a monograph to treat seriously, but you should at least be aware of it. There are those (I am one of them) who think that Chomsky is a master at (certain aspects of) manipulative control of language, in what are often the wrong ways, I would suggest. I think that his use of terms such as "creative use of language" in connection with generative grammar, especially during the second half of the 1960s, is such a case; the use of the term "deep structure," and later "Universal Grammar," are similar cases. To take the first example for a moment, that of "creative use of language"; the use of formal terms to allow for recursive structures, out of which potentially infinite sets of structures could be generated, does not give us insight into creative use of anything. There are some allusions to poetic extensions of ordinary language in *Aspects* and writings of that period, but real creativity has never been the kind of phenomenon that Chomsky's style of theorizing is designed for, nor is it the sort of thing that interests him as a scientist. I think this is obvious to anyone who knows his theories; it's not really a matter of interpretation, as I see it. "Deep structure" has a much more remarkable history. Chomsky put together a very elegant model in Chapter Two of *Aspects*, providing a deep explanation of an important observation that Charles Fillmore had published in 1964

(as I recall), in a Mouton monograph, and Chomsky made a number of interesting predictions based on this new model. But it was wildly misunderstood and
misquoted, often taken to be universal, and certainly understood as containing
somehow the essence and the language-independent meaning of the sentence, not
at all central to Chomsky's technical theory at the time.[5]

One source of confusion, which leads to the misunderstanding that
Goldsmith describes, is Chomsky's references to creative use of language,
and creativity more broadly defined, in response to specific questions
about freedom expressed through artwork. In this realm, freedom is
inscribed into a preexisting system, a kind of liberty within the context
of a rule-bound social system. Therefore, "if a person just throws cans
of paint randomly at a wall, with no rules at all, no structure, that is not
artistic creativity, whatever else it may be." This suggests that there is a
kind of intentionality involved in Chomsky's vision of art; for him, "it
is a commonplace of aesthetic theory that creativity involves action that
takes place within a framework of rules, but is not narrowly determined
either by the rules or by external stimuli. It is only when you have the
combination of freedom and constraint that the question of creativity
arises" (*Language and Politics* 144). The rules, therefore, are far more
recognizable and self-conscious than those described by Marc Angenot,
which tend as we shall see to reflect historical and discursive conditions.
This is not an anomaly in Chomsky's work; in fact, it is fair to suggest
that artistic works are seldom viewed beyond the sociopolitical realm in
which they are created.

For this reason, Chomsky seems to suggest that it is necessary to
understand literature according to the constraining system, which is
the dominant sociopolitical context within which the artistic work is
received. This context contains powerful legislation and methods of
policing public activities. A revealing example for an understanding of
Chomsky's work is the reception and the teaching of George Orwell's
novel *1984*. He describes this text as an unimaginative, tenth-rate work
that does not approach the true nature of our own system. We have suppressed, according to Chomsky, the fact that this work was a description of what Orwell had "expected to happen in the industrial
democracies, and as a prediction that was very bad, that hasn't happened." He then suggests that for these very reasons, it is sanctioned
by the authorities in our society since it can be read as an anti-Soviet

treatise that points out apparent flaws in the *enemy's* society. "The U.S. public relations industry had already gone very beyond Orwell when he wrote *1984*. In fact, you might ask yourself why Orwell's *1984* is a popular book. Why does anybody bother reading it? One reason is because it's obviously modelled on an enemy. It's about the Soviet Union, a very thinly disguised account of the Soviet Union, and anything bad that you say about an official enemy is fine" (*Language and Politics* 727). This is Chomsky the sociologist of literature, describing the reception, the sale, and the use of a literary text by the ruling classes. The power that he ascribes to this ruling elite is remarkable, and serves as a bridge between his thinking about literature and his analysis of propaganda.

Suppose that Orwell had written a more interesting book. It's kind of trivial to write about the Soviet Union, with its obvious forms of indoctrination. Suppose he'd written an interesting book, namely about us. That's much more interesting than about somebody else. Suppose he had exposed the kind of indoctrination that goes on here, like that I've just mentioned. You bet your life that wouldn't be a best-seller. Nobody would have heard of Orwell. Nobody would have published it and it would have gone right down the "memory hole"—his "memory hole." The very fact that you [the interviewer] even think of Orwell is already a sign of how indoctrinated you are. Not that it's your fault. From kindergarten you just get deluged with this stuff until you just don't know how to think any more. (ibid.)

The text by Orwell that Chomsky does appreciate is *Homage to Catalonia*, a nonfiction work that describes Orwell's personal experiences as a member of POUM (Partido Obrero de Unificación Marxista—Worker's Party of Marxist Unification) during the Spanish Civil War. In discussing this text, Chomsky describes the context of its publication:

The history of that book is itself interesting and revealing. The book appeared in 1937. It was not published in the United States. It was published in England, and it sold a couple of hundred copies. The reason that the book was suppressed was because it was critical of communists. That was a period when pro-communist intellectuals had a great deal of power in the intellectual establishment. It's similar to the kind of control that many people called "pro-Israel," although I think it's a bad term, but people who are called pro-Israel" have media and expression today. They're similar in many respects. They succeeded in preventing Orwell's book from appearing. It did appear about 15 years later, and it appeared as a Cold War tract, because it was anti-Russian and fashions had changed. That was a really important book. I think there were things wrong with it, but I think it was a book of real great significance and importance. It's probably the least known of Orwell's major political books. (*Language and Politics* 629)

There is no mention here of the epistemology of literature or what is specifically literary about a text (its so-called *literariness*), that is, what would differentiate *1984* from *Homage To Catalonia*, and in fact Chomsky rarely discusses aesthetics in his work, and he certainly does not offer a clear sense of what literature is or does. Nevertheless, he seems to suggest here that one would read, say, Orwell's work, simply in order to learn sociological, political, or historical truths, so the form, style, vocabulary, and rhetoric of the literary text have no place in Chomsky's discussions. For example: "Existing Soviet society and its terror have been very well described by factual analyses not very well known here, but they existed. People like Maximov, for example, the anarchist historian, had given excellent detailed analyses of Leninist and Stalinist institutionalized terror going back to the Revolution. You didn't have to go to Orwell and fantasy to find this out. Orwell's fictionalized account was in my view no contribution and also not very well done" (ibid.). In this discussion, Chomsky gives the impression that the measure of greatness of a novelist is the degree to which he or she is able to step outside of the prevailing system of thought control and describe to the readers the actual workings of society. "On the other hand, [Orwell] was an honest man. He did try to, and often succeeded in extricating himself from the systems of thought control, and in that respect he was very unusual and very praiseworthy. But the one great book that he wrote, in my view, is that one that I mentioned, *Homage to Catalonia*" (*Language and Politics*, 630). And this, in my opinion, is where Chomsky's ideas about literature become intriguing and where his ideas find interesting overlap with those of Marc Angenot, whom I will cite at length to provide a source of comparison:

Literature does not provide meaning in that it would illuminate a contradictory world and transform these contradictions into certainties, and that is why . . . literature is useless. And it is true that it is, if you have a friend whose child has just died, you cannot tell her to go read Joyce and find some kind of answer to the scandal of death. Literature is a device that helps us decipher not only the world, but the text which is part and parcel of the world in a more honest way than most of the monosemic, non-contradictory paradigms that are available to us. You would come up with some kind of answer, therefore, that wouldn't be so paradoxical, that literature cannot transform the world, as so many nice people including Gide and Malraux have suggested in the twentieth century, that literature could do something to emancipate human life. Since these people are not naive on the one hand and are quite aware of the logic of aesthetic writing on the other, that means that the temptation of finding a solution was extreme. So literature does not provide an answer to the paradox 'Why is it useful?' Because it does not. . . . [T]o the extent that literature is innocuous and in a way, impotent to the evils of the world, we need it in order not to fool ourselves. . . . But if I do like literature, I'm not sure I like literature departments or literary teaching as such, the way it is usually done. I don't like the fetishization of this specific sector of symbolic inventiveness that seems entailed in your studying a canon of great texts, or not so great texts, or even a canon of texts produced by the oppressed, the workers or the women or whatever. . . . It's the same attitude, which is to isolate a segment of this whole intertextual array of social discourse, and whatever you do you will have to fetishize it. . . . I don't think that literary departments as such are a very good thing; they correspond to a very obsolete concept of division of labor in academia, and of course even your being interested in literature is no justification to the same extent as it would be ridiculous to say that your interest in sex makes you a sexologist. Disciplines do not deal with objects, they deal with questions. So, the kind of object that we are dealing with in a discipline is a set of questions. My set of questions makes me encounter at given moments, and occasionally frequently, literary texts. But never exclusively them, and never centrally them. And for some subsets of questions that I may have in mind that are part and parcel of the problems I tried to explain, literature is decidedly irrelevant.[6]

Angenot appeals to an idea, present as well in Chomsky's work, that literature is a discourse practice without a particular knowledge claim, so it doesn't make sense to isolate or study literature as a particular subject; rather, literary texts offer the kinds of insights one might be looking for to understand sociological or historical issues. Nevertheless, since literature is also devoid of any single underlying ideological or institutional basis, its creativity and inventiveness can be more insightful than the assertions that are made in other discursive realms. As such, Chomsky can, when pressed, imagine ways in which literature could play a role that goes beyond its sociological function in society. To begin, there is a valuable interview in *The Chomsky Reader* that will serve as the basis for my remarks concerning how Chomsky perceives the role of the literary text, and there is an important interview with Mitsou Ronat in *Language and Responsibility*, that will serve as the basis for descriptions of the epistemology literature.

James Peck, the editor of *The Chomsky Reader*, and the interviewer for the opening discussion concerning Chomsky's personal background and *cheminement* (pathway), begins with a somewhat cryptic but vitally important question: "You've rarely written much on the kinds of experiences that led to your politics, even though, it seems to me, they may have been deeply formed and influenced by your background. . . . For example, I am struck by how seldom you mention literature, culture, culture in the sense of a struggle to find alternative forms of life through artistic means; rarely a novel that has influenced you. Why is this so? Were there some works that did influence you?" (3). Chomsky replies by stating that he rarely "writes about these matters" because they "don't seem particularly pertinent to the topics I am addressing." Literature affects him, he says, inasmuch as certain notions "resonate" when he reads, but overall his "feelings and attitudes were largely formed prior to reading literature." "In fact," says Chomsky, "I've been always resistant consciously to allowing literature to influence my beliefs and attitudes with regard to society and history." In sum, therefore, literary renditions of social or political situations do not offer privileged *information* concerning the actual events or the power structure with which Chomsky is concerned. However, he does admit that literature can offer a far deeper insight into another realm of knowledge, the study of what James Peck in this interview calls "the full human person" (ibid 3–4).

Furthermore, according to Chomsky, literature provides more insightful information about the full human person than does any mode of scientific inquiry. This is a notable exception to his sense of the power and value of pure sciences over social sciences, and it is in perfect accord with Mikhail Bakhtin's belief that dialogism, which is most adequately expressed in the dialogic novel, is the only means to adequately represent what he calls "the whole human being." However, Chomsky is nonetheless reticent about drawing "any tight connections" between literature and knowledge because he can not really say whether literature has ever "changed [his] attitudes and understanding in any striking or crucial way:" "[I]f I want to understand, let's say, the nature of China and its revolution, I ought to be cautious about literary renditions. Look, there's no question that as a child, when I read about China, this influenced my attitudes—*Rickshaw Boy*, for example. That had a powerful effect when I read it. It was so long ago I don't remember a thing about it, except the impact. . . . Literature can heighten your imagination and insight and understanding, but it surely doesn't provide the evidence that you need to draw conclusions and substantiate conclusions" (4).

Literature from this standpoint does not reflect either the overall social discourse of a given society or particular elements thereof, but rather is a means through which experiences can be, as Angenot pointed out, questioned, reread and, potentially, reviewed. It is difficult (if not impossible due to variations depending upon the person) to assess whether the attitudes developed by the reader with regard to a particular subject preceded the reading of literary texts, or whether the literary texts themselves helped form the attitudes (as Chomsky suggests by his discussion of the role that literary texts played for him when he was a child). But the actual relationship between literary knowledge and empirical facts is clearly problematic for Chomsky, to the point where he "consciously" blocks out any effects that literary texts might have for his analysis of particular situations. But this blockage of literary knowledge happens on the level of methodology, and it does not imply that literary discourse has no role to play in describing the contextual reality within which it is situated or read.

When Peck says to Chomsky: "you have rarely written much on the kinds of experiences that led to your politics, even though . . . they may have been deeply formed and influenced by your background," Chomsky replies that "I've not thought about it a great deal." When the question of the novel *Rickshaw Boy* comes up with respect to a discussion of China, Chomsky says that he doesn't "remember a thing about it, except the impact." When pushed on whether literature can sensitize someone "to areas of human experience otherwise not even asked about," Chomsky replies that "people certainly differ, as they should, in what kinds of things make their minds work" (4). For Chomsky, there is no rich homogeneous reservoir of intact memories that are or are not open-ended, because the reservoir itself is not filled with a homogeneous liquid that dissolves all elements in the same way, and even if there was it would only be interesting inasmuch as it could help us understand how the mind works, a capacity that we are nowhere near finding out at this point in our evolution.

Explanatory Principles

This returns us to Chomsky's refusal to bring together his work on political discourse and his work in the field of linguistics, which in this sense is based upon a belief that the former is purely observational and the latter is scientific. This has consequences for his understanding of literary texts because, as we saw earlier, Chomsky claims to consciously resist allowing literature to affect his beliefs and attitudes with regard to history. When, in his interview with Mitsou Ronat in *Language and Responsibility*, Chomsky speaks to knowledge claims, we can see why he might hold the views of literature just described: "A discipline is defined in terms of its objects and its results. Sociology is the study of society. As to its results, it seems that there are few things one can say about that, at least at a fairly general level. One finds observations, intuitions, impressions, some valid generalizations perhaps. All very valuable, no doubt, but not at the level of explanatory principles. Literary criticism also has things to say, but it does not have explanatory principles. Of course ever since the ancient Greeks people have been trying to find general principles on which to base literary criticism, but while I'm far from an authority in this field, I'm under the impression that no one has yet succeeded in establishing such principles. . . . That is not a criticism. It is a characterization, which seems to me to be correct. Sociolinguistics is, I suppose, a discipline that seeks to apply principles of sociology to the study of language; but I suspect that it can draw little from sociology, and I wonder whether it is likely to contribute much to it." Mitsou Ronat replies that "in general one links a social class to a set of linguistic forms in a manner that is almost bi-unique," to which Chomsky replies: "You can also collect butterflies and make many observations. If you like butterflies, that's fine; but such work must not be confounded with research, which is concerned to discover explanatory principles of some depth and fails if it does not do so" (57).

All of this is quite comical, and speaks to Chomsky's take on "theory" in the social sciences, and, moreover, on those who try to employ it to resolve important questions relating to social issues. More important, though, and this applies to the question of intellectual work within and beyond the Ivory Tower, is the question of what intellectuals can and should be doing to promote the values of freedom and liberation. Any deliberate distortion, concealment or obfuscation of ideas has the nefarious effect of directing our attention away from what is truly important for our own lives and for those of persons around us. From this standpoint, Chomsky's approach recalls Orwell's words on the subject of

"Politics and the English Language": "In our time, political speech and writing are largely the defense of the indefensible. Events like the continuance of British rule in India, the Russian purges and deportations, and the dropping of the atom bombs on Japan can indeed be defended, but only by arguments that are too brutal for most people to face, and which do not square with the professed aims of the political parties. Thus political language has to consist largely of euphemism, question-begging, and sheer vagueness. Defenseless villages are bombarded from the air, the inhabitants driven out into the countryside, the cattle machine-gunned, the huts set on fire with incendiary bullets: this is called *pacification*. Millions of peasants are robbed of their farms and sent trudging along the roads with no more than they can carry: this is called *transfer of population* or *rectification of frontiers*. People are imprisoned for years without trial, or shot in the back of the neck, or sent to die of scurvy in Arctic lumber camps: this is called *elimination of unreliable elements*. Such phraseology is needed if one wants to name things without calling up mental pictures of them."[7] And, yet again, this recalls Rudolph Rocker's approach to anarchism in practice versus anarchism in theory. As Graur writes, "Syndicalist activists viewed the role of the theorist mainly as an educational one. The theorist should explain the motivation that leads to action. He should raise the awareness of the workers about the nature of their action, but he should neither impose his philosophy on the syndicates nor try to influence them. . . . Rocker, although viewed by many as the major theoretician of anarchy-syndicalism, did not regard himself as one. . . . He was a journalist, a propagandist, a teacher, and a historian. In his writings he exposed the sociological background in which the syndicates operated, thereby making workers aware of their power and their capacity to change their miserable circumstances through their direct action" (161).

This discussion about the role of research and its relationship to the kinds of observations one might make in different fields, such as sociology or literature, relates to Angenot's comments concerning the epistemology of literature; literature cannot "know" anything in terms of explanatory principles, and to look for such principles in literary texts would be an error. Some literary theorists—and, I might add sociologists, political scientists, anthropologists, and so forth—cringe at Chomsky's use of seemingly derogatory descriptions of their work. But they could use Angenot's position that *all* knowledge domains, including pure science's claim to a monopoly on what Chomsky calls "explanatory principles," are culturally and socially contingent in the same way that Chomsky claims that literary knowledge is.

Acceptable Discourse

Literature also reveals, in its canonical versions in particular, the relationship between acceptable and unacceptable discourse, or what Pierre Bourdieu in his work on *Language and Symbolic Power* describes in terms of what is *sayable* and what is *hearable*. This ties into other discussions Chomsky had about what can pass in the public discourse, and why:

NC: Well, I once asked another editor I know at the *Boston Globe* why their coverage of the Israeli/Palestinian conflict is so awful—and it is. He just laughed and said, "How many Arab advertisers do you think we have?" That was the end of the conversation.

Man: That's not true, unless he was joking.

NC: It *is* true, and he wasn't joking. That wasn't joking.

Man: The editor doesn't pay attention to the advertising—he doesn't care about the advertising.

NC: Are you kidding? If he doesn't care about the advertising, he will not be the editor any longer.

Man: You're saying that the *Globe's* editorial decisions are based on trying to keep advertising revenue from—what?

NC: From dropping. It means retailers aren't going to advertise there and the *Globe's* going to go under.

Man: But the *Globe* has a monopoly market.

NC: They do not.

Man: What are they going to do, advertise in the *Herald*?

NC: Absolutely.

Man: I think that really is simplistic, I really do.

NC: This actually happened, it's happened a few times. Most of the time, it never happens, because the newspapers never deviate. . . .

Man: I guess I don't know what it's like on a big paper. I have a great deal of autonomy as a reporter working for a small local paper.

NC: A small local paper's a different story. But suppose you start doing things that are harmful to local business interests—I think you'll find that it's not easy to keep doing it. You can probably do good reporting on international affairs if you want, just because they don't care so much in a small-town paper.

Man: I don't know—I don't take those interests into account at all. I'm the business writer for my county, I can do what I want.

NC: You think you can do what you want; see, Tom Wicker at the *NYT* thinks he does what he wants, too—and he's right. But what he wants is what power wants. [8]

Literary critics, or others, may take issue with some of this, but what is notable here is how similar Chomsky's views are across disciplines, from media to literature (from the *Boston Globe* to *1984*), from literature to society, and how despite our viewing his work as anomalous and discordant we are able to find links to other disciplines and by extension to the difficult questions posed in a variety of contexts. This polyglot nature of his work is in fact something that people find appealing and becomes a reason for his finding such an audience in those looking for inspiration on how to rethink their worlds, or even just how to dramatize this learning process, which leads to the idea of Chomsky not as teacher but as muse.

Chomsky as Literary Inspiration

Chomsky has himself inspired people to not only think creatively or think for themselves but also to write literature. This brings us back to the first chapter of this book, in which we saw that rock musicians have used Chomsky's work as an inspiration for songwriting and certain forms of social action, and it recalls as well the idea of what an anarchist education ought to be like; a combination of useful knowledge and inspiration. The ways in which he acts to inspire us will lead us in the next chapter to think about the role of the intellectual beyond the ivory tower; but for the moment, it suffices to think about the range of ways he inspires people to actually work and think creatively. For example, like any popular intellectual, Chomsky is the subject of myths, gossip, and storytelling, and there are those who, ruminating upon his work, his influence, his approach, have found it appropriate to think about him as this "Ol' Man Chomsky:"

Ol' Man Chomsky (to the tune *of* "Ol' Man River"), from the 1982 LSA Summer Institute

Ol' man Chomsky
That ol' man Chomsky—
His thoughts keep changin'
And rearrangin'
He just keeps writin'
He keeps on writin' them books.

He don't know German,
Much less Warlpiri,
And he won't learn 'em
Till they fit his theory!
He just keeps writin'
He keeps on writin' them books.

You and me must struggle through
Government, and binding too.
Bind that node!
Drop that PRO!
I don't believe it, but Noam says so.

I gits tired;
My eyes git weary—
Another damn extension
To the Standard Theory!
But Ol' Man Chomsky
He keeps on writin' them books.

Says John Goldsmith, of the University of Chicago, in response to my sending him this piece: "'Old Man Chomsky'? How did you run into that? I lived in a dorm house during the summer of 1982, and [as] was our wont in those days (the dregs of the 60s) we wrote lots of songs, sometimes to the tunes of songs we knew. I wrote that in about 15 minutes one night. This was at the University of Maryland." It's a tune I have run across variously, and it reflects that combination of irreverence and attraction, so much a part of the Chomsky Effect in the popular realm.

A concomitant phenomenon is to find a Chomsky-like character in one's readings, as I find happens when reading Norman Mailer (in whose nonfiction novel *Armies of the Night* Chomsky actually appears), Philip Roth (in for example *Operation Shylock*), in Gore Vidal's writings, or, in the same vein, Neal Stephenson's novel *Cryptonomicon*.[9] For example, when

Randy says, "You asked me earlier what is the highest and best purpose to which we could dedicate our lives. And the obvious answer is 'to prevent future Holocausts'." Avi laughs darkly. "I'm glad it's obvious to you, my friend. I was beginning to think I was the only one." "What? Get over yourself, Avi. People are commemorating the Holocaust all the time." "Commemorating the Holocaust is not, not not not not NOT, the same thing as fighting to prevent future holocausts. Most of the commemorationists are just whiners. They think that if everyone feels bad about past holocausts, human nature will magically transform, and no one will want to commit genocide in the future." "I take it you do not share this view, Avi?" "Look at Bosnia!" Avi scoffs. "Human nature doesn't change, Randy. Education is hopeless. The most educated people in the world can turn into Aztecs or Nazis just like that." He snaps his fingers. "So what hope is there?" "Instead of trying to educate the potential perpetrators of holocausts, we try to educate the potential victims. They will at least pay some fucking attention.

This passage gives particular pause because of what it suggests about higher purposes in life, but also because of the pedagogical approach claimed, which relies heavily upon a Stephen Pinker–style approach (particularly in books like *The Blank Slate*) in which we find ourselves biologically preprogrammed, even down to very specific details, to act and think in particular ways. This is a crucial area of consideration for anyone interested in Chomsky's work because of the tension that exists therein between biological determinism and the role of, say, social activism. We are clearly not blank slates at birth, but we clearly need some form of discussion and interaction with the world to hone our attitudes; the degree to which these attitudes can be changed, through information, experience, or encounters, may be severely limited by innate attitudes at some level below that of individual experience. Implications of this tension will be discussed in the final chapter of this book, in which I consider varying approaches to respectable work beyond the ivory tower, but is also at issue here in the question of how to dramatize the issues that Chomsky discusses.

Really Off-Broadway

In addition to thinking about literature and inspiring some poetry, Chomsky has also been the subject or inspiration for several dramatic works, which in their presentations have turned into fascinating events in themselves. In 1991 Daniel Brooks[10] and Guillermo Verdecchia[11] published a play that was inspired by Noam Chomsky's (and Edward

Herman's) "language and analysis," called *The Noam Chomsky Lectures*[12]. It was performed for the first time as part of the Buddies in Bad Times Rhubard! Festival at the Annex Theatre in Toronto, in February 1990, and was then expanded for the World Stage Festival in July 1990; the text that became the book is based upon a version presented from March 12–22 at the Backspace, Theatre Passe Muraille in Toronto. Chomsky enjoyed the work and even suggested, rather hopefully, that "maybe a new genre is in the making." *The Socialist Worker* described the text as "an anti-imperialist primer," and *Theatrum* stated that "it reaffirms the theatre as a place of dissent." These reviews suggest that when Chomsky's work is appropriated artistically it can have an impact beyond the pale of linguistics and politics, and into the world of literature and theatre.

Another work was undertaken by the Groupe de Création Théâtrale Mécanique Générale in Montreal, called *Chomsky, quelques bruits et la danse de Saint-Guy: Dérives hallucinatoires d'une activiste* [Chomsky, Some Noises and the Dance of Saint-Guy: Hallucinatory Derivations of an Activist]. This play, never published, is the comical story of gangsters who kidnap Chomsky but are unable to find anyone willing to put up the ransom for his release. It was developed by Luc Dansereau and performed by Estelle Clareton, Michèle Dansereau, Michel Côté, and Luc Dansereau from April 28–May 2, 1998. Given the approach that Chomsky has developed, and the effects that he has had upon such a great range of people, one can imagine, and in my sense one can truly hope, that such creative output will long be one of the results of his great efforts.

More recently, *The Loneliness of Noam Chomsky (A Performance)*, was presented in New York City, February 27–28, 2004, at the Arts Space at Chashama. This work was based entirely upon Chomsky's writings and found significant sympathy among the reviewers. Matthew Murray in *Off Broadway* reports: "The comprehensively researched piece (the program cites 24 sources, from Chomsky's books to a 1994 This Modern World comic strip) may be an unusual tribute to a surprising subject, but it's as confrontational and thought provoking as theatre of this type should be. It's interesting that the real Chomsky's reaction to being informed about the work even made it into the show—

while he claims that Salzman's endeavor is beyond his normal field of understanding, the wit, intelligence, and care with which it's been presented suggest that *The Loneliness of Noam Chomsky (A Performance)* is something of which he would no doubt approve."[13] Other descriptions seem to suggest a more mitigated or subdued response:

The performance begins with Chomsky (played with remarkable accuracy and great skill by the Asian-American actress Aya Ogawa) seated center stage, looking away from the audience at a wall of mirrors. The stage is all white, surrounded by a low barrier that looks as if it were constructed from military-issue wooden crates. On top the barrier are two video monitors that swivel and move on tracks. The back walls of the theater are entirely mirrored and the only set piece is the single Aeron-style rolling chair on which Chomsky is seated. When Chomsky begins talking it is in the slow, halting, nearly inaudible patterns that are familiar to those who have heard him speak. He discusses the very problem of being filmed and televised, how he is troubled by the focus on him. He says he never watches his televised or filmed appearances as they make him queasy and he only focuses on what he could have done better or said differently.

Enter "The Media": Judson Kniffen and Alanna Medlock dressed as newscasters, replete with napkins tucked into their collars, as if they had just left the make-up table and sat down behind the newsdesk. A Tom Tomorrow cartoon appears on the monitors as Kniffen and Medlock perform the dialogue from the strip:

"Brad, you're going to love what I bought you for your birthday!"

"What is it? A subscription to The Nation or Z Magazine? A new water filter? No, I know what it is—a tie-dyed Friends of the Rainforest T-shirt!"

"Uh-uh. You can put away all your other toys Brad, now that you've got this!"

"Oh Susan, you shouldn't have. A Chomsky doll!" As Medlock pulls out a small two-foot high skeleton and proceeds to hang it from a noose front and center. This sets the contradictory tone of reverence and self-mockery that makes "The Loneliness of Noam Chomsky" such a compelling performance. While the performance is generally sympathetic towards Chomsky, it establishes a tension between the perceived and real Chomsky that is almost menacing. The performance then uses this tension to aggressively question the nature of the "perceived" and "real" in contemporary politics and more gently question the extent of Chomsky's self-awareness.[14]

It is in many ways appropriate that the theater be the art form where Chomsky's ideas are batted around. The 1930s work for the Federal Theater Project[15] attempted to educate workers about issues of concern by encouraging an active engagement within workplaces and neighborhoods; it would seem, given the huge popularity of Chomsky's own talks, that theatrical presentations of his ideas might contribute to a much-

needed release of ideas and debates so hushed up in an area of con-
sumerist-driven media and entertainment.

Noam Chomsky's David Letterman–style Humor

The principle of laughter destroys . . . all pretence of an extratemporal meaning
and unconditional value of necessity. It frees human consciousness, thought, and
imagination for new potentialities.[16]

One of the reasons Chomsky's work is subjected to the types of spoofs
we see in *The Postmodern Haircut* comics is that he at times challenges
the reader's ability to synthesize concepts from myriads of facts, and the
subjects he addresses in his work can sometimes lead the reader or lis-
tener to despair, if only because the facts he presents so often indicate
the duplicity, hypocrisy, violence, and waste that comes in the trail of
power. He does harp upon the progress we have made and the optimism
he has when he sees people working together to overturn strategies of
oppression, in such passages as:

The world is pretty awful today, but it is far better than yesterday, not only with
regard to unwillingness to tolerate aggression, but also in many other ways,
which we now tend to take for granted. There are very important lessons here,
which should always be uppermost in our minds-for the same reason they are
suppressed in the elite culture. Without forgetting the very significant progress
towards more civilized societies in past years, and the reasons for it, let's focus
nevertheless on the notions of imperial sovereignty now being crafted. It is not
surprising that as the population becomes more civilized, power systems become
more extreme in their efforts to control the "great beast" (as the Founding
Fathers called the people). And the great beast is indeed frightening.[17]

Nevertheless, the general picture of the world is bleak, and no matter
how enthused we might get about the occasional triumph of resistance,
it is hard not to feel that in the end we are just going to go up in some
horrifying puff of all-consuming nuclear or hazmat fire. But if the overall
effect of Chomsky's words were despair tempered by flashes of successful resistance, it would be hard I think for him to sustain his own engage-
ments, never mind draw huge crowds to his words. In truth, with his
deadpan humor, his self-described dull delivery style, and his lucid
anti–status quo ravings, Chomsky can sometimes come across as a successful crossing of Woody Allen and David Letterman. His style, even
when he discusses the horrors of American imperialism, is at times *funny*,

and his humor, which usually takes the form of his stating the facts, or his labeling some institution or individual as "Stalinist," "commissar," or his insisting that we look together into the logic of some statement or event, is sarcastic and caustic. The following, from *Propaganda and the Public Mind*, is once again worth considering as a priceless example of Chomsky at work; a discussion about a aforementioned White House public statement concerning the Multilateral Agreement on Investment, in which they said that "domestic constituencies had been informed" of proceedings, Chomsky says:

So now we can carry out a little exercise in logic. Who are the domestic constituencies? It plainly wasn't Congress. In fact, undoubtedly people in Congress knew, but Congress in general wasn't even informed. Twenty-five representatives wrote a letter to the White House asking, 'How come you've been negotiating this for three years without telling us?' According to the Constitution, international commerce is the province of the Congress. They got the kind of letter that you get if you write a letter to the White House, saying, "Dear David, Thank you for your interesting comments." It's written by some computer. That's the kind of letter they got back. So, Congress wasn't a constituency. The public plainly wasn't a constituency. In fact, it was kind of like a negative constituency. The idea was to keep them out of it, keep them off our back. So the public isn't a constituency. Congress isn't a constituency. But the US Council for International Business is. They were informed all the way and were intimately involved. The corporate sector was involved. The White House is telling us plainly and clearly who their domestic constituencies are. It's very rare that political leaders are so frank in such a clear and vulgar fashion about exactly the way they perceive the world. It's an accurate perception. But that's not what you're supposed to teach in eighth-grade civics or graduate courses in political science at the University of Colorado. It's just the truth. So it's nice that they said it. I think the media were smart enough to keep it quiet and suppress it. Maybe somebody would think it through. (9–10)[18]

Why is this humorous? And, a related question, why is it an effective way of representing the facts of this case? One of the tactics employed here is the use of unexpected juxtapositions, the idea that domestic constituencies is everyone other than who it should be, or that what was demonstrated in the example is not what one is supposed to teach either to high school kids or to political science students because it's "just the truth." His antitheatrics are also very effective, notably in his ability to mimic the various voices of those party to the event, including the "Dear David" computer that writes letters (to members of Congress!) from the White House. These kinds of revelations lead audience members to grin, to shake or nod their heads, or to quite literally burst out laughing, a kind of laughter that's as dark as it is enlightening. This is the force of the humor that Chomsky uses, and, moreover, this is the power that humor has. The "clown," like David Letterman, can say anything, including the truth, and he can get away with it. The "humbled victim," like Woody Allen, can pour his wretched self into the script, and we can find both pity and self-realization in his words. We all know about laughter, we all laugh, and we all use humor, in some way or another, but it's rare to think about the effects and roles that humor plays, the way in which it can, quite literally, "bring things down to earth" so that we can truly examine them in their material, naked, and often pitiful form. When we laugh at statements that we might otherwise take very seriously, such as "we need to have a war in that country in order to bring peace," or "we need to destroy the city in order to save it," or "we need to precisely calculate how much weaponry we need to construct to engage in a tactical nuclear battle," we do not have to resort to the degrading or dehumanizing tactic of accepting preposterous terms for a debate before even considering the issues at stake. We can simply laugh at how ridiculous the whole discussion is before we even engage it. Laughter is from this standpoint creative, in part because it first allows us to destroy the artifice that is being presented to us, often by a figure of authority.

One of the few individuals who has paused to reflect in a sustained way upon the multifarious characteristics of humor is Mikhaïl Bakhtin, whose work on language has implications for almost all areas of contemporary humanities and social sciences, which is why he appears from time-to-time in this text. Surprisingly, up until 1929 only one short article, in an obscure provincial newspaper, had appeared under his own name even though he had by then elaborated an entire philosophical project that was to encompass every domain of everyday life, from literature to law to religion. To think about the approach he took to language, laughter, and human interaction helps shed light upon the power of Noam Chomsky's work, and, as we'll see, the ways in which Chomsky's humoristic "clowning around" can be seen as a very carefully calculated effort aimed at bringing his readers and his public to experience unexpected insight.

Bakhtin is a particularly interesting person to consider when assessing Noam Chomsky because of his sense of how we learn or create "dialogically," that is, in interaction and not through obedience to authority. For Bakhtin, the truly interesting aspect of a dialogic interaction is not the perspective of one speaker or another, but the way that their dialogue produces unexpected utterances, ideas, and notions not typical of either speaker. One person directs his or her ideas toward the perceived other, who understands the utterance according to a particular set of contextual elements and then responds, taking for granted certain kinds of contextual constants but adding to what was just said. In this manner, the conversation creatively constructs dialogue in the space that exists between the two speakers. In such a model, no single speaker is complete because each needs the other to *fill-in* the spaces that he or she cannot see and he or she needs to become *answerable* for the utterances of the other.

Bakhtin also helps us to understand Chomsky's use of different voices and registers in the quote above with reference to his work on *speech genres*, which denote the ways that speech is organized or cast in particular situations in terms of genre, length, and compositional structure. Speech genres go beyond their linguistic cousins *registers* to include social elements of speech, and we use them to orient our language properly for particular situations. There are many kinds of speech genres, from greetings, congratulations, wishes, or inquiries about somebody's well-being. A novel will contain many of these genres, sometimes couched in particular forms of expression, so one finds in, say, the work of Charles Dickens, imitations of parliamentary discourse, the banter of criminals, pious declarations of the self-satisfied bourgeoisie, and so on. In the example of Chomsky's speech, these speech genres are often subverted, sometimes through parody, sometimes through overt disrespect, sometimes through interruption, and sometimes through the general hullabaloo—subversions that seldom occur in the more rigid world of daily life. These subversions and strange juxtapositions provoke laughter amongst the audience in part because they work with the mirror opposites of death and rebirth, negation and affirmation, which mocks, derides, and affirms, simultaneously. In this sense, laughter is "also directed at those who laugh," and accordingly, it becomes an outlet for the audience, a way for people to publicly affirm their own incompleteness. In laughing, they do not exclude themselves from the wholeness of the world. Bakhtin says that like the world, "they, too, are incomplete, they also die and are revived and renewed" (12). The way in which laughter turns upon us, the "people" in Chomsky's writings, is in part that we come to realize our own folly in believing what we are told or buying into what is obviously a tissue of fabrications. Once again, from the book *Propaganda and the Public Mind*:

In the 1970s, there was a lot of concern that incompetent management meant the United States was falling behind the Japanese particularly, but the Europeans, too. It wasn't developing flexible manufacturing techniques. They were way behind because of management failures. What happened? The Pentagon stepped into the breach. It understands its place, it started a program called Manufacturing Technology, ManTech. It was a new program to design what they called the 'factory of the future,' with integrated production, computer control of equipment, flexible technology, and so on. That was then greatly expanded in the Reagan years, because the Reaganites were extreme statists, strongly opposed to market principles, more so than the norm. It was finally handed over to private industry. So that's American rugged individualism and consumer choice in the market as compared with the failure of the state-managed East Asian system. The whole discussion, from one end to the other, has been a tissue of fabrications. It's not a simple story, and if you look at it closely, there are all kinds of complexity; but if that picture had been written in Pravda, people would have laughed.[19]

This double image, of us realizing that we had thought of Reagan as supporting "free markets," when in fact it was the mirror opposite, is given an extra helping of humor with the idea that those who read *Pravda* in the Eastern Bloc countries would never have been so gullible as we in the "free world" are! These moments in Chomsky's writings are quite literally spaces in which one is compelled to smile knowingly, or in which we watch ourselves laughing at ourselves. In another example, describing how the Reaganites instilled fear into the population to carry on their misdeeds with impunity: "Nicaragua was 'two days' marching time from Texas'—a dagger pointed at the heart of Texas, to borrow Hitler's phrase. Again, you'd think the people would collapse with laughter. But they didn't. That was continually brought up to frighten us— Nicaragua might conquer us on its way to conquer the hemisphere. A national emergency was called because of the threat posed to national security by Nicaragua. Libyan hitmen were wandering the streets of

Washington to assassinate our leader—hispanic narco-terrorists. One thing after another was conjured up to keep the population in a state of constant fear while they carried out their major terrorist wars."[19] That the population was not doubled over in hysterics was proof that public laughter was successfully kept at bay by the authorities, and that the black humor of it all was never reported by the media. And this present administration, a particularly humorless bunch, seems to enforce not just the tough-guy "I'll shoot you in the face if you get in the way of my hunting quails" image, but the closed, devout, quiet image as well, giving the impression that the interior of the White House resembles a mausoleum, even as the Pentagon plans thunderous performances of noisy blazing firebombs to "shock and awe."

Utopia and Laughter

To think about humor as a tactic, it is useful to think about the very idea of laughter in official circles, and beyond. Bakhtin theorizes about laughter with respect to the "carnival laughter" of the late Middle Ages or the early Renaissance, which is captured in, for example, the writings of Francois Rabelais or the theater of Shakespeare. Why this period in particular? Bakhtin writes, in *Rabelais and His World*:

The Renaissance conception of laughter can be roughly described as follows: Laughter has a deep philosophical meaning, it is one of the essential forms of the truth concerning the world as a whole, concerning history and man; it is a peculiar point of view relative to the world; the world is seen anew, no less (and perhaps more) profoundly than when seen from the serious standpoint. Therefore, laughter is just as admissible in great literature, posing universal problems, as seriousness. Certain essential aspects of the world are accessible only to laughter (66).

Important as well is the fact that this laughter happened in very particular ways during the carnival before Lent:

In the Middle Ages folk humor existed and developed outside the official sphere of high ideology and literature, but precisely because of its unofficial existence, it was marked by exceptional radicalism, freedom, and ruthlessness. Having on the one hand forbidden laughter in every official sphere of life and ideology, the Middle Ages on the other hand bestowed exceptional privileges of license and lawlessness outside these spheres: in the marketplace, on feast days, in festive recreational literature. And medieval laughter knew how to use these widely (72).

The laughter of carnival is "genetically" linked to the most ancient forms of ritual laughter, which was "always directed toward something higher: the sun (the highest god), other gods, the highest earthly author-ity were put to shame and ridiculed to force them to renew themselves" (127). Furthermore, Bakhtin explains that the most "ancient rituals of mocking at the deity have survived" in carnival laughter, but they have acquired a new essential meaning. What was "purely cultic and limited has faded away, but the all-human, universal, and utopian element has been retained" (12).

To make it "human," Chomsky refuses the distance that is incurred between "us" and "them" in political discourse, a characteristic that infuriates his critics but is done for specific effect. In a discussion on what to do about Bin Laden, for instance, he says: "Every case is different, but let's take a few analogies. What was the right way for Britain to deal with IRA bombs in London? One choice would have been to send the RAF to bomb the source of their finances, places like Boston, or to infiltrate commandos to capture those suspected of involvement in such financing and kill them or spirit them to London to face trial. Putting aside feasibility, that would have been criminal idiocy" (62). Or "take the bombing of the federal building in Oklahoma City. There were imme-diate calls for bombing the Middle East, and it probably would have happened if even a remote hint of a link had been found. When it was instead discovered to be a domestically devised attack, by someone with militia connections, there was no call to obliterate Montana and Idaho, or the 'Republic of Texas,' which has been calling for secession from the oppressive and illegitimate government in Washington."[20]

According to Bakhtin, in ancient times and in the Middle Ages, all forms of ritual laughter were linked with death and rebirth, with the reproduc-tive act, and with symbols of the reproductive force; as such, ritual laughter was a "reaction to crises in the life of the sun (solstices), crises in the life of a deity, in the life of world and of man (funeral laughter). In it, ridicule was fused with rejoicing," and ancient ritualistic laughter served to define "the privileges of laughter in antiquity and in the Middle Ages." That is, like in the world of carnival, in the form of ritualistic laughter, "much was permitted . . . that was impermissible in serious form," such as mocking the gods or parodies of sacred religious texts. Carnival laughter, a descendent of ritual laughter, is also directed toward something higher, "toward a shift of authorities and truths, a shift of world orders." Similar to ancient ritual laughter, carnivalesque laughter is connected with crisis, it "embraces both poles of change, it deals with the very process of change, with crisis itself" (127). We have only to think of the somber etiquette of contemporary political speeches, where every detail of the speech, right down to the applause at just the right moments, has been choreographed into the rhetoric; the whole speech becomes a dance of supposed sincerity and truth-telling that is literally fed off of a teleprompting device. We are not far from the Middle Ages when we realize that the official world is so tightly wound, while truth is told by the tricksters and the clowns, like David Letterman, much deeper into the night. This is because power is well disciplined, but so too, according to Chomsky, is the media: "It took considerable discipline at the NATO [fiftieth] anniversary for participants and commentators 'not to notice' that some of the worst ethnic cleansing of the 1990s was taking place within NATO itself, in south-eastern Turkey; and furthermore, that these massive atrocities relied on a huge flow of arms from the West, overwhelmingly from the United States, which provided about 80 percent of Turkey's arms as the atrocities peaked by the mid-1990s" (11).[21] How can there be such a rift between official and unofficial discourses? Again, Bakhtin's words are ominous, and they help explain where Chomsky's approach to this "discipline" in official circles comes from:

As we have said, laughter in the Middle Ages remained outside all official spheres of ideology and outside all official strict forms of social relations. Laughter was eliminated from religious cult, from feudal and state ceremonials, etiquette, and from all the genres of high speculation. An intolerant, one-sided tone of seriousness is characteristic of official medieval culture. The very contents of medieval ideology—asceticism, somber providentialism, sin, atonement, suffering, as well as the character of the feudal regime, with its oppression and intimidation—all these elements determined this tone of icy petrified seriousness. It was supposedly the only tone fit to express the true, the good, and all that was essential and meaningful. Fear, religious awe, humility, these were the overtones of this seriousness" (73).

If this sounds familiar to those who have heard of the current administration's prayers before meetings, or the constant invocation, implied or explicit, of God's will in the administration's explanations of policy, it is for good reason.

The point of directing the laughter toward something higher is of course crucial, since it helps us to humanize the ethereal, and to "bring down to earth" that which gains power from hovering above us. Once again, Chomsky employs this against those in power, but also demonstrates the ways in which those in power try to do the same thing to foster an image of their folksy proximity to the voters:

Right before the 2004 election, about 10 percent of voters said their choice would based on the candidate's "agendas / ideas / platforms / goals"; 6 percent for Bush voters, 13 percent for Kerry voters. For the rest, the choice would be based on what the industry calls "qualities" and "values." Does the candidate project the image of a strong leader, the kind of guy you'd like to meet in a bar, someone who really cares about you and is just like you? It wouldn't be surprising to learn that Bush is carefully trained to say "nucular" and "misunderestimate" and the other silliness that intellectuals like to ridicule. That's probably about as real as the ranch constructed for him and the rest of the folksy manner. After all, it wouldn't do to present him as a spoiled frat boy from Yale who became rich and powerful thanks to his rich and powerful connections. Rather, the imagery has to be an ordinary guy just like us, who'll protect us, and who shares our "moral values," more so than the windsurfing goose-hunter who can be accused of faking his medals.[22]

Unlike Bakhtin, Chomsky does not theorize or reflect in any prolonged fashion his use of humor, although from time to time he does make observations about his own approach to transmitting messages:

It was a very good meeting [at a recent talk in Cambridge], very constructive, and was really going places. Groups were forming to organize things. There was the usual fringe of sectarian left parasites whose main function for years has been to disrupt popular movements. One line was, "I've got to get up and organize the working class to smash capitalism. Nothing else does any good." I think I said something like, "I agree. I think it would be a great idea to get the working class to smash capitalism, but obviously this isn't the place to do it, so what you ought to be doing is going to the nearest factory—I'll be happy to pay your carfare." It's not a new strategy. I never had an old one.

DB: Using humor to deflect arguments like that is sometimes very effective.

NC: It wasn't intentional. It was spontaneous.

DB: It got the guy to shut up.

NC: Maybe it works.[23]

Despite Chomsky's tendency to avoid talking about his approach, it is interesting to note that *Z Magazine*'s Lydia Sargent has made some remarks about this phenomenon that are remarkably apropos to Bakhtin's approach and applicable to Chomsky's:

There's lots of exciting things about using comedy and drama in organizing. I'm not talking about bringing in "professionals" or established groups, although that can be done as well. I'm talking about five or six people in activist projects or organizations forming troupes to provide information, inspiration, and humor in dramatic form. Doing this keeps the people involved active and informed. Participants have to follow the news and dig around for the facts, the details, the background, etc. It encourages solidarity and ties with local groups as scripts can be put together about their concerns and struggles; or groups can help them write and perform their own scripts. It involves lots of humor so it gets people laughing together, which is a nice alternative or compliment to more traditional speeches and workshop panels. Productions can provide material for radio and TV, not just the stage. It costs almost nothing and doesn't have to take lots of time. It's portable. We've performed in cafeterias, nursing homes, basements, classrooms, and union halls. As we continue to fight the good fight, perhaps we could prioritize the building of hundreds of small, diverse theater troupes of women and men of all ages spreading out through communities to entertain and inform. What could be more exciting and inspiring? Besides, after this last election, we could use a good (collective) laugh.[24]

Laughter is a remedy, a source of hope, a provocation, and a catalyst, all aimed, as Bakhtin concludes in his chapter about laughter, at the descent of those currently ruling from on high:

However, medieval laughter is not a subjective, individual and biological consciousness of the uninterrupted flow of time. It is the social consciousness of all the people. Man experiences this flow of time in the festive marketplace, in the carnival crowd, as he comes into contact with other bodies of varying age and social caste. He is aware of being a member of a continually growing and renewed people. This is why festive folk laughter presents an element of victory not only over supernatural awe, over the sacred, over death; it also means the defeat of power, of earthly kings, of the earthly upper classes, of all that oppresses and restricts. (92)

A noble cause indeed, which has vast implications for our own era of ever-present security measures and reinforced borders. To combine Chomsky's approach with Bakhtin's insights is to help us realize we are living in a period of time that is increasingly resistant to the festive and rejuvenating public space. Indeed, whatever benefits we could be gaining from public or collective efforts (including public initiatives in education, transportation, or medical care) are forsaken on account of the officially sanctioned fear of the "anarchy" of public spaces where growth and renewal occur. From this perspective, the intellectual's foray into the public space is all the more crucial, as we will see in the next chapter.

8

The Effective "Public" Intellectual

Q: Do you vote?

NC: Do I? well, differentially. I mean, I almost always vote for lower-level candidates, like school committee representatives and things like that—because there it makes a difference, in fact. But as you get more and more remote from popular control, it makes less and less of a difference. When you get to the House of Representatives—well, it's sort of academic in my case, because I live in one of these single-member districts where the same guy always wins, so it doesn't really matter whether you vote or not. When you get to Senator, it begins to become pretty symbolic anyway. At the level of President, half the time I don't even bother—I think those are usually very subtle judgments. I mean, it's a difficult judgment to try to figure out whether Nixon or Humphrey is going to end the Vietnam War sooner [in 1968], that's an extremely subtle judgment to make; I actually didn't vote on that one, because I figured that Nixon probably would. I did vote against Reagan, because I thought the guys around Reagan were extremely dangerous—Reagan himself was irrelevant, but the people in his administration were real killers and torturers, and they were just making people suffer too much, so I thought it might make a difference. But these are usually not very easy judgments to make, in my opinion.[1]

To be a public intellectual is to undertake work beyond the ivory tower, variously construed, a conscious or conscientious effort that has been going on ever since the advent of a complex line between an academy for intellectuals, and the rest of society. In Europe and North America, those involved with criticism of the established order of society have come from a broad array of backgrounds and, inspired by Greek, Roman, Renaissance or Enlightenment thinkers, have imagined themselves spreading ideas and approaches that foster some sense of the common good. As a consequence, many of those who have worked beyond the rarefied atmosphere of academia have embraced one or several social projects captured under such headings as Saint-Simonians, Marxists, feminists,

socialists, Utilitarians, Fabians, existentialists, social democrats, libertarians, radicals, anarchists, and, in more recent times, civil rights activists, Trotskyites, Maoists, muckrakers, and a whole host of causes ranging the entire left-right spectrum.[2] Rather than focusing upon how allegiances or resistances to particular programs play out, this book has focused upon Chomsky's own work and his ideas about the responsibilities that intellectuals have as intellectuals and that he has as a privileged academic, which in some ways leads us to question the relationship between the "public" and the "intellectual." This dynamic suggests to Howard Zinn that intellectuals have a tacit public responsibility "to earn our keep in this world. Thanks to a gullible public, we have been honored, flattered, even paid, for producing the largest number of inconsequential studies in the history of civilization: tens of thousands of articles, books, monographs, millions of term papers; enough lectures to deafen the gods. Like politicians we have thrived on public innocence, with this difference; the politicians are paid for caring, when they really don't; we are paid for not caring, when we really do."[3] This of course assumes that intellectuals possess some kind of special and potentially useful knowledge, or else, as Chomsky suggests, that "intellectuals are in a position to expose the lies of governments, to analyze actions according to their causes and motives and often hidden intentions." This position is accorded to them "from political liberty, from access to information and freedom of expression." For the privileged few who are in this situation, Western democracy "provides the leisure, the facilities, and the training to seek the truth lying hidden behind the veil of distortion and misrepresentation, ideology and class interest, through which the events of current history are presented to us."[4] The goal of this concluding chapter is to look to Chomsky, but also to the broader issues relating to work beyond the ivory tower, to examine the relationships that exist between Chomsky's approach and that of the precursors and contemporaries who give varied meaning to the idea of the public intellectual.

Discernment and "Cultural Criticism"

This ability to "seek the truth" implies some kind of special skill, tied to training, facilities, and leisure, which is best described as *discernment*.

How this actually works is never made terribly clear in Chomsky's work, beyond the idea that people need to avoid lying and use their common sense, but this begs the question of what role the contemporary intellectual can play in the so-called real world (as opposed, to, I suppose, the fictional one). Émile Zola is a good place to start in this discussion because he could use his notoriety and his literary talents to put forth his version of the truth, and the very literature he wrote could challenge prevailing ideas by saying, in Marc Angenot's words, "this doesn't make any sense, this is not the whole story, there is not just that," or in Hamlet's words, "there are more things on Heaven and Earth" or, to recall Gershwin's *Porgy and Bess,* "it ain't necessarily so."[5] But the power of Zola, Shakespeare, or Dickens, ironically enough, derives from their status as fiction writers who are gloriously disconnected from ordinary realms of discourse. Indeed, the power Zola wielded as a journalist was in some ways derived from his authority as a creator of literature, which Angenot describes as "deviance and subversion that is *tolerated, ostentatious* language expenditures, a satire that is protected by the Powers that be." [Ibid.] So although Edward Said or Noam Chomsky or Murray Bookchin might take their cue from Zola, they are nevertheless one step removed from the creative realm. This in some instances can be a liability, since they don't have the popular power accorded to fiction writers like Albert Camus, Charles Dickens, Umberto Eco, Philip Roth, Jean-Paul Sartre, or Émile Zola.

The fact that literature has its own realm can become a source of power, because as commentary about fiction and language, it does not bear any obligation to impose some kind of quick fix to complex social problems. This can provide an alibi for setting oneself off from the problems of the world, which literature itself is apt to remind the reader. A good example is the hilarious scene in Kingsley Amis's novel *Lucky Jim,* in which Dixon is asked to recall the title of the scholarly article he had submitted for review: "It was a perfect title, in that it crystallized the article's niggling mindlessness, its funereal parade of yawn-enforcing facts, the pseudo light it threw upon non-problems. Dixon had read, or begun to read, dozens like it, but his own seemed worse than most in its air of being convinced of its own usefulness and significance. 'In considering this strangely neglected topic,' it began. This what neglected topic? This strangely what topic? This strangely neglected what? His thinking all this without having defiled and set fire to the typescript only made him appear to himself as more of a hypocrite and fool" (14–15).

Literary criticism suffers from this sense of uselessness, but it can also offer a safe realm to discuss serious issues with the cultural clout accorded the likes of Fredric Jameson or Edward Said. Said in particular set for himself a series of tasks as an intellectual and a critic in the broader sense of the terms: "At bottom the intellectual in my sense of the word, is neither a pacifier nor a consensus builder, but someone whose whole being is staked on a critical sense, a sense of being unwilling to accept easy formulas, or ready-made clichés, or the smooth ever-so-accommodating confirmations of what the powerful or conventional have to say, and what they do. Not just passively unwilling, but actively willing to say so in public."[6]

Jim Merod, who has written' in a vein that is strongly supported by Chomsky's work, suggests that North American literary critics can play a positive role because they "have amassed the knowledge to move beyond positive and negative assessments of literary study (and the role of knowledge in promoting social change). Critical awareness has achieved sufficient intellectual sophistication to undo its professional self-encasement by constructing both the conceptual and the institutional means for evaluating the ways in which research of every kind gains legitimacy, mainly in the university, to enforce its technical or professional authority within society as a whole." Merod, unlike Chomsky, does suggest that the literary realm carries within it special knowledge, if only in this sphere of "critical awareness" (25). How this awareness is defined, or the uses to which it can and has been applied, is far more difficult to pin down.

Others are more skeptical about the value of their professional knowledge, to judge from a recent collection of work about the uses of sociology beyond the classroom, but at least one, Charles Derber, finds that, if nothing else, their professional work and their profession provide them with an audience of students around the country: "Professional sociology seeks a restricted, credentialed audience, for the essence of professionalism is to monopolize knowledge and create a knowledge base inaccessible to the uninitiated. In contrast, the essence of public sociology is the quest for knowledge accessible to the public."[8] The assumption here is that if the objective is to create a public knowledge base, rather than to appeal to particular categories of knowledge of expertise, then the whole idea of the profession breaks down: "Marx, Weber, and Durkheim—the most important public sociologists—practiced an intellectual craft spanning the contemporary fields of history, politics, sociology and economics, challenging today's narrow professional segmentation of knowledge. Public sociology is really public intellectualism that is not only inter-disciplinary, but anti-disciplinary."[9]

Howard Zinn writes from this same standpoint when he suggests that a scholar who wishes to make a difference in the public sphere needs to become an "activist-scholar" who "thrusts himself and his works into the crazy mechanism of history, on behalf of values in which he deeply believes. This makes of him more than a scholar; it makes him a citizen in the ancient Athenian sense of the word."[10] For the historian to "thrust himself" into such work suggests the power of words which, for Carlos Fuentes,[11] can be used to unseat illegitimate power because "today, for the first time, the writer's valid words prove that the words of power are invalid. The credibility gap that pursued Lyndon Johnson, until he was forced to forgo a second chance at the presidency for the sake of maintaining the system, had no other meaning." Thinking back to the Vietnam era, Fuentes optimistically reminds us "that the head of the most powerful nation in the world was run out of his post by the students, intellectuals, journalists, writers, by men with no other weapon than words. And it is because words today do not fit within the perpetuated and renewed foundation order of the United States." As such, "words have become the enemy of Power: Norman Mailer, William Styron, Arthur Miller, Susan Sontag, Robert Lowell, Joan Baez. . . ." (114). All of this suggests that public intellectuals bear the arms of reason or common sense, and need only to seek out appropriate battlegrounds and valuable motivations for action.

Motivations for Action

The intellectual attempting to contribute something beyond the ivory tower does so with a range of possible justifications or motives, depending upon the issues and the individual's (perceived) expertise. An ideal-istic approach would be to imagine that ideas have power in themselves, and therefore intellectuals attempt to spread useful knowledge for its own sake. Others have suggested that academics have a unique access to knowledge sources that provide them with the tools for public engage-ment, and also the responsibility to get involved with crucial issues. Whether they choose to do so, or whether they are successful in their efforts, leads to interest in those who purvey the ideas, rather than the ideas themselves, which can either help or hinder the cause to which the personality in question chooses to engage. The personal implications of this engagement are also part of this equation, particularly when the intellectual takes a stand that threatens his or her reputation, career, or even safety. In his introduction "Representations of the Intellectual," Edward Said put together two ideas, about taking personal risks in the name of moral issues, and about the value of willed disconnection from the realm of political power, to describe the value of true intellectual pursuit: "It involves a sense of the dramatic and of the insurgent, making a great deal of one's rare opportunities to speak, catching the audience's attention, being better at wit and debate than one's opponents. And there is something fundamentally unsettling about intellectuals who have neither offices to protect nor territory to consolidate and guard; self-irony is therefore more frequent than pomposity, directness more than hemming and hawing. But there is no dodging the inescapable reality that such representations by intellectuals will neither make them friends in high places nor win them official honors. It is a lonely condition, yes, but it is always a better one than a gregarious tolerance for the way things are."[12] Said seemed in his writing and his actions to be not only willing to forego whatever advantages public fawning of the powerful might procure but, on the contrary, willing to bait the most visible icons of his own government and indeed the popular media in the hope, of course never satisfied, of coming to verbal debate with them or at least having access to the media. Numerous examples of intellectual courage could be cited, but an article from the weeks leading up to the second Iraq war is particularly powerful as we bear witness to the continued tensions in Iraq: "It has finally become intolerable to listen to or look at news in this country. I've told myself over and over again that one ought

to leaf through the daily papers and turn on the TV for the national news
every evening, just to find out what 'the country' is thinking and planning, but patience and masochism have their limits." His own responsibility, which is self-imposed, herein meets the limits of his personal
abilities, and pushes him outward to the public domain: "Every one of
us must raise our voices, and march in protest, now and again and again.
We need creative thinking and bold action to stave off the nightmares
planned by a docile, professionalized staff in places like Washington,
Beijing, or Tel Aviv. For if what they have in mind is what they call
'greater security' then words have no meaning at all in the ordinary
sense. That Bush and Sharon have contempt for the non-white people of
this world is clear. The question is, how long can they keep getting away
with it?"[13]

Indeed Said embodies many of the qualities of the public intellectual,
partly because he has tried to apply the professional knowledge he has
accrued as a literary scholar to practical problems, and partly because
he has used his professional reputation and institutionally-sanctioned
power to fight for unpopular causes, such as the rights of Palestinians,
and in so doing has put himself at personal risk. In a 1999 *Boston Globe*
interview he explained this approach by suggesting that "I've always felt
that if someone was a person of privilege . . . the least you could do was
help those who were not as fortunate as you." His work on behalf of
Palestinians was in his words an "individual commitment. Which I don't
regret at all."[14] Indeed, the regret would have kicked in had Said done
nothing, because he felt he had not only the ability but indeed the responsibility to speak out on contemporary issues. But what was this ability
that he felt compelled to employ? Moreover, what can a humanist, a literary critic, or a philologist contribute to contemporary debates on political, legal, or social issues? Said's *Orientalism* offers some suggestions,
including the effort to "use humanistic critique to open up the fields of
struggle, to introduce a longer sequence of thought and analysis to
replace the short bursts of polemical, thought-stopping fury that so
imprison us in labels and antagonistic debate whose goal is a belligerent
collective identity rather than understanding and intellectual exchange"
(xxii). This is what Said calls "humanism," which specifically attacks the
new critical rarefication of literature in favor of engagement and which

he describes as dissolving "Blake's mind-forg'd manacles so as to be able to use one's mind historically and rationally for the purposes of reflective understanding and genuine disclosure."[15]

This certainly brought Edward Said down from the university setting within which literary criticism often operates, in part because his humanistic endeavors were "sustained by a sense of community with other interpreters and other societies and periods" (*Orientalism* xxiii). But his work remains steadfastly within his own discipline because of his conscientious insistence upon using the critical tools of history, philology, and language studies to assess Rudyard Kipling, on the one hand, and Condoleezza Rice, on the other. For this reason, the Said of *Orientalism* specifically assesses the ways in which literature and classical philology are fraught with or have unmediated political significance; moreover, he lifts literature from the rarefied world of polite conversation by describing "how the general liberal consensus that 'true' knowledge is fundamentally non-political (and conversely, that overtly political knowledge is not 'true' knowledge) obscures the highly if obscurely organized political circumstances obtaining when knowledge is produced." For Said, in short, "we are *of* the connections, not outside and beyond them. And it behooves us as intellectuals and humanists and secular critics to understand the United States in the world of nations and power from *within* the actuality, as participants in it, not detached outside observers who, like Oliver Goldsmith, in Yeats's perfect phrase, deliberately sip at the honeypots of our minds."[16]

Truman Nelson, in a provocative text titled "On Creating Revolutionary Art and Going Out of Print,"[17] finds on the one hand that revolutionary morality runs through the American fabric "with a greater purity and continuity than anywhere else," but that it is nevertheless increasingly ignored or downplayed, which causes him to reflect upon his era. "Why were our heroic personalities, the carriers and reinforcers of the lifeline to a future beyond the chaos of greedy and irrational society, so denigrated, so deprincipled that they could no longer fortify the hope that we can establish a rational world of peace and beauty?" For Nelson, it is not only that there is some kind of conspiracy against memory, as Chomsky is wont to invoke, because "as the great names come to mind, now on far-off shores, dimly seen, the names of Sumner,

Theodore Parker, Garrison, John Brown, Wendell Phillips, Frederick Douglass, Atgeld, Debs. . . . I began to realize that these men have been exorcised because they understood and dramatized those crises which came at the peak of the flowering of a young and vigorous capitalist democracy, dramatized them in ways which led to the unmasking and sharpening of the very contradictions which will cause this bloom to fade and flower into yet higher social forms" (93). This reminds us that when it comes to such categories as the role of the intellectual, context is key, and in the current political climate, the pantheon is as likely to be called upon to reinforce the status quo as to challenge it, as we see in Michael Ignatieff's overt support for Bush's policies in Iraq, which seem to so clearly betray ideas about human rights and the role of the United Nations in emerging conflicts. This political function is famously invoked in Beauvoir's earlier fictional work *The Mandarins,* and, of course, in the updated nonfictional version thereof penned early on by Noam Chomsky.[18]

New Mandarins

Truman Nelson speaks of the "exorcision" of "heroic personalities" as though it happened from the outside, whereas in fact it is clear that that academics are often part of, or wedded to, the powerful segments of society. Despite the obvious advantages of having intellectuals play a strong role in the moral or political fabric of society, there are some risks and downsides as well. First, there is a danger in according specific powers to intellectuals or academics if their own interests are tied to those of the ruling classes, something we see whenever politicians are looking for justification for some foolhardy military mission, for example. Intellectuals from prestigious universities or think tanks are always being called upon to justify some military escapade or another, just as other intellectuals who stand on the opposite side of these issues can be scorned by virtue of their privileged place in society, as though their ivory tower status makes them "out of touch" with the masses and therefore not worth the attention of a general public. This ambivalence is shared by large portions of the population in the United States, who on the one hand hope to educate their children at Harvard or Yale or

Vanderbilt, but on the other feel a kind of class scorn for the liberal humanism that might occasionally leak out from the faculty at such prestigious institutions. This contrast is captured by the distinction between the vision of the "intellectual" versus the person who is "studying" at a "prestigious place," whereby the former is deemed to be out of touch, while the latter is admired and envied. What counts in the latter, though, is the label or the bumper sticker, and not the humanist values that these prestigious institutions claim to promote.

Similar distinctions were made in earlier times between the labels "radical" and "member of the Communist Party" which have been and still are used by different sides to different ends. Addressing the conflicted status of the radical but nonparty member in the 1940s, George Orwell remarked that "the very word 'Intellectual' has become a term by which left-wing politicians try to discredit each other and any common rival. The effect of this policy has been to strengthen the hold of leaders over parties and political groups, because any person who takes an independent stand and refuses to follow the party line can be discredited as an 'intellectual,' who is out for his own ends and has nothing in common with the workers." Orwell, who has now been subjected to this very revisionism postmortem, could recall his own words: "I have actually seen this method at work in many left-wing movements. The demagogic use of such a line of argument is obvious. It serves effectively to keep the rank and file segregated from any individual writer who may think on original lines, and so it preserves the party dogma—and, incidentally, its dogmatists—from the effects of free criticism" (*The Collected Essays* 16). Herbert Marcuse, no stranger to this type of debate on account of his own relations to both the labor movement and the ivory tower, calls upon his experience of efforts made, by design or not, to discredit viable opposition, which he describes in "Liberation from the Affluent Society": "We all know the fatal prejudice, practically from the beginning, in the labor movement against the intelligentsia as catalyst of historical change. It is time to ask whether this prejudice against the intellectuals, and the inferiority complex of the intellectuals resulting from it, was not an essential factor in the development of the capitalist as well as the socialist societies: in the development and weakening of the opposition."[19]

Within the Actuality

The question of speaking on behalf of a segment of the population begs questions about who can represent whose actuality, and on what basis. This has been a crucial consideration for African Americans, for whom the late Ray Charles, W. E. B Dubois, Ralph Ellison, Martin Luther King, Malcolm X, and many others represent both icons and particular political approaches. Contemporary intellectuals, such as Kwame Anthony Appiah, Stephen Carter, Henry Louis Gates, Stuart Hall, bell hooks, Leroi Jones, Toni Morrison, Shelby Steele, Alice Walker, Cornell West, and Patricia Williams, set the tenor of the discussion by engaging on a whole range of fronts the crucial intellectual and public challenges of the African American, and more broadly, the African continent. The actuality for them is the discrimination they experienced throughout their lives, and now, as they occupy positions of privilege, they have set out to define responsible work within and beyond their respective disciplines. This means that the African American intellectual task demands a range of institutional and public obligations: redefining the canon and contributing to it; rethinking the university and erecting or contributing to new programs within it; (re)building ties between the community and the ivory tower and then serving themselves as bridges; and at every turn attempting to raise the consciousness that traditional methods are not always the right ones, all the while demonstrating that they can thrive in and transform institutions as staid and traditional as, say, the (Ivy League) university.

The challenge for the female public intellectual is, perhaps, less clearly defined, even if there is an overlap with some of the issues set out thus far. Speaking within the female actuality is to represent a massive diversity of voices, which would lead one to expect that there would be a roughly equivalent split between male and female intellectuals engaged beyond the confines of the university. For what they are worth, two studies have amassed, based on varying criteria, lists of public intellectuals in the United Kingdom and the United States, and neither puts women beyond 15 percent of the overall count of public intellectuals. In the case of the *Prospect Magazine* list of the "100 worthies," there are only 12 women: religious historian Karen Armstrong; critic, essayist, and novelist A. S. Byatt; historian Linda Colley; pharmacologist and director of the Royal Institute Susan Greenfield; writer and academic Germaine Greer; historian Lisa Jardine; moral philosopher Mary Midgley; philosopher Onora O'Neill; author and columnist Melanie Phillips; biographer Gitta Sereny; philosopher and public ethicist Mary Warnock; and novelist Jeanette Winterson. Pondering the list's absences, David Herman wonders, "Is this the result of institutional . . . sexism in the media and universities? Or is it rather an acknowledgement that the big battles have been won, that sexism [is] no longer [one of the] key fault lines in our intellectual culture?"[20] A July 2, 2004, *Guardian* article by Laura Barton titled "Here's a few you missed"[21] suggests that Herman's query "rather supposes that we would only see a large number of women on such a list if women's rights were still contentious—if we were still entitled to a sympathy vote. And if the good fight is over, then we ought to get back to the kitchen." It then goes on to cite Steve Fuller, professor of sociology at Warwick University and author of *How To Be An Intellectual*,[22] who suggests "that male intellectuals tend to reinforce each other more than women do. The old boy network permeates the intelligentsia just as much as any other aspect of British society." Furthermore, he has found that female public intellectuals are not regarded with the same respect as their male counterparts, and they are scrutinized more severely, and on different grounds, including "Susan Greenfield's mini skirts, or the personal life of Germaine Greer. 'Women intellectuals certainly appear on enough pages,' says Fuller, but often this can slightly devalue their intelligence in the public's perception. Men, by comparison, 'don't get hurt by being around a lot.' It seems that even in the intellectual world there are slags and there are studs." The *Guardian* adds a list of its own 101 who are missing from the pantheon, including literary critic Elaine Showalter; academic Gillian Beer; actor and campaigner Vanessa Redgrave; author Doris Lessing; psychoanalyst and author Juliet Mitchell; author Naomi Klein; director of Liberty Shami Chakrabarti; television producer, author, member of the ICA council Lisa Appignanesi; broadcaster and author Bonnie Greer; leader of the House of Lords Lady Amos; editor of the *London Review of Books* Mary Kay Wilmers; director of think tank Politeia; and author Sheila Lawlor.

As part of his own effort to document the public intellectual, Richard Posner also offers a list in *Public Intellectuals*, this time of 607 public intellectuals in America.[23] Slightly more complete and systematic, Posner includes categories of description for each candidate, including whether they are female, Black, Jewish, academically affiliated (and in which domain), government affiliated, scholarly citations, and the number of web hits their names draw. A survey of this list includes a relatively small number of female public intellectuals including Renata Adler, Hannah Arendt, Martha Bayles, Simone de Beauvoir, Ruth Benedict, Sissela Bok, Judith Butler, Rachel Carson, Lynn Chaney, Anne Coulter, Laura D'Andrea Tyson, Angela Davis, Midge Decter, Andrea Dworkin, Barbara Ehrenreich, Jean Bethke Elshtain, Barbara Epstein, Cynthia Fuchs Epstein, Susan Estrich, Susan Faludi, Frances Fitzgerald, Elizabeth Fox-Genovese, Betty Frieden, Carol Gilligan, Mary Ann Glendon, Doris Kearns Goodwin, Linda Greenhouse, Lani Guinier, Amy Gutmann, Elizabeth Hardwick, Vicki Hearne, Carolyn Heilbrun, Lillian Hellman, Gertrude Himmelfarb, bell hooks, Ada Louise Huxtable, Carol Iannone, Pauline Kael, Mary Lefkowitz, Catharine MacKinnon, Janet Malcolm, Mary McCarthy, Deirdre McCloskey, Margaret Mead, Kate Millett, Martha Minow, Jessica Mitford, Toni Morrison, Martha Nussbaum, Joyce Carol Oates, Cynthia Ozick, Camille Paglia, Virginia Postrel, Francine Prose, Hilary Putnam (!), Ayn Rand, Diane Ravitch, Adrienne Rich, Elaine Scarry, Eve Kosofsky Sedgwick, Nancy Sherman, Judith Sklar, Elaine Showalter, Theda Skocpol, Christina Hoff Sommers, Susan Sontag, Gloria Steinem, Kathleen Sullivan, Abigail Thernstrom, Diana Trilling, Barbara Tuchman, Katrina Vanden Heuvel, Rebecca West, Patricia Williams, Ellen Willis, Roberta Wohlstetter, and Naomi Wolf. Notice that of these 78, 13 are dead and one (Hilary Putnam) is a man. This means that of the 604 public intellectuals in Posner's pantheon, only 10 percent or so are women who are still alive, a number that is consistent with the *Prospect Magazine* effort.

A sense of how one might act in the face of such power dynamics and the institutional apparatuses that mirror them is captured very nicely in the work of Camille Paglia,[24] who in a talk at MIT invoked her situation and her sex as she performed a combination of a stand-up comedy routine and a provocative feminist-informed attack on the elite scientific institution: "Now, speaking here at M.I.T. confronted me with a dilemma. I asked myself, should I try to act like a lady? I can do it. It's hard, it takes a lot out of me. I can do it for a few hours. But then I thought, *naw*. These people, both my friends and my *enemies* who are here, aren't coming to see me act like a lady. So I thought I'd just be myself—which is, you know, abrasive, strident, and obnoxious. So then you all can go outside and say 'What a bitch!' " (250). This is fun, and it follows both the idea of the catalyst, you have the right to your own thoughts and who cares what authority thinks, and nurturing, in that you have to grow and work in your own way, informed but independent. Paglia continues: "Now, the reason I'm getting so much attention: I think it's pretty obvious that we're in a time where there's a kind of impasse in contemporary thinking. And what I represent is independent thought. What I represent is the essence of the Sixties, which is free thought and free speech. And a lot of people don't like it. A lot of people who are well-meaning on both sides of the political spectrum want to shut down free speech. And my mission is to be absolutely as painful as possible in every situation" (250). Her primary goal here is to denounce rather than uphold some kind of social program, and she does so, typically, by challenging the authoritative voices who would claim to speak on behalf of the audience.

One amusing example, and notice the role of humor in this type of approach, is in her discussion about multiculturalism's rise as an à la mode subject, suddenly preached by those least likely to recognize its implications. "Whereas people like, um Stanley Fish—whom I call 'a totalitarian Tinkerbell'—that's what I call him. Uh-huh. Okay? How *dare* he? What a hypocrite! People at Duke telling us about multiculturalism—those people who have never had anyone outside of a prep school in their classes. It's unbelievable—the preaching! That whole bunch of people at Duke—all of them in flight from their ethnicity—every one of them—trying to tell us about the problem of the old establishment was that it was WASP. So what's the answer to that? Be *ethnic*! Okay? Every one of them—every one of them—look at the style that they write—this kind of gameplaying, slick, cerebral style. Those people have an identity problem!" (255). To separate herself from these people involves her acknowledging the soil in which she was raised, which brings her gardening into public view: "I'm probably the only major voice right now in academe who's actually taught factory workers. As opposed to these people who are the Marxists [makes prancing, dancing, hair-preening gestures], oh yes, these Marxists, like Terry Eagleton at Oxford. Do you know what he makes? Do you know the *salary* that man makes? Oh, it just disgusts me. This is why he has to wear blue jeans, to show "Oh, no, I don't have the money." These people are hypocrites! They really are. It's all a literary game. There's no authentic self-sacrifice, no direct actual experience of workers or working-class people. It's appalling, the situation. It's everywhere, it's everywhere in the Ivy League" (255). The tensions and contradictions herein abound, and Paglia herself, guru, self-fashioned populist, writer, Yale graduate, on a podium at the Massachusetts Institute of Technology in front of a hoard of adoring fans, embodies whole realms of them. From a more social perspective, those who work from this standpoint recall Herbert Marcuse's or Howard Zinn's ideas that intellectuals need, to recall Zellig Harris's term, to "de-fool" the population, in part by offering the humor required to save us from drowning in the media and popular culture sea of misrepresentation.

The Intellectual Life Buoy

To draw upon intellectual work to combat this hypocrisy demands engagement with quite complex ideas and issues represented in the aforementioned Jim Merod book on the political responsibility of the (literary) critic,[25] in which he provocatively ask how humanists can "turn the rather elegant and complicated readings of cherished texts into politically productive knowledge for a society immersed in consumer junk and drowning in images of false liberation." If this is the goal, then one of the many challenges is to uphold the sometimes obscure project of criticism in the humanities while extending its worth to useful work, which in some ways demands that it be transformed at least in its language to perform this redemptive function: "In all its forms, the question is how criticism can become practical without losing clarity and analytic skill, become democratic (or democratically useful) and not evasive" (89).

The corpus from which a humanities critic like Merod can draw for such efforts is often some combination of political philosophy and literary or language theory, and generally includes references to a well-established pantheon including the likes of Jürgen Habermas, Russell Jacoby, Fredric Jameson, Julia Kristeva, Edward Said, and Gayatri Spivak, who, despite their differences, make a case for bringing the substance of their academic writings to bear upon contemporary problems. These are the writers who tend to leave the ivory tower without leaving it behind, by addressing current structural problems that are serving as obstacles toward the establishment of a good society. The constant problem, however, involves the translation of these critical approaches into concrete action, which in most forums leads people to conclude with some statement about how there is a need to address questions from several different angles at once, and that at least one of them should be academic. Judging by the difficult nature of the prose in such efforts, however, the academic side of things can sometimes cause as many problems as it addresses, and there is a long history of writers and scholars making lucid pleas for sensible and productive scholarship instead of self-serving, obliquely indecipherable political obfuscation.

Russell Jacoby finds in his nostalgic book *The Last Intellectuals* that the problem is not so much in the obscurity of the language as in the fact that the modern university takes the soul out of the intellectual; laboring for a discovery for which they will receive recompense, contemporary academics find their work becoming narrower, their quest more single-minded, and their ends more bureaucratic.[26] In his poorly reviewed[27] 2001 study titled *Public Intellectuals*, Richard Posner is equally critical of the university, but he has no desire to return to an era of committed intellectuals who fought the good fight, favoring instead a more utilitarian approach that actually lauds the assessment that ideas are commodities fighting it out on the open market and supporting those ideas that can be put to work for liberal purposes over more utopian-style analyses.[28] This calls to mind Pierre Bourdieu's idea that discourse is bought and sold on a symbolic marketplace of ideas as commodities, except that Bourdieu emphasizes in most of his work the degree to which the legitimate discourse against which utterances are judged tends to favor power rather than the exchange of useful information.[29]

A number of studies have pointed to nefarious connections between so-called rarefied university quarters and the more hard-nosed business practices, such as the trade in arms,[30] and it is obvious, looking at the number of PhDs and former professors who people current government offices and the number of high-placed government officials in important university offices, that the tower is not so separate from other high places. Bill Readings goes further in the *University in Ruins*,[31] claiming that the "ideal community" in the university no longer "provides a model of the rational community, a microcosm of the pure form of the public sphere;" indeed, Readings claims that the Humboldt-inspired university has lost "its privileged status as the model of society," and it has not regained it "by becoming the model of the absence of models." Instead, the university "becomes one site among others where *the question of being-together is raised*, raised with an urgency that proceeds from the absence of the institutional forms (such as the nation-state), which have historically served to mask that question for the past three centuries or so" (20).

Contemporary Concerns

The range of criticisms of how intellectuals engage public issues often speaks to a divide between the interests of the academic and the day-to-day concerns of the people on whose behalf the academic is trying to speak. In some cases, the speech or the writings of these academics are so obscure and complex that the public feels excluded rather than assisted. Writers such as Homi Bhabha or Gayatri Spivak, for example, specifically employ complex ideas from the realms of deconstruction or Lacanian psychoanalysis and the specialized privilege they procure within their respective universities to better understand postcolonial society. The often contradictory mission of speaking from within the university and using complex theory, like deconstruction, to useful ends, like relieving discrepancies in wealth, is invoked in different contexts. Sonia Shah's Znet article titled "Our Deeply Twisted Understanding of the World" represents this perspective: "Right now, people are dying from western capitalism; they're getting poisoned by industrial chemicals and flooded out of their homes by mega-dams. Women are being forced to service an international sex industry, work in sweatshops, and undergo painful mutilations. We don't need to know a lot about how these people live because the question right now is survival itself. . . . It's too important to leave to the lofty intellectuals in their ivory towers."[32]

Since it is too important to leave it to the "lofty intellectuals," but it is also beyond the interests of most people to start deconstructing misinformation, the only hope is to bring scholars' work to bear upon contemporary issues. This is Jean-Paul Sartre's approach, which demands engagement in contemporary issues because "the writer has no way of escaping, we want him to embrace his era—tightly. It is his only chance; it was made for him and he was made for it".[33] This idea challenges many of the practices of the ivory tower, at least in its effort to shelter or validate work deemed obscure or disconnected, unless it is accompanied by some version of social engagement. The writer, therefore, is not some New Critical construct, a gloriously disconnected genius who owes nothing to his time or his surroundings. Says Sartre, "The writer is *situated* in his time; every word he utters has reverberations. As does his silence. I hold Flaubert and the Goncourts responsible for the repression that followed the Commune because they didn't write a line to prevent it. Some will object that this wasn't their business. But was the Calas trial Voltaire's business? Was Dreyfus's sentence Zola's business? Was the administration of the Congo Gide's business? Each of those authors, at a particular time in his life, took stock of his responsibility as a writer. The Occupation taught us ours. Since we act upon our time by virtue of our very existence, we decide that our action will be voluntary."[34]

So for Sartre, there is a real obligation to write to the issues of the day, and it is indeed incumbent upon the academic to venture outside the scholarly confines or bear the consequences, if only through his or her silence, of actions taken in the outside world. Many who have written on the social responsibility of the academic hold to this idea, often taking for granted that the issues are fundamentally economic and, in many cases, solvable only through some kind of profound upheaval leading up to a reconfiguration of economic powers in the country. This is certainly the case for writers like Cornelius Castoriadis,[35] who bemoans intellectualism without true intellectual engagement. One example he provides is that so many "Marxist" and "leftist" intellectuals "continue to spend their time and energy writing on and on about the relation between Volume 1 and Volume 3 of *Das Kapital*, commenting on and reinterpreting this or that comment on Marx by this or that interpreter of Marx, heaping glosses on glosses of *books*," rather than addressing "actual history, the effective creation of forms and meanings in and through the activity of people" (255). One reason for this is clearly professional, as Paul Street suggests:

As one genuinely radical professor told me years ago, his colleagues "spend most of their time writing long love letters to each other." The "love letters" referred, of course, to the academics' parade of specialized self-refereed and self-referential books and articles, . . . long and involved life works that rarely attain anything but the most select insider readership They excel mainly at enabling their authors to gain tenure and promotions and at gathering dust on the shelves of university libraries. Meanwhile, those professors who focus on teaching, on communicating with and inspiring the thousands of students out in their classrooms and lecture halls, the children of people who pay professors' salaries, are ridiculed for not knowing who the real audience is. At the same time, the radical potential of academia is badly diluted by the profoundly anti-intellectual super-specialization and subdivision of knowledge and labor across diverse academic departments and programs. The modern university's artificial separation (reflected in an academic lecture I once heard on "Marx the sociologist, Marx the political scientist, Marx the economist, Marx the historian, and Marx the anthropologist") of thought makes it difficult for academics and students to make the connections essential for meaningful intellectual work and radical criticism. The few who rise above it . . . are often denounced for speaking outside their little assigned corner of academic expertise.[36]

As we have seen, Chomsky has certainly been the subject of such critique for his writing about foreign policy, economics, and social sciences. Howard Zinn has made similar observations about the projects of historians in his article titled "Historian as Citizen,"[37] but rather than considering professional advancement he focuses instead on personal responsibility:

I am suggesting that blame in history be based on the future and not the past. It is an old and useless game among historians to decide whether Caesar was good or bad, Napoleon progressive or reactionary, Roosevelt a reformer or a revolutionist. True, certain of these questions are pertinent to present concerns; for instance, was Socrates right in submitting to Athens? But in a recounting of past crimes, the proper question to ask is not "Who was guilty then?" unless it leads directly to: "What is our responsibility now?" (513).

The idea for these approaches, each in its own way associated with revolutionary thinking, is to distinguish between lived history and the "history of ideas," narrowly construed, because history is not just the array of historical "facts"; what matters, from a revolutionary point of view, "is the *interpretation* of these facts, which cannot be left to the historians of the university establishment."[38] From this vantage point, academics have a responsibility, but they are not necessarily to be trusted to carry out their role adequately, and they should not expect that they can serve as anything more than catalysts, as Herbert Marcuse points out:

Can we say that the intelligentsia is the agent of historical change? Can we say that the intelligentsia today is a revolutionary class? The answer I would give is: No, we cannot say that. But we can say, and I think we must say, that the intelligentsia has a decisive preparatory function, not more; and I suggest that this is plenty. By itself it is not and cannot be a revolutionary class, but it can become the catalyst, and it has a preparatory function—certainly not for the first time; that is in fact the way all revolution starts—but more, perhaps, today than ever before. Because—and for this too we have a very material and very concrete basis—it is from this group that the holders of decisive positions in the productive process will be recruited, in the future even more than hitherto."[39]

The Seymour Melman Approach

A key figure in this discussion is Seymour Melman, an old friend and indeed a mentor of Noam Chomsky. Throughout his career Melman wrote some of the saddest texts imaginable, not only about what is happening in a world of "pentagon capitalism" but what is happening elsewhere in society as a consequence of those actions. I always feel like crying when reading Melman's work, both for what is and what could be, particularly in his last book, *After Capitalism*, a masterpiece that was virtually ignored (in part because it came out within days of the tragedy of 9/11). When he died he was working on a new book, from which I offer this segment as a sense of the kinds of facts Melman accumulated and looked to change. In a chapter titled "The Human and Industrial Cost of Defense," Melman offers his view of the tasks that stand before those who wish to work beyond the ivory tower:

From 1990 to 2000, the United States government spent $2,956 billion on the Department of Defense. This sum of staggering size (try to visualize even one billion of anything) does not express the cost of the military establishment to the nation as a whole. The true cost is measured by the "opportunity cost," by what has been foregone, by the accumulated deterioration in many facets of life, by the inability to alleviate human wretchedness of long duration.

Here is part of the human inventory of depletion:

1. By 2001, huge numbers of U.S. homes were decaying. 2 million homes have severe physical problems. 13 million have leaks from outside the structure. 1 million homes have holes in their floors. 1 million homes are infested with rats. 72,000 homes have no electricity.

2. In 2002, 9.3 million people in the United States were classified as "hungry" by the U.S. Department of Agriculture. Furthermore, almost 35 million people— 12.5 percent of U.S. households—had no secure supply of food, due to lack of resources.

3. In 2002, 34.8 million people in the U.S. lived in poverty. This is 12.4 percent of the population, and an increase of 1.4 million from 2001.

4. 2.3–3.5 million people (including 1.3 million children) in the U.S. experience homelessness each year.

5. 41.2 million people in the U.S. lacked health insurance during the entire year 2001. In 2002, 18,000 uninsured Americans died due to lack of treatment.

6. 14 million children go to class in deteriorating public schools. Two thirds of all public schools have troublesome environmental conditions.

Melman then notes that "The human cost of military priority is paralleled by the depletion of industrial technology caused by the concentration of manpower and capital on military technology and in military industry." For example:

1. In 1996, over 60% of the machine tools used in U.S. industry were 11 + years old.

2. Congestion of roads causes 5.7 billion hours of delay in the U.S. each year. This is equivalent to 650,684 years of time wasted.

3. U.S. railways have become antiquated. Now the electrification of 60,000 miles of track is required before the U.S. can use the modern, fast and efficient trains that exist in other countries.

As civilian industrial technology deteriorates or fails to advance, productive employment opportunity for Americans diminishes.

To carry out the role that Melman as an industrial engineer assigned to himself, he as an intellectual had to be engaged, in the Sartrean sense of *engagé*, in issues of the day, and to do so he had to be willing to extend the scope of his work by taking risks in the real world. The danger, however, is that intellectuals come to be seduced, or "bewitched," by ideologies that in their implications can be murderous even if their ambitions seem lofty. In his controversial book *The Opium of the Intellectuals*, Paul Aron berated those who mercilessly attack the failings of contemporary democracies while providing intellectual asylum for those who support the "proper" doctrines, no matter how murderous. His target was often Marxism, of course, but it is the intoxicated intellectual who seems most guilty of upholding, legitimizing, and promoting ideologies versus his own humanist-inspired commonsense approach to contemporary concerns.

Speaking Out as a Radical Intellectual

Is there a link between the type of critique leveled and the access provided to organs aimed at the diffusion of information? Although the media is quick to deny it (pace the March 2006 *NYRB* editorials by *New York Times* and *Washington Post* editors who vociferously deny charges that they were purposely deaf to evidence that the Iraq invasion was so clearly built on a dubious WMD case), some critics do note the obvious link between who speaks publicly and what they have to say. Edward S. Herman and David Peterson, for example, write in Znet that "an intellectual who has generous media access is often funded by the American Enterprise or Manhattan Institutes, Heritage Foundation, or the Hoover Institution, as in cases of Dinesh D'Souza, the Thernstroms, Christina Hoff Sommers, Shelby Steele, and Heather MacDonald. More generally, those who enjoy access can be relied on to say what the establishment wants said on the topics of the day—'civility,' 'political correctness,' race, free trade, and 'humanitarian intervention,' and the civilizing mission of the United States and West."

For Herman and Peterson, power dynamics rather than public service characterizes "the work of intellectuals such as Alan Wolfe, Charles Murray, Paul Krugman, Robert Kaplan, David Rieff, and Michael Ignatieff, who have been relatively ubiquitous figures over the past decade, enjoying bylines, radio and television appearances, and favorable book reviews. Given their service to the powerful we categorize these preferred intellectuals as 'power' rather than 'public' intellectuals. It is a distinction that captures a crucial feature of the U.S. system of selective promotion or marginalization of intellectuals and their ideas throughout the public sphere."[40] This is a very useful distinction, and begs the question of whether there is in fact a good or positive way to carry out useful work beyond the ivory tower by conscientiously serving particular interests, and without inadvertently or perhaps consciously serving as a *tool* for a particular constituency.

The problem is, it is difficult to come down on one side or another of these debates without realizing that each position is fraught with potential pitfalls, and that one's own work can be misread and come to support a side in the debate that the author had, overtly or not, hoped to discredit, particularly with the evolution of a political situation or series of events. As such, the status of Solzhenitsyn's corpus has been variously vilified and revived, as have seminal texts such as George Orwell's *1984*, which seem either predictive or contiguous with status quo thinking. One way out of this conundrum is to recall the previous idea of working to catalyze useful action, rather than dictating its direction. Another approach, often favored by libertarian thinkers or those associated with certain veins of anarchist thought, is to focus on the creative and nurturing function that the intellectual can play.

Herbert Marcuse's opening lines in "Liberation from the Affluent Society" begin with the words: "I am very happy to see so many flowers here and that is why I want to remind you that flowers, by themselves, have no power whatsoever, other than the power of men and women who protect them and take care of them against aggression and destruction" (276). Sartre as well finds that "a politically active individual has no need to forge human nature; it is enough for him to eliminate the obstacles that might prevent him from blossoming."[41] This vision of individuals as seedlings that simply need decent soil and adequate sunlight in order to flourish in their own way is scattered throughout the literature, as we have seen, and is often linked to the idea of promoting individual creativity. This idea is related to some sense of consciousness raising, on the one hand respecting individual makeup and approach, and on the other promoting valuable exchange of ideas to sensitize people as to how to best direct their energies.

As we have seen, Chomsky has a special affiliation with intellectuals who take personal risks, who are willing to stand up for and speak out on behalf of valued convictions. But public intellectuals need as well to be humble, so those who work beyond the ivory tower need to seriously consider the limitations of their work and the role that powerful interests play in forming public opinion. For this reason, intellectuals must draw from strengths and experience, they must foster a nurturing environment in the society to which they address their work, they must act as catalysts to awaken that which is existent in the human brain, and they must be midwives for creativity. But they must also face up to the obstacles and counteract the multitude of attempts to miseducate us for other agendas, particularly today when this effort is so pervasive, and so well funded. In short, there is no single version of the ivory tower, any more than there is one way in which scholars work beyond its walls. The task of identifying characteristics of those who work within and beyond the ivory tower is therefore informed by reference to extraordinarily influential examples from past eras, but the challenge of adequately representing the various faces of the ensconced intellectual is also to acknowledge present trends in university life.

The Most Important Public Intellectual in the World

This discussion returns us to the opening of this book, in which I noted that Noam Chomsky was voted by 20,000 people as "the most important public intellectual in the world today" by the British monthly *Prospect* and the Washington-based conservative magazine *Foreign Policy*.[42] So much of what we have seen about Chomsky's approach and effect are echoed in the particularities of the article that was produced about this event, especially Chomsky's own commentary:

NC: "It's not the first time this happened," says Chomsky. "But you have to really ask questions in depth to know what they mean. So back in the early '70s, there was some kind of poll . . . among American intellectuals, about who was the most influential American intellectual, just in politics, and I think that I appeared first or close to the top in that. But there was another poll where they asked further questions which made sense. They said, 'Who would you pay attention to?' Or something like that—I was way down at the bottom."

Q: Who would you say is the most important living intellectual?

NC: "That's really hard to say. The people I find impressive are mostly not intellectuals. For example, Father Javier Giraldo, the Jesuit priest who runs the [Intercongregational Commission for Justice and Peace] in Colombia, which is the major human rights center there. Colombia has by far the worst human rights record in the hemisphere and of course is the leading recipient of U.S. military aid. Those two things correlate very closely. You know, especially the military and the paramilitaries have been carrying out hideous massacres and so on.

Father Giraldo is exposed to a lot of them and has in some cases forced people to accept international investigation. And he provides protection to people, he's in great danger. He's under constant death threats . . .
"Last time [I saw him], he brought to see me a leader of a town, San Jose, that had a strong peace community, that was the first of the peace communities that declared themselves zones of peace. They don't want to be bothered by the military . . . He brought the leader of the group to see me in Bogota, which was dangerous; the town was at that time under military siege and had been for several months. [The leader] was describing to me how they were starving, children were starving; every once in a while the military or paramilitary would come into town and just shoot people just to show them they were still there. And he was pleading for help, he said do something about it, help us. Anyway, just a few months ago, the military went in and he was murdered, along with several others. But Father Giraldo is still there. He's not the only one. But there are people like that all over the world."[43]

This slap in the face to the mainstream thinking about intellectuals in the Western world is also trademark Chomsky in that it upholds as valuable the *real* work of those individuals, usually unrecognized outside of small activist circles, who battle with conviction "on the ground" and in doing so take real personal risks. Consistent as well with all we have seen is the way in which he steps outside of the accolades to assess their true meaning:

They have that paranoid image of me being the most influential person . . . but they hated me. I mean, if you want to know what American intellectuals, especially liberal intellectuals, think—take a look at the house journal of liberal American intellectuals, Cambridge intellectuals; it's called the *American Prospect*, and it's for people around here. It's really left-liberal. Now they had a very comical front cover . . . [earlier] this year, depicting the embattled American liberals, and there are two snarling figures right at their throats. One is Dick Cheney. The other is me. They're caught between these two immense forces.

In light of it all, the pressures, the criticisms, even the adoration and the incredible demands it places upon his life, one would imagine that Chomsky might be tempted to slow down. If what I have suggested in this book is accurate, he can perhaps do so with the sense that he and others have catalyzed sufficient energies and ideas to leave this world in somewhat better hands than did the previous generations, intellectuals and otherwise. Instead, the powerhouse that is Chomsky looks forward to more of the same:

Q: Assuming you have 50 more years of work, what would you like . . .

NC: "[That's] not likely—120 is the most you get."

Q: I don't know. It's one of the things people say, you know. Why, what would you like to do in the next 50 years if you work?

NC: "More of what I'm doing now. I'm happy to go on like that as long as I can."[44]

Noam Chomsky. Ever the optimist, ever the hard worker, forever the champion of the underdog. I for one hope that the end is nowhere in sight.

Notes

Preface

1. See www.prospect-magazine.co.uk/intellectuals/results (accessed 2/12/07).

2. The speech by Chavez began with the following remarkable tribute: "Representatives of the governments of the world, good morning to all of you. First of all, I would like to invite you, very respectfully, to those who have not read this book, to read it. Noam Chomsky, one of the most prestigious American and world intellectuals, Noam Chomsky, and this is one of his most recent books, 'Hegemony or Survival: The Imperialist Strategy of the United States.'" [Holds up book, waves it in front of General Assembly.] "It's an excellent book to help us understand what has been happening in the world throughout the 20th century, and what's happening now, and the greatest threat looming over our planet. The hegemonic pretensions of the American empire are placing at risk the very survival of the human species. We continue to warn you about this danger and we appeal to the people of the United States and the world to halt this threat, which is like a sword hanging over our heads. I had considered reading from this book, but, for the sake of time," [flips through the pages, which are numerous] "I will just leave it as a recommendation. It reads easily, it is a very good book, I'm sure Madame [President] you are familiar with it. It appears in English, in Russian, in Arabic, in German. I think that the first people who should read this book are our brothers and sisters in the United States, because their threat is right in their own house." Available at http://www.newsmax.com/archives/articles/2006/9/20/123752.shtml (accessed 2/13/2007).

3. Cited at http://www.chomsky.info/interviews/1992—02.htm (accessed 2/13/07).

4. *Understanding Power: The Indispensable Chomsky,* ed. Peter R. Mitchel and John Schoeffel (New York: The New Press, 2002), p. 98.

5. Ibid., p. 98.

Chapter One

1. http://storms.typepad.com/booklust/2005/05/im_drawn_to_noa.html (accessed 2/13/2007). I should mention at this point that whenever possible I will provide

URLs for references, to allow the reader a sense of how important Chomsky has become on the Internet, and to provide access to his and related materials to the broadest possible audience.

2. See my *Noam Chomsky: A Life of Dissent* for discussions of the goals of these groups. I will devote considerable attention to them in my forthcoming *Zellig Harris's America* (Cambridge: MIT Press, 2008).

3. "Old Wine, New Bottles: Free Trade, Global Markets and Military Adventures," University of Virginia, February 10, 1993, available online at http://www.zmag.org/chomsky/talks/9302-uva.html (accessed 2/13/2007).

4. Cited in Otero's *Radical Priorities,* p. 24.

5. Mina Graur, *An Anarchist Rabbi: The Life and Teachings of Rudolph Rocker* (Jerusalem: Magnes Press, 1997), pp. 61–62.

6. See http://www.kibbutz.org.il/eng/kbaeng.htm (accessed 2/13/2007).

7. Amsterdam: Querido Verlag, 1934.

8. "Addresses on Reconstruction in Palestine," in *Ideas and Opinions by Albert Einstein,* based on *Mein Weltbild,* ed. Carl Seelig, and other sources, new translations and revisions by Sonja Bargmann (New York: Wings Books, 1954), p. 179.

9. Graur, *An Anarchist Rabbi,* p. 46.

10. Cited in *Le Monde* Sept. 1, 1998 (my translation).

11. Here again is an overlap between Chomsky and Rocker (and indeed between Chomsky and a range of anarchists, who tend to excel at envisioning the effects of world events upon larger issues). For example, Mina Graur reminds us that Rocker "was much quicker than most of his anarchist friends to recognize that the Bolshevik revolutionary myth was just that, a myth, and it was not going to yield any real social betterment" (131).

12. In the *Baltimore Sun,* January 3, 1999.

13. Available online at http://www.chomsky.info/onchomsky/19880201.htm (accessed 2/13/2007).

14. http://www.nytimes.com/2002/10/10/garden/10PETE.html?ex=1035622770 &ei=1&en=9027e0d53aa62770 (accessed 2/13/2007).

15. From http://www.zmag.org/chomsky/rage/rageQA.html (accessed 2/13/2007): "Rage Against the Machine is a popular rap-metal band, explicitly critical of U.S. power and capitalist rule. Their recent album *Evil Empire* hit #1 on the Billboard charts when it first came out. Noam Chomsky, professor of linguistics at MIT and well-known dissident intellectual, is highly admired by the group. Guitarist Tom Morello comments that Chomsky's books are the most popular on the Rage tour bus, and a couple of his works appear on the inside cover of their latest album. The following interview between Morello and Chomsky was conducted via phone during the summer of 1996. It was broadcast nation-wide during the *Radio Free LA* program in January 1997."

16. The Daily Whopper, "Noam Chomsky—America's #1 Traitor," October 11, 2001.

17. See "To Noam Is to Love Him" (Chomsky "Rocks" on Film), by Mickey Z., Dissident Voice, December 2, 2002, http://www.dissidentvoice.org/Articles/MickeyZ_Chomsky.htm, accessed 2/13/2007.

18. *Heterodoxy*, March 1996.

19. http://www.zmag.org/ZMag/articles/feb2000MCCHESNEY.htm (accessed 2/13/2007).

20. http://www.zmag.org/ZMag/articles/jan2000carter.htm (accessed 2/13/2007).

21. http://www.interpunk.com/item.cfm?Item=71234& (accessed 2/13/2007).

22. Ibid.

23. Ibid.

24. http://www.amazon.com/gp/richpub/syltguides/fullview/1HKKP08I8F8ZB (accessed 2/13/2007).

25. Ibid.

26. http://www.largeheartedboy.com/blog/archive/2003/04/eddie_vedder_bu .html (accessed 2/13/2007).

27. http://www.punkvoter.com/guest/guest_detail.php?GuestColumnID=23 (accessed 2/13/2007).

28. Ibid.

29. http://www.punkvoter.com/guest/guest_detail.php?GuestColumnID=15 (accessed 2/13/2007).

30. See www.realchangenews.org/pastissuesupgrade/2004_10_14/issue/current/ features/coverstory.html (accessed 2/13/2007).

31. http://www.aversion.com/bands/interviews.cfm?f_id=199 (accessed 2/13/2007).

32. "*Manufacturing Consent* Portrays Noam Chomsky's Ideas," Noam Chomsky interviewed by Pat Dowell et al., *Morning Edition*, National Public Radio, May 24, 1993, available at http://www.chomsky.info/interviews/19930524.htm (accessed 2/13/2007).

33. Cited in *Understanding Power*, but also available online, http://www .chomsky.info/books/power02.htm (accessed 2/13/2007).

34. Ibid.

35. Ibid.

36. http://www.digitallyobsessed.com/showreview.php3?ID=7341 (accessed 2/13/2007).

37. http://www.dvdtown.com/review/noamchomskyrebelwithoutapause/15963/2853 (accessed 2/13/2007).

38. http://www.dissidentvoice.org/Articles/MickeyZ_Chomsky.htm (accessed 2/13/2007).

39. http://www.dissidentvoice.org/Articles/MickeyZ_Chomsky.htm (accessed 2/13/2007).

40. Cited in the *Boston Globe Magazine* November 19, 1995, p. 25, available at http://www.chomsky.info/onchomsky/19951119.htm (accessed 2/13/2007).

41. Personal correspondence with the author, May 28, 2000.

42. Anthony Flint, "Divided Legacy, *Boston Globe Magazine* November 19, 1995, p. 25, available at http://www.chomsky.info/onchomsky/19951119.htm (accessed 2/13/2007).

43. Personal correspondence with the author, May 28, 2000.

44. *Boston Globe Magazine*, November 19, 1995, p. 25, available at http://www.chomsky.info/onchomsky/19951119.htm (accessed 2/12/2007).

Chapter Two

1. *The Daily Whopper*, "Noam Chomsky—America's #1 Traitor," October 11, 2001, by J. B., online at http://www.democraticunderground.com/whopper/01/10/11_chomsky.html (accessed 02/13/2007).

2. A recent example occurs in the February 1, 2007 review of Jacques Bouveresse's book *Peut-on ne pas croire? Sur la vérité, la croyance et la foi*, published by the Agone group, which concludes with the following:"Etait-il besoin d'ajouter à ce panthéon une personnalité aussi controversée que Noam Chomsky, dont les opinions, parfois baroques, quoique célébrées dans le monde du militantisme 'alter,' suscitent des adhésions passionnelles plutôt que raisonnées? Acte de foi, sans doute . . ." "[Was it necessary to add to this pantheon a personality as controversial as Noam Chomsky, whose opinions,—often baroque, even though they are celebrated in the world of "alter" militantism,—promote passionate rather than reasoned adherence? An act of faith, no doubt. . . ." (my translation). A further illustration of the Chomsky Effect appears on February 5, when a reader remarks that "Il est curieux de voir dans un article portant sur un ouvrage de haute tenue comme celui de Bouveresse que la seule réserve concerne la référence à Chomsky, ce qui n'a aucune portée critique étant donné qu'on se contente de signaler qu'il s'agit d'une personnalité 'controversée' alors qu'on attendrait plutôt l'examen de la pertinence des citations de cet auteur dans le contexte spécifique de cette réflexion sur la foi et la croyance. Depuis quand la référence à un auteur est-il un 'acte de foi'?" ["it is curious to see in an article about a high-level work like that of Bouveresse that the only reservation concerns the reference to Chomsky. This critique has no critical weight given that [the author] is satisfied to note that [Chomsky] is a 'controversial' author, whereas we would have expected an examination of the pertinence of the quotes from this author in the specific context of this reflection upon faith and belief. Since when is the reference to an author an 'act of faith'?" (my translation).

3. *Boston Globe Magazine,* November 19, 1995, p. 25.

4. "The Chorus and Cassandra," *Grand Street,* Autumn 1985, available at http://www.zmag.org/chomsky/other/85–hitchens.html (accessed 02/13/2007).

5. http://www.mekong.net/cambodia/hitchens.htm (accessed 02/13/2007).

6. http://www.thenation.com/doc.mhtml?i=20011008&s=hitchens (accessed 02/13/2007).

7. http://www.counterpunch.org/chomskyhitch.html (accessed 02/13/2007).

8. http://www.thenation.com/doc.mhtml?i=20011015&s=hitchens20011004 (accessed 02/13/2007).

9. "The Chorus and Cassandra," available online at http://www.zmag.org/chomsky/other/85-hitchens.html (accessed 2/13/2007).

10. *Understanding Power,* p. 205.

11. For details on his life, see my *Noam Chomsky: A Life of Dissent.*

12. *Propaganda and the Public Mind,* pp. 92–93.

13. Matt Nesvisky, "Looking Right for the Revels of the Hippy Left of Yesteryear," *Jerusalem Post,* June 2, 1995, p. 4.

14. A Web site devoted to books that document these policies, by the likes of Noam Chomsky, Norman G. Finkelstein, Israel Shahak, and Edward Said, is online at http://www.radioislam.org/historia/zionism/index_books.html (accessed 02/13/2007).

15. See my *Arguing and Justifying* for a long discussion of this complex issue.

16. http://www.zmag.org/content/showarticle.cfm?SectionID=11&ItemID=4780 (accessed 2/13/2007).

17. Published in Peter Collier and David Horowitz, eds., *The Anti-Chomsky Reader* (Encounter Books, 2004) and online in an abridged form at http://www.acpr.org.il/ENGLISH-NATIV/04–issue/bogdanor-4.htm (accessed 02/13/2007).

18. My book *Arguing and Justifying* contains detailed discussions about what led Soviet and Israeli citizens to flee their countries to claim refugee status in Canada, and it documents the interesting events that led to Israel becoming a leading source country for claimants in the mid-1990s.

19. This complex debate is discussed at length in my *Zellig Harris's America,* forthcoming, and is set forth in a range of interesting books including Yosef Gorny's *Zionism and the Arabs 1882–1948.*

20. I include the more inflammatory and contentious remarks that Ben-Gurion makes in this letter to offer a full sense of the context within which this debate occurred, and the rationales, not always edifying, for Ben-Gurion's approach. The letters cited are from the Jacob Rader Marcus center at Hebrew Union College of Cincinnati, which documents Jewish life in the United States. Information about the collection is at http://www.americanjewisharchives.org/aja/ (accessed 02/13/2007).

21. For some of the many writings on this subject, see articles Edward Said contributed to Al-Ahram Weekly, http://weekly.ahram.org.eg/2003/657/edsaid.htm (accessed 02/13/2007).

22. Paul Bogdanor cited at http://www.acpr.org.il/English-Nativ/04-issue/bogdanor-4.htm (accessed 02/13/2007).

23. Chomsky, cited in his book *Peace in the Middle East?*, p. 37.

24. http://www-tech.mit.edu/V122/N25/col25dersh.25c.html (accessed 02/13/2007).

25. http://www.lewrockwell.com/wall/wall26.html (accessed 02/13/2007).

26. In personal correspondence of August 20, 1998. David Heap notes that R. Kayne has now left Paris-8, so "French generativism remains both somewhat beleaguered and internally divided."

27. John Goldsmith takes issue with this point in personal correspondence: "It seems to me that this perspective of Chomsky's is a rewriting of history in the way that I am not at all happy about. It was Ruwet's espousal of Chomsky's generative grammar—which was contagious and enormous in the period following May 1968—which made the difference and which made Chomsky virtually a household name in 1968, and it was he who set up the department at Vincennes and who brought Richie Kayne (the student Chomsky is referring to) to Paris. But Ruwet has in years since been quite critical of Chomsky's linguistics, and so Chomsky won't acknowledge the work that Ruwet did, successfully supporting Chomsky's view's spreading in Western Europe. I am very critical of this attitude on Chomsky's part; it seems very ungrateful, to my eyes, and I think gratitude and appreciation is a not unimportant trait. The language is indicative of his views of the French scene, and in particular his sense that there is a strong measure of control exerted by organizations like universities, publishing houses and research institutes."

28. (Paris: Odile Jacob, 1998.) Didier Eribon writes in *Le Nouvel observateur* that "Peut-être ce livre de Barsky, en restituant tout le parcours de Chomsky, avec ce qu'il faut bien appeler ses "accidents," permettra-t-il de lui redonner la place éminente qui est la sienne. Ce qui n'empêchera pas de soumettre ses prises de position à la vigilance critique à laquelle tout son discours nous incite à ne jamais renoncer." (12–18 February 1998.) "Maybe this book by Barsky, by recalling Chomsky's pathway, along with what should be called the 'accidents' that occurred along the way, will allow Chomsky to reclaim the eminent place that is his due. This doesn't impede our vigilant criticism of his positions, which he himself insists that we never renounce" (my translation).

29. http://www.city-journal.org/html/12_3_urbanities-americas_dumbe.html (accessed 02/13/2007).

30. *Cultural Semantics: Keywords of Our Time* (Amherst: University of Massachusetts Press, 1998).

31. http://www.vho.org/aaargh/engl/chomsky.engl.html. This text is no longer online, but it nonetheless appeared in my computer from previous searches, with

the following descriptor: This is Google's cache of http://www.vho.org/aaargh/arab/arab.html as retrieved on 24 Dec 2006 15:38:05 GMT. The text came accompanied with the following information: "This text has been displayed on the Net by the International Secretariat of the Association des Anciens Amateurs de Récits de Guerre et d'Holocauste (AAARGH) in 1998. The URL of the Secretariat http://abbc.com/aaargh/. Address: Box 81475, Chicago, IL 60681-0475".

32. Online at http://www.chomsky.info/onchomsky/19850622.htm (accessed 2/13/2007).

33. "His Right to Say it," *The Nation*, February 28, 1981, available online at http://www.zmag.org/chomsky/articles/8102-right-to-say.html (accessed 2/13/2007).

34. Cited in *The Problem of the "Gas Chambers", or "the Rumor of Auschwitz"*, a pamphlet published by the Ridgewood Defense Fund. Available online at http://www.ihr.org/jhr/v19/v19n3p40_Faurisson.html (accessed 2/18/2007).

35. The apparently now-defunct AAARGH site suggested that it is wrong to attribute "to Thion or the Vieille Taupe Group the initiative of a petition, signed by Chomsky, to demand the respect of the right of Professor Faurisson. Even Chomsky himself seems to believe this! It was the doing of Mark Weber, who later rose to become the present-day director of the Institute of Historical Review. This petition reached Paris only later." This is repeated by Thion in his "Notes du texte *Serge Thion et Chomsky*," note 61, in which he writes: "Certains ont cru et écrit que j'étais à l'origine de cette pétition (dont le texte figure dans *Vérité historique ou vérité politique?*, p. 163) ou que j'avais demandé à Chomsky de la signer. Il n'en est rien. J'ai appris par la suite qu'elle avait été lancée par un jeune révisionniste américain, Mark Weber; elle n'a circulé qu'aux Etats-Unis, après que la presse américaine ait rapporté que le professeur Faurisson avait été suspendu et interdit d'enseignement." "Some people believed and wrote that I was at the origin of this petition (the text of which appars in *Vérité historique ou Vérité Politique?* p. 163) or that I had asked Chomsky to sign it. This is not the case. I learned afterwards that it had been initiated by a young American revisionist by the name of Mark Weber; it was only circulated in the United States, after the American media had reported that Professor Faurisson had been suspended from his job and denied the right to teach" (my translation).

36. "The Treachery of the Intelligentsia: A French Travesty," cited in *Language and Politics* and available online at http://www.chomsky.info/interviews/19811026.htm (accessed 02/13/2007).

37. In *Assassins of Memory: Essays on the Denial of the Holocaust*.

38. See Francois Lyotard's book *The Differend: Phrases in Dispute*, translated by Georges van den Abbeele, University of Minnesota Press, 1989.

39. Available online at http://www.zmag.org/chomsky/articles/8102-right-to-say.html (accessed 2/13/2007).

40. AAARGH comments on Roy on their site: "What we always found striking was the need in which Chomsky's opponents found themselves to invent and lend him opinions they found thus easier to fight. It has been the case of a particularly disgusting underdog called Claude Roy who, as a former royalist, fascist, Stalinist, socialist, turned liberal, was a usual writer in *Le Nouvel Observateur*."

41. AARGH reports that "in 1980, Serge Thion had to vigorously intervene to dismantle his [Roy's] castle of lies and deception. In a more general way, he had analyzed the attacks against Chomsky published in the French press in an article published in a monthly called *Esprit*. This issue of September 1980 was something of a monument: The opening was the attack, now a classic of sorts, by Vidal-Naquet against Faurisson and the Vieille Taupe Group called "A paper Eichmann" had refused to communicate in advance to Thion because he was fearing a reply. At the same time, Thion felt compelled to reply to a particularly debased article written by Leopold Labedz in the London based *Encounter*, a journal that had been used to receive CIA funds. This reply was titled: "A strange Revisitor." This is Google's cache of http://www.vho.org/aaargh/fran/revu/TI98/TI981021.html as retrieved on 1/13/2007 22:56:47 GMT.

42. Guillaume has been accused of publishing this text without authorization, which he has variously denied, notably in a series of letters written to the director of the newspaper *Le Monde* and published to the net. They are of some historical interest as regards the affair; the one that follows is dated November 30, 1993:

Monsieur le Directeur,

Mis en cause en tant qu'éditeur de textes de Noam Chomsky par une allégation de Jean-Michel Frodon d'autant plus inexplicable que cette allégation est précisément réfutée par Chomsky lui-même dans le film dont le journaliste rend compte, je vous prie de bien vouloir insérer conformément à la loi du 29 juillet 1881—article 13 (L. 29 sept. 1919) le droit de réponse suivant:

Dans *Le Monde* du 24 novembre 1993, sous le titre "La guerre de Noam," Jean-Michel Frodon a écrit: "Chomsky s'explique également sur l'affaire, qui fit grand bruit en France lorsqu'un de ses textes en faveur de la liberté d'expression fut utilisé, sans son accord, en préface à un livre du révisionniste Robert Faurisson."

Cette allégation me met gravement en cause en ce qu'elle insinue qu'en tant qu'éditeur du *Mémoire en défense* du professeur Faurisson j'aurais abusé Chomsky. Cela a été démenti à de nombreuses reprises, et par Chomsky lui-même, notamment dans le film dont il est rendu compte. Cela a été démenti par mes soins, notamment dans mon livre *Droit et histoire* où un chapitre est consacré à mes relations avec Chomsky.

On ne s'explique d'ailleurs pas par l'opération de quel Saint Esprit un avis sur la liberté d'expression, évoquant précisément l'affaire Faurisson, écrit par Chomsky, aurait pu parvenir dans mes mains "sans l'accord de l'auteur."

On s'explique encore moins pourquoi Chomsky m'aurait confié l'édition française de son livre *économie politique des droits de l'homme* (publiée dans la collection que je dirigeais aux éditions J.-E. Hallier-Albin Michel), et l'édition de ses *Réponses inédites à mes détracteurs parisiens,* (parues dans une livraison des Cahiers Spartacus financée par mes soins et précédées d'une introduction signée P. G.) si il estimait avoir été abusé par moi et s'il m'avait retiré sa confiance.

Le seul regret que manifeste explicitement Chomsky dans le film, c'est précisément de s'être laissé influencer par la cabale d'une coterie d'intellectuels parisiens, acharnés à refuser à leurs adversaires la liberté d'expression qu'ils réclament pour eux-mêmes, et de s'être interrogé un instant sur l'opportunité de publier cet avis dans le livre-même de Faurisson. Cette interrogation, confiée à titre privé à l'un de ces intellectuels parisiens, dénaturée et sortie de son contexte, a fait l'objet d'une exploitation médiatique sans vergogne et mensongère, et continue à prospérer en dépit des démentis et de l'évidence. C'est pourquoi j'affirme, je confirme, et je répète: Chomsky était pleinement averti de la publication de son texte sur la liberté d'expression en tête du *Mémoire en défense* de Faurisson, dont il ne partage pas les thèses, et il n'a jamais retiré son accord, ni manifesté de regrets.

En vous priant d'agréer, monsieur le directeur, l'expression de mes salutations distinguées

Pierre Guillaume.

Note: This is Google's cache of http://www.vho.org/aaargh/fran/archVT/bullVT/bullVT11a.html as retrieved on 1/3/2007 14:01:00 GMT.

43. *Réponses inédites à mes détracteurs parisiens,* published by Spartacus.

44. "En ce sens, la prise de position de Chomsky rejoint celle de Voltaire sur la défense du droit d'exprimer des opinions qu'il juge, par ailleurs, exécrables" Larry Portis, "Noam Chomsky, l'état et l'intelligentsia française," *L'Homme et la Société* (1997) pp. 123–124, my translation.

45. A fascinating anecdote: according to Burdette Kinne, it was E. Beatrice Hall, better known under her pseudonym S. G. Tallentyre, who uttered those words, not Voltaire! "Voltaire Never Said It!," *Modern Language Notes* 58 (November 1943): 534–535.

46. This discussion is taken up again in "On Faurisson and Chomsky," available online at http://www.anti-rev.org/textes/VidalNaquet81b/, accessed 02/13/07.

47. Cf. Nadine Fresco, "Les redresseurs de morts," *Le temps modernes* (June 1980) for comments regarding Faurisson's literary theories and their relationship to his revisionism.

48. From "The Chorus and Cassandra," *Grand Street Magazine,* Autumn 1985.

49. In Edmond Y. Lipsitz, ed., *Canadian Jewry Today: Who's Who in Canadian Jewry* (Downsview, Ont.: J.E.S.L. Education Products, 1989), pp. 30–36.

50. This text is available online at http://www.nizkor.org/ftp.cgi/orgs/canadian/canadian-jewish-congress/ftp.py?orgs/canadian/canadian-jewish-congress//holocaust-denial-today (accessed 02/13/2007).

51. See http://www.peaceworkmagazine.org/pwork/0699/0602.htm (accessed 2/13/2007).

52. This text is cited at http://www.vho.org/aaargh/fran/revu/TI98/TI981021 .html (accessed 02/13/2007), and comes from the International Secretariat of the Association des Anciens Amateurs de Récits de Guerre et d'Holocauste (AAARGH) in 1998. On issues relating to the French media they are generally in agreement with Chomsky's own experiences: "The standard of French journalism is among the lowest on this planet, we are sad to report. After that, the French press and the French 'intellectuals' built a wall of silence around Chomsky. This wall broke down only last month with the *Le Monde* interview, and we do not know for sure why it broke down."

53. *Ordres et raisons de la langue* (Paris: Le Seuil, 1982).

54. http://www.news.harvard.edu/gazette/daily/2005/11/30–chomsky.html (accessed 02/13/2007).

55. November 7, 1980, p. 31, column D.

56. http://www.abbc.com/aaargh/fran/chomsky/STrevisitor.html (accessed 02/13/ 2007).

57. http://www.radioislam.org/totus/1963-1980/139revisitor.html (accessed 02/13/ 2007).

58. Ibid.

59. Ibid.

60. Ibid.

61. Available at http://www.mekong.net/cambodia/demcat.htm (accessed 02/13/ 2007).

62. Chomsky also says that "On events of the 1980s and since, and the issues you raise, I'd suggest that you consult publications by Michael Vickery, Ben Kiernan, Steve Heder, and others, who differ quite radically, and draw your own conclusions. It's pretty murky, in my opinion."

63. http://www.zmag.org/forums/chomchatarch.htm (accessed 02/13/2007).

64. *Understanding Power*, p. 210. See also *A New Generation Draws the Line: Kosovo, East Timor and the Standards of the West* (London: Verso).

Chapter Three

1. December 23, 1996; posted in response to a question from "Tom" at: http://www.zmag.org/chomsky/whose_world_order.htm (accessed 02/13/2007).

2. "Whose World Order: Conflicting Visions," (lecture, University of Calgary, September 22, 1998). Available online at http://www.zmag.org/chomsky/ whose_world_order.htm (accessed 02/13/2007).

3. "Eight Questions on Anarchism" http://www.zmag.org/chomsky/interviews/ 9612–anarchism.html (accessed 02/13/2007).

4. Ibid.

5. Andrew Hook, "Philadelphia, Edinburgh and the Scottish Enlightenment," in Richard B. Sher and Jeffrey R. Smitten, *Scotland and America in the Age of the Enlightenment* (Princeton: Princeton University Press, 1990), p. 230.

6. David Daiches, "Style Périodique and Style Coupé: Hugh Blair and the Scottish Rhetoric of American Independence" in Sher and Smitten p. 224.

7. *The Papers of Benjamin Franklin*. Ed. Leonard W. Labaree, volume 15 (New Haven, Conn, Yale University Press, 1959–, p. 530.

8. Ferguson, Adam. *Principles of Moral and Political Science, being chiefly a retrospect of lectures delivered in the College of Edinburgh,* 2 vols., Edinburgh, 1792, 1:42–43.

9. Available online at http://www.islandnet.com/~contempo/library/mai/chomsky2.html (accessed 02/13/2007).

10. As Lyotard suggests in the *Postmodern Condition*, translated by Geoff Bennington and Brian Massumi, (Minneapolis MN: University of Minnesota Press, 1984).

11. In such books as *The Gulf War Did Not Take Place*, by Baudrillard, translated by Paul Patton (Bloomington: Indiana University Press, 1995).

12. "Politics and the English Language," cited in *The Norton Anthology of English Literature* (New York: Norton, 1993), 2:2240. Available online at http://www.mtholyoke.edu/acad/intrel/orwell46.htm (accessed 02/13/2007).

13. In Sher and Smitten, *Scotland and America in the Age of Enlightenment,* p. 102.

14. Ibid., p. 225.

15. http://www.cooperativeindividualism.org/chomsky_commongood.html (accessed 02/13/2007).

16. Daiches, "Style Périodique and Style Coupé," p. 223.

17. http://www.cooperativeindividualism.org/chomsky_commongood.html.

18. Daiches, "Style Périodique and Style Coupé," p. 223.

19. http://www.cooperativeindividualism.org/chomsky_commongood.html.

20. *Language and Mind,* p. 21.

21. *Language and Responsibility,* pp. 77–78, available online at http://www.ukzn.ac.za/undphil/collier/Chomsky/ChomskyLRall.html (accessed 02/13/2007).

22. From the November 25, 1992, audiotape recording of a talk Chomsky gave in Barcelona, 1992 titled "Creation and Culture", Alternative Radio, www.alternativeradio.org (accessed 02/13/2007).

23. A selection of Chomsky's posts from the ChomskyChat Forum and available online at http://www.zmag.org/ScienceWars/forumchom.htm (accessed 02/13/2007).

24. See my *Noam Chomsky: A Life of Dissent,* chapter 3.

25. *The Chomsky Reader,* p. 152.

26. Wilhelm von Humboldt, *The Limits of State Action*. Translation by J. W. Burrow. (London: Cambridge University Press 1969). This text is available online at http://oll.libertyfund.org/Texts/Humboldt0128/SpheresAndDuties/HTMLs/0053_Pt02_Part2.html (accessed 02/13/2007).

27. Chomsky, "Creation and Culture," 1992.

28. Personal correspondence, August 8, 1994.

29. Much of Ginsberg's poetry is available online at sites including http://www.rooknet.com/beatpage/writers/ginsberg.html (accessed 02/13/2007).

30. *Nationalism and Culture*, p. 157. This book is available online at http://www.anarchyisorder.org/CD%234/TXT-versions/Rocker%20Rudolf%20-%20Nationalism%20and%20Culture%20(partly_%20no%20lay-out).txt (accessed 02/13/2007).

31. Ibid.

32. See the excellent description of this case and its implications in Herbert Mitgang's *Dangerous Dossiers: Exposing the Secret War Against America's Greatest Authors* (New York: Donald I. Fine, 1988), pp. 13–26.

33. This passage is available online at http://www.ala.org/ala/oif/ifissues/issuesrelatedlinks/amendmentsconstitution.htm (accessed 02/13/2007).

34. http://www.zmag.org/chomsky/interviews/9612–anarchism.html (accessed 02/13/2007).

35. Letter to author, September 9, 1997.

36. Cited in Chomsky's *Towards a New Cold War*, pp. 60–61.

37. *The Spanish Anarchists* (San Francisco, AK Press, 1998), pp. 26.

38. Rudolph Rocker, *Nationalism and Culture*, trans. Ray E. Chase (St. Paul, Minn.: Michael E. Coughlin, 1985). This work first appeared in Spanish *as Nacionalismo y cultura,* translated by Diego Abad de Santillán, in three volumes published by Tierra y Libertad, Barcelona, 1935–1937. The first North American edition, translated by Ray E. Chase, was published by Covici-Friede, New York, in 1937.

39. Rudolph Rocker, *Anarchism and Anarcho-Syndicalism* (London: Freedom Press, 1988). It was written in 1937, one year after the Spanish Civil War and Revolution broke out, and was translated into English in March 1938.

40. Ibid. p. 3 and available online at http://sunsite.utk.edu/FINS/Doctrines_Injustice/Fins-DI-03.htm (accessed 02/13/2007).

41. "Creation and Culture," audiotape, Alternative Radio, recorded November 25, 1992.

42. All cited in Rocker, *Nationalism and Culture,* pp. 148–149, available online at http://flag.blackened.net/rocker/liberal.htm (accessed 02/13/2007).

43. *Powers and Prospects: Reflections on Human Nature and the Social Order* (Delhi, Madhyam Books, 1996), pp. 73–74, excerpts online at http://www.tribuneindia.com/2000/20000702/spectrum/books.htm (accessed 01/13/2007).

44. This preface is available online at http://www.geocities.com/CapitolHill/Lobby/2554/rudolf.html (accessed 02/13/2007).

45. NYRB volume 17 number 11.

46. This makes Zellig Harris's posthumous book on the subject worth examining in this regard. Zellig Harris, *The Transformation of Capitalist Society* (Lanham, UK: Rowman and Littlefield Publishers, 1997).

47. Letter to the author, September 9, 1997.

48. This section picks up on and elaborates similar issues discussed in my *Noam Chomsky: A Life of Dissent* chapter 2.

49. http://www.upenn.edu/gazette/0701/hughes.html   (accessed   02/13/2007), *The Pennsylvania Gazette*, The Alumni Magazine of the University of Pennsylvania, July/August edition.

50. This doesn't apply to linguistics alone, of course, but perhaps the vehemence with which people either or adore or reject Noam Chomsky, and the stakes and constraints of studies relating to language and its relation to human nature make for some surprisingly vicious attacks and counterattacks.

51. *Pennsylvania Gazette*.

52. Chomsky, *Chomsky Reader*, p. 8.

53. Cited in *Pennsylvania Gazette*.

54. Chomsky, *Chomsky Reader*, p. 8.

55. Ibid.

56. Cited in Randy Allen Harris, *The Linguistics Wars* (New York: Oxford University Press, 1993), p. 31.

57. Chomsky, *Language and Mind,* pp. 3–4, available online at http://www.cambridge.org/us/catalogue/catalogue.asp?isbn=9780521858199&ss=exc (accessed 02/13/2007).

58. *Pennsylvania Gazette*.

59. Personal correspondence to the author, December 13, 1994.

60. Chomsky, *Knowledge of Language,* p. 64.

61. Cited in Otero, ed., *Noam Chomsky: Critical Assessments* vol. I.I, 292.

62. Personal correspondence from Hoenigswald to the author, July 8, 1997.

63. Personal correspondence, from Chomsky to the author, April 3, 1995.

64. Personal correspondence, from Chomsky to the author, December 13, 1994.

65. Ibid.

66. Personal correspondence, July 8, 1997.

67. I should note that it is this exact quote that led me to write this biography of Harris, forthcoming with MIT Press.

68. Personal correspondence, June 23, 1993.

69. http://www.zmag.org/chomsky/interviews/9612-anarchism.html.

70. http://www.zmag.org/chomsky/interviews/9612-anarchism.html (accessed 02/13/2007).

Chapter Four

1. There is a range of articles by and about Chomsky that deal with law, but most of his work in this area uses law as a launching point for other more concrete discussions about state terrorism, imperialism, the misuse of international law, and current affairs in a properly historical perspective. See for example Noam Chomsky, "The Intifada and the Peace Process," *The Fletcher Forum of World Affairs* 14, no. 2 (Summer 1990): 345–353; "World Order and Its Rules: Variations on Some Themes," *Journal of Law and Society* 20, no. 2 (Summer 1993): 145–165; James G. Wilson, "Noam Chomsky and Judicial Review," *Cleveland State Law Review* 44, no. 4 (Fall 1996): 439–472. For a more general discussion, see as well *The Nature and Process of Law: An Introduction to Legal Philosophy*, edited by Patricia Smith (New York: Oxford University Press, 1993). "Why American business supports third world fascism: our president is campaigning for "human rights" abroad, but for 30 years our government and corporations have been supporting precisely the opposite," Chomsky, Noam; Herman, Edward S. *Business-and-Society-Review,* Fall 1977, pp. 13–21; Noam Chomsky and Edward Herman, "The United States versus Human Rights in the Third World," *Monthly Review* 29 (August 1977): 22–45; "World Order and Its Rules: Variations on Some Themes," *Scandinavian Journal of Development Alternatives* 13, no. 3 (September 1994): 5–27; World Order and Its Rules: Variations on Some Themes" *Journal of Law and Society* 20, no. 2 (summer 1993): 145–165.

2. (Oxford: Oxford University Press, 1986).

3. (Buffalo: Prometheus Books, 1982).

4. Howard Zinn, *The Zinn Reader* (New York: Seven Stories Press, 1997), p. 372.

5. *Deterring Democracy* (Boston: South End Press, 1991), p. 199–200, available online at http://www.zmag.org/Chomsky/dd/dd-c06-s10.html (accessed 02/13/2007).

6. "The Gulf Crisis," January 1991, reprinted in *Z Magazine,* February 1991, available online at http://www.zmag.org/zmag/articles/chomgu.htm (accessed 02/13/2007).

7. *The Prosperous Few and the Restless Many* (Interviews with Noam Chomsky) by David Barsamian, online at http://www.zmag.org/CHOMSKY/pfrm/pfrm-06.html (accessed 02/13/2007).

8. See http://www.un.org/aboutun/charter/ (accessed 02/13/2007).

9. "Market Democracy in a Neoliberal Order: Doctrines and Reality," Davie Lecture, University of Cape Town, May 1997, available online at http://www.zmag.org/zmag/articles/chomksydavie.htm (accessed 02/13/2007).

10. ZNet Commentary, May 9, 1999, "Chomsky Answers Some Queries About Moral Principles and International Law" Available online at http://www.zmag.org/Sustainers/Content/1999-05/may_9chomsky.htm (accessed 02/13/2007).

11. http://www.zmag.org/ZMag/Articles/jan02albertchomsky.htm (accessed 02/13/2007).

12. *Necessary Illusions* (Boston: South End Press, 1989). See especially chapter 2: "Containing the Enemy."

13. Online at http://www.zmag.org/Chomsky/ni/ni-c02-s04.html (accessed 02/13/2007).

14. For instance: "The U.N. session just preceding the 'wondrous sea change' (Winter 1989–90) can serve to illustrate. Three Security Council resolutions were vetoed: a condemnation of the U.S. attack on the Nicaraguan Embassy in Panama (U.S. veto, Britain abstained); of the U.S. invasion of Panama (U.S., U.K., France against); of Israeli abuses in the occupied territories (U.S. veto). There were two General Assembly resolutions calling on all states to observe international law, one condemning the U.S. support for the contra army, the other the illegal embargo against Nicaragua. Each passed with two negative votes: the U.S. and Israel. A resolution opposing acquisition of territory by force passed 151 to 3 (U.S., Israel, Dominica). The resolution once again called for a diplomatic settlement of the Arab-Israeli conflict with recognized borders and security guarantees, incorporating the wording of U.N. resolution 242, and self-determination for both Israel and the Palestinians in a two-state settlement; the U.S. has been barring such a settlement, virtually alone as the most recent vote indicates, since its January 1976 veto of this proposal, advanced by Syria, Jordan, and Egypt with the backing of the PLO. The U.S. has repeatedly vetoed Security Council resolutions and blocked General Assembly resolutions and other U.N. initiatives on a whole range of issues, including aggression, annexation, human rights abuses, disarmament, adherence to international law, terrorism, and others." *Deterring Democracy*, p. 198, available online at http://www.zmag.org/CHOMSKY/dd/dd-c06-s09.html (accessed 02/13/2007).

15. "Domestic Constituencies," online at http://www.zmag.org/zmag/articles/chomskymay98.htm (accessed 02/13/2007).

16. From Chomsky's essay "On the Limits of Civil Disobedience," in *The Berrigans*, ed. William Van Etten Casey, S. J., and Philip Nobile (New York: Avon Books, 1971), pp. 39–41, available online at http://www.zmag.org/Chomsky/mc/mc-supp-020.html (accessed 02/13/2007).

17. From Howard Zinn's *Declarations of Independence*, available online at http://www.ecn.cz/temelin/JEF_ZIN.HTM (accessed 02/13/2007).

18. Ibid., p. 402.

19. Ibid.

20. See Fons Elders, ed. "Reflexive Water: The Basic Concerns of Mankind," (London: Souvenir Press, 1974).

21. The entire discussion is available online at http://www.chomsky.info/debates/ 1971xxxx.htm (accessed 02/13/2007).

22. *Necessary Illusions*, appendix V, "The C1ontinuing Struggle," 177, available online at http://www.zmag.org/chomsky/ni/ni-c10-s30.html (accessed 02/13/ 2007).

23. *9/11* (Boston: Seven Stories Press, 2001), p. 25, The interview that is reproduced in *9/11* was originally published in *Monthly Review* and is available online at http://www.monthlyreview.org/1101chomsky.htm (accessed 02/13/2007).

24. Ibid., p. 80 and available online at http://www.zmag.org/chomskygsf.htm (accessed 02/13/2007).

25. Ibid., p. 118 and available online at http://www.zmag.org/albintchom.htm (accessed 02/13/2007).

26. A term used in the justice administration when a process is not public.

27. "Is Peace at Hand?" November 1987, reprinted in Z *Magazine*, January 1988, and available online at http://www.zmag.org/zmag/articles/chompe.htm (accessed 02/13/2007).

28. "Middle East Diplomacy: Continuities and Changes," November 5, 1991, reprinted in Z *Magazine,* December 1991) and available online at http:// www.chomsky.info/articles/199112–.htm (accessed o2/13/2007).

29. "Limited War in Lebanon," Z *Magazine*, September 1993, cited online at http://www.zmag.org/zmag/articles/chomlimwar.htm (accessed 02/13/2007).

30. John Dunn, "Our Insecure Tradition," *Times Literary Supplement*, October 5, 1990.

31. http://www.chomsky.info/articles/199102—02.htm (accessed 02/13/2007).

32. "Old Wine, New Bottles: Free Trade, Global Markets and Military Adventures," (lecture, University of Virginia, February 10, 1993), available online at http://www.zmag.org/chomsky/talks/9302-uva.html (accessed 02/13/ 2007).

33. "Democracy Enhancement" Z *Magazine*, May 1994, http://www.zmag.org/ chomsky/year/year-c03-s13.html (accessed 02/13/2007).

34. http://www.counterpunch.org/chomsky01242006.html (accessed 02/13/2007).

35. http://www.commondreams.org/headlines04/0607-08.htm (accessed 02/13/ 2007) published Monday, June 7, 2004, by *Democracy Now!*

36. "Market Democracy in a Neoliberal Order: Doctrines and Reality" (Davie Lecture, University of Cape Town, May 1997), available online at http:// www.zmag.org/zmag/articles/chomksydavie.htm (accessed 02/13/2007).

37. This is a term that was employed by Zellig Harris and maintains its currency through the work of Chomsky and others.

38. "Market Democracy in a Neoliberal Order," available online at http://www.zmag.org/zmag/articles/nov97chomsky.htm (accessed 02/13/2007).

39. "Is Peace at Hand?," online at http://www.zmag.org/zmag/articles/chompe.htm (accessed 02/13/2007).

40. 16, no. 1 (January 2–15, 1999), online at http://www.zmag.org/chomsky/interviews/9901-frontline-iraq.htm (accessed 02/13/2007).

41. Cited at http://www.myantiwar.org/Channel/id/20/pn/3 (accessed 02/13/2007) and reproduced in *Chronicles of Dissent* (Monroe, Me.: Common Courage Press, 1992).

42. "Is Peace at Hand?" November 1987, and available online at http://www.zmag.org/zmag/articles/chompe.htm (accessed 02/13/2007).

43. *Deterring Democracy*, (Boston: South End Press, 1991), chapter 6: "Nefarious Aggression," Available online at http://www.zmag.org/Chomsky/dd/dd-c06-s10.html (accessed 02/13/2007).

44. ZNet Commentary, May 9, 1999, available at http://www.zmag.org/ZMag/chommorality.htm l.

45. Stephane Courtois, Nicolas Werth, Jean-Louis Panne, Andrzej Paczkowski, Karel Bartosek, Jean-Louis Margolin, Mark Kramer (translator), Jonathan Murphy (translator) (Cambridge: Harvard University Press, 1999).

46. See Ana Mari Smith, *Laclau and Mouffe: The Radical Democratic Imaginary* (New York: Routledge, 2004).

47. "The administrative state is an immense and tutelary power, in which the will of man is not shattered, but softened, bent, and guided; men are seldom forced by it to act, but they are constantly restrained from acting. Such a power does not destroy, but it prevents existence; it does not tyrannise, but it compresses, enervates, extinguishes, and stupefies a people, till each nation is reduced to nothing better than a flock of timid and industrious animals, of which government is the shepherd" (cited in Boesche, *The Strange Liberalism of Alexis de Tocqueville* [Ithaca: Cornell University Press, 1987], p. 251).

48. (Cambridge: MIT Press, 1994.)

49. Neumann, "The Concept of Political Freedom," cited in Scheuerman p. 165.

50. In his work, *Laws of Ecclesiastical Polity*, published in 1593.

51. "Market Democracy in a Neoliberal Order," available online at http://www.zmag.org/Zmag/articles/chomskysept97.htm (accessed 02/13/2007).

Chapter Five

1. Cited online at http://www.hinduonnet.com/fline/fl1826/18260750.htm (accessed 02/13/2007).

2. Murray Bookchin, *The Spanish Anarchists: The Heroic Years 1868–1936* (Edinburgh: AK Press, 1998 [1977]).

3. Sam Dolgoff, *The Anarchist Collectives: Workers' Self-Management in the Spanish Revolution* (Montreal: Black Rose Books, 1990).

4. J. G. Casas, *Anarchist Organization: The History of the FAI* (Montreal: Black Rose Books, 1986).

5. Bookchin, *The Spanish Anarchists*, p. 12.

6. Bookchin, *To Remember Spain: The Anarchist and Syndicalist Revolution of 1936.* (San Francisco: AK Press), p. 9, available online at http://www.spunk.org/library/writers/bookchin/sp001642/overview.html (accessed 02/13/2007).

7. Emma Goldman, *Red Emma Speaks,* (New York: Random House, 1972), p. 96.

8. Michael Albert and Noam Chomsky, from Znet, online at http://www.zmag.org/chomsky/interviews/9301-albchomsky-1.html (accessed 02/13/2007).

9. *Understanding Power,* p. 274, online at http://www.nooranch.com/synaesmedia/wiki/wiki.cgi?FreedomOfExpressionVsFeministCondemnationOfPornography (accessed 02/13/2007).

10. Available online at http://www.calresco.org/texts/mutaid8.htm (accessed 02/13/2007).

11. This is notable given Emma Goldman's actual training and practice as a midwife!

12. http://www.zmag.org/ZMag/articles/may01barsamian.htm (accessed 02/13/2007).

13. http://www.zmag.org/forums/chomchatarch.htm (accessed 02/13/2007).

14. "Old Wine, New Bottles: Free Trade, Global Markets and Military Adventures," (lecture at University of Virginia, February 10, 1993).

15. On the relationship between Chomsky's approach and that of the education theorist Jean Piaget, see Noam Chomsky, *The Debate Between Chomsky and Piaget* (Cambridge: Harvard University Press, 1980).

16. Online at http://www.zmag.org/chomsky/talks/9410-education.html (accessed 02/13/2007).

17. *Tom Lane December 23, 1996* http://members.tripod.com/anarclan/9612–anarchism.html.

18. *Propaganda and the Public Mind,* p. 20, online at http://www.thirdworldtraveler.com/Chomsky/Propaganda_PublicMind.html (accessed 02/13/2007).

19. "A Walk in Noam's Garden," *The Peak,* Simon Fraser University's Student Newspaper, 92, no. 10 (March 11, 1996), available online at http://www.peak.sfu.ca/the-peak/96-1/issue10/chomsky.html (accessed 02/13/2007).

20. *Propaganda and the Public Mind,* p. 217.

21. This is published as chapter 2 of Humboldt's *The Limits of State Action*, edited with an introduction and notes by J. W. Burrow, Cambridge, Cambridge University Press, 1969. This chapter and the first half of the next first appeared in Schiller's *Neue Thalia* II, 131–169 (1792). Available online at http://oll.libertyfund.org/Home3/BookToCPage.php?recordID=0053 (accessed 02/13/2007).

22. Burrow notes that this passage was singled out for quotation by John Stuart Mill in *On Liberty*.

23. A contribution to the 1975 collection edited by Walter Feinberg and Henry Rosemont, Jr., called *Work, Technology and Education: Dissenting Essays in the Intellectual Foundations of American Education* (Urbana: University of Illinois Press, 1975).

24. Available online at http://www.thirdworldtraveler.com/Chomsky/Propaganda _PublicMind.html (accessed 02/13/2007).

25. Imperial Presidency: Strategies to Control the Great Beast, on Znet, and available online at http://www.thirdworldtraveler.com/Chomsky/Imperial _Presidency.html (accessed 02/13/2007).

26. Tom Lane, December 23, 1996, http://members.tripod.com/anarclan/9612 –anarchism.html.

27. Rudolph Rocker, *Nationalism and Culture*, trans. Ray E. Chase (St. Paul, Minn.: Michael E. Coughlin, 1985), p. 157, available online at http://books .google.com.

28. John Stuart Mill, *On Liberty* (London, Everyman's Library, 1968), p. 118.

29. Chomsky, "Democracy and Education," available online at http://www .zmag.org/chomsky/talks/9410-education.html (accessed 02/13/2007).

30. "Democracy and Education," Mellon Lecture, Loyola University, Chicago, October 19, 1994.

31. See *Powers and Prospects,* p. 75 ff.

32. Chomsky's "Goals and Visions," online at http://www.geocities.com/ capitolhill/5065/goals.html (accessed 02/13/2007).

33. Ibid. For a wide-ranging elaboration of these issues, see Robert F. Westbrook's book *John Dewey and American Democracy* (Ithaca, N.Y.: Cornell University Press, 1991).

34. Originally published in *The School Journal* 54, no. 3 (January 16, 1897): 77–80, and reprinted in *Dewey on Education: Selections*, introduction and notes by Martin S. Dworkin (New York: Bureau of Publications, Teachers College, Columbia University, 1959). This text is available online at http://www .infed.org/archives/e-texts/e-dew-pc.htm (accessed 02/13/2007), and it is from here that I quote.

35. "Goals and Visions."

36. (New York: Hart Publishing, 1960.)

37. From the MIND brochure, MIT; all quotes are from that same pamphlet.

Chapter Six

1. David Barsamian, *Propaganda and the Public Mind: Conversations with Noam Chomsky* (Boston: South End Press, 2001), p. 107.

2. The best source for understanding Chomsky's work in linguistics is Chomsky's own writings. Nevertheless, there are as well many reviews of his work, from which I have chosen a few in English as a measure of the range and applications of "minimalism," one of the approaches he advocated in the mid-nineties and to which he still in some ways adheres. Robert Frieden, "The Minimalist Program," *Language* 73, no. 3 (1997): 571–582. Grangio Graffi et al. "The Minimalist Program," *Lingua e Stile* 32, no. 2 (1997): 335–343. Alan Munn, "The Minimalist Program," *Studies in Second Language Acquisition* 19, no. 1 (1996): 121–123. Tal Siloni, "The Minimalist Program," *Journal of Pragmatics* 27, no. 2 (1997): 250–254. Elly Van Geldern, "The Minimalist Program," *English Studies* 78, no. 4 (1997): 397–399. Jan-Wouter Zwart, "The Minimalist Program," *Journal of Linguistics* 34, no. 1 (1998): 213–226. Youngjun Jang, "Minimal Feature-movement," *Journal of Linguistics* 33 (1997): 311–325. Norbert Hornstein, "An Argument for Minimalism: The Case of Antecedent-Contained Deletion," *Linguistic Inquiry* 25, no. 3 (1994): 455–480. David Johnson and Shalim Lappin, "A Critique of the Minimalist Program," *Linguistics and Philosophy* 20, no. 3 (1997): 273–333. David Kathman, "Infinit . . . ? Complements in a Minimalist Theory . . ." *Studies in the Linguistic Sciences* 24, no. 1–2 (1994): 293–302. Svetla Koeva, "A Minimalist View on NP Raising," *Contrastive Linguistics* 20, no. 4–5 (1995): 5–9.

3. *Language* 33, reprinted in Gilbert Harman, ed., *On Noam Chomsky: Critical Essays* (Amherst: University of Massachusetts Press, 1982), pp. 37–38. Available online at http://www.jstor.org/view/00978507/ap020131/02a00060/0 (accessed 02/13/2007).

4. See R. A. Harris *The Linguistic Wars* (NY: Oxford University Press, 1997) and, moreover, John A. Goldsmith and Geoffrey J. Huck, *Noam Chomsky and the Deep Structure Debates* (Chicago: University of Chicago Press, 1995).

5. K. L. Billingsley, "Noam Chomsky, Punk Hero," in *Heterodoxy*, (March 1996).

6. Mark Achbar, ed., *Manufacturing Consent: Noam Chomsky and the Media* (Montreal: Black Rose Books, 1994), p. 30, online at http://www.zmag.org/Chomsky/mc/mc-supp-030.html.

7. *Understanding Power,* p. 210.

8. I'd like to thank Stephen Anderson and Noam Chomsky for their invaluable input, and, especially, to acknowledge the Franklin Institute for the unsigned report that served as the basis for the preceding discussion of Chomsky's importance for the field of computer sciences and from which I have taken much of the language here.

9. A talk at the American University in Washington, cited in Mark Achbar, *Manufacturing Consent: Noam Chomsky and the Media*, p. 43.

10. ZNet Posting, online at http://www.zmag.org/forums/chomchatarch.htm (accessed 02/13/2007).

11. Noam Chomsky, *A New Generation Draws the Line: Kosovo, East Timor and the Standards of the West* (London: Verso, 2000), pp. 94–95, available online at http://www.zmag.org/ZMag/articles/chomskyapril2000.htm (accessed 02/13/2007).

12. Personal correspondence with Goldsmith, May 28, 2000.

13. "Democracy and Education," http://www.zmag.org/chomsky/talks/9410 -education.html.

14. Ibid.

15. Pierre Bourdieu, *Language and Symbolic Power*, ed. with an introduction by John B. Thompson; trans. Matthew Adamson (Cambridge: Harvard University Press, 1991), p. 7.

16. Julia Kristeva, *The Portable Kristeva*, ed. Kelly Oliver (New York: Columbia University Press, 1977), p. 32.

17. See Lyotard's book by the same name.

18. "A Sociological Theory of Postmodernity," p. 149; see also http://shaunbest. tripod.com/id4.html (accessed 02/13/2007).

19. In "Derrida's Politics," *New York Review of Books,* October 25, 1998, available online at http://mural.uv.es/arolla/dpolitics.html (accessed 02/13/2007).

20. Charles Jencks, *What is Post-Modernism* (London: Academy Editions, 1996).

21. My thanks to Marsha for her crucial input in this section.

22. Lilla, "Derrida's Politics."

23. Jean-François Lyotard, "On the Post Postmodern." *Eyeline* 6 (Nov. 1987): 3–22. There is an interesting discussion of these issues available online at http://muse.jhu.edu/journals/pmc/v011/11.3spinks.html (accessed 02/13/2007).

24. Chomsky's quotes are from a letter to the author, dated 03/31/1994.

25. http://www.zmag.org/chomsky/interviews/9301-albchomsky-2.html (accessed 02/13/2007).

26. http://www.zmag.org/ScienceWars/forumchom.htm (accessed 02/13/2007).

27. Ibid.

28. Jean Bricmont and Alan Sokal, *Intellectual Impostures*, (London: Profile Books, 1998).

29. Available online at http://www.physics.nyu.edu/faculty/sokal/weinberg.html (accessed 02/13/2007).

30. Available online at http://www.nybooks.com/articles/1409 (accessed 02/13/ 2007).

31. Ibid.

32. Ibid.

33. This article is available online at http://www.nyu.edu/gsas/dept/philo/faculty/boghossian/papers/bog_tls.html (accessed 02/13/2007).

34. This quote appears in several texts by Sokal and Bricmont and is available online in Sokal's Afterword to his *Social Text* article at http://www.virtualschool.edu/mon/SocialConstruction/SokalSocialTextAfterword.html (accessed 02/13/2007).

35. "Exposing the Emperor's New Clothes: Why We Won't Leave Postmodernism Alone," in *Free Inquiry* 18 (Fall 1998).

36. Available online at http://www.zmag.org/chomsky/year/year-c11-s05.html (accessed 02/13/2007).

37. A selection of Chomsky's posts from the ChomskyChat Forum, online at http://www.zmag.org/ScienceWars/forumchom.htm (accessed 02/13/2007).

38. Ibid.

39. A publisher of Chomsky's work in France explained to me recently that the Barsamian interviews are virtually unreadable in France because of the always-supportive tone and approach of the interviewer. For him, the French expect that their journalists take a critical stance toward the interviewee, so Barsamian's pro-Chomsky bias is difficult to swallow.

40. Mikhail Bakhtin, *Dialogic Imagination,* edited by Michael Holquist, translated by Caryl Emerson and Michael Holquist (Austin: University of Texas Press, 1981) p. 431.

Chapter Seven

1. See Mikhail Bakhtin, *Rabelais and His World,* trans. Helene Iswolsky (Bloomington: Indiana University Press, 1984).

2. See my *Marc Angenot and the Scandal of History*, available online at http://muse.jhu.edu/journals/yale_journal_of_criticism/toc/yale17.2.html (accessed 02/13/2007).

3. David Barsamian and Noam Chomsky, *Propaganda and the Public Mind,* (Boston, MA: South End Press, 2001), pp. 79–80.

4. Noam Chomsky, *Language and Politics* (Montreal: Black Rose Books, 1988); *Language and Responsibility*, trans. John Viertel (New York: Pantheon, 1979); *Problems of Knowledge and Freedom: The Russell Lectures* (New York: Vintage, 1972.

5. Personal correspondence with author.

6. "Conversation between Robert F. Barsky and Marc Angenot," *Marc Angenot and the Scandal of History*, a special issue of the *Yale Journal of Criticism* 17, no. 2 (2004).

7. Cited online at http://www.mtholyoke.edu/acad/intrel/orwell46.htm (accessed 02/13/2007).

8. *Understanding Power*, pp. 22–23.

9. Neal Stephenson, *Cryptonomicon* (NY: Avon, 1999). This reference was suggested to me in the course of conversations with Michel Pierssens.

10. Born in 1958, Daniel Brooks studied theater in Toronto, "the Method" in New York, clown in Paris, dance in Buenos Aires, and puppet theater in Brazil.

11. Guillermo Verdecchia is a playwright, actor, director and translator whose work has been seen and heard across Canada and around the globe. Born in Argentina, Guillermo Verdecchia currently lives and works in Vancouver, B.C.

12. The play has been published in Toronto by Coach House Press, 1991.

13. http://www.talkinbroadway.com/ob/02_27_04.html (accessed 02/13/2007).

14. http://www.culturebot.org/archives/2004/02/28/TheLonelinessOfNoam-Chomsky.php (accessed 02/13/2007).

15. For information on this New Deal initiative see http://memory.loc.gov/ammem/fedtp/fthome.html (accessed 02/13/2007).

16. Caryl Emerson and Gary Saul Morson, *Mikhaïl Bakhtin: Creation of a Prosaics* (Stanford: Stanford University Press, 1990), p. 49.

17. Cited online at http://www.chomsky.info/articles/20041129.htm (accessed 02/13/2007).

18. Available online at http://www.radioproject.org/transcript/1998/9838.html (accessed 02/13/2007).

19. Noam Chomsky, "Chomsky on the Anti-War Movement: An Interview in the *Guardian*," *Guardian*, February 4, 2003, available online at http://www.zmag.org/content/showarticle.cfm?SectionID=1&ItemID=2962 (accessed 02/13/2007).

20. Noam Chomsky, *9/11*, p. 63, available online at http://www.zmag.org/chomcalmint.htm (accessed 02/13/2007).

21. Chomsky, *A New Generation Draws the Line: Kosovo, East Timor and the Standards of the West* (London: Verso, 2000).

22. "Imperial Presidency: Strategies to Control the 'Great Beast'," online at http://zmagsite.zmag.org/Feb2005/chomsky0205.html (accessed 02/13/2007).

23. Barsamian and Chomsky, *Propaganda and the Public Mind*, p. 73.

24. Lydia Sargent, "Humor, Theatre and Social Change," online at http://zmagsite.zmag.org/Feb2005/sargent0205.html (accessed 02/13/2007).

Chapter Eight

1. *Understanding Power*, p. 56.

2. Much of this list breaks down by country, since national traditions often dictate the form and style of work within and beyond the ivory tower, just as there exists a huge variation in different conceptions of what it means to be an intellectual who is *engagé*, or politically active. An indication of this spectrum can be found in the contrast between a recent book describing the history of

American muckraking (*Exposés and Excess: Muckraking in America 1900/2000,* by Cecilia Tichi, (Philadelphia: University of Pennsylvania Press, 2003) and, say, Zeev Sternhell's explosive book about the French Intellectual tradition, *Neither Right nor Left,* translated by David Maisel. (Princeton: Princeton University Press, 1995).

3. Howard Zinn, "The Uses of Scholarship," *Saturday Review*, October 18, 1969, reproduced in *The Zinn Reader: Writings on Disobedience and Democracy.* (New York: Seven Stories Press, 1997), pp. 499–500.

4. February 23, 1967, article in the *New York Review of Books* and published in *American Power and the New Mandarins* and available online at http://www.chomsky.info/articles/19670223.htm (accessed 02/13/2007).

5. Marc Angenot, "The Scandal of History," special issue of the *Yale Journal of Criticism*, cited online at http://muse.jhu.edu/login?uri=/journals/yale_journal _of_criticism/v017/17.2barsky01.pdf (accessed 02/13/2007).

6. Edward Said, *Representations of the Intellectual* (New York: Pantheon, 1994), pp. 12–13.

7. In *The Social Responsibility of the Critic*, (Ithaca: Cornell University Press, 1987).

8. Charles Derber, "Public Sociology as a Vocation," *Social Problems*, February 2004, p. 119.

9. Ibid., p. 120.

10. Howard Zinn, "Historian as Citizen," *Zinn Reader*, p. 510.

11. Carlos Fuentes, "The Enemy: Words," in George Abbott White and Charles Newman, eds., *Literature in Revolution* (Chicago: Northwestern University Press, 1972).

12. From Edward Said's Reith lectures, "Representations of the Intellectual," broadcast on the BBC in 1993 and reproduced in *Representations of the Intellectual* (New York: Pantheon Books, 1994), p. 18.

13. Edward Said, "A Monument to Hypocrisy," *Counterpunch*, February 15, 2003, online at http://www.counterpunch.org/said02152003.html.

14. Cited in the *Boston Globe* obituary marking the passing of Edward Said, available online at http://www.boston.com/news/education/higher/articles/ 2003/09/26/edward_said_critic_scholar_palestinian_advocate_at_67/ (accessed 02/13/2007).

15. "Window on the World," *Guardian Unlimited*, August 2, 2003, cited in an article called "Response to Christopher Hitchens Weasel words," by Clare Brandabur, that is critical of Christopher Hitchens's attacks against Said, at http://www.dissidentvoice.org/Articles8/Brandabur_Hitchens.htm (accessed 02/13/2007).

16. Edward Said, "Representing the Colonized: Anthropology's Interlocutors" *Critical Inquiry* 15, no. 2 (Winter 1989): 205–225, cited online at http://links.jstor.org/sici?sici=0093–1896(198924)15%3A2%3C205%3ARTCA I%3E2.0.CO%3B2-5 (accessed 02/13/2007).

17. In White and Newman, *Literature in Revolution*.

18. *American Power and The New Mandarins*.

19. Herbert Marcuse, *Liberation from an Affluent Society* (Boston, Mass.: Beacon Press, 1971), p. 285.

20. David Herman, "Thinking Big," *Prospect Magazine*, July 2004, online at http://www.prospect-magazine.co.uk/article_details.php?id=6227 (accessed 02/13/2007).

21. Online at http://www.guardian.co.uk/gender/story/0,11812,1252410,00.html (accessed 02/13/2007).

22. Steve Fuller, *How to Be an Intellectual* (London: Icon Books, 2004).

23. Online at http://home.uchicago.edu/~rposner/TABLE%20II.pdf (accessed 02/13/2007).

24. Camille Paglia, *Sex, Art and American Culture* (New York: Vintage Books, 1992).

25. Jim Merod, *The Political Responsibility of the Critic* (Ithaca: Cornell University Press, 1987).

26. Russell Jacoby, *The Last Intellectuals: American Culture in the Age of Academe* (New York: Basic Books, 1987).

27. See http://www.complete-review.com/reviews/posnerr/publicis.htm (accessed 02/13/2007).

28. See Posner's approach to such things is well illustrated in his recent listing of the 607 public intellectuals in America, online at http://home.uchicago.edu/~rposner/TABLE%20II.pdf .

29. On this point see as well David Damrosch, *We Scholars* (Cambridge: Harvard University Press, 1995).

30. See for example Jonathan Feldman's *Universities in the Business of Repression* (Boston: South End Press, 1998).

31. Bill Readings, *The University in Ruins* (Cambridge: Harvard University Press, 1996).

32. Sonia Shah, *Z Magazine*, November 21, 1999, online at http://zmag.org/ZSustainers/ZDaily/1999–11/21shah.htm (accessed 02/13/2007).

33. Jean-Paul Sartre, "Introducing *Les Temps modernes*," originally published in October 1, 1945, reproduced in Jean-Paul Sartre and Steven Ungar, *What Is Literature and Other Essays* (Cambridge: Harvard University Press, 1988), p. 252.

34. Ibid., pp. 252–253.

35. Cornelius Castoriadis, *Political and Social Writings*, ed. and trans. David Ames Curtis, vol. 3 (University of Minnesota Press, 1993).

36. "Defending Civilization and the Myth of Radical Academia," July 15, 2002. http://www.zmag.org/content/print_article.cfm?itemID=2116&sectionID=37 (accessed 02/13/2007).

37. Howard Zinn, "Historian as Citizen," *New York Times*, September 25, 1966, in the *Zinn Reader*.

38. Castoriadis, *Political and Social Writings*, p. 255.

39. Herbert Marcuse, *The Dialectics of Liberation* (London: Pelican Books, 1968), cited online at http://www.marcuse.org/herbert/pubs/60spubs/67dialecticlib/67LibFromAfflSociety.htm.

40. Edward Herman and David Peterson, "Public Versus Power Intellectuals," part I, *Z Magazine,* May 11, 2001, cited online at http://www.zmag.org/sustainers/content/2001-05/11peterson.htm (accessed 02/13/2007).

41. Jean-Paul Sartre, *What Is Literature?* p. 257.

42. See www.prospect-magazine.co.uk/intellectuals/results.

43. The interview was conducted by Shira Hadad Haaretz, and was cited online at http://www.zmag.org/content/showarticle.cfm?SectionID=1&ItemID=9121 (accessed 02/13/2007).

44. Ibid.

Bibliography

Abt, Lawrence E., and Stanley Rosner. *The Creative Experience*. New York: Grossman Publishers, 1970 (cf. s. v. Chomsky).

Achbar, Mark, ed. *Manufacturing Consent: Noam Chomsky and the Media*. Montreal: Black Rose Books, 1994.

d'Agostino, Fred. *Chomsky's System of Ideas*. Oxford: Clarendon Press, 1986.

Albert, Michael. *What Is to Be Undone?* Boston: Porter Sargent, 1974.

———, et al. *Liberating Theory*. Boston: South End Press, 1986.

———, and Robin Hahvel. *Looking Forward: Participatory Economics for the 21st Century*. Boston: South End Press, 1991.

———, and Robin Hahvel. *The Political Economy of Participatory Economics*. Princeton: Princeton University Press, 1991.

Allen, J., ed. *March 4: Scientists, Students, and Society*. Cambridge: MIT Press, 1970.

Avrich, Paul, and Barry Patemen. *Anarchist Voices, Anarchist Portraits*. Princeton: Princeton University Press, 2005.

———. *The Haymarket Tragedy*. Princeton: Princeton University Press, 1986.

———. *The Russian Anarchists*. Princeton: Princeton University Press, 1967.

———. *Sacco and Vanzetti: The Anarchist Background*. Princeton: Princeton University Press, 1991.

Avukah. *An Approach to Action: Facing The Social Insecurities Affecting The Jewish Position*. Avukah Pamphlet Service. New York: Avukah, 1943.

———. *Avukah Cooperative Summer School. Summer of 1941 Lectures* (featuring contributions from Shmuel Ben-Zvi, D. Mcdonald, I. Mereminski, Alfred Kahn, A. Rosenberg, Nathan Glazer, Adrien Schwartz). New York: Avukah, 1941.

———. *Avukah Student Action*. Avukah Pamphlet Service. New York: Avukah, 1938.

———. *Program for American Jews*. Avukah Pamphlet Service. New York: Avukah, 1938.

——. *A Short History of Zionism*. By Suzanne Harris Sankowsky. Avukah Pamphlet Service. New York: Avukah, s.d.

——. *What Can Be Done*. Avukah Pamphlet Service. New York: Avukah, 1940.

Bakhtin, Mikhail Mikhailovitch. *Dialogic Imagination,* edited by Michael Holquist. Translated by Caryl Emerson and Michael Holquist. Austin: University of Texas Press, 1981.

——. *Rabelais and His World,* trans. Helene Iswolsky. Bloomington: Indiana University Press, 1984.

Barsky, Robert F. *Arguing and Justifying: Assessing the Convention Refugee Choice of Moment, Motive and Host Country*. Aldershot, UK; Ashgate, 2001.

——. "Interview Between Marc Angenot and Robert F. Barsky." *Marc and the Scandal of History, Yale Journal of Criticism* 17, no. 2 (Fall 2004).

——. *Noam Chomsky: A Life of Dissent*. Cambridge: MIT Press, 1997.

——. *Noam Chomsky: Une voix discordante,* translated by Geneviève Joublin Paris: Odile Jacob, 1998.

——, editor. Anton Pannekoek, *Workers Councils*. Introduction by Robert F. Barsky and Noam Chomsky. San Francisco: AK Press, 1998.

Barsamian, David, and Noam Chomsky. *Propaganda and the Public Mind*. Boston: South End Press, 2001.

Baudrillard, Jean. *The Gulf War Did Not Take Place*. Translated by Paul Patton. Bloomington: Indiana University Press, 1995.

Bauman, Zygmunt. "A Sociological Theory of Postmodernity." *Between Totalitarianism and Postmodernity*. Edited by Peter Beilharz, Gillian Robinson, and John Rundell. Cambridge: MIT Press, 1992.

Billingsley, K. L., "Noam Chomsky, Punk Hero," *Heterodoxy*, March 1996.

Boesche, Roger. *The Strange Liberalism of Alexis de Tocqueville*. Ithaca: Cornell University Press, 1987.

Bookchin, Murray. The Ghost of Anarcho-Syndicalism. *Anarchist Studies*. Volume I. Cambridge: The White Horse Press, 1993, pp. 3–24.

——. "Looking Back at Spain," in Dimitrios Rossopoulos, ed., *The Radical Papers*, 1987, pp. 53–96.

——. *The Spanish Anarchists: The Heroic Years 1868–1936*. Edinburgh: AK Press, 1998 [1977].

——. *To Remember Spain: The Anarchist and Syndicalist Revolution of 1936*. San Francisco: AK Press, 1996.

Botha, Rudolf. *Challenging Chomsky*. London: Blackwell, 1989.

Bourdieu, Pierre. *Language and Symbolic Power*. Edited with an introduction by John B. Thompson; translated by Matthew Adamson. Cambridge: Harvard University Press, 1991.

Bracken, H. *Mind and Language: Essays on Descartes and Chomsky*. Dordrecht: Foris, 1984.

Bricianer, Serge. *Pannekoek and the Workers' Councils.* St. Louis, Mo.: Telos, 1978.

Bricmont, Jean, and Alan Sokal, *Intellectual Impostures.* London: Profile Books, 1998.

———. "Exposing the Emperor's New Clothes: Why We Won't Leave Postmodernism Alone." *Free Inquiry* 18 (Fall 1998).

Brooks, Daniel, and Guillermo Verdecchia. *The Noam Chomsky Lectures.* Toronto: Coach House Press, 1991.

Bruggers, H. "Stages of Totalitarian Economy." *Living Marxism* 6, no. 1 (Fall 1941): 15–24.

Carling, Christine. *Understanding Language: Towards a Post-Chomskyan Linguistics.* London: Macmillan, 1982.

Casas, J. G. *Anarchist Organization: The History of the FAI.* Montreal: Black Rose Books, 1986.

Castoriadis, Cornelius. *Political and Social Writings*, vol. 3. Edited and translated by David Ames Curtis. University of Minnesota Press, 1993.

Chandra, T. V. Prafulla, and L. S. Ramaiah. *Noam Chomsky: A Bibliography.* Gurgaon, Haryana (India): Indian Documentation Service, 1984.

Chomsky, Noam. *American Power and the New Mandarins.* New York: Pantheon, 1969.

———. *A New Generation Draws the Line: Kosovo, East Timor and the Standards of the West.* London: Verso, 2000.

———. "An Interview With Noam Chomsky." *Working Papers in Linguistics* 4, Supplement (Spring 1978): 1–26.

———. *Aspects of the Theory of Syntax.* Cambridge: MIT Press, 1965.

———. *At War With Asia.* New York: Pantheon, 1970.

———. *Barriers.* Cambridge: MIT Press, 1986.

———. "Cambodia Year Zero." To the Editor. *Times Literary Supplement,* January 4, 1980, p. 14, and January 15, 1980, p. 177.

———. "Creation and Culture." Alternative Radio cassette recording. Barcelona, 1992.

———. "The Creative Experience." *The Creative Experience.* Eds. Stanley Rosner and Lawrence E. Abt. New York: Grossman Publishers, 1970, pp. 71–87.

———. *Cartesian Linguistics: A Chapter in the History of Rationalist Thought.* New York: Harper and Row, 1966.

———, "Chomsky on the Anti-War Movement: An Interview in the *Guardian*." *Guardian,* February 4, 2003.

———. *The Chomsky Reader.* Edited by James Peck. New York: Pantheon, 1987.

———. *Chronicles of Dissent.* Introduction by Alexander Cockburn. Monroe, Me.: Common Courage Press/Stirling, Scotland: AK Press, 1992.

—— (with Edward S. Herman). *Counter-Revolutionary Violence; Bloodbaths in Fact and Propaganda*. Preface by R. Falk. Andover, Mass.: Warner Modular Publications, 1973.

——. *The Culture of Terrorism*. Boston: South End Press/Montreal: Black Rose Books, 1988.

——. *Current Issues in Linguistic Theory*. The Hague: Mouton, 1964.

——. *The Debate Between Chomsky and Piaget*. Cambridge: Harvard University Press, 1980.

——. "Democracy and Education," Mellon Lecture given at Loyola University, 1994.

——. *Deterring Democracy*. Boston: South End Press, 1991.

——. *Écrits politiques 1977–1983*. Peyrehorade: Acratie, 1984.

——. *Essays on Form and Interpretation*. New York: North-Holland, 1977.

——. *The Fateful Triangle: The United States, Israel and the Palestinians*. Boston: South End Press, 1983/Montreal: Black Rose Books, 1984.

——. *For Reasons of State*. New York: Pantheon, 1973.

——. (with van Riemsdijk and Huybregts). *The Generative Enterprise*, Dordrecht, Foris, 1982.

——. *Generative Grammar: Its Basis, Development and Prospects*, Kyoto: Kyoto University of Foreign Studies, 1987.

——. "His Right to Say It." *The Nation*, February 28, 1981.

——. "Is Peace at Hand?" November 1987, Z *Magazine*, January 1988.

——. *Keeping the Rabble in Line*. Monroe, Me.: Common Courage, 1994.

——. *Knowledge of Language: Its Nature, Origin and Use*. New York: Praeger, 1986.

——. *Language and Information: Selected Essays on the Theory and Application*. Reading, Mass.: Addison-Wesley/Jerusalem: The Jerusalem Academic Press, 1964.

——. *Language and Mind*. New York: Pantheon, 1968; enlarged edition New York: Harcourt, 1972.

——. *Language and Politics*. Edited by C. P. Otero. Montreal: Black Rose Books, 1988. Cf. 1981, RP.

——. *Language and Problems of Knowledge: The Managua Lectures*. Cambridge: MIT Press, 1987.

——. *Language and Responsibility*. Translated from the French by John Viertel [*Dialogues avec Mitsou Ronat*. Paris: Flammarion, 1977]. New York: Pantheon, 1979.

——. *Language in a Psychological Setting*. Tokyo: Sophia U, 1987.

——. *Lectures on Government and Binding: The Pisa Lectures*. Dordrecht: Foris, 1981; corrected edition, 1982.

——. *Letters from Lexington: Reflections on Propaganda*. Monroe, Me.: Common Courage Press, 1993.

——. "Linguistics and Politics." *New Left Review* 57 (September-October 1969): 21–34.

——. *Logical Structure of Linguistic Theory*. New York: Plenum, 1975 [1955–56].

—— (with Edward S. Herman). *Manufacturing Consent: The Political Economy of the Mass Media*. New York: Pantheon, 1988.

——. "Market Democracy in a Neoliberal Order: Doctrines and Reality," Davie Lecture, University of Cape Town, May 1997.

——. *A Minimalist Program for Linguistic Theory*. Cambridge: MIT Deptartment of Linguistics, 1992.

——. *The Minimalist Program*. Cambridge: MIT Press, 1995.

——. *Modular Approaches to the Study of the Mind*. Distinguished Graduate Research Lecture Series I, 1980; California State University Press, 1984.

——. *Necessary Illusions*. Boston: South End Press, 1989.

——, *9-11*. London: Open Media, 2001.

——. "Noam Chomsky Interviewed by Eleanor Wachtel." *Queen's Quarterly* 101.1 (Spring 1994): 63–72.

——. "Old Wine, New Bottles: Free Trade, Global Markets and Military Adventures," University of Virginia, February 10, 1993.

——. *On Power and Ideology: The Managua Lectures*. Boston: South End/ Montreal: Black Rose Books, 1987.

——. "On the Limits of Civil Disobedience." In *The Berrigans*, edited by William Van Etten Casey, S. J., and Philip Nobile, Avon Books, 1971, pp. 39–41.

——. *Peace in the Middle East? Reflections on Justice and Nationhood*. New York: Pantheon, 1974.

——. *Pirates and Emperors: International Terrorism and the Real World*. New York: Claremont Research and Publications, 1986; Montreal: Black Rose Books, 1987.

—— (with Edward S. Herman). *The Political Economy of Human Rights*. Boston: South End Press/Montreal: Black Rose Books, 1979, 2 vols.

——. "Political Pilgrims." To the Editor. *Times Literary Supplement,* January 22, 1982, p. 81.

——. *Powers and Prospects: Reflections on Human Nature and the Social Order*. Delhi: Madhyam Books, 1996.

——. *Problems of Knowledge and Freedom: The Russell Lectures*. New York: Pantheon, 1971.

——. *The Prosperous Few and the Restless Many*. Berkeley: Odonian Press, 1993.

——. "Psychology and Ideology." *Cognition* I (1972): 11–46.

——. *Radical Priorities*. Edited, introduction, and notes by Carlos P. Otero, Montreal: Black Rose Books, 1981; enlarged edition 1984.

——. *Réponses inédites à mes détracteurs parisiens*. Paris: Spartacus, 1984.

——. *Rethinking Camelot; JFK, the Vietnam War and US Political Culture*. Boston: South End Press/Montreal: Black Rose Books, 1993.

——. "Review of Skinner, *Verbal Behaviour. Language* 35 (1959): 26–58.

——. "Review of Skinner, *Beyond Freedom and Dignity. New York Review of Books*, December 30, 1971.

——. "Roots of Progressive Thought in Antiquity," transcription of a speech given on Capital Hill on January 9, 1997.

——. *Rules and Representations*. New York: Columbia University Press, 1980.

—— (with Morris Halle). *The Sound Pattern of English*. New York: Harper & Row/Cambridge: MIT Press, 1968.

——. *Secrets, Lies and Democracy*. Berkeley: Odonian Press, 1994.

——. *Syntactic Structures*. The Hague: Mouton, 1957.

——. *Studies on Semantics in Generative Grammar*. The Hague: Mouton, 1972.

——. *Terrorizing the Neighbourhood: American Foreign Policy in the Post-Cold War Era*. Stirling, Scotland: AK Press, 1991.

——. "The Gulf Crisis" January 1991, *Z Magazine* February 1991.

——. "The Tragedy of Political Science." To the Editor. *Times Literary Supplement*, April 19, 1985, p. 1437.

——. *Towards a New Cold War. Essays on the Current Crisis and How We Got There*. New York: Pantheon, 1982.

——. *Turning the Tide: U.S. Intervention in Central America and the Struggle for Peace*. Boston: South End Press, 1985; enlarged edition subtitled *The U.S. and Latin America*, 1987.

——. *Understanding Power: The Indispensable Chomsky*. Edited by Peter R. Mitchel and John Schoeffel. New York: The New Press, 2002.

——. *What Uncle Sam Really Wants*. Berkeley: Odonian Press, 1992.

——. "Whose World Order: Conflicting Visions," September 22, 1998, The University of Calgary.

——. *World Orders Old and New*. New York: Columbia University Press, 1994.

——. *Year 501: The Conquest Continues*. Boston: South End Press/Montreal: Black Rose Books, 1993.

——. "The Intifada and the Peace Process," *Fletcher Forum of World Affairs* 14, no. 2 (Summer 1990): 345–353.

——. "World Order and its Rules: Variations on Some Themes," *Journal of Law and Society* 20, no. 2 (Summer 1993): 145–165.

—— (with Edward S. Herman). "Why American business supports third world fascism: our president is campaigning for 'human rights' abroad, but for 30 years our government and corporations have been supporting precisely the opposite." *Business-and-Society-Review,* Fall 1977, pp. 13–21.

——, and Edward S. Herman. "The United States Versus Human Rights in the Third World." *Monthly Review* 29 (August 1977): 22–45.

——. "World Order and Its Rules: Variations on Some Themes," *Scandinavian Journal of Development Alternatives* 13, no. 3 (September 1994): 5–27.

——. "World Order and Its Rules: Variations on Some Themes." *Journal of Law and Society* 20, no. 2 (Summer 1993): 145–165.

——. "The United States versus Human Rights in the Third World," *Monthly Review* 29, no. 3 (July–August 1977): 22–45.

Chomsky, William. *Hebrew, the Story of a Living Language.* New York: Education Department, Zionist Organisation of America, 1947.

——. *Hebrew, the Eternal Language.* Philadelphia: Jewish Publication Society of America, 1957.

——. *How to Teach Hebrew in the Elementary Grades.* New York: The United Synagogue Commission on Jewish Education, 1946.

——, ann. and intro. *David Kimche's Hebrew Grammar (Mikhlol).* New York: Dropsie College for Hebrew and Cognate Learning, 1952/5713.

——. *Teaching and Learning.* Third edition. New York: Jewish Education Committee Press, 1959.

CIA study, *Kampuchea: A Demographic Catastrophe,* GC 80-0019U.

Cohen, Joshua, and Joel Rogers. "Chomsky's Social Thought." *New Left Review* (1991): 187.

Cohn, Werner. *The Hidden Alliances of Noam Chomsky.* New York: Americans for a Safe Israel, 1988.

Collier, Peter, and David Horowitz, eds., *The Anti-Chomsky Reader.* Encounter Books, 2004.

Cook, Vivien. *Chomsky's Universal Grammar: An Introduction.* Oxford: Basil Blackwell, 1988.

Cooper, David E. "Chomsky." *Times Literary Supplement,* October 1, 1976, p. 1255.

Cordemoy, Géraud de. *Discours Physique de la Parole.* Geneva: Slatkine Reprints, 1973 [1668].

Courtois, Stephane, Nicolas Werth, Jean-Louis Panne, Andrzej Paczkowski, Karel Bartosek, Jean-Louis Margolin, Mark Kramer, translator, Jonathan Murphy, translator. *The Black Book of Communism.* Cambridge: Harvard University Press, 1999.

Cowan, Marianne, ed. *Humanist Without Portfolio.* Detroit: Wayne State University Press, 1963.

Culler, Jonathan. *Structuralist Poetics: Structuralism, Linguistics and the Study of Literature.* London: Routledge, 1975.

Damrosch, David. *We Scholars.* Cambridge: Harvard University Press, 1995.

Dellinger, Dave. *The New Nonviolence.* Nashville, Tenn.: Southern Student Organizing Committee, 1968.

———. *What Is Cuba Really Like?* New York: Liberation, 1964.

Daiches, David. *Style Périodique and Style Coupé: Hugh Blair and the Scottish Rhetoric of American Independence.* In Sher and Smitten. *Scotland and America in the Age of the Enlightenment,* pp. 209–226.

De Leon, ed. *Contemporary American Activists: A Biographical Sourcebook, 1960 Onward.* Westport, Conn.: Greenwood Press, 1995.

Dershowitz, Alan M. *Chutzpah.* New York: Simon and Schuster, 1991.

Descartes, René. *The Philosophical Works of Descartes.* Translated by E. S. Haldane and G. R. T. Ross, 1955.

Dewey, John. *Dewey on Education: Selections,* introduction and notes by Martin S. Dworkin. New York: Bureau of Publications, Teachers College, Columbia University, 1959.

Dolgoff, Sam. *The Anarchist Collectives: Workers' Self-Management in the Spanish Revolution.* Montreal: Black Rose Books, 1990.

Dolgoff, S., ed., trans., intro. *Bakunin on Anarchy.* New York: Knopf, 1973.

Donaghue, Denis. "The Politics of Grammar." Review of Noam Chomsky, *Reflections on Language. Times Higher Education Supplement,* November 1976, p. 19.

Ehrlich, H., et al., eds. *Reinventing Anarchy: What Are Anarchists Thinking These Days?* London: Routledge and Kegan Paul, 1979.

Einstein, Albert. *Ideas and Opinions by Albert Einstein,* based on *Mein Weltbild,* ed. Carl Seelig, and other sources, new translations and revisions Sonja Bargmann. New York, Wings Books, 1954.

Elders, Fons, ed. *Reflexive Waters: The Basic Concerns of Mankind.* London: Souvenir Press, 1974.

Emerson, Caryl, and Gary Saul Morson, *Mikhaïl Bakhtin: Creation of a Prosaics.* Stanford: Stanford University Press, 1990.

Faurisson, Robert. "Letter to the New Statesman," *Journal of Historical Review* 1.2 (1980): 157–161.

———. *Mémoire en Défense contre ceux qui m'accusent de falsifier l'Histoire; la question des chambres à gaz.* Preface by Noam Chomsky. Paris: La Vieille Taupe, 1980.

———. *The Problem of the "Gas Chambers," or "the Rumor of Auschwitz,"* a pamphlet published by the Ridgewood Defense Fund, s.d., reprinted in *The Journal for Historical Review* 19.3 (May/June 2000).

Feinberg, Walter, and Henry Rosemont Jr., eds. *Work, Technology and Education: Dissenting Essays in the Intellectual Foundations of American Education.* Chicago: University of Illinois Press, 1975.

Feldman, Jonathan. *Universities in the Business of Repression.* Boston: South End Press, 1989.

Ferguson, Adam. *Principles of Moral and Political Science, being chiefly a retrospect of lectures delivered in the College of Edinburgh.* 2 volumes. Edinburgh, 1792.

Franklin, Benjamin. *The Papers of Benjamin Franklin.* Edited by Leonard W. Labaree et al. 27 volumes to date. New Haven, Conn., 1959–.

Freidin, Robert. *Foundations of Generative Syntax.* Cambridge: MIT Press, 1992.

Fresco, Nadine. "Les redresseurs de morts." *Le temps modernes,* June 1980.

Fuller, Steve. *How To Be An Intellectual.* London: Icon Books, 2004.

George, Alexander, ed. *Reflections on Chomsky.* Oxford: Basil Blackwell, 1989.

Goldman, Emma. *Red Emma Speaks: Selected Writings and Speeches by Emma Goldman.* Edited by Alix Kates Shulman. New York: Random House, 1972.

Goldsmith, John A., and Geoffrey J. Huck, *Noam Chomsky and the Deep Structure Debate.* Chicago: University of Chicago Press, 1995. Goreing, Andrew. "Enduring Champion of Ordinary People," *The Times Higher Education Supplement,* February 3, 1989, p. 15.

Graur, Mina. *An Anarchist Rabbi: The Life and Teachings of Rudolph Rocker,* Jerusalem: Magnes Press, 1997.

Guérin, Daniel. *Anarchism: From Theory to Practice.* Introduction by Noam Chomsky. New York: Monthly Review Press, 1970.

Habermas, Jurgen. *Lectures on the Philosophical Discourse of Modernity.* Cambridge: MIT Press, 1987.

Harman, Gibert, ed. *On Noam Chomsky.* Amherst: University of Massachusetts Press, 1982. Harris, Randy Allen. *The Linguistic Wars.* NewYork: Oxford University Press, 1997.

Harris, Zellig S. *A Grammar of English on Mathematical Principles.* New York: Wiley-Interscience, 1982.

———. *Language and Information.* New York: Columbia University Press, 1988.

———. *Linguistic Structure of Hebrew.* New Haven: American Oriental Society, 1941.

———. *Mathematical Structures of Language.* New York: Wiley-Interscience, 1968.

———. *Papers in Structural and Transformational Linguistics.* New York: Reidel, 1970.

———. *Papers on Syntax.* New York: Reidel, 1981.

———. *Structural Linguistics*. Chicago: University of Chicago Press, 1986 [1951].

———. *The Transformation of Capitalist Society*. Lanham, UK: Rowman and Littlefield Publishers, 1997.

———, and James A. Montgomery. *The Ras Shamra Mythological Texts*. Philadelphia: The American Philosophical Society, 1935.

———, et al. *The Form of Information in Science: Analysis of an Immunology Sublanguage*. Preface by Hilary Putnam. Dordrecht: Kluwer Academic Publishers, 1989. Hashomer Hatzair. *Pioneer Saga: The Story of Hashomer Hatzair*. New York: Hashomer Hatzair, 1944.

———. *What Is Hashomer Hatzair?* New York: Hashomer Hatzair, 1939.

Hassan, Ihab. *The Postmodern Turn: Essays in Postmodern Theory and Culture*. Columbus: Ohio State University Press, 1987.

Heny, Frank. Review of LSLT, In Otero, *Critical Assessments* 1, no. 1, 308.

Hekman, Susan J. (1990) *Gender and Knowledge: Elements of a Postmodern Feminism*. Boston: Northeastern University Press.

Herbert of Cherbury. *De Veritate*, 1624. Translated by M. H. Carré. Bristol: University of Bristol Studies no. 6, 1937.

Herman, Edward S. "Letter" [David Peterson], 12 August 1992.

———. "Pol Pot, Faurisson and the Process of Derogation." *Noam Chomsky*. Edited by Carlos P. Otero. Oxford: Blackwell, 1994, pp. 598 ff.

———, and Noam Chomsky. *Counter-Revolutionary Violence; Bloodbaths in Fact and Propaganda*. Preface by R. Falk. Andover, Mass.: Warner Modular Publications, 1973.

———, and Noam Chomsky. *The Political Economy of Human Rights*. 2 vols. Boston: South End Press/Montreal: Black Rose Books, 1979.

———, and Noam Chomsky. *Manufacturing Consent: The Political Economy of the Mass Media*. New York: Pantheon, 1988.

Hirsh, Arthur. *The French Left: A History and Overview*. Montreal: Black Rose Books, 1982.

Hitchens, Christopher. "American Notes." *Times Literary Supplement*, January 11, 1985, p. 36.

———. "The Chorus and Cassandra," *Grand Street Magazine*, Autumn 1985.

Hook, Andrew. "Philadelphia, Edinburgh and the Scottish Enlightenment." In Sher and Smitten, *Scotland and America in the Age of the Enlightenment*, pp. 227–241.

Hooker, Richard. *The Laws of Ecclesiastical Polity*. Edited by A. S. McGrade. Cambridge, UK: Cambridge University Press, 1989.

Horvat, B., et al. *Self-Governing Socialism*. 2 vols. White Plains, N.Y.: International Arts and Sciences Press, 1975.

Humboldt, Wilhelm von. (1767–1836). *The Limits of State Action*. Introduction by J. W. Burrow. London: Cambridge University Press, 1969.

——. *Linguistic Variability and Intellectual Development*. Philadelphia: University of Pennsylvania Press, 1972 [1836].

——. *Über die Verschiedenheit des Menschlichen Sprachbaues*, 1836. Facsimile ed. Bonn: F. Dümmlers Verlag, 1960.

Hutcheon, Linda (1988) *A Poetics of Postmodernism: History, Theory, Fiction*. New York: Routledge Kegan and Paul.

Huyssen, Andreas (1986) *After the Great Divide: Modernism, Mass Culture, Postmodernism*. Bloomington: Indiana University Press.

International Council Correspondence. Westport, Conn.: Greenwood Reprint, 1937 [1934].

Jacoby, Russell. *The Last Intellectuals: American Culture in the Age of Academe*. New York: Basic Books, 1987.

Jameson, Fredric (1991) *Postmodernism, or The Cultural Logic of Late Capitalism*. Durham, N.C.: Duke University Press.

Jay, Martin. *Cultural Semantics: Keywords of Our Time*. Amherst: University of Massachusetts Press, 1998.

Jencks, Charles (1996) "What is Post-Modernism," Laurence Cahoone (ed), *From Modernism to Postmodernism: An Anthology*, Cambridge, U.K.: Blackwell, pp. 471–480.

Jowitt, Ken. "Our Republic of Fear: Chomsky's Denunciation of America's Foreign and Economic Policy." *Times Literary Supplement,* February 10, 1995, pp. 3–4.

Kasher, Asa, ed. *The Chomskyan Turn*. Oxford: Basil Blackwell, 1990.

Kellner, Douglas, ed. *Karl Korsch: Revolutionary Theory*. Austin: University of Texas Press, 1977.

Kinne, Burdette. "Voltaire Never Said It!" *Modern Language Notes* 58 (November 1943): 534–535.

Koerner, E. F. Konrad, and Matsuji Tajima, with the collaboration of Carlos P. Otero. *Noam Chomsky: A Personal Bibliography, 1951–1986*. Philadelphia: John Benjamins, 1986.

Kristeva, Julia. *The Portable Kristeva*. Edited by Kelly Oliver. New York: Columbia University Press, 1977.

Kropotkin, Peter Alexeivich. *Modern Science and Anarchism*.

——. *Mutual Aid: A Factor of Evolution*. Introduction by George Woodcock. Montreal: Black Rose Books, 1989.

Laclau, Ernst, and Chantal Mouffe. *The Radical Democratic Imaginary*. New York: Routledge, 1998.

Lees, Robert. *The Grammar of English Nominalizations*. Bloomington: University of Indiana Press, 1960.

——. "Review of Noam Chomsky's *Syntactic Structures*." *Language* 33, no. 3 (1957).

Lilla, Mark. "The Politics of Jacques Derrida," *New York Review of Books*, June 25, 1998, p. 41.

Lipset, Seymour M. *Agrarian Socialism*. Berkeley: University of California Press, 1959.

Lipsitz, Edmond Y., ed. *Canadian Jewry Today: Who's Who in Canadian Jewry*. Downsview, Ontario: J.E.S.L. Education Products, 1989, pp. 30–36.

Lukes, Steven. "Chomsky's Betrayal of Truths." *Times* (London), November 7, 1980, p. 31.

Lyotard, Jean-François. *The Differend: Phrases in Dispute*, translated by Georges van den Abbeele, University of Minnesota Press, 1989.

——. "On the Post Postmodern." *Eyeline* 6 (November 1987): 3–22.

——. *The Postmodern Condition: A Report on Knowledge* Translated by Geoff Bennington and Brian Massumi. Minneapolis: University of Minnesota Press, 1984.

Lyons, John. *Chomsky*. London: Wm. Collins [Fontana Modern Masters] 3rd Expanded Edition, 1991 [1970, 1978].

Macdonald, Dwight. *Henry Wallace: The Man and the Myth*. New York: Vanguard, 1948.

——. *Memoirs of a Revolutionist: Essays in Political Criticism*. New York: Farrar, Straus and Cudahy, 1957.

——. *Against the American Grain*. New York: Random House, 1962.

——. *On Movies*. New York: Berkeley Medallion, 1971.

——. *Discriminations: Essays and Afterthoughts, 1938–1974*. New York: Grossman, 1974.

MacCorquodale, Kenneth. "On Chomsky's Review of Skinner's *Verbal Behaviour*." *Journal of the Experimental Analysis of Behaviour* 13 (1970): 83–99.

Marcuse, Herbert. *The Dialectics of Liberation*. London: Pelican Books, 1968.

——. *Liberation from an Affluent Society*. Boston: Beacon Press, 1971.

Matthews, P. H. "The Gene of Grammar." Review of Noam Chomsky *Rules and Representations*. *Times Literary Supplement*, November 21, 1981, pp. 13–14.

——. *Grammatical Theory in the United States from Bloomfield to Chomsky*. Cambridge: Cambridge University Press, 1993.

——. "Saying Something Simple." Review of Zellig Harris's *Language and Information*, *Times Literary Supplement*, December 23–29, 1988.

Mattick, Paul. *Anti-Bolshevik Communism*. White Plains, N.Y.: M. E. Sharpe, 1978.

——. "Two Men in a Boat—Not to Speak of the 8 Points." *Living Marxism* 6, no. 1 (Fall 1941): 24–79.

——. "Workers' Control." *The New Left*. Edited by Priscilla Long. Boston: Porter Sargent, 1969.

Melman, Seymour. *Decision-Making and Productivity*. Oxford: Blackwell, 1958.

——. *Pentagon Capitalism: The Political Economy of War*. New York: McGraw-Hill, 1970.

——. *The Permanent War Economy: American Capitalism in Decline*. New York: Simon and Schuster, 1974.

——. *Profits Without Production*. New York: Knopf, 1983.

——. *War Inc.*, unpublished manuscript.

Merod, Jim. *The Social Responsibility of the Critic*. Ithaca, N.Y.: Cornell University Press, 1987.

Mill, John Stuart. *On Liberty*. London, Everyman's Library, 1968.

Miller, Thomas P. "Witherspoon, Blair and the Rhetoric of Civic Humanism." In Sher and Smitten, *Scotland and America in the Age of the Enlightenment*, pp. 100–119.

Milner, Jean-Claude. *Ordres et raisons de la langue*. Paris: Le Seuil, 1982.

Mitgang, Herbert. *Dangerous Dossiers: Exposing the Secret War Against America's Greatest Authors*. New York: Donald I. Fine, 1988.

Modgil, Celia, and Sohan Modgil, eds. *Noam Chomsky: Consensus and Controversy*. Barcombe: Lewes, Falmer Press, 1987.

Morris, Brian. *Bakunin: The Philosophy of Freedom*. Montreal: Black Rose Books, 1993.

Neill, A. S., *Summerhill: A Radical Approach to Child Rearing*. New York: Hart Publishing, 1960.

Nelkin, D. *The University and Military Research: Moral Politics at MIT*. Ithaca: Cornell University Press, 1972.

Nesvisky, Matt. "Looking Right for the Revels of the Hippy Left of Yesteryear," *Jerusalem Post*, June 2, 1995, p. 4.

Newman, Charles, and George Abbott White, eds., *Literature in Revolution*. Chicago: Northwestern University Press, 1972.

Norris, Christopher. *Uncritical Theory: Postmodernism, Intellectuals and the Gulf War*. London: Lawrence and Wishart, 1992.

——. *What's Wrong With Postmodernism: Critical Theory and the Ends of Philosophy*. Baltimore: Johns Hopkins Press, 1990.

Orwell, George. *Homage to Catalonia*. San Diego: Harcourt, Brace, Jovanovich, 1980.

——. *The Collected Essays, Journalism and Letters of George Orwell*. Edited by Sonia Orwell and Ian Angus. London: Secker and Warburg, 1968, 5 vols.

——. "Politics and the English Language," cited in *The Norton Anthology of English Literature* volume 2. New York: Norton, 1993, 2233–2242.

Otero, Carlos P. *Behavioral and Brain Sciences* (December 1990): 747ff.

——. *Chomsky's Revolution: Cognitivism and Anarchism.* Oxford: Blackwell 1999.

——. *Noam Chomsky: Critical Assessments.* Edited by Carlos P. Otero. London: Routledge, 1994, 4 vols.

——. "The Third Emancipatory Phase of History." Introduction to Chomsky, *Language and Politics*, 22–81.

——, and Noam Chomsky. *Radical Priorities.* London: AK Press, 2003.

Paglia, Camille. *Sex, Art and American Culture.* New York: Vintage Books, 1992.

Pannekoek, Anton. *Lenin as Philosopher: A Critical Examination of the Philosophical Basis of Leninism.* New York: Breakout Press, 1975.

——. *Workers Councils: The Way to Workers' Control.* Melbourne: ILP, 1950.

Parini, Jay. "Noam is an Island." *Mother Jones* (October 1988): 36–41.

Peck, Jim. "Noam Chomsky: An American Dissident." *Progressive* (July 1987): 22–25.

Ponchaud, François. *Cambodge, année zéro.* Paris: éditions Kailash, 1998.

Portis, Larry. "Noam Chomsky, l'état et l'intelligentsia française," *L'Homme et la Société* (1997): 123–124.

Rai, Milan. *Chomsky's Politics.* London: Verso, 1995.

Readings, Bill. *The University in Ruins.* Cambridge: Harvard University Press, 1996.

Rendall, Jane. *The Origins of the Scottish Enlightenment.* London: Macmillan, 1978.

Robinson, Ian. *The New Grammarians' Funeral: A Critique of Noam Chomsky's Linguistics.* Cambridge: Cambridge University Press, 1975.

Rocker, Rudolf. *Anarchism and Anarcho-Syndicalism.* London: Freedom Press, 1988.

——. "Anarchism and Anarcho-Syndicalism." In Paul Eltzbacher, ed., *Anarchism.* London: Freedom Press, 1937.

——. *Anarcho-Syndicalism.* Preface by Noam Chomsky. London: Pluto Press, 1989.

——. *The London Years.* Translated Joseph Leftwich. London: Robert Anscombe, 1956.

——. *Nationalism and Culture.* Translated by Ray E. Chase. St. Paul, Minn.: Michael E. Coughlin, 1985.

——. *The Tragedy of Spain.* New York: Freie Arbeiter Stimme, 1937.

Rosenberg, Arthur. *The Birth of the German Republic.* Oxford: Oxford University Press, 1931.

———. *Democracy and Socialism: A Contribution to the Political History of the Past 150 Years.* New York: Knopf, 1939. Reprinted by Beacon Press, 1965.

———. *A History of Bolshevism.* Oxford: Oxford University Press, 1934.

Rousseau, Jean-Jacques. *First and Second Discourses.* Introduction by R. D. Masters. New York: St. Martin Press, 1964.

Russell, Bertrand. *The Autobiography of Bertrand Russell.* 3 volumes. London: George Allen and Unwin, 1968.

Said, Edward. *Representations of the Intellectual.* New York: Pantheon, 1994.

———. *Unpopular Essays.* London: George Allen and Unwin, 1950.

Salkie, Raphael. *The Chomsky Update: Linguistics and Politics.* London: Unwin Hyman, 1990.

Sampson, Geoffrey. "Human Language Debates." Review of Noam Chomsky, *Rules and Representations. THES,* September 19, 1980, p. 14.

Sartre, Jean-Paul, and Steven Ungar. *What Is Literature and Other Essays.* Cambridge: Harvard University Press, 1988.

Schachtman, Max (1903–1972). *Sacco and Vanzetti: Labor's Martyrs.* New York: International Labor Defense, 1927.

Schelling, F. W. J. *Philosophical Inquiries into the Nature of Human Freedom.* Translated and edited by James Gutmann. Chicago: Open Court Publishing, 1936.

Scheuerman, William. *Between the Norm and the Exception: The Frankfurt School and the Rule of Law.* Cambridge: MIT Press, 1994.

Schlegel, August Wilhelm. "De l'étymologie en général." In E. Böcking, ed., *Oeuvres écrits en Français.* Leipzig, 1946.

Searle, John R. "Reflections on Language." To the Editor. *Times Literary Supplement,* October 22, 1976, p. 1330.

———. "The Rules of the Language Game." Review of Noam Chomsky, *Reflections on Language. Times Literary Supplement,* September 10, 1976, pp. 1118–1120.

Sgroi, Claudia. *Noam Chomsky: Bibliografia 1949–1981.* A cura di Salvatore Claudio Sgroi. Padova: CLESP editrice, 1983.

Shenker, Israel. "Experts Labor to Communicate on Animal Talk. *New York Times,* September 25, 1975, pp. 45, 74.

———. "Noam Chomsky." *Horizon* 13, no. 2 (Spring 1971): 104–109.

———. *Words and Their Masters.* Photographs by Jill Krementz. Garden City, N.Y.: Doubleday, 1974.

Sher, Richard B., and Jeffrey R. Smitten. *Scotland and America in the Age of the Enlightenment.* Princeton: Princeton University Press, 1990.

Singh, Chhatrapati. *Law From Anarchy to Utopia.* Buffalo, N.Y.: Prometheus Books, 1982.

Skinner, B. F. *Beyond Freedom and Dignity*. New York: Knopf, 1971.

——. *Verbal Behaviour*. Englewood Cliffs, N.J.: Prentice Hall, 1957.

——. "Verbal Behaviour." Letter to *Times Literary Supplement*, March 9–15, 1990, p. 253.

Smart, D. A. *Pannekoek and Gorter's Marxism*. London: Pluto, 1978.

Smith, Adam. *An Inquiry into the Nature and Causes of the Wealth of Nations*. Edited by R. H. Campbell, A. S. Skinner, and W. B. Todd. 2 volumes. Oxford: Oxford University Press, 1976.

Smith, Patricia, ed. *The Nature and Process of Law: An Introduction to Legal Philosophy*. New York: Oxford University Press, 1993.

Smith, Neil, and Deirdre Wilson. *Modern Linguistics: The Results of Chomsky's Revolution*. Harmondsworth: Penguin, 1979.

Spiro, George. *Marxism and the Bolshevik State, Workers Democratic World Government Versus National Burocratic* [sic] *"Society" and Capitalist Regimes*. New York: Red Star Press, 1951.

Steffens, Lincoln. *The Autobiography of Lincoln Steffens*. New York: Harcourt, Brace and Co., 1931.

Stephenson, Neal. *Cryptonomicon*. New York: Avon, 1999.

Sternhell, Zeev. *Neither Right nor Left*, Translated by David Maisel. Princeton: Princeton University Press, 1995.

Summers, Laura J. "Chomsky and the Cambodian Regime." Letters to the Editor. *THES* December 19, 1980, p. 22.

Terrace, Herbert. *Speaking of Apes*. New York: Plenum Press, 1980.

Tichi, Cecilia. *Exposés and Excess: Muckraking in America 1900/2000*. Philadelphia: University of Pennsylvania Press, 2003.

Townshead, Charles. "In the Name of Liberty." *Times Literary Supplement*, July 15–21, 1988, p. 777.

Vidal-Naquet, Pierre. *Assassins of Memory: Essays on the Denial of the Holocaust*. Translated and foreword by Jeffrey Mehlman. New York: Columbia University Press, 1992.

——. *Holocaust Denial in France: Analysis of a Unique Phenomenon*. New York: The Project for the Study of Anti-Semitism, 1995.

——. and David Ames Curtis. *The Jews*. New York: Columbia University Press, 1998.

Vincent, John. "Cambodia Year Zero." To the Editor. *Times Literary Supplement*, January 18, 1980, p. 63.

Watson, George. "Chomsky: What Has It to Do with Literature?" *Times Literary Supplement*, February 14, 1975, pp. 164–165.

Weiskind, Ron. "Chewing Up the Pacifier." *Pittsburgh Post-Gazette*, October 15, 1993, p. 4.

Westbrook, Robert F. *John Dewey and American democracy,* Ithaca, N.Y.: Cornell University Press, 1991.

Whitfield, Stephen J. *A Critical American: The Politics of Dwight Macdonald.* Hamden, Conn.: Archon Books, 1984.

Wilson, James G. "Noam Chomsky and Judicial Review," *Cleveland State Law Review* 44, no. 4 (Fall 1996): 439–472.

Woodhouse, C. M. "The Anti-American Case." Review of Noam Chomsky, *Towards a New Cold War. Times Literary Supplement,* July 23, 1982, p. 784.

Zinn, Howard. *A People's History of the United States.* New York: Perennial, 2001.

——. *The Zinn Reader.* New York: Seven Stories Press, 1997.

——. *Student Nonviolent Coordinating Committee: The New Abolitionists.* Boston: Beacon Press, 1968.

Index

AARGH (Anciens Amateurs de Récits de Guerre et d'Holocauste), 31, 35, 56, 68, 87, 330–331, 332nn40–41, 333n42, 334nn52

Achbar, Mark, xvii, 28, 30, 31, 33, 228, 344n6

Activism, ix, 12, 18, 19, 107, 172, 225, 284

Agone Press, 63, 164, 328n2

AK Press, xvi, 17, 19, 20

Alami, Mussa, 56

Albert, Mike, xvii, 3, 157, 197, 203, 246

Allen, Woody, 287, 289

Althusser, Louis, 238

American Enterprise, 319

Amis, Kingsley, 300

Anarchism, 5–8, 10, 21, 36, 41, 68, 76, 82–83, 98, 104, 105, 109–110, 118–121, 129–131, 133, 135, 136–144, 156, 163–164, 167, 170, 181, 187, 189, 193–196, 198–199, 205, 210, 212, 225, 257, 260, 262, 275, 280, 282, 320. *See also* Anarchists; Anarchy; Anarcho-syndicalism; Anarcho-syndicalists; Libertarianism

Anarchists, xv, xvi, 3, 7, 9, 11, 15, 17, 26, 40, 50, 66, 105, 107, 109–110, 127–130, 135, 142, 153, 156, 167, 172, 193, 195–196, 204–205, 299, 326n11

Anarcho-syndicalism, 129, 130, 142, 157, 280

Anarcho-syndicalists, xv, 3

Anarchy, 6–7, 15, 27, 129, 161, 163, 177, 191, 194, 198–199, 201, 257, 296

Anderson, John, 111

Anderson, Stephen, 344n8

Angenot, Marc, 237, 267–271, 275–278, 280–281, 300

Angola, 97

Angry Young Men, 241

Anti-Flag, 21, 23

Antony, Louise, 47

Appiah, Kwame Anthony, 308

Appignanesi, Lisa, 309

Arab-Jewish cooperation. *See* League for Arab Jewish Cooperation

Arabs, 5, 8, 39, 53, 55–58

Arendt, Hannah, 310

Aristotle, 105, 113

Armstrong, Karen, 308

Arnold, Matthew, 118

Art, artists, 13, 25, 35, 168, 201, 224, 239, 260–263, 270, 273, 277, 285

Artificial intelligence (AI), 138–140, 227

Aslan, Amir, 57

Asner, Ed, 12

Atlantic Monthly, 86

Attali, Jacques, 96, 97, 237

Australia, 72